PURE FOOD

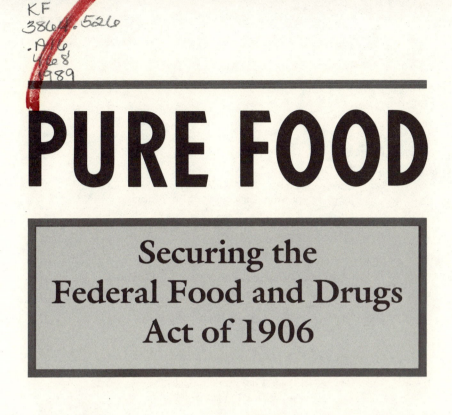

PURE FOOD

Securing the Federal Food and Drugs Act of 1906

JAMES HARVEY YOUNG

PRINCETON UNIVERSITY PRESS

PRINCETON, NEW JERSEY

Copyright © 1989 by Princeton University Press. Published by Princeton University Press, 41 William Street, Princeton, New Jersey 08540. In the United Kingdom: Princeton University Press, Oxford

Library of Congress Cataloging-in-Publication Data
Young, James Harvey.
Pure food : securing the Federal Food and Drugs Act
of 1906 / James Harvey Young.
p.   cm.
Includes index.
ISBN 0-691-04763-4
1. United States. Food and Drugs Act.
2. Food law and legislation—United States.
3. Drugs—Law and legislation—United States.
I. Title.
KF3864.526.A16Y68 1989
344.73'0423—dc19   89-30355
[347.304423]   CIP

This book has been composed in Linotron Galliard

Clothbound editions of Princeton University Press books are printed on acid-free paper, and binding materials are chosen for strength and durability. Paperbacks, although satisfactory for personal collections, are not usually suitable for library rebinding.

Printed in the United States of America
by Princeton University Press,
Princeton, New Jersey

To
My Grandchildren

Heather Caldwell Young
and
Samuel Townsend Young

Contents

vii

Preface

The research required for *The Toadstool Millionaires* and *The Medical Messiahs*, in which I traced health quackery through the American experience, led me to the Food and Drug Administration, the federal agency primarily responsible for regulating health fraud as represented by adulterated and misbranded drugs, foods, and devices. As a result of my interest in this phase of the FDA's mission, Commissioner George P. Larrick appointed me to the National Advisory Food and Drug Council. For nearly four years in the 1960s, during the concluding part of Mr. Larrick's commissionership and the beginning of James L. Goddard's tenure in that office, I learned about the full range of the Food and Drug Administration's regulatory responsibilities at their cutting edge. This experience caused me to expand my research goals beyond quackery to the broader theme of food, drug, device, and cosmetic regulation in the United States. The roots of an agency that regulates products for which consumers today pay twenty-five cents of every dollar they spend seemed worth pursuing. In the intervening years I have written a number of articles and one small book, *American Self-Dosage Medicines: An Historical Perspective*, based on my new research. The present volume begins a more systematic exploration of the subject.

Broad-scale federal regulation came with the Food and Drugs Act of 1906. Some six decades of relevant background, including nearly three decades of congressional consideration, preceded enactment of this pioneering law. Through the final thirty years a motley band of campaigners, all desiring a law although sharply divided as to its nature, waved the banner of "pure food." Earlier historical works have tended to emphasize some periods to the neglect of others, and to stress some elements at the expense of others, often so as to buttress a given theory of

ix

Progressivism. The present book presents a fuller and broader account and, it is hoped, a more balanced one, while not neglecting the drama inherent in the sweep of events. During the 1980s, when the manuscript was nearing completion, there has occurred, to my surprise and delight, a veritable outburst of publication directly relevant to the background of the Food and Drugs Act and the simultaneous meat-inspection amendments of 1906. I have taken account of this recent scholarship and am greatly indebted to its authors.

The main primary sources in a legislative history of this kind must be the documents of the Congress, the *Record* and its predecessors, the hearings of committees, committee reports, and other official documents. Both for insight and for vividness, I have sought to exploit the verbatim nature of hearings and of debate in the Senate and House of Representatives. In the book also, I have gone outside these chambers, trying to give the legislative consideration of food and drugs a proper setting, taking account of important developments in food processing and in drug therapy and production, and of trends in public opinion.

Major research for the book—and for my other publications, past and future, in this field—began while I held a fellowship from the John Simon Guggenheim Memorial Foundation. Later I was provided substantial support by the Food and Drug Administration, first by an extended research appointment under the Intergovernmental Personnel Act, then through a contract between the FDA and Emory University providing me with released time from teaching to continue research and writing. Finally, after my retirement from Emory, I was able to complete my research and revise my manuscript—and to continue research for its sequel—while serving as Visiting Historical Scholar in the History of Medicine Division of the National Library of Medicine in Bethesda. For all this generous assistance, permitting a professor busy with teaching and committeeing the free time to make progress toward his research goals, I express my profound gratitude.

The persons who deserve my thanks for helping me bring this volume to publication probably exceed the number of pages it contains. Some of them receive credit in my notes. Others I will mention here. Emory University librarians who have aided me in a thousand ways include Carol A. Burns, Virginia H. Cain, R. Alan Clark, Linda Matthews, Elizabeth McBride, Eric R. Nitschke, Marie M. Nitschke, Nena K. Perry, and Ruth Walling. Leon Benham, Patricia MacArthur, and George E. Sims, as research assistants, scanned magazine files for my benefit.

Wallace F. Janssen of the Food and Drug Administration has for more than thirty years talked fruitful shop with me as we have both pursued our historical endeavors. Others at the FDA whose continuing interest and assistance have been most helpful include Henry H. Dausch, J. Paul Hile, Sharon H. Holston, Maurice D. Kinslow, Fred L. Lofsvold, Gerald F. Meyer, Barbara J. Mooney, Robert G. Porter, Nancy K. Ross, Paul J. Sage, George R. White, and Suzanne R. White.

Members of the staff of the National Library of Medicine who gave me signal assistance as I worked in their pleasant company were James H. Cassedy, Carol Clausen, Madeline Crisci, Margaret Donovan, Dorothy Hanks, Margaret Kaiser, Lucinda Keister, Jan Lazarus, John L. Parascandola, Karen Pitts, Philip M. Teigen, Elizabeth Tunis, and Celia Volen.

Many friends have answered questions and volunteered suggestions. I express my appreciation for such thoughtfulness to Rima D. Apple, Edward C. Atwater, Saul O. Benison, Gert H. Brieger, Gerald Carson, David L. Cowen, Caroline Hannaway, Victoria A. Harden, Michael R. Harris, William H. Helfand, Robert J. T. Joy, Edward F. Keuchel, Ramunas A. Kondratas, Dorothy I. Lansing, Ronald L. Numbers, Peter D. Olch, William C. Pratt, Todd L. Savitt, Dale C. Smith, Glenn Sonnedecker, Ernst W. Stieb, Helen Finneran Ulibarri, Patricia Spain Ward, and Eugene J. Watts. I remember with gratitude my many helpful conversations with the late Oscar E. Anderson, author of the admirable biography of Harvey W. Wiley.

David L. Cowen, Edward F. Keuchel, Fred L. Lofsvold, John Harley Warner, and two anonymous readers for Princeton University Press have done me the great favor of reading and commenting on my manuscript. Their suggestions have been most helpful in my revision. They are, of course, absolved from whatever faults the book may still contain.

Patricia Stockbridge has put the manuscript into the memory of her word processor and has willingly modified that memory many times as the manuscript has moved along the path toward publication.

Gail Ullman and Wendy Wong of Princeton University Press, as well as copyeditor Jeff Beneke, merit grateful mention for moving my manuscript along the course toward production.

As with all my books and articles, my wife Myrna has shared in the research and in the typing of drafts. Moreover, this book, in its concepts and language, has profited immensely from her critical reading of its evolving text.

JAMES HARVEY YOUNG
Emory University
October 1988

Acknowledgments

Quotations from the typescript of an oral history interview with Upton Sinclair entitled, "Reminiscences about Some of His Novels and about His Political Career," conducted by several interviewers at Claremont Graduate School, Claremont, California, in 1963, are used by permission of the Honnold Library.

Permission has also been given me to use in this book in revised form material that I have published previously. The Johns Hopkins University Press has given me permission to use two articles from the *Bulletin of the History of Medicine*: my Fielding H. Garrison Lecture, " 'This Greasy Counterfeit': Butter versus Oleomargarine in the United States Congress, 1886" 53 (Fall 1979), and "The Pig That Fell into the Privy: Upton Sinclair's *The Jungle* and the Meat Inspection Amendments of 1906" 59 (Winter 1985). The editor of *FDA Consumer* has granted permission for me to use "The Long Struggle for the 1906 Law" 15 (June 1981). Princeton University Press has given permission for me to include several revised passages from my earlier book, *The Toadstool Millionaires: A Social History of Patent Medicines in America before Federal Regulation* (1961).

Acknowledgment of the sources of illustrations is given in the captions.

PURE FOOD

I

A "Murderous Traffic"
in Imported Drugs

> The cool-blooded, deliberate, studied, and fatal deception prac-
> ticed in articles designed for the relief of suffering and disease,
> can admit of no palliation—can find no excuse.
> —House Report 644, 30th Congress, 1st Session, 1848[1]

Preview: Toward the Food and Drugs Act of 1906

Federal regulation of food and drugs in the United States began, in a
broad, across-the-board way, with the Pure Food and Drugs Act of
1906. The preliminaries to that law, however, ran far back to the time
beyond memory when unscrupulous bakers and vintners began to adulterate bread and to water wine.[2] Such practices persisted through the
centuries, and rulers issued various decrees aimed at curtailing deceptions. Legislatures in the British American colonies imitated statutes
earlier enacted in the mother country seeking to protect the purses and
safeguard the health of their citizens.[3]

After the American Revolution, through the first half of the nineteenth century, states and towns renewed such laws sporadically. Officials of the federal government, however, did not pose the question
whether the quality of food eaten by the American people or of medicines with which they were dosed might fall within federal responsibility and jurisdiction.[4] Not until the Mexican War did a crisis over medi-

---

[1] *Imported Adulterated Drugs, Medicines, &c.*, 30 Cong. 1 ses., House Report 664 (1848),
23.

[2] Ernst W. Stieb, *Drug Adulteration: Detection and Control in Nineteenth-Century Britain*
(Madison, WI, 1966), 3–24; F. Leslie Hart, "A History of the Adulteration of Food before
1906," *Food, Drug, Cosmetic Law Journal* 7 (1952), 5–22; Peter Barton Hutt and Peter Barton
Hutt II, "A History of Government Regulation of Adulteration and Misbranding of
Food," *ibid.* 39 (1984), 3–35.

[3] Wallace F. Janssen, "America's First Food and Drug Laws," *FDA Consumer* 9 (June
1975), 12–19.

[4] An early show of interest in vaccination may constitute an exception to this generalization. In 1813, as a result of the advocacy of James Smith, a Baltimore physician and early

cations for the troops prompt Congress, without fanfare or delay, to enact a law aimed at banning adulterated drugs offered for import. Three decades passed before Congress began to consider a general food and drug measure, and almost three decades more before the pure-food campaign came to fruition in the 1906 law. Seven *C*'s underlay the enactment of this pioneering statute: change, complexity, competition, crusading, coalescence, compromise, and catastrophe.[5]

Change suggests the "research revolution." Scientific discovery accelerated during the last third of the nineteenth century, nurturing technology. These forces, interacting with all of society's institutions, brought countless planned and unforeseen consequences, not least those involving food and drugs. "The research revolution," Hunter Dupree has said, "is a social phenomenon, and hence of many orders greater complexity than the nucleus of the atom."[6]

The second *C* stands for complexity. All concerns of humankind grew more complex during these turbulent years, and a particular kind of complexity became wedded early to the question of how the federal government might confront deceptions and hazards in the food and drug supply. Almost from the start, bills proposed in Congress were omnibus bills, encompassing food, drink, and drugs. All food and drink and virtually all drugs entered the body through the mouth, and all were subject to similar adulterations. So it was natural to face the problem all at once. Britain had done so, and its example provided precedent. Many interest groups were potentially subject to an omnibus law, with producing and processing units located in every congressional district. A long and tortuous legislative process became inevitable.

Competition in the marketplace, the third *C*, lay behind the earliest omnibus bills. By a sort of Gresham's law, adulterated foods that could be sold cheaply threatened to drive out sounder fare. Alarmed, the more

user of Edward Jenner's vaccine for smallpox, the Congress enacted a law authorizing the president "to appoint an agent to preserve the genuine matter, and to furnish the same to any citizen of the United States, whenever it may be applied for, through the medium of the post office." President James Madison appointed Smith to this post. Smith's troubles and his considerable success in dispatching agents throughout the nation, especially into the West, to vaccinate citizens, are ably described in Whitfield Bell, Jr., "Dr. James Smith and the Public Encouragement for Vaccination for Smallpox," *Annals of Medical History* ser. 3, 2 (1940), 500–517. *Annals of Congress*, 11 Cong. 3 ses., 839; 12 Cong. 2 ses., 96, 98, 101, 106, 107, 958, 1080–81, 1336–37 (text of law).

[5] This patterning I explored in "Social History of American Drug Legislation," in Paul Talalay, ed., *Drugs in Our Society* (Baltimore, 1964), 217–29, and in "The Long Struggle for the 1906 Law," *FDA Consumer* 15 (June 1981), 12–16.

[6] A. Hunter Dupree, "Comment," in *The Government and the Consumer: Evolution of Food and Drug Laws* (Washington, 1963), 40.

reputable wing of the expanding processed-food industry appealed for help to Congress. Farmers complained too, upset by a new invention from France, oleomargarine, which posed a grave threat to butter. Producers aggrieved by adulterating rivals could bring omnibus bills before Congress but could not get them passed, for competitors spoke with different voices, all heard in Washington. Early legislative success crowned a few particular bills, which stuck to a single subject—drug imports and oleomargarine, for example—and received impassioned support from agitated pressure groups, physicians and pharmacists in the case of drugs, dairy farmers in the case of margarine.

The public had not yet become much aroused. The achievement of this required crusading, the fourth *C*. When the early omnibus bills first appeared in Congress, the loudest crusading voice came from a Massachusetts lawyer, George T. Angell. Angell thought business-sponsored omnibus bills too unmindful of the consumer, whereas businessmen thought Angell a devilish alarmist. Thus, early developed a polarized controversy that has been recurrent ever since.

The major figure in the pure-food crusade came to be Harvey Washington Wiley. A chemist and physician, Wiley became in 1883 head of the Division of Chemistry in the Department of Agriculture. He made a study of adulteration his bureau's principal business and early saw the need for a protective law. Sensing a stalemate in Congress, Wiley successfully expanded the coalition espousing food and drug reform. He consolidated his allies and recruits—segments of business, state agricultural chemists, physicians, women's club members, reform-minded journalists—into an effective pressure group. Coalescence is the fifth *C*. Wiley and his supporters turned the pure-food cause into a crusade broadening public awareness.

Even though one bill passed the Senate in 1892, divided business interests and constitutional scruples kept omnibus bills from becoming law. Compromise, the sixth *C*, offered the traditional American route to legislative success. During the last years of the century, Wiley tried in three national voluntary pure-food congresses, composed of delegates from widely diverse interests, to work out in the private sector a consensus broad enough to transfer into the Congress and thus secure enactment of a law. Delegates labored diligently and made much progress, but not enough. Some commercial differences seemed too deep and bitter to bridge. As the new century dawned, efforts at compromise continued, but again in their customary setting, the halls of Congress. By this time the majority of food and drug processors and distributors wanted a national law, or at least recognized its inevitability, and each element lobbied to shape the law so as to retain or gain competitive advantage.

As compromise continued, crusading accelerated. In the end, however, it took the seventh *C*, catastrophe, to fuse a final compromise that became the 1906 law. That perceived disaster came in reaction to Upton Sinclair's socialist novel *The Jungle*; his few pages describing the filthy conditions in which the nation's meat supply was prepared turned the public's stomach, cut sales in half, angered President Theodore Roosevelt, and pushed through the Congress both a meat-inspection bill and the food and drug law.

The pure-food campaign leading to the 1906 law, here sketchily mapped without taking note of controversies in interpretation, warrants deliberate exploration. The significant point of departure is the law of 1848 by which Congress sought to protect the nation's soldiers and citizens from the consequences of adulterated drugs imported from overseas.

The Drug Importation Act of 1848

A week before President James K. Polk proclaimed the treaty ending the war with Mexico, he signed the Drug Importation Act of 1848.[7] The war and the law were not unrelated. During the brief debate given the bill by members of the Congress, Representative Washington Hunt of New York noted that "the importation of deleterious drugs has been very injurious to our army during the war, . . . and hence some action . . . was loudly demanded."[8] Adulteration, insisted a House committee report, had forced army doctors to prescribe "herculean portions of active medicines" to the "gallant troops" and was itself a major factor in the "lamentable mortality."[9]

Adulteration of drugs, in fact, warranted only a very small share of the blame for troop mortality in the deadliest war in American history. For every fighting man killed in action, seven died of disease. The death rate from disease was 110 per year per thousand soldiers, diarrhea and dysentery striking the severest blows, with yellow fever, respiratory ailments, and cholera also significant killers. An inadequate supply of medical officers, inattention to camp sanitation, improper clothing for the extremes of weather, and an unbalanced diet played primary roles in the high death rates during this prebacteriological war. Troops were treated with medicines standard in civilian practice and believed efficacious by

[7] 9 U.S. Stat. 237 (June 26, 1848).
[8] *Cong. Globe*, 30 Cong. 1 ses. (June 2, 1848), 810.
[9] *Imported Adulterated Drugs, Medicines, &c.*, 20.

both doctors and patients: alcohol, opium, camphor, and powerful purgatives like calomel, jalap, and rhubarb. From a later perspective it is clear that these drugs, even if unadulterated, could not have done much to hold the grim reaper at bay. Yet, at the time, suspicion of adulteration's part in the lamentable disaster exercised members of the Congress.[10]

While patriotism helped speed enactment of an innovative law, long-standing concern on the part of American pharmacists and physicians about the purity of the drugs they compounded and prescribed had led to the measure's introduction. A century earlier the *Boston News-Letter* had reflected complaint about persistent importation of "a very bad Sort of Rhubarb," sold "for the best." Increasing worry about adulteration helped stimulate many private initiatives. The perceived dangers of spurious drugs underlay the publication in 1820 of the first *Pharmacopoeia of the United States*. Control of drug quality furnished a major motivation for the establishment of the nation's first two colleges of pharmacy, in Philadelphia in 1820 and in New York eight years later. Thus professional institutions were erected that could furnish support for law when individual endeavor seemed not to be making headway at combating the flow of shoddy drugs deliberately dispatched from abroad to American shores. "Good enough for America," asserted British pharmacy leader and member of Parliament Jacob Bell, was a phrase that had "long been applied to designate articles reduced by decay or ingenuity to American price."[11]

American professional journals, growing in number during the early nineteenth century, began to make clear that Europeans also suffered from adulterated drugs. What was more promising news to doctors and druggists, the journals reported that European scientists worked constantly to improve means for detecting such sophistications. Alexandre Bussy's notable French treatise of 1829, for example, received careful American review.[12]

[10] Thomas R. Irey, "Soldiering, Suffering, and Dying in the Mexican War," *Journal of the West* 11 (1972), 285–98; John Porter Bloom, "With the American Army into Mexico, 1846–1848" (Emory University dissertation, 1956), 202–8.

[11] *Boston News-Letter*, August 16, 1750; Glenn Sonnedecker, *Kremers and Urdang's History of Pharmacy*, 4th ed. (Philadelphia, 1976), 256–57, 260–63; Sonnedecker, "Contributions of the Pharmaceutical Profession toward Controlling the Quality of Drugs in the Nineteenth Century," in John B. Blake, ed., *Safeguarding the Public: Historical Aspects of Medicinal Drug Control* (Baltimore, 1970), 98–99; David L. Cowen, "A Store, Mixt, Various, Universal," *Journal of the Rutgers University Library* 25 (1961), 4; Bell cited in Clarke Ridgway, "Good Enough for America! The Drug Import Law of 1848" (University of Wisconsin seminar paper, 1986).

[12] Edwin D. Faust, "Original and Select Observations on the Detection of Adultera-

American scientists adopted the ever-improving European techniques of analytical chemistry—as in due course they would employ the achromatic microscope—which advanced the art of detecting adulterants beyond the centuries-old organoleptic tests of inspection by the unaided sight, taste, smell, and feel. A major landmark was published in New York strategically two years before the 1848 law, Lewis Caleb Beck's *Adulteration of Various Substances Used in Medicine and the Arts, with the Means of Detecting Them: Intended as a Manual for the Physician, the Apothecary, and the Artisan*. This treatise, according to a modern scholar, "seems to have been the first *comprehensive* work in English" on the subject.[13]

A life filled with diligent scientific endeavor preceded Beck's preparation of his adulteration volume. Soon after acquiring his medical degree, at the age of nineteen, by an apprenticeship in Schenectady and study at the College of Physicians and Surgeons in New York, Beck went to St. Louis. Instead of setting up a practice, he roamed Illinois and Missouri, studying their botany, geology, climate, health, and social customs, acquiring information that he assembled into an impressive *Gazetteer*. At the request of the New York governor, Beck assessed the advancing cholera epidemic of 1832. Beck settled down to permanent connection with both Rutgers College, as professor of chemistry and natural history, and Albany Medical College, as lecturer on pharmacy and chemistry.[14]

Soon after publishing a chemistry textbook in 1831, Dr. Beck was chosen by the New York legislature to investigate potash manufacture in the state, an industry with an annual value of a million dollars. Beck found that much potash reaching the market showed unmistakable evidence of adulteration. Producers frequently added "various substances, . . . ostensibly for the sole purpose of facilitating manufacture, but

tions," *American Journal of Science and Arts* 19 (1831), 70–87; Alexandre A. B. Bussy, *Traité des moyens de reconnaître les falsifications des drogues simples et composées et d'en constater le degré de pureté* (Paris, 1829).

[13] James E. Cassedy, "The Microscope in American Medical Science, 1840–1860," *Isis* 67 (1976), 76–97; Lewis Caleb Beck, *Adulteration of Various Substances Used in Medicine and the Arts* (New York, 1846); Stieb, *Drug Adulteration*, 249.

[14] Alden March, "Lewis C. Beck," in S. D. Gross, *Lives of Eminent Physicians and Surgeons of the Nineteenth Century* (Philadelphia, 1861), 679–96; Gustavus A. Weber, *The Bureau of Chemistry and Soils* (Baltimore, 1928), 10; Lyman F. Kebler, "Beck, Lewis Caleb," in Allen Johnson and Dumas Malone, eds., *Dictionary of American Biography*, 20 vols. and index (New York, 1928–37), vol. 2, 116; Kebler, "A Pioneer in Pure Foods and Drugs, Lewis C. Beck, A.B., M.D.," *Industrial and Engineering Chemistry* 16 (1924), 968–70; Ellis Kellert, "The Doctors Beck of Schenectady and Albany," *New York State Journal of Medicine* 48 (1948), 1015–19.

which really have the effect of increasing the weight of the resulting mass at the expense of its purity." Such fraud, Beck argued, jeopardized valuable markets overseas.[15]

The potash assignment, as well as his experience with medicines as a practicing physician, turned Beck's attention to the theme of drug adulteration. With characteristic intensity, thoroughness, and dispatch, he mastered the growing body of literature, foreign and domestic, applied his skills as an analytical chemist, and wrote his treatise.[16]

In alphabetical order Beck discussed the medications that physicians employed, giving both common and pharmacopoeial names, describing common adulterants, and suggesting organoleptic and analytical tests by which to expose them. In his preface Beck cited the authorities he relied on, in addition to his own experiments. He also acknowledged the limitations of his work. He did not intend to provide directions for "accurate quantitative analysis," just simple instructions by which "even . . . the tyro in chemistry" might determine "the nature" of adulterants "and in some cases an approximation of the proportions in which they exist." Beck included mineral remedies, such as calomel and tartar emetic, and paid heed to the recently discovered alkaloids of traditional botanicals, morphine, quinine, and strychnine. Mainly, however, he treated vegetable remedies, running the gamut from asafetida through dragon's blood and false dragon's blood to rhubarb. Rhubarb continued to be badly adulterated, its worm holes often filled with a paste concocted from powdered rhubarb and mucilage.

"There is no article in which frauds have been more extensively practiced," Beck asserted, "than in opium." Even of the best Turkish opium in the market, a quarter part usually consisted of impurities. One of Beck's sources stated that not a single cake of opium left the Near East that had not been mixed, when soft and fresh, with crushed grapes. Other adulterants included extract of licorice, gum arabic, aloes, sand, small stones, and pieces of lead. The cruder deceptions might be easily detected, but subtler ones that often deprived opium entirely of its active principle proved almost impossible to discover. Only "by actual trial upon the system" could the proportion of morphine, and hence the quality of a sample of opium, be determined.

Beck's careful, sober volume, Ernst W. Stieb believes, "provided the necessary documentation leading to" the 1848 law.[17] Getting legislation on the books, however, required more than dispassionate chemical anal-

[15] Lewis C. Beck, "Researches on the Commercial Potash of the State of New York," *American Journal of Science* 29 (1836), 260–73.
[16] Beck, *Adulteration of Various Substances Used in Medicine and the Arts*.
[17] Stieb, *Drug Adulteration*, 249.

ysis. It demanded also a sense of outrage that spurred pressure upon the Congress by organized groups whose voices warranted heeding. Drug adulteration seemed to be worsening as the decade of the forties wore on. In New York City, whose port received three-quarters of the nation's drug imports, prominent pharmacists associated with the New York College of Pharmacy, especially John Milhau and George Coggeshall, sensed that adulteration had assumed alarming proportions. They came to believe a federal law might be needed to achieve reform. Rallying physicians, including the membership of the New York Academy of Medicine, behind their campaign, the coalition also managed to place a physician ally in a crucial place, as examiner of drug imports passing through customs at the port of New York.[18]

The New York pharmacists and physicians had appealed to Secretary of the Treasury John C. Spencer, in whose domain the customs service fell, for help with the drug problem. He promised aid, but his retirement was too near to let him carry through. His successor, however, when approached, immediately deemed drug adulteration a subject of "great importance" and persisted in his shrewd support until a law was passed.[19] Robert J. Walker, a Pennsylvanian by birth and education, had gone to Mississippi as a young man, served that state in the United States Senate, and then entered the cabinet of President Polk. A passionate supporter of the war against Mexico, Walker also held free-trade ideas and devised the low-level tariff of 1846.[20] The secretary accepted the suggestion made by the New Yorkers that he appoint an outspoken critic of adulteration, Dr. M. J. Bailey, to inspect drugs offered for admission at the New York port. Bailey began his labors in December 1846. He could not only judge with scientific authority the state of drugs he was required to admit, he could also castigate the adulteration evil with warm conviction. He soon had an opportunity to make his case at the loftiest level.[21]

[18] Curt P. Wimmer, *The College of Pharmacy of the City of New York* (New York, 1929), 192–205; Edward R. Squibb, "Remarks upon the Practical Working of the U.S. Drug Law," *Transactions of the American Medical Association* 15 (1864), 142–50; M. J. Bailey, *Report on the Practical Operation of the Law Relating to the Importation of Adulterated and Spurious Drugs, Medicines, &c.* (New York, 1849), 4. In the 1848 House Report, *Imported Adulterated Drugs, Medicines, &c.*, this key figure's surname is spelled Baily.

[19] *Imported Adulterated Drugs, Medicines, &c.*, 16, 21–22.

[20] James P. Shenton, *Robert John Walker: A Politician from Jackson to Lincoln* (New York, 1961); Leonard D. White, *The Jacksonians: A Study in Administrative History, 1829–1861* (New York, 1954), 173. I owe debts of appreciation to Gilbert S. Guinn and to Clarke Ridgway for pointing out the significance of Walker's role, Guinn in "Between the People and the Pestilence: The Walker-Baily-Edwards Drug Import Bill of 1848" (University of South Carolina seminar paper, 1969), and Ridgway in "Good Enough for America!"

[21] *Imported Adulterated Drugs, Medicines, &c.*, 5, 8, 16, 21.

The urban New Yorkers, as part of their campaign, found in the House of Representatives a rural Ohioan willing to introduce a drug importation bill and to work zealously for its enactment. Born in Maryland, Thomas Owen Edwards had studied medicine at the University of Maryland, and had then settled in Lancaster, Ohio. After a decade of practice, he won election in 1846 to the Thirtieth Congress. At the insistence of the New York physicians and pharmacists, Dr. Edwards proposed his bill. He was made chairman of a House select committee, the majority of whose members were also physicians, to inquire more deeply into the quality of imported drugs.[22]

Secretary Walker shared in this legislative strategy. Dr. Bailey held conferences with Walker and other Treasury officials, apprising them of his discoveries while working in New York. Walker's tariff of 1846 sought both to raise more revenue by lowering rates and to protect nascent industries, and the secretary sensed merit in a drug import bill that might advance these goals. He also saw political advantages in such a measure. Sectional tensions were worsening during the war, and Polk's veto of an internal improvements bill had cost him popularity in the West. The West and the South, where drug adulteration seemed most prevalent, might be grateful to an administration that enacted a law protecting medications.[23]

Walker, it seems obvious, helped the campaign along by requesting friends in the Mississippi legislature to secure a resolution instructing the state's senators and representatives in Washington to suggest the need for a law banning the importation of adulterated drugs. Such drugs, the resolution asserted, now "pass daily through the custom-houses, to be disseminated by ignorant or unprincipled dealers, to the great detriment of the people."[24]

What Bailey had reported to Walker became public knowledge when the appraiser appeared as key witness before Dr. Edwards's committee.

---

[22] *Ibid.*, 1, 23; "Edwards, Thomas Owen," *Biographical Directory of the American Congress, 1774–1971* (Washington, 1971), 902; Charles C. Miller, ed., *History of Fairfield County and Representative Citizens* (Chicago, 1912), 311–12; Donald Shira, "A Few Early Ohio Doctor-Statesmen," *Ohio State Medical Journal* 35 (1939), 301; unidentified Wheeling, WV, newspaper clipping [Feb. 5, 1876], Archives-Manuscripts Division, Ohio Historical Society, Columbus. The Ohio references were provided to me by Eugene J. Watts.

[23] *Imported Adulterated Drugs, Medicines, &c.*, 2, 21; Ridgway, "Good Enough for America!"; Eugene Irving McCormac, *James K. Polk: A Political Biography* (Berkeley, 1922), 260; Joel H. Silbey, *The Shrine of Party: Congressional Voting Behavior, 1841–1852* (Pittsburgh, 1967), 47, 83–97; Charles Sellers, *James K. Polk, Continentalist, 1843–1846* (Princeton, 1966), 451–68.

[24] *Resolutions of the Legislature of Mississippi Relative to the Importation of Adulterated Medicines and Chemicals*, 30 Cong. 1 ses., House Misc. Doc. 65 (1848).

Having spurned bribes to suppress the truth, Bailey presented a forthright report of his year's observations at the New York port. He testified:

> More than one-half of many of the most important chemical and medicinal preparations, together with large quantities of crude drugs, come to us so much adulterated, or otherwise deteriorated, as to render them not only worthless as a medicine, but often dangerous.[25]

Bailey said he had not seen a single shipment of pure Aleppo scammony and only one of real myrrh. In one three-month period, the customhouse had admitted seven thousand pounds of rhubarb root, not one pound of it "fit, or even safe." Opium departing from Smyrna already had been deprived of two-thirds of its active principle and had been adulterated with Spanish licorice paste and a bitter extract. Often, moreover, opium was "infested with living worms." As for imported bottled and packaged preparations, like compound extracts and calomel, Bailey warned, never trust labels, for "fictitious" ones were rife, falsely purporting to designate products made by prestigious European manufacturing chemists. American dealers also practiced this deception, Bailey charged, importing empty bottles, filling them with adulterated wares, then affixing allegedly respectable European labels really printed in some New York shop.

"These base deceptions are rapidly multiplying," Bailey told the committee. Laws against adulteration in many European nations made the unprotected United States a welcome substitute market. American agents for foreign processors of specious drugs had increased the vigor of their promotion. Further, manufacturers displayed "evidence . . . of increased proficiency in the deceptive art." "This country," Edwards's committee concluded after hearing Bailey, had "become the grand mart and receptacle of all the refuse merchandise, . . . not only from European warehouses, but from the whole eastern world." The cost of such deceptions included the loss of "many valuable lives every year." Those blessings of providence, the medicines in nature provided by the "All-Wise Being," should not be circumscribed by man's greed.

Dr. Edwards and his committee proceeded to assert with confidence:

> The day of incantations and charms, of sympathetic and mesmeric cures, has passed. Medicine, in its practice and relations, is now a natural science . . . [and] has fully kept pace with its kindred sciences. . . . But in vain do we push investigations into the laws of disease; in vain does *materia medica* open its vast and various trea-

[25] *Imported Adulterated Drugs, Medicines, &c.*, 5–6, 8–16, 21–23.

sures; in vain may pharmacy and chemistry point out and provide the curative agency of means, if those means themselves, through mercenary fraud, are despoiled of their power to heal.[26]

A law regulating drug imports seemed an indispensable first step toward ultimate reform. If only authentic drugs entered the country, Dr. Bailey believed, American processors would not dare to expand adulteration. Such wickedness would soon be revealed, and the force of public opinion would soon punish the perpetrator. If this force proved insufficient, state laws could be enacted to suppress such "domestic evils."[27]

The committee concurred in this perspective, holding that the federal law they proposed, despite arguments to the contrary in the commercial press, fell well within the power of Congress to enact. Occasional exceptions to the free-trade principle must be conceded, and medicines fell into this category. The citizen could stand the risk of encountering a fraudulent coat or a fraudulent wine. "But a mistake in the strength of a confessedly valuable medicine, may be followed by consequences at which humanity may mourn, but its tenderest sympathies are lost on the sufferer."[28]

A precedent for such exceptional legislation existed in the tariffs of 1842 and 1846, which forbade importation of indecent and immoral books and pictures. Why, queried Dr. Edwards's report rhetorically, did the law make counterfeit bills, but not counterfeit medicines, a crime? Why "punish the use of a dagger" but not protect the "community from violence not less fatal, but better concealed?" In a phrase, the committee summed up its principles for handling adulterated drugs offered for import: "Condemnation, re-exportation or destruction."[29]

Dr. Edwards's report was astutely drafted, both in describing the problems and in stressing the proposed law's advantages to the West and South and to the infant American drug industry. Secretary Walker's close collaboration with the committee may be assumed.[30]

Considering its innovative nature and considerable opposition in the business community, the bill's path to passage proceeded smoothly. Debate was neither extended nor acrimonious.[31] Senator Daniel S. Dickinson of New York stated that, while he would not oppose the bill, he "had no faith" in it; it "belonged to that class of legislation which at-

[26] *Ibid.*, 17–18.
[27] *Ibid.*, 15.
[28] *Ibid.*, 19–20.
[29] *Ibid.*, 18.
[30] Ridgway, "Good Enough for America!"
[31] *Cong. Globe*, 30 Cong. 1 ses. (April 11, 1848), 593, (June 19), 855, (June 20), 858, (May 8), 730, (May 11), 761, (June 2), 810, (June 21), 861.

tempts to put the bell on the cat." Dickinson's New York colleague, James A. Dix, favored the bill, pointing to a resolution supporting it from a convention of the American Medical Association. Dr. Edwards had gone to Baltimore to attend the AMA meeting explicitly to urge such a statement of sentiment.[32] Senator John C. Calhoun of South Carolina feared the proposed law would not end the evil. Senator Jefferson Davis of Mississippi, a close acquaintance of Secretary Walker, supported the measure. Conversations with doctors in New York, Davis said, had led him to think it sound. No forthright word of opposition was reflected in the *Congressional Globe*, and the bill passed quickly into law.

Effective immediately, all drugs and medicinal preparations offered for import at six major ports of entry—New York, Boston, Philadelphia, Baltimore, Charleston, and New Orleans—received appraisal by "suitably qualified" special examiners. Checking for "quality, purity, and fitness for medical purposes," the examiner was empowered to reject drugs adulterated or deteriorated below the standards set in "the United States, Edinburgh, London, French and German pharmacopoeias and dispensatories," and hence "improper, unsafe, or dangerous to be used for medicinal purposes." Thus, right at the start of federal drug legislation, the *United States Pharmacopoeia* acquired quasi-official status. The importer could challenge the examiner's decision and, at his own expense, secure a reexamination by a competent analytical chemist chosen by the customs collector. A final judgment that the drug should be rejected gave the importer the option of reexporting within six months. Otherwise the drug was destroyed.[33]

Secretary Walker promptly appointed well-qualified chemists to the examiner posts. After the law had been in effect for some months, its proponents proclaimed it a success. Dr. Edwards, after failing at reelection to the House, received from the secretary of the treasury a roving commission to visit the ports and assess the law's impact. Under the "diligent, faithful, and capable" administration of the new examiners, he concluded, the entry of adulterated and deteriorated drugs had been prevented entirely. News of strict enforcement had reached European exporters, so fewer bad drugs and more of high quality were being shipped to America. Challenges of examiners' initial judgments had been few, and in only one case had a decision been partly overturned upon review. A few problems required ironing out, especially the need for uniform standards among the ports, but overall results justified the

[32] "Report of the Committee on Adulterated and Sophisticated Drugs," *Trans Amer Med Assoc* 2 (1849), 655–61.

[33] 9 U.S. Stat. 237 (June 26, 1848).

optimism with which physicians had greeted the law's passage. Even the fear of a loss in tariff revenue seemed groundless, because of the greater monetary value possessed by drugs of excellent quality.[34]

Dr. Bailey, who retained his post at the New York port, shared Dr. Edwards's ebullience. Despite "threats of vengeance," Bailey had barred the door when need be. Now that the "murderous traffic" in imported drugs was ending, attention could be turned to "home adulterations," for no longer could domestic perpetrators of such "iniquitous business" escape through the loophole of blaming shoddy American medicines on the state of imported raw material. Bailey made several concrete suggestions about how to proceed, but another federal law was not on his list of remedies.[35]

Such euphoria, however, proved premature. Within only two years, evidence of a lack of enforcement zeal at some ports, blamed partly on political interference and partly on the lack of effective drug standards and methods of analysis, prompted the New York College of Pharmacy to convene delegates from pharmacy colleges to confront the danger of revived adulteration. This meeting led to another in 1852, at which the American Pharmaceutical Association was born. The association repeatedly complained about unqualified examiners, but conditions at the ports did not improve.[36] By 1864 a new foe of adulteration, Edward R. Squibb, could write that the "wise and beneficent law" of 1848 had been done to death by politics. The initial period of rigorous enforcement had ended. Adulterated products made their way past examiners into the marketplace. Or, rejected by one examiner, a shipment would be reexported, then brought back to another American port at which the examiner was more lenient. Men of competence and conscience, like Dr.

[34] Ridgway, "Good Enough for America!"; R. J. Walker, "Circular Instructions to Collectors and the Officers of Customs," *Pharmaceutical Journal and Transactions* 8 (1848), 102–4; *Report of the Secretary of Treasury with the Report of Dr. Edwards . . .* , 30 Cong. 2 ses., Senate Exec. Doc. 16 (1849).

[35] Bailey, *Report on the Practical Operation of the Law*. See also, Bailey, "United States Customs," *New York Journal of Pharmacy* 1 (1852), 289–95, and C. B. Guthrie, "General Report upon the Results and Effects of the 'Drug Law,' Made to the Secretary of the Treasury," *ibid.*, 264–72. Some early state pharmacy laws sought to control fraudulent drug adulteration, but weak penalties and low budgets severely limited their effectiveness. Sonnedecker, *Kremers and Urdang's History of Pharmacy*, 214–16, 220.

[36] Sonnedecker, "Contributions of the Pharmaceutical Profession," 100; J. H. Beal, "The American Pharmaceutical Association as a Factor in American Food and Drug Legislation," *Journal of the American Pharmaceutical Association* 26 (1937), 747–48; F. W. Nitardy, "Notes on Early Drug Legislation," *ibid.*, 23 (1934), 1124; Lyman F. Kebler, "The Examination of and Standards for Imported Drugs from 1790 to 1908," *Journal of the American Pharmaceutical Association, Scientific Edition* 30 (1941), 25–30.

Bailey, gave way to men with "no qualifications or fitness for the office," chosen only because of "political party influence."[37]

Doubts that the law had enhanced American medicines also arose in the Navy Department. Criticism of adulteration had led the navy's Bureau of Medicine and Surgery to set up in 1845 a small laboratory in Brooklyn to make its own pharmaceuticals, so as to be sure of their strength and purity. By 1854 the laboratory supplied virtually all medications used in the entire navy, on shore and ship, and at low cost. The chief of the bureau was glad that this state of affairs had come about, for it might be questioned, he asserted, whether the 1848 law had "accomplished the humane purposes suggested for it." Even if adulterated imports had been curtailed, the law could not suppress "the manufacture and sale of adulterated medicines in our own country."[38]

By 1860 the 1848 law was "rarely administered at all." Such was the judgment of Edward Squibb, physician, chemist, former director of the navy laboratory, and as of 1858 manufacturer of drugs and chemicals, most of which, with the outbreak of the Civil War, went to the Union army.[39]

With the inauguration of Abraham Lincoln, Squibb became a leader in a nationwide campaign to restore to the 1848 law its pristine bite. In a letter to the new president, officers of New York medical and pharmacy organizations wrote: "This law, if thoroughly executed, is a great public safeguard and benefit; but if administered through venality, incompetency or carelessness, it becomes mischievous." In a companion letter to Secretary of the Treasury Salmon P. Chase, the health leaders attested to "an absolute knowledge that the law is badly administered." Both letters urged that port examiners be graduates of either a regular medical college or a college of pharmacy, their competency judged by the medical boards of the army or navy.[40]

[37] Squibb, "Remarks upon the Practical Working of the U.S. Drug Law," *Trans Amer Med Assoc* 15 (1864), 139–50.

[38] *Reports of the Navy Department Bureau of Medicine and Surgery*, 31 Cong. 2 ses., Senate Exec. Doc. 1 (1850), 366; 33 Cong. 2 ses., Senate Exec. Doc. 1 (1854), 579–80; 34 Cong. 3 ses., Senate Exec. Doc. 1 (1856), 734; 35 Cong. 3 ses., Senate Exec. Doc. 1 (1857), 932.

[39] Squibb, "Remarks upon the Practical Working of the U.S. Drug Law"; Squibb, "Report of the Special Committee upon the United States Drug Law," *Transactions of the Medical Society of the State of New York* (1862), 423–30; Lawrence G. Blochman, *Doctor Squibb* (New York, 1958); George Winston Smith, *Medicines for the Union Army* (Madison, 1962). Squibb became interested in drug adulteration when, as a navy doctor in Gibraltar, he found that the rhubarb with which he was treating himself for a stomach disorder was badly worm-eaten. See Tom Mahoney, *The Merchants of Life: An Account of the American Pharmaceutical Industry* (New York, 1959), 49.

[40] Squibb, "Remarks upon the Practical Working of the U.S. Drug Law."

Dr. Squibb was deputized to take Chase's letter to Washington and present it personally to the secretary. Chase was too busy to see Squibb, who instead made his case before a sympathetic assistant secretary. Later Squibb learned that Chase had been given the message "in a strong and true light." When the secretary appointed an examiner for the New York port, however, he selected "for strong political reasons" a "money broker of Wall street." True, the broker in early life had been a druggist, but for seventeen or eighteen years he had had nothing to do with the drug market.

Thus, the campaign of persuasion by medical and pharmacy leaders, trying to combat the spoils system, had come to naught. Chase, like several of his predecessors, had appointed unqualified men and thus had been, as Squibb charged, "the first to break the law." The atrocious state of the import market proved that most drug examiners had to "forswear themselves" in taking an oath to be faithful in the performance of their duties.

For the remainder of the century appointments for the sake of politics and consequent loose enforcement of the 1848 law continued. In due course, these very circumstances became factors impelling a new generation of physicians and pharmacists to labor in behalf of broader and stronger laws to control the quality of drugs used to dose the citizens of the republic.[41]

[41] Kebler, "The Examination of and Standards for Imported Drugs."

▌▌

Mercury, Meat, and Milk

[T]he crowd loves medicines.
—WILLIAM LAWRENCE, 1819[1]

The New York and Brooklyn milkman stands forth as the great
modern Herod, the wholesale slaughterer of the innocents!
—*Frank Leslie's Illustrated Newspaper*, 1858[2]

American Ways of Medication

In concluding his 1864 report on the ineffective enforcement of the 1848
drug importation law, Dr. Edward R. Squibb pointed with alarm to a
looming threat, which he deemed, in some measure, a consequence of
the shoddiness of drugs available to American physicians. "The profession appears to be rapidly, and doubtless justly, losing much of their
former reliance upon drugs," he wrote. It worried Squibb that the trend
might accelerate into a "pernicious . . . absolute scepticism" with respect
to drug therapy.[3]

Dr. Squibb correctly noted voices within the ranks of the nation's
physicians raising trenchant questions about American ways of medication. In his fears, however, he overestimated the proportion of such
critics, exaggerated the extent of their skepticism, and distorted the reasons that prompted it. As a motivation for skepticism, drug adulteration
played only a minor and tangential role. While Squibb did sense accurately that the ranks of the critics were destined to increase, he did not
take into sufficient account the power of the medicine-taking habit in
the sick or the centrality of medicine prescribing in the physicians' conception of their role.

Four years before the date of Squibb's report, the most articulate of
the doubters, Dr. Oliver Wendell Holmes, autocrat of the breakfast table
and professor of anatomy at Harvard Medical School, had expressed a
judgment destined to become famous from frequent repetition:

[1] Cited in Oswei Temkin, "Historical Aspects of Drug Therapy," in Talalay, ed., *Drugs
in Our Society*, 9.
[2] *Frank Leslie's Illustrated Newspaper* 5 (1858), 359.
[3] Squibb, "Remarks upon the Practical Working of the U.S. Drug Law," 149–50.

Throw out opium, . . . throw out a few specifics which our [phy-sicians'] art did not discover, and is hardly needed to apply; throw out wine, which is a food, and the vapors which produce the mir-acle of anaesthesia, and I firmly believe that if the whole materia medica, *as now used*, could be sunk to the bottom of the sea, it would be all the better for mankind,—and all the worse for the fishes.[4]

Dr. Holmes paid tribute to a few predecessors in the land, especially Jacob Bigelow, who had expressed a preference for the physician's mild supportive aid to nature's recuperative powers as against bold intrusion through the prescribing of potent medicinals. Yet Holmes recognizes the boldness of his central theme, how it runs counter to prevailing ther-apeutic concepts.[5] The doctrine nonetheless remains far short of the bor-ders of nihilism. Opium, Holmes notes, "The Creator himself seems to prescribe, for we often see the scarlet poppy growing in the cornfields, as if it were foreseen that wherever there is hunger to be fed there must also be pain to be soothed."[6] He retains also wine and ether and such specifics as cinchona, colchicum, sulphur, iodine, and arsenic. As for the rest of the materia medica destined for dumping beneath the waves, Holmes italicizes his controlling phrase, "*as now used*." With these words he means to rebuke the contemporary disciples of Dr. Benjamin Rush, a major portion of orthodox practitioners, for their gross overdosing.

With considerable sympathy Holmes understands Rush in his histor-ical setting, as much as he abhors the continuing power of Rush's heroic doctrines forged in the aftermath of the American Revolution. "As to nature," Rush had once opined, "I would treat it in a sick chamber as I would a squalling cat—open the door and drive it out."[7] Rush, in his employment of massive bleeding and purging, Holmes believes, "gave a direction to the medical mind of the country more than any other one man." Holmes asks rhetorically:

How could a people which has a revolution once in four years, which has contrived the Bowie-knife and the revolver, which has

---

[4] Holmes, *Medical Essays, 1842–1882* (Boston, 1891), 202–3. John Harley Warner elucidates the complexity of the revived trust in nature that developed during these years in " 'The Nature-Trusting Heresy': American Physicians and the Concept of the Healing Power of Nature in the 1850's and 1860's," *Perspectives in American History* 11 (1977–1978), 289–324. Holmes coined the phrase "nature-trusting heresy," *Medical Essays*, 183.

[5] *Ibid.*, 173–208. Bigelow's 1835 essay on "Self-limited Diseases" is reprinted in Gert H. Brieger, ed., *Medical America in the Nineteenth Century: Readings from the Literature* (Bal-timore, 1972), 98–106.

[6] Holmes, *Medical Essays*, 202.

[7] Cited in Warner, " 'The Nature-Trusting Heresy,' " 294.

chewed the juice out of all the superlatives in the language in Fourth of July orations; . . . which insists in sending out yachts and horses and boys to out-sail, out-run, out-fight, and checkmate all the rest of creation; how could such a people be content with any but "heroic" practice? What wonder that the stars and stripes wave over doses of ninety grains of sulphate of quinine, and that the American eagle screams with delight to see three drachms of calomel given at a single mouthful?[8]

Deeper roots than an excess of patriotic zeal lay beneath the American practice of heroic medicine. Holmes pointed to the power of one of these forces: "the public itself . . . insists on being poisoned." An ancient superstition still strongly influenced the popular mind, "that disease is a malignant agency, or entity, to be driven out of the body by offensive substances." Medicine taking was a habit deeply implanted in the human psyche. To fulfill the patient's expectations and bolster his confidence, even cautious physicians prescribed medicines liberally.[9]

Rush and his disciples, of course, were anything but cautious. The Philadelphia physician's therapeutic practices formed a logical part of his medical system, rooted in the conviction that all diseases were caused by excess excitability of the blood vessels, and relief of this pressure by bleeding and purging constituted the sole means of cure. Other monistic rational systems flourished in Europe, where biologists and physicians had sought to imitate the beautiful precision of physics as that discipline had emerged from the scientific revolution. However, the greater complexity of biological phenomena, as well as taboos governing research on the human body, had thus far not permitted medicine to discover encompassing principles. Individual empirical observations could sometimes themselves give rise to excessive theorizing. Competing theorists engaged in acrimonious debate. In America, Rush's ideas became quickly dominant, and, despite eventual attack, continued to exercise wide influence.[10]

The "extravagance" of heroic therapy as practiced by Rush's heirs Holmes hoped to curtail. His espousal of moderation was not a re-

[8] Holmes, *Medical Essays*, 192–93. Paul Starr, *The Social Transformation of American Medicine* (New York, 1982), 3, agrees with Holmes that Americans possessed an "activist therapeutic mentality."

[9] Holmes, *Medical Essays*, 186–87; William G. Rothstein, *American Physicians in the Nineteenth Century: From Sects to Science* (Baltimore, 1972), 9; Temkin, "Historical Aspects of Drug Therapy," 9.

[10] Richard Harrison Shryock, *The Development of Modern Medicine* (New York, 1947), 3–78; Erwin H. Ackerknecht, "A Short Survey of Drug Therapy Prior to 1900," in Blake, ed., *Safeguarding the Public*, 51–58.

sponse to the adulteration of drugs, which Squibb believed had furnished motivation to skeptics, but to the overuse of drugs. To be sure,
adulteration thwarted the practitioner aiming to get a certain effect
from a given dosage, because he could not be sure how much of the
active ingredient a given lot of Peruvian bark or calomel might contain.
Since adulteration reduced the active principle, it fostered the prescribing of larger doses and thus strengthened the tenure of heroic practice.
Particularly in the South and West, into which imported drugs came
only after passing through several dealers, providing successive opportunities for "home adulteration," did the tradition of mammoth dosages
persist.[11]

Holmes represented the extreme expression of a different tradition
from that of Rush, a return, as Holmes believed, to the Hippocratic
concept of the physician's role, siding with nature's healing power and
avoiding drastic interference. He opposed Rush's heroic therapy on
grounds of ineffectiveness, indeed of a counterproductiveness that too
often killed patients. Careful empirical observation played some part in
his convictions, but also Holmes, like Bigelow, had brought back from
his medical training with Pierre Louis in Parisian hospitals awareness of
a statistical kind of observation that was new to medical evaluation.
Louis's experiments had raised questions about the utility of several hallowed therapies, bloodletting in particular. Holmes himself, sharing
"the observing and computing mind" of his century, employed such
evidence to recognize the contagiousness of puerperal fever. Increasing
use of the numerical method in the decades ahead would enlist in
Holmes's camp the most perceptive minds in American medicine.[12]

Sweeping changes in society that brought a decline in the social es-
teem and educational status of the medical profession also influenced

[11] Holmes, *Medical Essays*, 93; Madge E. Pickard and R. Carlyle Buley, *The Midwest Pioneer: His Ills, Cures & Doctors* (New York, 1946), 98–114.

[12] Holmes, *Medical Essays*, 103–208; James H. Cassedy, *American Medicine and Statistical
Thinking, 1800–1860* (Cambridge, MA, 1984), 60–67, 82–83, 230–38. My summary of thera-
peutic currents during roughly the first two-thirds of the nineteenth century owes debts,
not always easy to document, to John S. Haller, Jr., *American Medicine in Transition, 1840–
1910* (Urbana, IL, 1981); Robert P. Hudson, *Disease and Its Control: The Shaping of Modern
Thought* (Westport, CT, 1983); Joseph F. Kett, *The Formation of the American Medical
Profession: The Role of Institutions, 1780–1860* (Westport, CT, 1980); Rothstein, *American
Physicians*; Shryock, *The Development of Modern Medicine*; Starr, *The Social Transformation
of American Medicine*; Temkin, "Historical Aspects of Drug Therapy"; and John Harley
Warner, *The Therapeutic Perspective: Medical Practice, Knowledge, and Identity in America,
1820–1885* (Cambridge, MA, 1986). Warner, 33–35, comments on how Holmes's bold phrasing upset many physicians. As David L. Cowen points out, pragmatic observations by
some physicians, even unbolstered by statistics, led to skepticism about heroic practices:
Medicine and Health in New Jersey: A History (Princeton, NJ, 1964), 28–36.

patterns of prescribing. After the American Revolution, though most physicians continued to acquire their training by apprenticeship, Benjamin Rush and his peers associated with the nation's first medical schools formed a patrician elite. They used their prestige and power to strengthen within the states a licensing system to control admission to the profession. Their authoritative pretensions, and also their therapeutic concepts, met severe challenge during the combined democratic and romantic onslaughts that began during the very years that drug adulteration assumed the proportion of a major problem.[13]

The egalitarian currents of Jacksonian America swept away the general acceptance of a stable, ranked society and brought the former traditional, educated leadership under siege. "The priest, the doctor, and the lawyer," wrote an untutored New Englander, Samuel Thomson, all stood convicted of "deceiving the people."[14] All that orthodox physicians ever learned about the nature of medicine, he charged, was "how much poison . . . [could] be given without causing death." A medical journalist concluded several decades later that medicine had become "the most despised of all the professions."[15]

The heroic therapy of the regular physician became a major point of attack for critics upset by his dominant position. The state "Black Laws" by which orthodoxy sought to monopolize medical practice irked especially a growing breed of irregulars.[16] "We go for free trade in doctoring," a Cincinnatian wrote in 1848; "medicine, like theology, should be divorced from the State, and, . . . as in the different sects of religionists, the various medical systems . . . [should] be treated alike."[17]

With followers of Thomson's botanical system playing a leading role, opponents of orthodoxy swept licensing laws from the statute books. The public wanted no discrimination against untaught sectarians and graduates of mushroom medical schools.[18] By midcentury only four

[13] Martin Kaufman, *American Medical Education: The Formative Years, 1765–1910* (Westport, CT, 1976), 36–108; Richard Harrison Shryock, *Medical Licensing in America, 1650–1965* (Baltimore, 1967), 3–42; Alexander Wilder, *History of Medicine . . . and Especially a History of the American Eclectic Practice of Medicine* (New Sharon, ME, 1901), 448–511; Kett, *The Formation of the American Medical Profession*, 14–30.

[14] Samuel Thomson, *New Guide to Health; or Botanic Family Physician* (Boston, 1835), 24–95, 201.

[15] Editorial in *Medical Record*, 1869, cited in Starr, *The Social Transformation of American Medicine*, 7.

[16] Wilder, *History of Medicine*, 448–511.

[17] Cited in Charles E. Rosenberg, "The American Medical Profession: Mid-Nineteenth Century," *Mid-America* 44 (1962), 169.

[18] Wilder, *History of American Medicine*, 468–71; Shryock, *The Development of Modern Medicine*, 261; Shryock, *Medical Licensing*, 30–31; David L. Cowen, "Louisiana, Pioneer in

states still made any pretense of trying to regulate who should and who should not practice medicine. In his 1850 pioneering report on the condition of the public health in Massachusetts, Lemuel Shattuck ironically summed up the extent of the popular victory over the medical establishment. "Any one, male or female, learned or ignorant, an honest man or a knave, can assume the name of physician, and 'practice' upon any one, to cure or to kill, as either may happen, without accountability. It's a free country!"[19] One of the defeated aristocrats gloomily declared that the Goths and Vandals of modern barbarism had invested the last strongholds of science.[20]

Not an invading Vandal but that native usurper Samuel Thomson built a medical system depending on American botanicals which required of patients a courage equivalent to that needed for the heroic therapy of the regulars. Thomsonian principles spread across the country, their major impact being in the South and West. So popular were the doctrines that many regular physicians modified their practices in a Thomsonian direction. A Mississippi doctor began to carry orthodox medicines in one saddlebag, Thomsonian remedies in the other. A more widespread and significant response of regular physicians to Thomsonianism and other sects, however, was fervent reassertion of the truths of orthodox doctrine, including traditional therapeutics.[21]

The wave of primitivism accompanying the romantic movement also fostered unorthodoxy. Such a climate, Grete de Francesco has written, favors "all sorts of nature cults" and "the development of a new kind of imposture: a falsification of Nature through overemphasis on the natural."[22] All over America, as well as in Europe, lay healers in rustic settings employed a variety of "natural" remedies, water being especially prominent. Those bemoaning the increasing artificiality of life became preoccupied with a "natural" diet. Not that critique of the prevailing diet was undeserved, but some sages went much further. Sylvester Graham plot-

the Regulation of Pharmacy," *Louisiana Historical Quarterly* 26 (1943), 339–40; Rosenberg, "The American Medical Profession: Mid-Nineteenth Century," 163–71.

[19] Lemuel Shattuck, *Report on the Sanitary Commission of Massachusetts, 1850* (Cambridge, MA, 1948), 58.

[20] Rosenberg, "The American Medical Profession: Mid-Nineteenth Century," 169.

[21] Thomson, *New Guide to Health*; Alex Berman, "The Thomsonian Movement and Its Relation to American Pharmacy and Medicine," *Bulletin of the History of Medicine* 25 (1951) 405–28, 519–38; James Harvey Young, *The Toadstool Millionaires: A Social History of Patent Medicines in America before Federal Regulation* (Princeton, 1961), 44–57; Rothstein, *American Physicians*, 125–51; Haller, *American Medicine in Transition*, 104–29; Starr, *The Social Transformation of American Medicine*, 51–54; Kett, *The Formation of the American Medical Profession*, 97–131; Warner, *The Therapeutic Perspective*, 182.

[22] Grete de Francesco, *The Power of the Charlatan* (New Haven, CT, 1939), 188.

ted a dietary regimen that he hoped might restore the pristine conditions of the Garden of Eden. Graham's ideas influenced the prescriptions of unorthodox physicians and the doctrines of new religions.[23]

The romantic outlook helped homeopathy take firm root. A set of
ideas formulated in the late eighteenth century by Samuel Christian
Hahnemann, a regular German physician, homeopathy entered the
United States in 1825 and flourished as free trade in medical ideas became
the rage. The sect's stress on the therapeutic value of infinitesimal doses
attracted patients timid about confronting regular medicine's heroism.
Oliver Wendell Holmes ridiculed homeopathy's theories at the opposite
extreme from heroic medicine, pointing scornfully to the therapeutic
inconsequence of a potion achieved by a series of seventeen dilutions
requiring, if made in full measure, enough alcohol to "equal in quantity
the waters of ten thousand Adriatic seas." It offended Holmes's reason
to disguise noninterference with nature by such folderol.[24]

The spirit of medical laissez-faire also accentuated the ancient tradition of medical self-help. Indeed, a strong do-it-yourself component
characterized hydropathy, homeopathy, and Thomsonianism. Thomson's rallying cry made "Every man his own physician," aided by counsel
in his *New Guide to Health*. Other domestic manuals represented almost
every prevailing shade of medical theory, although, until the late nineteenth century, not differing significantly from each other in therapeutic
guidance. John C. Gunn's *Domestic Medicine, or Poor Man's Friend*, for
example, which ran through a hundred editions between 1830 and 1870,
appealed to the wisdom of the common people, while citing heroic regulars and recommending mammoth doses of calomel and jalap.[25]

[23] Harry B. Weiss and Howard R. Kemble, *They Took to the Waters* (Trenton, NJ, 1962);
Weiss and Kemble, *The Great American Water-Cure Craze* (Trenton, 1967); William B.
Walker, "The Health Reform Movement in the United States, 1830–1870" (Johns Hopkins
University dissertation, 1955); James C. Whorton, *Crusaders for Fitness: The History of
American Health Reformers* (Princeton, 1982); Sylvester Graham, *Lectures on the Science of
Human Life* (New York, 1883); Harvey Green, *Fit for America: Health, Fitness, Sport, and
American Society* (New York, 1986), 45–53; Ronald L. Numbers, *Prophetess of Health: A
Study of Ellen G. White* (New York, 1976).

[24] Martin Kaufman, *Homeopathy in America: The Rise and Fall of a Medical Heresy* (Baltimore, 1971), 15–92; Holmes, *Medical Essays*, 1–102, quotation at 53; Rothstein, *American
Physicians*, 152–74; Haller, *American Medicine in Transition*, 104–22; Starr, *The Social Transformation of American Medicine*, 96–102; Kett, *The Formation of the American Medical Profession*, 132–64.

[25] John B. Blake, "From Buchan to Fishbein: The Literature of Domestic Medicine,"
11–30, and Ronald L. Numbers, "Do-It-Yourself the Sectarian Way," 49–72, in Guenter
B. Risse, Ronald L. Numbers, and Judith Walzer Leavitt, eds., *Medicine Without Doctors:
Home Health Care in American History* (New York, 1977); John C. Gunn, *Gunn's Domestic*

Medical democracy also spurred a great increase in self-dosage with patent medicines. American nostrum brands had come on the market during the cultural nationalism following the Revolution, fabricated in imitation of old English patent medicines that had gained American popularity during the eighteenth century. During the age of the common man, developments made it easier for the nostrum maker to appeal to and supply his customers. The newspaper press boomed, and patent-medicine promoters became the most prolific national advertisers. When Dr. Thomas Edwards, a year after shepherding through Congress the drug importation law, headed a House committee to look into patent medicines, he discovered that one pill manufacturer was spending a hundred thousand dollars a year to promote his purgative. The expansion of public elementary education in the North and West, another accompaniment of Jacksonian democracy, better equipped the ordinary citizen to read the gory symptoms and glorious cures flamboyantly presented in nostrum advertising.[26]

Like the sectarians, patent-medicine promoters belabored regular physicians for murderous bleeding and purging, promising instead swift and sure cures for diseases great and small to be wrought by mild, pleasant-tasting remedies. In fact, their concoctions were often loaded with opium or alcohol, unbeknownst to the customer, and not infrequently contained much mercury, even while advertising condemned the regulars for using it.[27]

Orthodox physicians, outraged at the imposture, pointed out the evils of the patent-medicine business. Holmes, for example, campaigned from the lyceum rostrum against "the toadstool millionaires."[28] Such critical voices, however, were buried beneath an avalanche of advertising.

Medicine, with an introduction by Charles E. Rosenberg (Knoxville, 1986; originally published 1830).

[26] Young, *The Toadstool Millionaires*, 3–110; James Harvey Young, "American Medical Quackery in the Age of the Common Man," *Mississippi Valley Historical Review* 47 (1961), 579–93; Young, "Patent Medicines and the Self-Help Syndrome," in Risse, Numbers, and Leavitt, eds., *Medicine Without Doctors*, 95–116; James Harvey Young, "The Marketing of Patent Medicines in Lincoln's Springfield," *Pharmacy in History* 27 (1985), 98–102; *Patent Medicines*, 30 Cong. 2 ses., House Report 52 (1849), 31.

[27] Young, *The Toadstool Millionaires*. See also the revealing series of articles by J. Worth Estes that relate the therapeutic promises made by nineteenth-century patent-medicine proprietors to the concepts prevailing among regular physicians: "Public Pharmacology: Modes of Action of Nineteenth-Century 'Patent' Medicines," *Medical Heritage* 2 (1986), 218–28; "Selling Massachusetts Medicines," *Historical Journal of Massachusetts* 14 (1986), 122–34; "The Pharmacology of Nineteenth-Century Patent Medicines," *Pharm Hist* 30 (1988), 3–18.

[28] Holmes, *Medical Essays*, 186.

The times were not ripe for even so modest a step as denying the patent privilege to nostrums. Such a step Dr. Edwards and the fellow members of his House committee pondered during 1849. To be sure, very few "patent medicines" were offered for patent, either in England, where the name and policy had originated, or in the United States. Patenting required a revelation of ingredients, and to the shrewd proprietor secrecy seemed a safer and more profitable stance. Patent applications came, by and large, from simple folk not used to the wily ways of commerce. The relatively few patented medicines, none of them useful, and the vast horde of unpatented nostrums, the House committee reported, harmed "poor and illiterate" citizens especially, for they of all people most "eagerly and credulously accepted" the "false and treacherous doctrine of 'every man his own doctor.'" Denying that legal restraints on quackery were "anti-republican," Dr. Edwards's committee urged that at least the "immoral and pernicious" practice of granting patents to nostrums be eliminated. The proposal received no consideration on the House floor.[29]

Besides stimulating sectarianism and quackery, the climate of untrammeled freedom encouraged the proliferation of proprietary medical schools. In exchange for modest fees, a group of physicians of perhaps no notable competency would give a short course of lectures to what recruits they could muster and thereby convert them into doctors. For most matriculants at such schools, bemoaned a well-educated physician, it was "but a short step from the plough-handles to the diploma." Efforts by the most skilled and conscientious wing of the medical spectrum to improve the situation proved unavailing until toward the close of the nineteenth century.[30]

Amid all the turmoil surrounding medical practice earlier in that century, a remarkable circumstance prevailed. Despite the controversy among existing camps of regular physicians and between orthodoxy and sectarianism, the most important point, as Charles Rosenberg has argued cogently, is what all agreed about.[31] Physicians, and their patients

[29] *Patent Medicines*, 30 Cong. 2 ses., House Report 52; Lyman Kebler, "United States Patents Granted for Medicines during the Pioneer Years of the Patent Office," *J Amer Pharm Assoc* 24 (1935), 485–89.

[30] Kaufman, *American Medical Education*, 36–162, quotation at 111. Kett argues that the spread of medical education, even though proprietary medical schools had abominable standards, led the public in time generally to desire treatment by educated physicians and to abandon sectarians. See *The Formation of the American Medical Profession*, 178–80.

[31] Charles E. Rosenberg, "The Therapeutic Revolution: Medicine, Meaning, and Social Change in Nineteenth-Century America," in Morris J. Vogel and Charles E. Rosenberg, eds., *The Therapeutic Revolution: Essays in the Social History of Medicine* (Philadelphia, 1979), 3–25.

too, shared a set of convictions about illness and its treatment, the product of a long tradition extending back to the rationalistic speculations of classical antiquity. These ideas worked their way into a formalized social pattern of physician-patient relationships governing what both parties anticipated and how both performed. However chaotic and obscurantist early nineteenth-century medical practices may seem as viewed from late twentieth-century perspectives, and, despite the arguments at the time about particulars, the system seemed eminently sensible to those who took it for granted and who were persuaded that in most cases it worked.[32]

The human body, this traditional doctrine held, sailed like a frail bark upon an uncertain sea amid stormy winds, always at risk. Its state of health at any moment depended on the degree of equilibrium maintained among a host of forces, some relating to constitutional endowment, some to habits of living, others linked to the environment, such forces as air, food, water, climate, working conditions. A person required a balanced vital economy, a proper income of breath and nourishment, a proper outgo of energy expenditure and wastes. Each individual strove to lead the mode of life most conducive to equilibrium, but too often sickness revealed a balance disturbed. Then, often after self-treatment, the patient sought a physician to play his customary role. The doctor felt morally obligated to intervene, using his best judgment as to therapy. He might modify intake by dietary counsel, but regulating excretions was his essential task, striving to alter the course of the ailment and to restore the body's balance and hence its health by promoting perspiration, urination, defecation, and by removing blood. Such procedures provided both physician and patient with visible evidence that something was happening. When balance had been righted, tonics built up the patient's strength.[33]

Since each patient possessed a different constitution from every other, and also encountered varying circumstances through time, each crisis for every patient required a different combination of prescribed therapies. Nor were diseases constant. It was not only Samuel Thomson who

[32] *Ibid.* Other works especially useful in correcting the tendency to disparage unduly the past for its medical ignorance from the perspective of the enlightened present are Hudson, *Disease and Its Control*, and Lester S. King, *Medical Thinking: A Historical Preface* (Princeton, 1982).

[33] Rosenberg, "The Therapeutic Revolution," 3–25, and Warner, *The Therapeutic Perspective*, 13–15, 58–80, provide the most detailed descriptions of this point of view. The vigor and the nature of the physicians' intervention, of course, varied. Martin S. Pernick stresses the enlarging role of a "conservative professionalism" which stressed a more careful calculation of the benefits and risks of possible therapies. See *A Calculus of Suffering: Pain, Professionalism, and Anesthesia in Nineteenth-Century America* (New York, 1985).

could claim that his mother had died of measles turned into "galloping consumption." Orthodox physicians held that "painless diarrhea," if not properly treated, shifted into cholera. Disease was protean, dynamic, unspecific. "Scarcely any two cases of disease are to be treated exactly alike," asserted the editors of a Boston medical journal in 1858. "The treatment in every case of disease is to be varied according to a thousand varying circumstances." Prescription files reveal that the physician tended to reassess the condition of each patient frequently, changing prescriptions, often radically, day by day. Therapy, rendered with solemn ceremony, usually in the home, provided reassurance to patients and their families. More often than not, treatment seemed to prove its efficacy, sustaining faith in the system, because the patient survived.[34]

Drugs, then, were not considered specifics to treat particular ailments, but rather tools to achieve calculated physiological effects. Indeed, the concept of a specific was held in general disdain as ethically suspect. Even the new quinine was deemed a tonic, given for many conditions besides malaria. In treatises on the materia medica, the classification of drugs testifies to this perspective, formulated in the previous century, for they were arranged in such categories as astringents, cathartics, emetics, diaphoretics, diuretics, sedatives, and stimulants. Patent-medicine makers, botanical irregulars, authors of self-help manuals, and various branches of orthodox physicians, whatever their differences, shared common inherited assumptions about the dynamics of disease. Drug therapy played a central role for all, even, in theory, despite their minute dosages, for the homeopaths.[35]

The materia medica resorted to by healers of various stamps ran a very broad gamut of time and space. Botanicals predominated, some of ancient origins like opium and rhubarb, which had reached Europe from the Orient; others, like cinchona bark and ipecac, discovered in the Americas during the age of exploration. The new chemistry had increasingly isolated the active principles of vegetable drugs, finding morphine in opium and quinine in cinchona, thus making dose response somewhat more predictable, and the hazards of adulteration more ominous.

[34] Rosenberg, "The Therapeutic Revolution," 3–25; Thomson, *New Guide to Health*, 24; Charles E. Rosenberg, *The Cholera Years: The United States in 1832, 1849, and 1866* (Chicago, 1962), 65, 74; Warner, *The Therapeutic Perspective*, 58–80, citing *Boston Medical and Surgical Journal*, 64; David L. Cowen, Louis D. King, and Nicholas G. Lordi, "Nineteenth Century Drug Therapy: Computer Analysis of the 1854 Prescription File of a Burlington Pharmacy," *Journal of the Medical Society of New Jersey* 78 (1981), 760–61.

[35] Rothstein, *American Physicians*, 157–58, 187–89; Haller, *American Medicine in Transition*, 113–14; Temkin, "Historical Aspects of Drug Therapy," 5; Warner, *The Therapeutic Perspective*, 62–63.

Chemical remedies from mineral sources, especially preparations of mercury, arsenic, and antimony, had become increasingly important following the sixteenth-century Paracelsian revolution.[36]

To illustrate one localized instance of a pattern, physicians in a small New Jersey city, Burlington, according to a recent computer analysis of their prescriptions from 1854, prescribed drugs of vegetable origin almost twice as often as chemical and mineral drugs. Opium led the botanical list, followed by ipecac and camphor. Often opium and either ipecac or camphor were prescribed in combination. Other vegetable drugs prominent in the prescriptions were squill, acacia, cinchona compound, and rhubarb. Mercury led the mineral/chemical drugs, especially in the form of calomel. Quinine sulphate, potassium citrate, morphine acetate, and morphine sulphate headed the list of medications inherited from the pioneering days of pharmaceutical chemistry. Alkaloids, however, had not yet banished nature's forms. Prescribing in Burlington conformed with considerable consistency to the tenets of the *United States Pharmacopoeia* of 1850. At the time of the drug import law of 1848, imports still provided the major source of American medications.[37]

Despite the continued usage of traditional drugs, the persistence of the individual variability concept, and the tenacity of the belief that restoring a patient's balance constituted the physician's goal, therapeutic change did occur, gradually though decisively, during the first two-thirds of the nineteenth century. As John Harley Warner has elegantly demonstrated, changes took place in both attitudes and practices. Early in the century, while Rush's system maintained its strongest hold, physicians believed that prevailing diseases tended to overexcite the body, requiring bold depleting therapies like bloodletting and mineral cathartics. As heroism declined in favor, a more palliative regimen came into use, an approach according nature a greater role. The belief gained ground that the pattern of dominant diseases had shifted away from exciting to enfeebling, so that restoration of balance now required not heroic depletion but well-nigh heroic stimulation, through prescription of quinine, iron compounds, and, especially, large doses of beverage alcohol.[38]

Preserved during the change was an active intervention in the course

[36] Glenn Sonnedecker, *Kremers and Urdang's History of Pharmacy*, 39–45, 145–58, 172–74; Ackerknecht, "A Short History of Drug Therapy," 51–58; David L. Cowen, "The Impact of the Materia Medica of the North American Indians on Professional Practice," in Wolfgang-Hagen Hein, ed., *Botanical Drugs of the Americas in the Old and New Worlds* (Stuttgart, 1984), 51–63.

[37] Cowen, King, and Lordi, "Nineteenth-Century Drug Therapy," 758–61.

[38] Warner, *The Therapeutic Perspective*; see also Rothstein, *American Physicians*, 181–83.

of disease determined by the physician's judgment. The older therapies like venesection and calomel, while declining in frequency and vigor of use, were not rejected outright. Most physicians continued to defend the legitimacy of such therapeutic strategies. Nonetheless, prevailing theory was flexible enough to accommodate accumulating changes in prescribing practices and also a major shift in therapeutic epistemology. In the middle third of the century, Rush's rationalistic system had been largely supplanted by skeptical empiricism, so critical of the deadly dosing of earlier years. Holmes was an extreme spokesman for the new perspective.[39]

Holmes's region of New England made the transition away from heavy reliance on depleting drugs more rapidly than did the West and South. The comparative tracing of regional trends through intensive study of case records at Massachusetts General Hospital and Commercial Hospital of Cincinnati is one of Warner's notable achievements. Bloodletting peaked in Boston in the 1830s, in Cincinnati two decades later. A gradual and uneven decline at both hospitals then ensued. The aggressive use of calomel also persisted longer in the West. Moreover, the rationale behind bleeding and purging differed between the hospitals: in Cincinnati the intent was clearly to break up disease and force a cure; in Boston venesection was employed to ease pain, and cathartics to clear the way for nature to play its healing role. Stimulation therapy, through the use of alcohol, quinine, and other supportive drugs, and by an enriching diet, had become evident at Massachusetts General by the early 1850s. At Commercial Hospital these changes did not appear until the 1860s and never became so extensive as in Boston.[40]

Attacking the old rationalistic system and adopting empiricism gave many regular physicians hope that both their status and their practices might be enhanced, dispelling the gloom that earlier had enveloped the profession.[41] By the end of the Mexican War, when most citizens anticipated glorious prospects for an expanded United States,[42] some physicians like Congressman Edwards also looked cheerfully toward the future. The true science of medicine, he wrote in his House report, was advancing. "The causes of pestilential epidemics" had been found out and "the world . . . warned and protected against them." Millions of lives had been saved for valuable work. "A stringent medical police"

[39] Warner, *The Therapeutic Perspective*, especially 99, 221–24.

[40] *Ibid.*, 102–61.

[41] *Ibid.*, 51–54.

[42] Robert W. Johannsen, *A New Era for the United States: Americans and the War with Mexico* (Urbana, IL, 1975), 11–32.

protected the public health; "an army of devoted medical men stood between the people and the pestilence."[43]

That army, Edwards took for granted, required sound drugs to wage effective war against disease. Adulteration posed a major obstacle to continued medical progress. In an era when signs of the physiological activity of drugs held such a central place in the scheme of things, adulteration, which made incalculable a drug's power to puke or purge, or to stimulate a weakened constitution, seemed like a cardinal sin. The adulterator's violation of such hallowed doctrines explains why many physicians and pharmacists worked to secure a pioneering federal law barring adulterated drugs from entering American ports. When poor enforcement kept that law from being effective, organized pharmacy launched a new attack on drug adulteration by reviving state laws seeking to suppress such dangerous deception. Enforcement, however, was feeble, and achievements minimal.[44]

Growing Anxiety about the Food Supply

Besides worrying about adulterated drugs, mid-nineteenth-century Americans expressed increasing concern about the state of their food supply. In the treatise that made the drug import law seem scientifically feasible, Dr. Lewis Beck also paid heed to food and drink. Citing foreign and domestic authorities and his own analyses, Beck described the ingenious ways by which adulterators cheapened flour and sugar, chocolate and honey, beer, coffee, milk, tea, and wine. Writing straightforward prose devoid of rhetorical flourish, Beck let the facts speak for themselves.[45]

"Chocolate," for example, "is now extensively manufactured in Europe and America, and there are probably few articles that are more largely adulterated." Wheat flour, potatoes, beans, rice, peas, egg yolks, almonds, and soap were among the substances used for this purpose. While these materials posed no hazards, other adulterants could be poisonous, like red oxide of mercury, employed to enhance chocolate's color and add to its weight. A more frequent use of poisonous mineral and organic colors, Beck said, marked the confectionery industry. Even

[43] *Imported Adulterated Drugs, Medicines, &c.*, 30 Cong. 1 ses., House Report 664 (1848).
[44] Sonnedecker, *Kremers and Urdang's History of Pharmacy*, 214–17, 220, 381–82; Sonnedecker, "Legalization of Drug Standards under State Laws in the United States of America," *Food, Drug, Cosmetic Law J* 8 (1953), 741–60.
[45] Beck, *Adulteration of Various Substances Used in Medicine and the Arts.*

the paper wrappings could be dangerous to children because of metallic dyes.[46]

Beck's discussion of wheat flour brought about his appointment to a significant assignment. The same session of Congress that had enacted the drug import law also made the first federal appropriation in the nation's history to support a chemical analysis of agricultural products. The commissioner of patents was given one thousand dollars for a study of "vegetable substances produced and used for the food of man and animals in the United States." The commissioner selected Beck, telling him to concentrate on grains and flour. In his two reports on "breadstuffs," Beck focused entirely on wheat.[47]

In one report, Beck drew on European sources to describe frauds in breadmaking. Wheat flour could be cheapened by the addition of potato starch, ground peas and beans, buckwheat, and rice, thus cheating the customer but not threatening his health. Other adulterants posed dangers. Copper sulphate let bakers use poor flour, and the bread so made gained weight by taking up large amounts of water. Alum also disguised the use of inferior flour. Alkaline carbonates, chalk, pipe clay, and plaster of paris permitted bakers to counter the acidity of damaged flour, add weight, and produce deceptively white bread.[48]

What happened in Europe could also happen in America, but this theme Beck did not address. His major concern was the state of the export market in wheat and wheat flour. Already a booming business, such exports, Beck believed, could anticipate a glowing future. "There can be little doubt," he wrote, "that our country is destined to be the *granary of the world*."[49] For the moment, however, serious problems faced the farmer and the grain merchant. European importers complained that both grain and flour reached their ports in sadly deteriorated condition. Beck confirmed the truth of these charges, blaming carelessness in the handling of grain and flour while in storage and in transit. The main cause of the difficulty lay in excessive moisture in the grain and flour. Adulteration, consisting of a mixture of "good and bad kinds" of flour, did occur, Beck acknowledged, but rarely. Adulterators should be "promptly exposed" and "held up to merited reproach."[50]

[46] *Ibid.*, 53–55, 78–80.

[47] *Ibid.*, 256–62; Kebler, "A Pioneer in Pure Food and Drugs," 970; 9 U.S. Stat. 285, 30 Cong. 1 ses. (1848); Beck, *Report on the Breadstuffs of the United States . . .* , 30 Cong. 1 ses., House Exec. Doc. 59 (1848–49); Beck, *Second Report on the Breadstuffs of the United States*, 31 Cong. 1 ses., House Exec. Doc. 20 (1848–49).

[48] Beck, *Report on the Breadstuffs*, 257.

[49] *Ibid.*, 245.

[50] Beck, *Second Report on the Breadstuffs*, 63.

As with this first federal inquiry exposing food adulteration, however tangentially, concern about markets had stimulated earlier local interest in the quality of food. In studying food ordinances enacted in the city of New York, John Duffy gained "the impression that . . . officials were far more concerned with the city's commercial reputation than with what the citizens ingested."[51] In the seventeenth century numerous laws provided inspection of flour and meat intended for export, required the exporter's brand mark on flour barrels, and stipulated that "the best not be left out" when meat was put in casks. The details of such regulation proliferated as time went on, and the General Assembly of the colony of New York passed laws to buttress the city's ordinances. This parcel of laws passed virtually intact into the period of independence. As Beck's study showed, however, the inspection system did not protect European importers from the results of carelessness and fraud.

Other colonies developed similar systems. Massachusetts began to inspect exports of fish, beef, and pork routinely beginning with a statute passed by the General Court in 1641.[52] Special problems sometimes led to special laws. In 1688 Massachusetts banned use of an adulterated form of salt, "Turtoodas Salt," for packing fish, because it left "spots upon fish, by reason of shells and trash in it." Another export crisis, according to the later testimony of Benjamin Franklin, brought the enactment in 1723 of a statute by the Massachusetts legislature.[53] New England rum shipped south to North Carolina, Franklin wrote, "poison'd their People giving them the Dry-Bellyach, with a Loss of the Use of their Limbs." Protests provoked inquiry, and Massachusetts physicians concluded that the "Mischief" had resulted from rum contaminated with lead from distillery pipes. The law forbade such use.

If export concerns seemed to predominate, governing officials of early America were not unmindful of their citizens' purses and their health. English experience influenced American practice. In England control of the cost of bread dated back at least to Norman times. King John issued in 1202 the Assize of Bread, the first recorded regulation in a long series aimed at keeping the staff of life cheap enough to prevent Englishmen from starving. Some of these laws aimed also at curtailing adulteration. The American colonies adopted this tradition. In 1646 Massachusetts enacted an assize of bread, which controlled butter also. Bakers were told what each penny loaf of three qualities of bread—"white," "wheat,"

[51] John Duffy, *A History of Public Health in New York City, 1625–1866* (New York, 1968), 222–23, 31–32.

[52] Janssen, "America's First Food and Drug Laws," 12–19.

[53] John B. Blake, *Public Health in the Town of Boston, 1630–1822* (Cambridge, MA, 1959), 145.

and "ordinary"—should weigh when wheat was selling at stated prices. Every baker must place on each loaf his distinct mark, so that the bread inspectors in every town could trace to the proper source any underweight loaves they might find. The penalty for short weight and for failure to bear the maker's mark was forfeiture of the article. Three years later the governor and council of New Amsterdam passed a similar decree, and other colonies sought to protect their residents in the same way.[54]

Bakers occasionally used inferior wheat flour to bake their loaves, substituted cheaper grains for wheat, and added adulterants like chalk and ground beans. The colonies and, later, the states, passed more laws forbidding such practices.[55] Now and again a newspaper or a grand jury would renew charges against the bakers, although before 1850 complaints about bread quality or price were so few as to indicate either widespread indifference or, more likely, strict enough enforcement to make bad bread a minor problem.[56]

Bakers did not always rest easy under restraint. A "Loaf-Bread Baker" in New York, writing a pamphlet in 1827, exuded a rising spirit of laissez-faire. Quoting Adam Smith, he demanded that bread laws and other relics of the feudal British king's power be "shut up . . . in a leaden box, labelled '*not of freedom, nor '76*,' and . . . deposit[ed] . . . as *curious relics*, for the amusement of aristocrats, antiquarians, and visitors to . . . the American Museum."[57]

Early Americans found slaughterhouses more troublesome than bakeries. Again English precedent influenced American practice. Henry VII had removed slaughterhouses from cities and towns to prevent the engendering of illness. American towns passed ordinances fixing the location and curbing the practices of butchers, fishmongers, candle makers, and other noxious trades. In an era in which miasmas were rising into the position of chief environmental factor thought to be the cause of disease, "loathsome smells" and "effluvias" frightened the public into suppressive action. A Boston town meeting in 1797 determined to remove a slaughterhouse from its location and shut down all fish stalls in the market because the ground around them was "impregnated with the

[54] Frederick A. Filby, *A History of Food Adulteration and Analysis* (London, 1934); Janssen, "America's First Food and Drug Laws," 13–14; Duffy, *A History of Public Health in New York City, 1625–1866*, 13.

[55] Janssen, "America's First Food and Drug Laws," 12–19; Hutt and Hutt, "A History of Government Regulation," 35–38.

[56] Duffy, *A History of Public Health in New York City, 1625–1866*, 223–25, 426–27.

[57] A Loaf-Bread Baker, *Bread Laws Examined* (New York, 1827), 9, 16.

seeds of the plague."[58] Seven decades later slaughterhouses in Boston and surrounding towns became the first dramatic issue of controversy for the new State Board of Health. No changes in slaughtering methods had taken place during the past half century, asserted the board's secretary. Water and air polluted with animal offal, by lowering bodily resistance, portended, he feared, the most threatening consequences. After several years of pressure, the board persuaded the butchers to make a fresh start, replacing their several foul slaughterhouses with a single large abattoir.[59]

Stern measures also had their beginning in the colonial years against the sale of meat and fish deemed unfit for human consumption.[60] Tainted meat and meat inflated by blowing could not be marketed. The vending of oysters was prohibited during the summer months. In New York at the end of the eighteenth century no fresh meat or dead fish could be sold at public markets after ten o'clock in the morning. As New York expanded, its political chicanery increasing with its population, controls weakened. The few butchers who had earlier been licensed met increasing competition from a growing number of unlicensed shops. Council committees in the 1830s reported the widespread sale of meat diseased or otherwise unwholesome and suggested clamping down on unlicensed butchers. The same spirit of unfettered individualism that hampered orthodox physicians, however, made impossible a return to meat-market monopoly. In 1843 all butcher shops were legitimated. In ensuing decades one journalistic exposure after another condemned both public and private markets as "filthy and revolting sink-holes" from which the flesh of diseased cattle continually moved to the citizens' dinner tables. The worst of such meat came from cows living out their short lives in dairy herds attached to distilleries where the boiling hot waste products of the fermentation process, fed to the cattle, might yield added profit.[61]

As cities expanded, forcing dairy herds fed on grass ever farther from the customers who bought their milk, the swill-milk business burgeoned. By 1840, some sixty thousand families in New York City, including among them twenty-five thousand children under the age of five, used milk from distillery dairies as a staple of their diets.[62] Criticism

[58] Blake, *Public Health in the Town of Boston*, 11–16, 29–30, 104, 145, 161.

[59] Barbara G. Rosenkrantz, *Public Health and the State, Changing Views in Massachusetts, 1842–1936* (Cambridge, MA, 1972), 65–66.

[60] Janssen, "America's First Food and Drug Laws," 12–19.

[61] Duffy, *A History of Public Health in New York City, 1625–1866*, 223, 420–26.

[62] Robert M. Hartley, *An Historical, Scientific and Practical Essay on Milk As an Article of Human Sustenance* (New York, 1977; originally published 1842), 20.

of the dairies began in the late 1820s and renewed itself in periodic waves, breaking futilely over municipal officials linked politically to wealthy distillers.[63]

A staunch crusader against impure milk in the 1830s, Robert M. Hartley, appealed for its regulation, using arguments linking deep religious piety, a commonsense approach to the science of public health, and great compassion for the lot of the lowly.[64] A founder and director of the New York Association for Improving the Condition of the Poor, Hartley saw distillery milk as the primary cause of death among slum children. "The natural and healthy condition of . . . cows," open pasture with a diet of grass, produced good milk. Distillery dairies violated the animal economy and constituted a "grievous offense against God and high treason against humanity." The unnatural crowding and artificial diet of the cattle not only sickened them but made their milk "impure, unhealthy, and innutritious." In a book published in 1842, Hartley bemoaned the dreadful paradox involved in the diversion of good grain into whiskey and swill milk, a pair of poisons "by which the health and lives of multitudes are annually destroyed."[65] The city fathers did not harken unto Hartley's words.

In 1848 a committee of the New York Academy of Medicine took up the torch, drafting a hard-hitting report that blamed swill milk for the high infant death rate in the city. The total academy membership, however, was not yet ready to take an open stand on the issue, delaying publication of the report and tabling resolutions proposed by the committee that urged the city government to suppress the death-dealing business.[66]

Crusading journalism, a decade later, stirred the city and the nation to horror and outrage about the swill-milk scandal. The New York press had published occasional exposures earlier without making much impact.[67] On May 8, 1858, Frank Leslie, a British immigrant and pioneer of pictorial journalism, launched in the pages of *Frank Leslie's Illustrated Newspaper* a major continuing campaign.[68] A front-page woodcut showed ill-kempt men dragging a dead cow from the dark bowels of a

[63] Duffy, *A History of Public Health in New York City, 1625–1866*, 427–37; Norman Shaftel, "A History of the Purification of Milk in New York or How Now Brown Cow," *NY State J Med* 58 (1958), 911–28.

[64] Charles E. Rosenberg, *No Other Gods: On Science and American Social Thought* (Baltimore, 1976), 116–22.

[65] Hartley, *An . . . Essay on Milk*, 108–9, 330–31.

[66] Duffy, *A History of Public Health in New York City, 1625–1866*, 429–30.

[67] *Ibid.*

[68] *Frank Leslie's Illustrated Newspaper* 5 (1858), 353–54, 359–62, 368.

distillery dairy. Another picture displayed the stable yard, where milk cans lay among decaying carcasses near carts labeled "Pure Country Milk." Other cuts revealed cows covered with sores and possessed of only stumpy rotted-off tails, crowded into narrow stalls inside a distillery dairy. Such pictures, an editorialist asserted later, aroused the public in a way that mere words previously had been unable to do.[69] Nonetheless, Leslie bemoaned the inability of his artists fully to "depict the filth of the stables, their darkness and cobwebs, their close and fetid air, and the sickening stench which pervaded the entire place."[70]

From on the spot observation, often at risk to reporters, *Leslie's* provided detailed descriptions of major distillery dairies in Brooklyn and Manhattan. The cows stood crowded in long, low, wooden shanties, filthy from roof to floor.[71] Each cow lived out its life in a space measuring three by eleven feet. A reporter described the method of feeding:

> The distillery stuff, or swill comes rushing and foaming down into the troughs from an upper duct; . . . boiling hot and reeking with subtle poison, it splashes into the troughs, and the cows, at risk of scalding their mouths, thrust their heads into it. At first the cows revolt against the swill, but after a week or two they begin to have a taste for it, and in a short time we find them consuming from one to two, even three barrels of swill a day.[72]

Some dairies supplied a little hay to supplement the swill, but the swill so damaged the teeth of the cows that they could not chew the hay adequately. Dirt and confinement caused the cattle other, more severe health problems. A distemper had been endemic among them for some years, marked by grim symptoms, often leading rapidly to death. In an empirical effort to protect against this plague, dairymen had devised a sort of "inoculation" by which matter from a dead cow's lungs was inserted into a slit made in a living cow's tail. Sores generally developed, costing the animal much of her tail and spreading over her body. Sick and dying cattle continued to be milked. *Leslie's* pictured a cow, nearing death, yet still giving milk while supported by a sling. When a cow went dry or died, under these circumstances, the carcass was carried to a shambles for butchering to provide meat for the city's poor.[73]

The newspaper put detectives on the trail of swill milkmen, tracking them along their routes and printing exact addresses of their customers.

[69] *Ibid.*, 6 (1858), 184.
[70] *Ibid.*, 42.
[71] *Ibid.*, 5 (1858), 359.
[72] *Ibid.*, 6 (1858), 50–51.
[73] *Ibid.*, 5 (1858), 359; 7 (1859), 327–28.

Reporters quoted physicians reiterating the earlier charge that distillery milk was the leading cause of infant death. Another Academy of Medicine investigating committee cited case histories intended to verify this allegation.[74] Chemical analyses sought to distinguish the harmful thin bluish milk of distillery cows from the healthful thick creamy milk of grass-fed country cattle.

"The wildest excitement pervades all classes," *Leslie's* boasted of its own journalistic triumph.[75] Indeed, enough pressure had been generated by that weekly and the city's dailies to force municipal authorities into an appearance of action. After giving the swill-milk dairies time to clean up and to ship out the sickest cattle, a committee of the common council paid a brief visit to one establishment, drank whiskey with its proprietor, and announced that the danger had been vastly overrated.[76] Such callousness brought journalistic protest that prodded the board of health to appoint another committee, which made a more extensive, if no less biased, inquiry. Two aldermen on the committee seemed more intent, concluded *Leslie's*, on attacking the newspaper than on discovering the truth. They examined physicians in a manner "frivolous and harassing and impertinent," while treating in friendly fashion a distiller who testified that he once had saved the life of a child by feeding him swill milk.[77]

A minority member of the committee condemned the lethal quality of milk from distillery dairies.[78] The three-member majority, however, found the stables "as clean as it was possible for such places to be"; the cattle, in general, "in good condition"; and neither the milk nor the swill marred by the presence of any "deleterious or poisonous element." Nor had the majority been able "to ascertain a single instance in which a child . . . [had] sickened or died from the effects produced by drinking [swill] milk." Nothing more than improved ventilation and more space for each cow would be required to remedy outstanding difficulties. The entire board of health adopted the majority report by a vote of sixteen to eleven.[79]

Leslie's published a cartoon showing the three majority aldermen on the investigating committee in a swill milk stable literally whitewashing the walls, cows, and male milkmaids. A grand jury eventually dismissed libel complaints brought by the disgruntled aldermen against Frank

74 Duffy, *A History of Public Health in New York City, 1625–1866*, 435.

75 *Frank Leslie's Illustrated Newspaper* 5 (1858), 325.

76 *Ibid.*, 6 (1858), 22.

77 *Ibid.*, 43.

78 *Ibid.*, 90.

79 *Ibid.*, 120.

Leslie. The publisher did suffer the indignity of being ousted from a public banquet arranged by the aldermanic board to celebrate the successful completion of the laying of the Atlantic cable.[80]

Europe, in any case, could now get news more quickly about the swill-milk situation in New York. Indeed, the circumstances became a national and international sensation. New York City, however, made no real move to clean its Augean stables. "Don't you know," one cynic queried, "that every one of those cows has a vote?" A minor cosmetic cleanup by the dairymen was all the crusade by *Leslie's* had so far accomplished.[81]

Although polluted milk from dirty dairies held the spotlight, *Leslie's* reporters also paid heed to the watering of milk. The thin blue milk coming from the swill barns received additional dilution. A drawing showed two men, by dawn's early light, pouring water into milk cans beside a cart emblazoned "Pure Country Milk."[82] True-blue milk from the country, moreover, received the same attenuating treatment. To recapture the rich, creamy appearance, adulterants such as chalk, magnesia, and plaster of paris were employed.[83] As a health hazard, the surreptitious adding to milk of water from the handiest source loomed as large as dangers posed by swill milk itself.

Journalists, physicians, and members of Hartley's Association for Improving the Condition of the Poor went over the heads of city fathers to the state legislature. In 1862 a swill-milk bill was enacted into law. Although not defining the term with adequate precision, the law made it a misdemeanor to sell or exchange "impure, adulterated, or unwholesome milk." The law also forbade keeping cows in "crowded or unhealthy conditions" and feeding them food that made their milk impure. Milk dealers were required to mark their cans and their vehicles with their names and the localities from which the milk originated. Two years later a supplemental law specifically termed water—but not ice—an adulterant and defined milk coming from cows fed distillery swill as automatically impure.[84]

Contaminated milk would continue to bring children to their graves in ways unrecognizable to the reformers at midcentury, but a beginning at protection had been made.

[80] *Ibid.*, 110, 232, 296.

[81] *Ibid.*, 5 (1858), 378; 6 (1858), 34, 264.

[82] *Ibid.*, 5 (1858), 368.

[83] Duffy, *A History of Public Health in New York City, 1625–1866*, 427, 436.

[84] *Ibid.*, 436–37; Shaftel, "A History of the Purification of Milk in New York," 911–28; *Frank Leslie's Illustrated Newspaper* 14 (1862), 227.

III

A Broad Concern
Brought before the Congress

I prepared, with great care, a paper . . . in the highest degree
sensational. . . . I wanted to bring on a war of discussion, which
should wake the nation. Yet I was careful to state only what I
could prove. . . . I stated . . . that probably half the vinegar sold
in our cities was rank poison; that peppers and mustard were
adulterated with lead; . . . that sugars, sirups, and molasses were
dangerously adulterated.

—GEORGE T. ANGELL,
Autobiographical Sketches and Personal Recollections[1]

In view of the statements which . . . have from time to time been
made with regard to the prevalence . . . of adulterations of food
which are dangerous to health and life, and which have created
so much agitation in the public mind as to induce the National
Board of Trade to establish this competition, it is very gratifying
to find that none of the essayists produce any definite or satis-
fying evidence as to the widespread existence of such dangerous
adulterations in this country.

—Report of Committee of Award of the
National Board of Trade[2]

Fervent Foes of Adulteration

The attempt to secure a broad national law to protect citizens of the
United States from the expanding threat of adulterated food, drink, and
drugs began in 1879 and continued through a quarter century, by turns
waxing and waning in intensity, before reaching fruition in 1906. During this extended campaign, two kinds of voices urged the necessity for
action. The reform voice, sometimes shrill, concerns itself with the wel-

---

[1] George T. Angell, *Autobiographical Sketches and Personal Recollections* (Boston, 1892),
59–60.

[2] Report of Committee of Award, "Proposed Legislation on Adulteration of Food,"
National Board of Health Bulletin 2 (1881), 665.

fare of consumers, and, while bemoaning the way in which adulteration cheats the public, puts major stress on hazards to health. The business voice speaks in less frenetic tones, downplays danger, exempts from regulation harmless adulterants sanctioned by long trade practice, and defines more serious secret adulteration as a morally indefensible economic practice that pinches the consumer's purse and pushes the honorable entrepreneur, unable to compete, to the brink of bankruptcy. The reform and business voices criticize each other, as well as castigating their mutual enemies.

Such a debate marked the introductory efforts to seek a broad national law. Just as ancient British practice regulating bread making and butchering had guided American colonial and early state controls, so British experience in achieving national laws prodded Americans to consider similar action.

In 1820 a German chemist long resident in Britain published a critique of adulteration. Fredrick Accum's book was described a century later by Charles A. Browne, then chief administrator of America's 1906 law, as "the origin of the modern pure food movement."[3] Accum pioneered both as analyst and propagandist. A talented chemist, he taught the practical application of his skills to many aspiring students, including Americans. Accum based *A Treatise on Adulterations of Food* mainly on his own laboratory findings. "It is . . . lamentable," he wrote, "that the extensive application of chemistry . . . should have been perverted into an auxiliary to this nefarious traffic [in adulterated goods]. But, happily for the science, it may . . . be converted into a means of detecting the abuse." Bread and cheese, beer and wine, coffee and tea, candy and catsup, and many more articles of food and drink received exposure in Accum's pages. "Nine tenths of the most potent drugs and chemical preparations used in pharmacy," he further asserted, were "vended in a sophisticated state."[4]

Accum dramatized his alarm. Stamped on the cover of his treatise, a disturbing design revealed serpents bordering a web at the center of which a spider devoured a fly; at the top, a death's head rested on a pall, beneath which were warning words from the Old Testament, "There is death in the pot." On Accum's title page, bold type proclaimed the au-

[3] Charles Albert Browne, "The Life and Chemical Services of Fredrick Accum," *Journal of Chemical Education* 2 (1925), 829–51, 1008–34, 1140–49.

[4] Fredrick Accum, *A Treatise on Adulterations of Food, and Culinary Poisons, Exhibiting the Fraudulent Sophistications of Bread, Beer, Wine, Spirituous Liquors, Tea, Coffee, Cream, Confectionery, Vinegar, Mustard, Pepper, Cheese, Olive Oil, Pickles, and Other Articles Employed in Domestic Economy, and Methods of Detecting Them* (London, 1820), 13, 18. Accum devoted some attention to the adulteration of drugs.

thor's intent to treat of "Culinary Poisons." Echoing this somber sentiment, a device revealed an hourglass and the staff of life, both overturned, beside a flickering candle, around whose flame two moths hovered and at whose base a dead moth already lay.

It disturbed Accum that "the man who robs a fellow subject of a few shillings on the high-way, is sentenced to death, while he who distributes a slow poison to a whole community, escapes unpunished." He cited the lead in wine and in confectionery, the copper in pickles and catsup, the narcotic cocculus indicus in beer—"it never fails to shew its baneful effects at last"—as examples of dangerous adulterations met with every day.[5]

By later, more stringent scientific standards, Accum shirked documentation, depended more on organoleptic tests than on chemical analysis, and overgeneralized.[6] Yet in its own day Accum's *Treatise* provoked tremendous public excitement, leading rapidly to new editions and to reprinting throughout Europe. A pirated American edition soon appeared in Philadelphia.[7] In Browne's judgment, Accum's volume was "in all probability the most extensively reviewed book upon chemistry ever written."[8]

A series of imitative "Death" books kept public interest in adulteration alert.[9] However, comprehensive legislative remedies for social evils seemed inappropriate during the heyday of laissez-faire and caveat emptor. Like some of their American counterparts, British physicians and pharmacists saw relief not in new laws but in better education and higher professional standards. As the years passed, however, the deplorable living conditions of the poor engineered by urban industrialism, advancing more rapidly in England than in the United States, pricked the early Victorian conscience, spurred increasing concern about public health, and turned a still laissez-faire society toward law making. Compassion alone did not motivate measures improving city water supplies and sewage disposal. More significant was a gradually dawning awareness, accelerated by cholera epidemics, that matters affecting the public

[5] *Ibid.*, 15–16, 30, 209–10.

[6] Stieb, *Drug Adulteration*, 114–15; Mitchell Okun, *Fair Play in the Marketplace: The First Battle for Pure Food and Drugs* (DeKalb, IL, 1986), 6.

[7] The American edition did not reproduce on the title page Accum's pictorial design containing the quotation from 2 Kings.

[8] Browne, "The Life and Chemical Service of Fredrick Accum," 1028.

[9] Stieb, *Drug Adulteration*, 169–70. An important American example is Thomas H. Hoskins, *What We Eat: An Account of the Most Common Adulterations of Food and Drink with Simple Tests by Which Many of Them May be Detected* (Boston, 1861).

health influenced the whole economy. Insofar as disease could be prevented, sanitarians argued, industrial profits would expand.

By the 1850s, in the aftermath of the British Public Health Act of 1848 and other laws, legislative confrontation of adulteration seemed more plausible than in Accum's day. By midcentury also, the expanding use of the microscope gave a greater sense of authority to the work of analysts. As Lewis Beck's analyses underlay the 1848 American drug importation law, so the analyses of Arthur Hill Hassall opened the major campaign leading to Britain's first Adulteration Act of 1860.[10]

A young practicing physician in London, Hassall became impressed with apparent contradictions between foods as advertised and as displayed in shop windows. A first paper, published in 1850, exposed the extensive adulteration of coffee, and received wide publicity. Hassall then scrutinized brown sugar, the sweet used by most citizens. Current folk wisdom told of the grocer who called down to his assistant in the cellar: "Have you watered the treacle and sanded the sugar? . . . Then come up to prayers." Hassall's first examinations of brown sugar revealed not sand, but infestation with living and dead louse-like creatures responsible for an ailment called "Grocer's Itch."[11]

The carefulness of Hassall's methods impressed an older physician and radical reformer, Thomas Wakley, founder and editor of the *Lancet*, a medical journal, who had long criticized adulteration. Wakley offered Hassall the opportunity of publishing in this respected journal the results of intensive inquiries into adulteration, including the names of the guilty. The editor would pay expenses and assume legal risks. Between 1851 and 1854 the *Lancet* presented a long series of Hassall's reports, later revised into books, amounting to a veritable dictionary of adulteration. So accurate that only one legal suit was threatened—and that not brought to court—Hassall's careful analyses, combining chemistry and microscopy, gained vividness through an abundance of illustrations, wood engravings of views captured by a camera obscura of how adulteration appeared under the microscope.[12]

Hassall's prominence led to his becoming "first, last, and chief witness" before a Parliamentary Select Committee on Adulterations of

[10] Stieb, *Drug Adulteration*, 68–176.

[11] Arthur Hill Hassall, *The Narrative of a Busy Life: An Autobiography* (London, 1893), 43–44.

[12] This account of Hassall depends on *ibid.*, 43–58; Edwy Godwin Clayton, *Arthur Hill Hassall, Physician and Sanitary Reformer* (London, 1908), 11–444; and Hassall's books drawn from his *Lancet* articles: *Food and Its Adulterations* (London, 1855), and *Adulterations Detected; or, Plain Instructions for the Discovery of Frauds in Food and Medicine* (London, 1857).

Food in 1855 and 1856.[13] This inquiry had been launched on a motion by a member from Birmingham, prompted by an apothecary and surgeon, John Postgate, a vigorous agitator against adulteration. Hassall's testimony impressed the committee members, and eventually led Parliament to act.[14]

The British Adulteration Act of 1860 proved to the public that Parliament had taken note of a problem and furnished a precedent for broad regulation, but provided little in the way of an enforceable statute. It did not define adulteration. Authority was not centralized; local governing boards and councils had the option of appointing analysts and inspectors to enforce the act. Analysts were often inexperienced, their decisions conflicting. Conviction required proof that the seller of food or drink knew of the adulteration, a legal burden almost impossible to sustain. Under these circumstances, not much abatement of adulteration could be achieved.[15]

Therefore, the 1860 law in due course underwent amendment, first in 1872, mainly to add drugs to the articles covered. In 1875, following the report of a new Select Committee, the law received thorough recasting as the Sale of Food and Drugs Act. Enforcement authority remained with local governments, although a mild increase in central power occurred. Reluctant local areas could be forced to employ competent analysts, and a national body would serve as referee for disputed analyses. The analysts had the task of testing samples brought to them either by common citizens suspicious of wares they had bought or by local police and health inspectors assigned to surveillance of the market. Violators of the law's taboos were tried in court, with fines assessed for those guilty of first offenses and imprisonment possible for subsequent convictions.

The word "adulteration" did not appear in the 1875 law, and an absence of clear standards and precise definitions boded a continuation of enforcement difficulties. "No person," the law stated, should "mix, colour, stain, or powder" a food with "intent" to sell the sophisticated product. Also illegal was the mixing of other ingredients with a drug "so as to affect injuriously the quality or potency." The act of selling such mixtures also violated the law. Lack of knowledge by the seller that the foods or drugs had been tampered with still constituted a defense,

---

[13] Stieb, *Drug Adulteration*, 105.

[14] *Ibid.*, 176–77. Okun, *Fair Play in the Marketplace*, 16–18, challenges Hassall's reliability as a witness, charging that "he sometimes made exotic charges on mere hearsay" and that he had not made systematic and extensive investigations to warrant his charges of the "vast extent of adulteration."

[15] Stieb, *Drug Adulteration*, 126–28, 181–82.

but the new law required him to prove "that he could not with reasonable diligence have obtained that knowledge."

The law banned the depreciating of a food by abstracting any part of it so as to damage its "quality, substance, or nature." More generally it forbade the sale of foods and drugs that did not conform to the expectations of the consumer under the names he used in asking for them. Several exceptions permitted the use of nonpoisonous, nonfraudulent ingredients required in the process of production. A system of written warranties given by suppliers protected the vendor who, not knowing of a product's illegal state, "sold it in the same state as when he purchased it." The law specifically excluded from its purview proprietary medicines.

The analysts who would examine products predicted that the law's lack of standards would make enforcement troublesome.[16] The year before the law's enactment, this group of specialists had organized into a national body, the Society of Public Analysts, partly out of self-defense. The 1874 Select Committee of Parliament had blamed failures of the 1860 law partly on the inexperience of analysts and their conflicting analyses. The new society made its first order of business the formulating of definitions of adulteration that a revised law might properly contain. Although Parliament rebuffed the society's suggestions, the three-member drafting committee had not labored in vain. Through the venturesomeness of one of its members, the committee's recommendations shortly moved westward to America in an important episode of transatlantic persuasion.

By 1879, two generations after the publication of Accum's treatise and a generation after the enactment of the drug importation law, conditions in the United States had reached a stage at which some congressmen deemed it appropriate to begin considering broad bills to confront adulteration. Two separate groups, reformers worried about public health and businessmen worried about reformers, urged congressional attention to the problem. To these conflicting voices, the panicked appeal of the farmer soon was added.

During this first stage of a long contest, the most outspoken purefood crusader, George Thorndike Angell, brought to the cause promotional talents developed while pressing his primary lifelong concern, the prevention of cruelty to animals.[17] Born in Massachusetts, the son of a Baptist minister, Angell worked his way through Dartmouth and became a Boston lawyer. Within a quarter of a century he had made

[16] *Ibid.*, 131–32.
[17] Angell, *Autobiographical Sketches*.

enough money to give up his practice and devote his energies to the plight of dumb beasts. Slavery had been abolished, and other good works now seemed fitting for New Englanders of sensitive conscience. Angell brought to a secular crusade a religious zeal, "confident," as a eulogist wrote later, "that he was doing God's work just as truly as was the missionary abroad or the preacher in the pulpit."[18] Kindness to animals, Angell believed, led inevitably toward a better human world, one in which crime might be reduced and war abolished.[19] In 1868 he organized the Massachusetts Society for the Prevention of Cruelty to Animals and launched a publication, *Our Dumb Animals*.

The society took early and successful aim at the cruel treatment of animals held for butchering at the Brighton stockyards. Angell visited other stockyards incognito, then spoke out about the suffering of cattle. In Chicago his revelations led to the founding of the Illinois Humane Society. In Detroit he made explicit the linkage between dead and dying cattle and unclean beef, telling an audience, as he later remarked dryly, "much more about their meats than they had previously known." Angell testified in Washington in behalf of regulating the transport of animals in interstate commerce, even writing comments on this theme that were incorporated into the inaugural address of President Rutherford B. Hayes.[20]

In 1875 Angell learned that a marbleized ironware manufactured in New York contained soluble lead, posing grave danger to the health of families and hospital patients eating food cooked in such pots and pans. "When I found this out," he said, "it was clearly my duty to put a stop to this sort of thing, just as I would stop a driver from beating an overloaded horse." Angell's sharp criticism, carried in the press and backed up by the analysis of a Harvard chemist, led to the closing of the factory. Soon Angell spoke out against wallpapers colored with arsenical dyes.[21]

A next natural step in Angell's contest with what he called crimes against the public health brought him to adulterated foods. Assembling numerous examples from his reading and conversations, he went to the

[18] Guy Richardson, "Apostle of Peace and Justice to Animals—Centenary of George T. Angell," *Zion's Herald*, June 6, 1909. This and the following reference have been provided to me by Gerald Carson.

[19] Clipping of article by Thornton W. Burgess, in *Our Dumb Animals* 41 (March 1909), 145–46.

[20] Angell, *Autobiographical Sketches*, 38–40; Gerald Carson, *Men, Beasts, and Gods: A History of Cruelty and Kindness to Animals* (New York, 1972), 112.

[21] Angell, *Autobiographical Sketches*, 50, 51, 61; Burgess, in *Our Dumb Animals* 41; Lyman F. Kebler, "George Thorndike Angell, The Fearless Pioneer for Pure Food, Drugs and the Friend of Those Who Could Not Speak for Themselves," *J Amer Pharm Assoc* 19 (1930), 753–59.

1878 meeting of the American Public Health Association in Richmond hoping to arouse the concern of its members. A major yellow-fever epidemic, however, dominated the attention of both the convention and the nation.[22]

In January 1879 Angell succeeded in attracting the interest of the press to his deliberately sensational depiction of the adulteration evil. Addressing a meeting of the American Social Science Association in Boston, the reformer spoke of fraud and danger, stressing the latter: meat butchered from diseased animals, flour milled from unwholesome grain, pickles dyed with copper salts, cayenne pepper tinted with red lead, confectionery colored with metallic dyes. Falsely labeled butter and cheese made from the fat and bones of diseased animals contained living parasites to "enter and breed in human bodies." "Millions of dollars' worth of quack medicines" flooded the nation.[23]

Such adulterations were expanding every year, Angell charged:

> They poison and cheat the consumer; affect, and in many cases destroy, the health not only of the rich, but of the poor, whose health is their only capital. They are little or no profit to the seller, who, in ninety-nine cases out of a hundred, would prefer to sell honest goods, and enrich only those manufacturers and adulterators, some of whom, regardless of the laws of God and man, are little, if any, better than the pirates that plunder our ships on the ocean, or the highwaymen who rob and murder on the land.[24]

The nation's press, to which the speaker mailed this text, gave Angell's address prominent display. Other speeches followed. A trade paper compared Angell to an old clock that, once wound up, would never stop striking. His flamboyant attacks upset many citizens who considered themselves foes of adulteration, especially sanitarians and leading businessmen, who thought the Bostonian's charges extremely exaggerated. Their own analyses could not replicate the poisonous adulterants Angell pointed to with alarm. Albert R. Leeds, for example, a professor who had served on the New Jersey State Board of Health, credited Angell—although not naming him—for arousing increased "public interest" in adulteration. However, he deplored the extravagance of the charges as resting upon "a vast deal of misinformation posing as exact science." Leeds, the *New York Times* reported, thought that the current

[22] *Ibid.*; Angell, *Autobiographical Sketches*, 56–57.

[23] *Ibid.*, 59–62; Kebler, "George Thorndike Angell"; Angell, "Public Health Associations," *Sanitarian* 7 (1879), 126–31; *New York Times*, January 9 and November 11, 1879, and June 4, 1881.

[24] Angell, "Public Health Associations," 130.

alarm about adulteration, "industriously fostered by sensational statements," needed "correction in very essential particulars."[25]

When later in 1879 Angell repeated his charges at another meeting of the American Social Science Association, he faced rebuttal from another representative of the sanitarians, Henry Meyer, a New York sanitary engineer and publisher of a trade paper. To Angell's face and then in the *Sanitary Engineer*, Meyer stoutly denied claims of widespread and harmful adulteration. Terming Angell a rank amateur, Meyer bolstered his critique by citing distinguished figures in the nation's chemical profession.[26]

Food industry leaders also fought back. After the reformer's first major speech, Boston food processors called a meeting in Faneuil Hall to dispute Angell's alarms. He insisted upon attending the assembly and debating the adulteration issue with his critics. Angell continued to deliver inflammatory addresses that made headlines despite efforts, so he believed, by his antagonists to stifle the press.[27]

A major confrontation with his foes took place in 1880 at Saratoga before the Social Science Association. Thinking himself a solitary warrior pitted against oleomargarine and glucose interests that "could easily raise a million of dollars as a fighting-fund," Angell spent his vacation preparing for battle. He bolstered his earlier charges with new material provided by chemists, microscopists, and health officers in the West, especially Chicago, who asserted that they had come "to fear dangerous adulteration, in almost every article of the grocery kind."[28]

Taking the moderate view at Saratoga were chemists of the caliber of Ira Remsen of the Johns Hopkins University and Samuel W. Johnson of the Connecticut Experiment Station and of Yale. Surveying the evidence, Johnson conceded that adulteration was extensive and might be worse in the West and South than in the East. Yet, he asked, did the degree and nature of adulteration cause the nation's "purse and health" to "suffer" unduly? Johnson thought the answer "a qualified negative." He saw no overwhelming danger. Oleomargarine and glucose, key targets of the "rostrum reformers," could be respectable foods in their own right. While not naming Angell, Johnson gently chided those "excellent people whose apprehensions have been unduly excited" and who "have

[25] Angell, *Autobiographical Sketches*, 60–62, 64; *NY Times*, November 11, 1869; Okun, *Fair Play in the Marketplace*, 77.

[26] *Ibid.*, 91–92, 117–18.

[27] Angell, *Autobiographical Sketches*, 60–62.

[28] *Ibid.*, 67–68; *Journal of Social Science* 13 (1881), 99–132. The Chicago chemist quoted at 124 was G. A. Mariner.

scared the public with overdrawn pictures."[29] Angell, not persuaded, believed he had triumphed in the debate.

Countering Angell's alleged exaggerations from the perspective of the food vendor, Francis B. Thurber of New York City took the lead in the pages of his *American Grocer*. Brother-in-law of Henry Meyer, partner in the country's largest wholesale grocery firm, Thurber was destined to play a longer role than that of Angell—and a contrasting one—in the campaign for food and drug legislation. Buttressing his wholesale house, Thurber had set up canning factories and a coffee-processing plant. He had pioneered in oleomargarine production and had added glucose and pharmaceuticals to the wares he sold. Thurber had developed influence in a wide range of organizations in his city, state, and nation. Most, like the National Board of Trade, concerned business interests directly, but Thurber also played a weighty role in the New York Farmers' Alliance and in various associations of dairymen.[30]

More than self-interest motivated Thurber's energetic activity. His most sensitive interpreter, Mitchell Okun, considers Thurber a conservative reformer, anxious to "protect certain American traditions and values." Thurber had come to believe that new federal legislation was needed to safeguard citizens against huge corporations dominated by the railroads. "It is, perhaps, not strange," Thurber wrote, "that legislation for the protection of the public interest should have failed to keep pace with the enormous changes which steam, electricity, and machinery have wrought." The problem of adulteration might require such a law. Thurber's critique in *American Grocer* made it clear he agreed with neither Angell's analysis of adulteration nor his proposals for a federal law. Yet it was Angell's challenge that spurred Thurber to suggest the kind of law he favored and to propose a plan that might lead to legislation.[31]

American Grocer termed Angell's first speech "sensational and unreliable . . . [and] calculated to create needless alarm," and pitied the lecturer for resorting to such unfounded charges. Thurber's paper maintained this stance as Angell's continued disturbing allegations received wide coverage in the national press. Consumers were being done a vast disservice, Thurber said sadly, by being made suspicious of the entire food supply. Adulterations did occur, *American Grocer* conceded, but, with few exceptions like the watering of milk and the coloring of candy,

[29] Remsen's comments were not reported in detail. Johnson's text is given in *ibid.*, 99–123.

[30] Okun, *Fair Play in the Marketplace*, 97–105.

[31] *Ibid.*, 104–5.

adulterants did not harm the health of purchasers, though such fraud cast a shadow over food merchandising.[32]

In his first Boston address, Angell had spoken of the need for laws "prohibiting the manufacture and sale of these poisonous and dangerous articles under severe penalties, and compelling the manufacturers and sellers of adulterated articles to tell buyers the precise character of the adulterations." Enforcement authority, however, could not rest with established boards of health, for the task would be "beyond their power." Their efforts, however earnest, "would be opposed at once by combinations of capital and political influences which would either secure ... [the boards'] removal or paralyze their efforts." Only one course of action offered hope:

> the formation of "public health associations" in our cities, composed of influential citizens, supported by voluntary contributions, employing officers who cannot be bribed or removed by outside influence, and who would make it as dangerous to manufacture and illegally sell poisonous foods ... in our markets as it is now to cruelly beat horses or starve cattle.

Thurber, responding to Angell, dismissed his enforcement proposal as chimerical. Needed instead were American laws on both national and state levels modeled on English law which would ban only harmful adulterants, but would require harmless additives to be listed in labeling.[33]

Later in that same month of Angell's lecture and Thurber's rejoinder, January 1879, a Democratic congressman from Pennsylvania, Hendrick B. Wright, introduced into the House of Representatives the first broad bill aimed at protecting the purity of food and drink—drugs were not included—throughout the nation.[34] It was not likely direct influence of the Angell-Thurber debate that prompted Wright, rather the ripeness of adulteration as a theme for expanded public concern. Wright was aware of the British law of 1875, for his bill echoed some of its provisions. Only adulterations "injurious to ... health" were declared illegal. Even though the bill died in committee, it constitutes a significant precedent. No session of the Congress from this point on until 1906 failed to have before it for consideration one or more omnibus bills.

[32] *Ibid.*, 79, 118.

[33] Angell, "Public Health Associations," 130–31; *NY Times*, January 9, 1879; Okun, *Fair Play in the Marketplace*, 79.

[34] Wright introduced H.R. 5916 on January 20, 1879, *Cong. Record*, 45 Cong. 3 ses., 575. Lyman F. Kebler, "The Work of Three Pioneers in Initiating Federal Food and Drug Legislation," *J Amer Pharm Assoc* 19 (1930), 592–93; "Wright, Hendrick Bradley," *Biographical Directory of the American Congress* (Washington, 1950), 2047.

A southern representative, Richard Lee T. Beale of Virginia, brought before the Forty-sixth Congress in the spring of 1879 a bill that George Angell, raising his sights from the local to the national level, considered promising. Beale had served in the Congress that enacted the 1848 drug importation law, had left the Union to fight as a Confederate general, and now, soon after his postwar reelection, sponsored this first broad food and drug bill to receive a report from a committee of the Congress. Beale's measure needed changes, the House Committee on Manufactures asserted in offering a substitute, because the Constitution would not permit Congress to regulate the sale of food and drink within the borders of a state. Strong laws in all the states were needed, although this prospect lay "not within the range of reasonable hope." Congress did control interstate commerce, and under that power the committee proposed, not a complex bill like the laws of foreign nations, but a measure containing "only a few simple provisions of easy enforcement" that might "serve as a foundation for [whatever] fuller legislation" experience might show necessary. The bill forbade any person or corporation "knowingly" to transport in interstate commerce any article of food or drink mixed with a substance of less commercial value, or harmful to the consumer, unless the package bore a label naming the adulterants and providing the percentage of the ingredients in the mixture.

Such a beginning, reported the committee, was sorely needed:

> The rapid advance of chemical science has opened a wide doorway for compounding mixtures so nearly resembling nature's products that the senses are impotent to detect the difference. Human cupidity eagerly grasps the chances offered to turn a dishonest penny, and its greed for money becomes callous to human suffering. Not only are substances of less value commingled with those of greater, but such as are injurious to health, and we have no doubt often destructive of life, are freely used in manufacturing and preparing for consumption the necessaries and luxuries of life.[35]

The committee proceeded to cite examples of such hazards in an alarmist Angellic tone, much of the evidence chosen from that assembled by Angell concerning—as the inveterate reformer put it—"the as yet unfathomed and unfathomable sea of adulteration." On one alleged

[35] Beale presented H.R. 2014 on March 23, 1879, *Cong. Record*, 46 Cong. 1 ses., 1552. During the second session, the House Committee on Manufactures reported a substitute, H.R. 4738, on which a report was issued; the bill as amended was referred to the Committee of the Whole. No further action was taken. *Cong. Record*, 46 Cong. 2 ses., 1123–24, 1309; H.R. Report 346, *The Manufacture of Articles of Human Food and Drink*; Kebler, "The Work of Three Pioneers," 593–94; "Beale, Richard Lee Turberville," *Biographical Directory of the American Congress* (1950), 828.

danger the committee quoted Angell: "More than 90,000,000 pounds of oleomargarine butter and cheese were manufactured in this country in 1878, and I have microscopic photographs showing [in some of those pounds] the fungi, living organisms, and eggs resembling those of tapeworm."

Many memorials from honest merchants, the committee reported, had besought the Congress to "stay" the "ravages" of adulteration. Leading food merchants, however, Francis Thurber in particular, did not like the tone of the report or the terms of the revised Beale bill. They had a legislative plan of their own. The bill reported by the House committee, as the *New York Times* put it, was "an entirely different and much less respectable measure."[36]

A Prizewinning Bill

In December 1879 at its annual meeting, the National Board of Trade, a body founded a decade earlier to forward the mutual interest of its members, passed unanimously a resolution looking toward a national law. According to the preamble, "pure and wholesome food" posed a question "of great importance to the people," and the "public mind" had lately been "considerably agitated by the alleged general adulteration." Local regulatory efforts had failed because of "limited jurisdiction." Therefore, it was "important that wise laws (if possible national in character) should be enacted" to protect both "consumers and honest manufacturers." To help devise the text of such a law, "designed to prevent injurious adulteration . . . without imposing unnecessary burdens upon commerce," prizes would be awarded by the board for essays on the theme, each to include a draft of a model statute.[37]

The suggestion for the contest came from Henry Meyer, who persuaded his brother-in-law, Francis Thurber, to put up $1,000 in prize money. Thurber, who virtually ran the National Board of Trade, proposed the resolution announcing the essay awards to be funded with his money.[38]

The revised Beale bill prompted Meyer and Thurber's initiative. The bill bore too many traces of Angell's influence, especially in restricting harmless adulteration. Moreover, with a House committee's endorse-

[36] Okun, *Fair Play in the Marketplace*, 126–28, 160; *NY Times*, February 5, 1881.

[37] *Ibid.*, December 13, 1879; Okun, *Fair Play in the Marketplace*, 120–21.

[38] *Ibid.*, 103, 130; *American Grocer* 76 (July 4, 1906), 7, and (July 11, 1906), 9; *National Cyclopedia of American Biography*, vol. 22, 176; Oscar E. Anderson, *The Health of a Nation: Harvey W. Wiley and the Fight for Pure Food* (Chicago, 1958), 75; *Adulteration of Food*, 46 Cong. 3 ses., House Report 199 (1881), 17–18.

ment, the measure had some chance of enactment. So the sanitary engineer and the wholesale grocer hired a lobbyist to fight the bill, while they launched a plan to devise a measure suiting their own aims. Unless they could get "sensible bills" for Congress to consider, Meyer wrote a participant in the venture, that body would "likely pass one after . . . [Angell's] notions."[39]

The National Board chose as chairman of the prize committee to evaluate entries John Shaw Billings, an army physician then serving as vice president and most powerful member of another national board, this one a creation of Congress. The same yellow-fever epidemic that overwhelmed Angell's first effort to bring adulteration to public attention had led Congress to pass in 1879, to combat the saffron scourge, a measure drafted by Billings establishing a National Board of Health. Appointed to the board by the army, Billings became its leading figure. Known for his administrative skills, Billings was to play many important roles in emerging American scientific medicine, among them developing the Surgeon-General's Library, publishing a catalog of its holdings, and designing plans for the Johns Hopkins University Hospital. He sought to make of the National Board of Health something more than a mere quarantine-control body. To investigate a wide range of public-health problems, the board gave small expense grants to scientists, and adulteration of foods and drugs was among the topics studied. The board's first annual report contained hurriedly prepared reviews of the literature on food adulteration by Robert C. Kedzie, professor of chemistry at Michigan Agricultural College and president of the Michigan State Board of Health, and on drug adulteration by C. Lewis Diehl, president and professor at the Louisville College of Pharmacy. For the second report an army physician stationed in Washington, Charles Smart, who had written a novel on the Wild West, provided more detailed information on the state of the food supply. That condition was not so wild, Smart concluded, as sensationalist critics such as Angell charged. Some dyes used to color candies did pose danger, but most foods in the marketplace did not threaten health. That Billings should initiate and publish Smart's nonalarmist report in the *National Board of Health Bulletin* reflects that his own views on adulteration came close to coinciding with those of Thurber and Meyer.[40]

[39] Okun, *Fair Play in the Marketplace*, 126–28, 139, 158–60. Using manuscript and trade-press sources, Okun gives an excellent account of Meyer and Thurber's prize contest and of the subsequent drafting of proposed federal and state bills by members of the prize committee.

[40] A. Hunter Dupree, *Science in the Federal Government: A History of Policies and Activities to 1940* (Cambridge, MA, 1957), 258–63; Peter William Bruton, "The National Board of

The three men already knew each other. Billings had sought and secured Thurber's help in calming businessmen, members of the National Board of Trade, uneasy about how National Board of Health quarantine restrictions might disrupt commerce. When the plan arose to run a prize contest for a food bill, Meyer already had Billings serving on another *Sanitary Engineer* award committee, to judge entries for a model public-school building.[41]

The National Board of Trade had directed that its food law committee include a physician, a chemist, a lawyer, and a merchant. Chosen with Billings were Charles F. Chandler, president of the New York City Board of Health and professor of chemistry at Columbia University, the College of Physicians and Surgeons, and the New York College of Pharmacy; Benjamin Williamson, former chancellor of New Jersey and a corporate lawyer; and Alpheus H. Hardy, a Boston food merchant and president of that city's board of trade. The judges convened in New York City in late October 1880 to reach their verdict, having earlier been sent copies of the only four entries—essays with accompanying draft laws—that Meyer deemed worth considering.[42]

None of the contestants submitted a draft statute judged suitable by the committee members or by Meyer and Thurber for placing before the Congress. Chandler, indeed, had harsh comments—"Impossible law"—for the winning entry. Prizes, however, must be awarded; then the committee, using whatever helpful suggestions might be extracted from the proposals, would draft its own version of a law to bear the National Board of Trade imprimatur—or rather two similar laws, one

---

Health" (University of Maryland dissertation, 1974), 115–242; Wyndham D. Miles, "A History of the National Board of Health, 1879–1893," 2 vols. (manuscript in History of Medicine Division, National Library of Medicine, Bethesda, MD, 1970); Fielding H. Garrison, *John Shaw Billings, A Memoir* (New York, 1915), 162–66; Okun, *Fair Play in the Marketplace*, 105–11, 122–24, 128, 159–60; "Robert Clark Kedzie," in Clark A. Elliott, ed., *Biographical Dictionary of American Science: The Seventeenth through the Nineteenth Centuries* (Westport, CT, 1979), 143–44; William B. Bean, *Walter Reed, A Biography* (Charlottesville, VA, 1982), 57; Minutes of the Executive Committee of the National Board of Health, 1879–1882, January 15, 1881, Record Group 80, National Archives; C. Lewis Diehl, "Report on Deteriorations, Adulterations, and Substitutions of Drugs," in *Annual Report of the National Board of Health, 1879*, House Exec. Doc. 10, 46 Cong. 2 ses. (1879), 77–137; R. C. Kedzie, "The Adulteration and Deterioration of Food," *ibid.*, 137–48; Charles Smart, "Report on Deteriorations and Adulterations of Food and Drugs," in *Annual Report of the National Board of Health, 1880*, House Exec. Doc. 8, 46 Cong. 3 ses. (1882), 323–53.

[41] Okun, *Fair Play in the Marketplace*, 120–22.

[42] *Ibid.*, 125, 133–34; Haven Emerson, "Charles Frederick Chandler, 1836–1925: New York's First Public Health Chemist," *Science* 86 (1937), 453–61; "Benjamin Williamson," in Edward Q. Keasbey, *The Courts and Lawyers of New Jersey, 1661–1912* (New York, 1912), 731–36; Miles, "A History of the National Board of Health," chap. 20.

for consideration by Congress, the other for submission to state legislatures.[43]

Announced in November 1880, first prize went to a member of the three-man committee of the British Society of Public Analysts that had drafted definitions of adulteration rejected by Parliament in enacting the 1875 law. G. W. Wigner, who served as honorary secretary of the society and editor of its journal, kept close scrutiny on the working of the English law. The modifications of that law written into his draft for America thus represented the considered judgment of a top-ranking professional. Wigner's proposal, sounding more as if planned for a state than for a nation, defined adulteration explicitly, and made the offer to sell or the act of selling an adulterated article the offense, not requiring guilty knowledge on the seller's part. In his accompanying essay, Wigner assessed the state of the marketplace in a way congenial to the judges and their sponsors. Too many scare stories had been circulated about adulteration: even Hassall had been naive. Food tampering had never been so bad as often depicted, and the worst adulterations of earlier years had almost disappeared. Only in drug sophistications did serious danger lie.[44]

An almost identical perspective characterized the National Board of Trade committee report on the outcome of the contest. "None of our staple articles of food or drink," the committee concluded, "are so commonly adulterated as to be dangerous to health." Milk and confectionery might be exceptions. Adulterated food certainly posed less threat than did sophisticated drugs. Therefore, in the committee's judgment, although better state statutes and a national law seemed desirable, such laws should not "impose unnecessary burdens upon trade." The goals should be to "prevent deception, to furnish to the public authoritative information, and to nullify the operations of sensational alarmists, who damage the business interests of the country quite as much as do the evils of which they complain." It would be inadvisable to define adulteration in detail or to make penalties excessive. Legislation should emphasize "educational" over "punitive" objectives.[45]

Wigner's draft statute, as well as those of the second and third prizewinners, conceived of enforcement on the state level. Chandler was given the task of drawing up a state bill that accorded with the committee's views. Since the main purpose of the prize competition, however,

---

[43] *Ibid.*; Okun, *Fair Play in the Marketplace*, 133–37.

[44] *Ibid.*, 135–36; G. W. Wigner, "A Model Act Against Adulteration," *Sanitary Record* 12 (1880–81), 366–68; Stieb, *Drug Adulteration*, 115–16, 131–32; "Proposed Legislation on Adulteration of Food," *National Board of Health Bulletin* 2 (1881), 664–66.

[45] *Ibid.*; *Sanitary Engineer* 12 (1880–81), 366–68; *NY Times*, November 22, 1880.

had been to counter the threat of legislation in the Congress inimical to business interests, a national bill took top priority. Billings was assigned responsibility for drafting such a bill. Meyer coordinated the efforts of the two drafters, other members of the committee, and Thurber. Speed was deemed desirable, because Meyer wanted the results approved by the National Board of Trade before being presented to Congress and to state legislators.[46]

Billings assumed his drafting role eagerly, for he greatly desired a national food and drug law that would be enforced by his National Board of Health. The Congress had been so stingy at endowing the board with authority that Billings saw advantage in gaining control of what would certainly prove to be a major regulatory function. Billings's document satisfied the committee, Meyer, Thurber, and shortly the National Board of Trade. At the board's convention in Washington in December 1880, a unanimous resolution dispatched a copy of the bill to the Senate and the House, requesting its enactment. On January 31, 1881, Congressman Joseph R. Hawley of Connecticut introduced this version of food and drug legislation into the House.[47]

The Hawley bill prohibited interstate shipment of adulterated foods and drugs and forbade their manufacture and sale in the District of Columbia and other federal territories. Control over imported drugs, mandated by the 1848 law, was extended to cover foods. Convicted violators who had "knowingly" transgressed the law's provisions were guilty of a misdemeanor, subject for each offense to a fine not to exceed fifty dollars. These provisions owed a debt to the draft of the third-place contestant in the National Board of Trade contest, William H. Newell, a physician with the New Jersey State Board of Health.[48]

From Wigner's prizewinning draft Billings adapted the definitions of adulteration, reflecting the considered judgment of British analysts. Many of these definitions were to survive the quarter century of legislative effort and appear virtually unchanged in the act of 1906. Both "food" and "drug" were broadly defined: food as "every article used for food or drink by man," drug as "all medicines for internal or external use." Food was deemed adulterated if its quality or strength had been

[46] Okun, *Fair Play in the Marketplace*, 137–43.

[47] *Ibid.*, 137–43, 161; Miles, "A History of the National Board of Health," chap. 20; H.R. 7040, *Cong. Record*, 46 Cong. 3 ses., 1070. Chandler's state bill was not completed and agreed upon in time to submit to the National Board of Trade convention. Hawley had been governor of Connecticut and soon would become a senator from that state. See *Biographical Directory of the American Congress* (1950), 1286.

[48] Okun, *Fair Play in the Marketplace*, 125, 140, 143. Okun reprints the final text of the National Board of Trade Federal Bill, 299–302.

reduced by the addition or substitution of inferior ingredients, or by the removal of valuable constituents; if the product was "an imitation of or . . . sold under the name of another article"; if it should "consist wholly or in part of a diseased, or decomposed, or putrid, or rotten animal or vegetable substance"; if it was "colored or coated, or polished or powdered" so that it appeared "better than it really was"; or if it contained "any added poisonous ingredient, or any ingredient which may render . . . [it] injurious to the health of the person consuming it." Exempted from the law's jurisdiction were harmless "mixtures or compounds *recognized* as ordinary foods," if "distinctly labeled as a mixture, stating the components of the mixture." This was the proposed bill's sole allusion to misbranding. Billings's initial draft had contained a vague definition of food standards, but this was removed at Chandler's suggestion.

Certain drugs, however, must adhere to a set standard. If sold under a name listed in the *United States Pharmacopoeia*, a drug must not differ from "the standard of strength, quality, or purity laid down therein." Other pharmacopoeias and authoritative works on materia medica should also have considerable weight: drugs named in such volumes could not differ "materially" from their standards. As for all other drugs, they violated the law if their "strength or purity [should] fall below the professed standard" under which they were sold. This clause would cover proprietary medicines, their professed standard presumably to be judged by their labeled therapeutic claims.

The Treasury Department would retain jurisdiction over drug imports and gain jurisdiction over imported foods. But port inspectors must be chosen from a list of qualified persons submitted by the National Board of Health, and that agency would prepare instructions governing their work, subject to the secretary of the treasury's approval. As to food and drugs in interstate commerce and in areas under federal jurisdiction, Billings's board would be in control. The draft law gave the board authority to collect and examine specimens of food and drugs "in various parts of the country." The results of such analyses would be published in the board's weekly bulletin. Violative specimens would be reported by the board's secretary to the appropriate district attorneys, who should promptly launch prosecutions against violators.

Shortly before Hawley had introduced the National Board of Trade bill, George Angell had gone to Washington to agitate for stringent legislation. He had preceded his appearance with a letter to President Hayes, asking his help. Arriving in the capital, Angell found the climate chilly. His letter, he learned, had been sent by the president to the National Board of Health and turned over by that body to his enemies among the businessmen. An officer of the board told Angell that he could expect to accomplish nothing. A Washington lawyer agreed, terming Angell's mission "*as hopeless* as to *storm the rock of Gibraltar*." By persistent effort, the Boston reformer secured the promise of a hearing before the House Committee on Manufactures. When the appointed hour came, however, the committee stifled his plans by failing to assemble a quorum. "I knew some members of Congress who gave me kind words," Angell recalled, "but I had found no man who was willing to do battle against the political and financial power of adulteration."[49]

At length, however, the Yankee crusader found a southern congressman willing to sponsor his views. Casey Young of Tennessee chaired the Committee on Epidemic Diseases, concerned mainly with yellow fever and thus composed chiefly of southerners. As a result, as Angell saw it, these legislators did not fear "the political influence of either glucose or oleomargarine." Young took to the House a petition from Angell praying that a congressional commission be appointed to study the "enormous sale, in our markets, of articles poisonously and dangerously adulterated." Young got the petition referred to his committee and quickly issued a report composed almost entirely of Angell's fiery words. The reformer had five thousand extra copies printed and distributed across the nation.[50]

From this forum of a congressional report, Angell could not only repaint his dire picture of the nation's food supply; he could also draw a scandalous sketch of the combined machinations against the public interest of two national boards, one of trade, the other of health. In restating his case for the danger of adulteration, the Bostonian tellingly extracted evidence from the prize essays themselves, citing Wigner's catalog of threatening hazards still existing in Britain despite the law, and, from American runners-up, quoting references to lead in canned meats and vegetables, mercury in cheese, and copper in pickles. In light of the prize essays, Angell queried, how could the award committee possibly have asserted in its report to the National Board of Trade, a report reprinted in the National Board of Health's bulletin, that "none of our staple articles of food or drink are so commonly adulterated as to be

---

[49] Angell, *Autobiographical Sketches*, 69–71. The logging in of Angell's November 10, 1880, letter to the president, which was sent on to the National Board of Health, is noted on November 15 in Letters Received, National Board of Health, March 1880 to July 1881, Record Group 80, National Archives.

[50] Angell, *Autobiographical Sketches*, 72–74; Okun, *Fair Play in the Marketplace*, 161–64; Kebler, "George Thorndike Angell," 757–59; Kebler, "The Work of Three Pioneers," 596; "Young, Hiram Casey," *Biographical Directory of the American Congress* (1950), 2053; H.R. 7005 was introduced on January 24, 1881, *Cong. Record*, 46 Cong. 3 ses., 883, 1219, and Casey Young submitted his report on February 4: *Adulteration of Food*, House Report 199, 46 Cong. 3 ses.

dangerous"? Angell quoted a western editor parodying the reassuring conclusions reached by "the wise men from the east."[51]

The explanation of the paradox, Angell charged forthrightly, lay in "the power of dishonest, combined capital." If that power had become "so omnipotent" that "the people of this country cannot be protected, then republican government is a failure." The main elements in the combination consisted of the "giant" glucose and "its twin brother—oleomargarine." By adding a cent a pound to their prices, these industries could amass a "fighting fund" of five million dollars and "retain chemists and health officers and some portions of the public press, and make it exceedingly uncomfortable for those who attack" them. Editor Meyer and grocer Thurber, Angell asserted, initiators of the prize contest, ranked high among leaders of the conspiracy. Meyer had attacked Angell editorially; Thurber sold more oleomargarine than any other firm in New York City; Billings contributed regularly to Meyer's trade paper. The draft law that Billings's committee had written not only placed enforcement in Billings's National Board of Health, but incorporated the weak-kneed principles of the prize-committee report, favorable to members of the National Board of Trade.

Angell appealed to the Congress for a thorough investigation—not to be put in the hands of the National Board of Health—so that the full ramifications of the adulteration evil might be clearly shown. "There is a greater power" than the combined glucose and oleomargarine forces, Angell insisted, "namely, the American people, who are every day liable to eat these products." With the full evidence before them, the reformer implied, the people would demand the proper kind of law.

Angell's castigating characterization of the National Board of Health and of John Shaw Billings in particular may have been due to more than his belief that any linkage with businessmen on the National Board of Trade prevented purity of reformist zeal. Earlier Angell had sought out association with members of the National Board of Health, and while the essay contest was under way had sent Billings information on adulteration. In his letter to President Hayes, Angell had even suggested the National Board of Health as the proper body to operate a laboratory in which to study adulteration. Perhaps board members had rebuffed the Boston reformer, wounding his vanity. Whatever the cause, Angell's criticism may well have injured Billings's already meager chances to secure from Congress a food and drug law to be enforced by the National Board of Health.[52]

---

[51] *Adulteration of Food.*
[52] Miles, "The National Board of Trade," chap. 20.

Congressman Casey Young of Tennessee supported Angell's plan, and his southern committee recommended to the House authorization of a commission to make "a thorough and minute investigation" of adulteration. Nothing came of the proposal.[53]

Nothing immediate came of the National Board of Trade bill in Congress either. It did not emerge from the Commerce Committee during the Forty-sixth Congress, despite the lobbying of Meyer, Thurber, and Billings. In their trade papers Meyer and Thurber firmly opposed Congressman Young's bill to launch a probe of adulteration, but they concluded that continuing the shouting match with Angell would be counterproductive. Instead, they pledged to keep his name out of their publications. When the Forty-seventh Congress convened, Meyer and Thurber got their bill introduced again. Billings felt hopeful. He wrote a friend: "I think this Congress will pass a law with regard to adulteration of food and drugs which will give the Board new duties." The major threat to success, he thought, lay in the jealousy and hostility of the Marine Hospital Service, whose head, John B. Hamilton, had ambitions to expand the jurisdiction of his agency and saw the board as a threatening competitor. A year earlier Billings had written Meyer reporting the "petty and malicious" efforts of the Marine Hospital chief to enlist allies in his efforts to defeat the food and drug bill.[54]

A factor more fundamental than bureaucratic jealousy stifled chances for enactment of the National Board of Trade bill. Members of the House Committee on Commerce could not bring themselves to wield the interstate commerce clause of the Constitution as a weapon against adulteration. The amended version of the bill reported to the House dealt only with imported drugs. Domestic adulteration, the committee agreed unanimously, must be handled by the states. Thus, although the committee report contained considerable rhetoric about the ubiquity and even hazards of adulteration, its bill mustered minimum thrust. The measure would provide the secretary of the treasury—not the National Board of Health—power to appoint a board of analysts who would possess authority to "fix standards" for imports. When such standards became established, the Commerce Committee optimistically believed, they would soon be adopted by the states, thus serving the public interest, and, by creating a single national obligation, benefiting manufac-

[53] *Adulteration of Food.*

[54] Okun, *Fair Play in the Marketplace*, 164–65; H.R. 1080, 47 Cong. 1 ses., *Cong. Record*, 166, introduced December 16, 1881, by Roswell P. Flower of New York; Garrison, *John Shaw Billings*, 164–65; Billings to Meyer, December 22, 1880, Billings Papers, National Library of Medicine; Miles, "The National Board of Health," chap. 20; Ralph Chester Williams, *The United States Public Health Service, 1798–1950* (Washington, 1951), 475–77.

turers. Except in this indirect way, however, the bill abandoned federal intrusion into domestic commerce.[55]

This stand brought to a halt the campaign Meyer, Thurber, and Billings had launched for a national law. Meyer and Billings could only have recognized, states Mitchell Okun, that the substitute bill "rendered their efforts absurd." As for Thurber, the grocer

> had never sought so emasculated a bill. What the NBT had been after was not merely a paper tiger, but a reasonable, moderate, effective law. Thurber wanted to empower responsible professional sanitarians to hound the corrupt business competitor, yet leave space for the normal give and take of everyday trade while silencing the anxieties of a consuming public that had been aroused by men such as Angell and by exaggerations—and true revelations—of the press.[56]

Thurber would return to national pure-food campaigning later in the decade. Meyer and Billings would not. Congress had not accepted Billings's proposal to strengthen the National Board of Health by broadening its authority. Indeed, Congress proceeded to weaken the board in substantial ways, handing over its control of yellow-fever epidemics to the Marine Hospital Service and drastically reducing its appropriations. Billings resigned from the board, which became moribund, lingering on until 1893 when it expired.[57]

Until the National Board of Trade bill, thwarted by the House Commerce Committee, virtually all commentators had taken it for granted that control of domestic adulteration should be a state responsibility. The three prizewinning essayists had so assumed. So had Lewis Diehl in the paper he had prepared at Billings's request. Control over imports and restraints within the District of Columbia, he wrote, were as far as the federal government could "*directly*" go. These limitations meant that state laws must be improved. Many were ancient and most "very obscure, both in working and intent; none of them make suitable provision for their enforcement," relying on accidental discovery of adulteration. Pointing state authorities in the direction needed, Diehl appended to his report the rough draft of a law recently presented to the Medical Society of the State of New York. "No individual on this

[55] *Cong. Record*, 47 Cong. 1 ses., 1610; *Adulterated Food and Drugs*, 47 Cong. 1 ses., House Rep. 634 (1882); Okun, *Fair Play in the Marketplace*, 167.

[56] *Ibid.*

[57] *Ibid.*, 167–68; Miles, "The National Board of Health," chap. 20; Bruton, "The National Board of Health," 409–28.

side of the Atlantic," Diehl wrote, had "given the subject of adulteration more attention" than had its author, Edward R. Squibb.[58]

Like Diehl, Squibb recognized that the "most effective" antiadulteration measure would be a national law, but he regarded such a statute, "under the form of government of this country" as "inadmissible." So he aimed at making state legislation effective. Yet Squibb's key ideas came from studying the failures and successes of a national law, the British act of 1875. He urged New York state, in converting his rough draft into a polished statute, to send a legal expert to England for more probing inquiry. Squibb's analysis of British experience found three major weaknesses in the law, all of which his draft sought to avoid. Imprecise definitions of adulteration left too much to be decided in the courts. The offense, Squibb stated, must be so clearly defined as to be "plain to the understanding of the persons who adulterate," thus deterring them, or, if not, making convictions easier. Moreover, Squibb noted, requiring proof of intent to defraud on the part of the seller not only made enforcement virtually impossible but missed the point. Most adulterations resulted not from "malicious intention" but from "straining efforts to make money." "That the public is hurt and cheated is often but an accident." Squibb deemed it necessary to define the offense as consisting of "the act of debasement," not the evil motive of the debaser. Finally, he argued, putting the major initiative for enforcement on the aggrieved consumer brought meager results: "very few persons have either the inclination, time, or money to give to such prosecution, and . . . it is much cheaper for individuals to suffer than to prosecute." So Squibb proposed an elaborate enforcement procedure centered in a state board of health, including analysts and aggressive inspectors to initiate cases at law. Admittedly expensive, the plan, Squibb argued, would pay for itself by preventing the economic losses that adulteration cost the citizenry.[59]

Dr. Squibb's proposal stirred some debate, but seemed too costly and "burdensome," with its "army of Inspectors," to make immediate headway.[60] His prescient ideas, however, would enter into the broader dis-

[58] Diehl, "Report on Deteriorations, Adulterations, and Substitutions of Drugs," 118–19.

[59] E. R. Squibb, "Rough Draft of a Proposed Law to Prevent the Adulteration of Food and Medicine and to Create a State Board of Health," in *Annual Report of the National Board of Health, 1879*, 124–29. Squibb drafted his bill for a joint committee of representatives from the New York Academy of Sciences, the New York Academy of Medicine, the New York County Medical Society, the Therapeutical Society, the New York College of Pharmacy, the New York Medico-Legal Society, the American Public Health Association, and the American Chemical Society. Okun, *Fair Play in the Marketplace*, evaluates Squibb's proposal, 83–86.

[60] *NY Times*, February 7, 1879.

cussion stimulated by the prize proposals chosen by John Shaw Billings's committee.

The National Board of Trade strategists had also seen the need for improved state laws, providing protections that their federal bill could not cover. Charles Chandler's draft of a state bill was essentially the same as Billings's national bill. The one chief difference came in the realm of intent on the part of a violator of the law's provisions: Chandler omitted the word "knowingly." In this respect his draft resembled that of Dr. Squibb.[61]

Third-place prizewinner Newell saw to it that the National Board of Trade bill passed the New Jersey legislature in 1881, several days before it became law in Chandler's own state of New York. Chandler and Meyer had lobbied intensively in Albany, and Billings helped arrange support for the bill from sanitarians and physicians. Massachusetts became the third state to pass a law somewhat modeled on Chandler's draft, after which the thrust of the National Board of Trade legislative effort came to an end.[62]

Ironically George Angell took major credit for enactment of the Massachusetts law of 1882, which owed its structure to the draft arranged by his archenemies. Nor could the law have passed the legislature without support from antiadulteration business groups like those that Angell opposed in the national debate. The reformer nonetheless lobbied diligently and deemed the law "stringent." Indeed, it was stronger than its New Jersey and New York counterparts. The Massachusetts legislature made fewer changes in G. W. Wigner's draft than had the prize committee. Also, the Massachusetts law covered cosmetics and authorized prison sentences for knowing violators who vended adulterated food or drugs that were unwholesome or injurious. Angell probably deserves credit for this added rigor. This episode marked the close of the rostrum reformer's campaigning for the pure-food cause. No doubt disillusioned by his failures on the national level, Angell returned his full energies to the plight of dumb animals.[63]

Enforcement of the three state food laws derived mainly from Chandler's draft was skimpy, selective, and shadowed by both scientific and ethical uncertainties. Chandler's own role provides dramatic demonstration of why the laws had modest initial impact. As president of

[61] Okun, *Fair Play in the Marketplace*, 140, 143–44.

[62] *Ibid.*, 148–54; Squibb, "Rough Draft of a Proposed Law," 124–29; *NY Times*, May 7–14, July 2, 7, 20, 1881; "Sanitary Legislation in New Jersey," *National Board of Health Bull* 2 (1880–81), 795; "Adulteration of Food and Drugs," *ibid.* 3 (1881), 47–48. Okun provides the text of the New Jersey and New York laws, 303–6.

[63] Angell, *Autobiographical Sketches*, 76–77; Rosenkrantz, *Public Health and the State*, 10, 14, 111–26, 214–15; Okun, *Fair Play in the Marketplace*, 154–56.

the New York City Board of Health, Chandler became a member of the State Board of Health and chairman of its committee charged with enforcing the new law. Regulatory strictness was hampered by inadequate appropriations and a growing mood among sanitarians that adulteration, posing so few dangers to the public health, need not be their responsibility. The board's major restraint upon regulation, however, arose from Chandler's own decisive but dubious actions. A close associate of conservative business reformers like Thurber, Chandler had also contracted with various food manufacturers—makers of baking powder, glucose, and oleomargarine—to employ his skills at chemical analysis in their behalf. The producers then publicized Chandler's results, thereby trafficking on his prestige to enhance the stature of their wares. The chemist deemed this process proper, while condemning other chemists who permitted use of their names for outright product endorsement. Yet Chandler, however self-deceived, seemed compromised. His life-style transcended that of academicians subsisting on a professor's salary. He pressured his sanitarian colleagues on the board to acquiesce in setting food standards permitting harmless adulterations long sanctioned by trade practice. And he rarely took violators to court, confining cases to the retail level, exempting manufacturers and wholesalers who certainly bore more of the guilt. Chandler privately confessed his belief that the law was intended more to reassure the public than to clamp down stringently on business practices.[64]

While questioning Chandler's sincerity, Mitchell Okun does not conclude that the New York regulator and others of his type were "villains, . . . merely the corrupt minions of the business interests." If their judgments both as consultants to manufacturers and as public officials rested on "primitive and tentative" science, though often proffered with a tone of assurance not warranted by the facts, so too did business morality share a similar imprecision.[65]

The New York State Board of Health delayed enforcing the 1881 law for two and a half years while Chandler had a dozen analysts make a comprehensive examination of adulteration. The report embodying this information also forecast the board's intent to interfere with commerce as little as possible. When the shift from study to action came, milk was the first target. Despite earlier laws, no marked improvement had taken place. By general agreement milk was deemed the most adulterated food, although no unanimity marked judgments as to the best way to

[64] *Ibid.*, x–xii, 186–90, 217–20, 250, 287–88; Margaret W. Rossiter, "The Charles F. Chandler Collection," *Technology and Culture* 18 (1977), 222–30.

[65] Okun, *Fair Play in the Marketplace*, xi, 204, 293.

calculate skimming and watering. Chandler blocked efforts by dealers in skimmed milk to get a law permitting its sale, and he barred entrance of such milk into New York from New Jersey. The few prosecutions he launched, however, involved small dealers, and he avoided cases against the leading figures, some of them his friends, in a league of large milk concerns active in skimming and watering. Massachusetts regulators displayed greater zeal than did those in New York and New Jersey in seeking to protect the state's milk supply.[66]

As to other foods, Chandler followed his practice with respect to milk: a handful of prosecutions against small dealers while turning a blind eye to infractions by wholesalers and manufacturers. Coffee unduly mixed with chicory, mustard mingled with excessive flour, and cream of tartar cheapened with terra alba, none of these substitutions threatening health and all sold by retailers, formed the substance of the cases Chandler brought. At the same time he had manufacturers appear before the board to pressure its sanitarian members into accepting standards legitimizing some of these mixtures in more moderate measure. True hazard, as all commentators acknowledged, was posed by confectionery colored with dangerous chemicals. Yet Chandler and the New York board did little testing and brought no cases involving candy. New Jersey and Massachusetts seemed similarly indifferent.[67]

The same lack of concern during the early years of the three state statutes applied to drugs. Massachusetts and New York authorities discovered that a large proportion of drug samples examined revealed adulteration, but the former state took only a few cases to court, and New York none. Nor was New Jersey active in this field. Patent medicines, although covered by the definition of drugs in these laws, remained exempt from regulatory control.[68]

While state authorities gave their statutes minimal enforcement, the national Congress could not muster much concern about food and drug adulteration. Omnibus bills introduced anew in each successive session languished in committee and expired at session's end. It was not the broad front of adulteration that stirred Congress out of indifference and provoked impassioned interest in the issue of pure food. A single product, a product that had upset Angell and now increasingly enraged the nation's farmers, overcame congressional apathy and sparked a great debate.

[66] *Ibid.*, 188–203; Samuel W. Abbott, "Sixteen Years' Experience in Food and Drug Inspection," *Boston Med and Surg J* 142 (1900), 82–85.

[67] Okun, *Fair Play in the Marketplace*, 207–16, 223.

[68] *Ibid.*, 243–47.

IV

"This Greasy Counterfeit"

We face a new situation in history. Ingenuity, striking hands
with cunning trickery, compounds a substance to counterfeit an
article of food. It is made to look like something it is not; to
taste and smell like something it is not; to sell like something it
is not, and so deceive the purchaser.
— ROBERT M. LAFOLLETTE,
Congressional Record, 49 Cong. 1 ses., 1886[1]

Glucose

The most ardent foes of adulteration deemed especially insidious and
immoral what they called artificial foods, creations by man imitating and
selling as wares from nature's bounty. "The rapid advance of chemical
science," observed a House report of the Forty-sixth Congress, "has
opened a wide doorway for compounding mixtures so nearly resembling nature's products that the senses are impotent to detect the difference."[2] Worst of all were what George Angell termed "twin-brother[s],"
glucose and oleomargarine.[3] Campaigns got under way to suppress both
these alleged impostors. Efforts to restrain glucose failed, lacking support from a broad enough coalition of interests. Fueled by agrarian anger, the attempt to secure from Congress an antioleomargarine law succeeded.

In his testimony before Congressman Casey Young's Committee on
Epidemic Diseases, Angell described glucose as "a giant" that had
"grown in a few years to colossal proportions."[4] Its makers formed part
of a multimillion-dollar "ring." Angell cited an analytical chemist in Chicago as saying he had found in syrup made of glucose poisonous residues of tin, iron, calcium, and magnesia. Young introduced into the
Forty-seventh Congress a bill that would amend the internal revenue
laws so as to place a special levy on manufacturers of and dealers in

[1] *Cong. Record*, 49 Cong. 1 ses., appendix 223–26.
[2] *The Manufacture of Articles of Human Food and Drink*, 46 Cong. 2 ses., House Report
346 (1880), 2.
[3] *Adulteration of Food*, 46 Cong. 3 ses., House Report 199 (1881), 14.
[4] *Ibid.*, 2, 12–15.

66

glucose and to impose a tax of a dollar a gallon on glucose in its liquid form and ten cents a pound on grape sugar, its solid counterpart.[5] The bill got nowhere, but it provoked an influential study.[6]

Glucose had been invented during the height of Napoleon Bonaparte's power, when the emperor sought to bring Great Britain to her knees by banning her goods from entering the continent. With the cane sugar supply thus curtailed, chemists sought an alternate form of sweetening. Two German-born apothecary-chemists who spent their careers in Russia made the early discoveries. In 1792 Johann T. Lovits had first recognized dextrose, prepared from grapes, as a form of sugar different from that which came from cane. In 1811 Konstantin Kirchoff prepared dextrose from starch by the action of dilute sulfuric acid and quickly proposed methods for producing a sweetening agent in this manner. After Napoleon's defeat, the infant grape sugar industry sharply declined, then gradually revived. Starch sugar was made in Germany and France almost exclusively from the potato. When manufacturing began in the United States, the starch sugar came from Indian corn, maize.[7]

By the 1880s, the manufacture of glucose in the United States had become an important but unstable industry. Twenty-nine factories, most of them in the Midwest but with several large firms in New York state, could produce annually an estimated ten pounds of glucose per capita. The industry suffered sharp ups and downs depending on the relative prices of cane and corn. In making glucose, corn was first steeped in hot water to soften it. The starch was then separated from the husk and gluten. Finally, the starch was converted into glucose with an acid, usually sulfuric. Marble dust was added to neutralize the acid, and the resulting sulfate of lime filtered out. Further filtration through animal charcoal purified and decolored the evolving product, its final form—liquid or solid—determined by the duration and temperature of concentration in vacuum pans.[8]

Pure glucose possessed about two-thirds the sweetening power of cane sugar and, being cheaper, came to have a wide array of commercial uses. It was marketed as table syrup. It replaced sugar, in part or whole, in the making of confectionery, jellies, canned fruit and meat, and bak-

[5] H.R. 3170, *Cong. Record*, 47 Cong., 1 ses., 430, January 16, 1882; *Report on Glucose, Prepared by the National Academy of Sciences, in Response to a Request Made by the Commissioner of Internal Revenue* (Washington, 1884), 7; Okun, *Fair Play in the Marketplace*, 228.

[6] *Report on Glucose*.

[7] *Ibid.*, 9, 10, 15; N. Figurovsky, "Lovits (Lowitz), Johann Tobias," in Charles Coulston Gillespie, ed., *Dictionary of Scientific Biography*, vol. 8, 519–20; A. N. Shamin and A. I. Volodarsky, "Kirchoff, Konstantin Sigismundovich," *ibid.*, vol. 7, 378–79.

[8] *Report on Glucose*, 10–16, appendix B; Okun, *Fair Play in the Marketplace*, 213.

ery goods. It substituted for barley malt in brewing beer. Also, it served as an unacknowledged adulterant in cane sugar, cane and maple syrup, and honey. Some so-called honey consisted of nothing but glucose, sold in glass jars containing a small piece of honeycomb.[9]

Scarcely any commentator denied the widespread use of glucose as an adulterant. Both Robert Kedzie and Charles Smart in their reports for the National Board of Health thought this practice infrequent in white sugars but common in brown sugars and rampant in syrups. Four of the largest sugar refiners charged that new refineries entering the business in New York were engaging in adulteration.[10] Harvey Washington Wiley also contributed to the debate about glucose. Destined to be the principal actor in the pure-food drama, he had not yet come to Washington, the main theater. Still teaching chemistry and researching sweeteners at Purdue, Wiley estimated the adulteration of cane syrup at 90 percent. He agreed with the established sugar refiners in declaring the practice a fraud, warranting suppression by state laws.[11]

While the surreptitious employment of glucose cheated the public, glucose itself was widely proclaimed as wholesome. Only a handful of critics joined Angell in calling the corn sweetener a hazard to health, and then only when carelessly made, so that free sulfuric acid and some metallic residues might taint the final product. The prevailing view welcomed honestly promoted glucose to the national marketplace and diet. Harvey Wiley joined in: "Corn, the new American king, now supplies us with bread, meat, and sugar, which we need, as well as the whisky which we could do without."[12]

Angell's alarmist views on glucose, however, and the introduction by Congressman Young of a bill to impose a tax on the corn sweetener, prodded the commissioner of internal revenue to seek an investigation by the National Academy of Sciences. The academy had been created by Congress during Lincoln's presidency to provide the government with expert counsel on science, and now, in April 1882, the commissioner asked the academy's president to have a committee examine glucose to

[9] *Report on Glucose*, 17–18, 31.

[10] Kedzie, "The Adulteration and Deterioration of Food," *Annual Report of the National Board of Health, 1879*, 46 Cong. 2 ses., House Exec. Doc. 10 (1879), 145–47; Smart, "Report on Deteriorations and Adulterations of Food and Drugs," *Annual Report of the National Board of Health, 1880*, 46 Cong. 3 ses., House Exec. Doc. 8 (1882), 326–27; Wiley, "Glucose and Grape Sugar," *Popular Science Monthly* 19 (1881), 251–57; Anderson, *The Health of a Nation*, 21–23; Okun, *Fair Play in the Marketplace*, 224–25. Dr. Wiley is more fully introduced in the next chapter.

[11] Anderson, *The Health of a Nation*, 22–23.

[12] *Ibid.*, 22; Kedzie, "The Adulteration and Deterioration of Food," 16; Okun, *Fair Play in the Marketplace*, 226, 232.

determine its "composition, nature, and properties," to compare its sweetness with that of cane sugar or molasses, and especially to determine any "deleterious effect" when used as a food or drink or as a food ingredient.[13]

Five scientists from leading eastern universities constituted the committee. George F. Barker of the University of Pennsylvania served as chairman. A physicist and physiological chemist, Barker had broad interests, ranging from toxicology to solar eclipses. Active in the nation's scientific establishment, he became president of the American Chemical Society and the American Association for the Advancement of Science. William H. Brewer, chemist, geologist, and botanist, taught agriculture at Yale and was a member of the Connecticut State Board of Health. Oliver Wolcott Gibbs, Rumsford Professor at Harvard's Lawrence Scientific School, had helped establish the National Academy of Sciences and later served as its president. His studies included the toxic effect of organic compounds on animals. The other two committee members were Ira Remsen of Johns Hopkins and Charles Chandler of Columbia. The analyses Dr. Chandler performed for the committee no doubt revealed his technical skill, yet, in this, as in other matters, his judgment may not have been free of bias. In the year of the committee's appointment he had been employed by a glucose manufacturer to testify at a House committee hearing. Moreover, Francis Thurber, whose wholesale grocery vended vast quantities of glucose, asked Chandler to use the city and state boards of health to test arguments being used to secure the tax. Thurber hoped Chandler would come up with evidence to counter allegations of the unwholesomeness of glucose. If the contrary proved true, Thurber offered to join in the campaign for suppressive legislation.[14]

The academy committee, in a report that took two years to complete, presented chemical analyses and confronted the question: "Is the use of 'glucose,' or 'grape-sugar,' injurious to health?" Chandler and Gibbs tested glucose for its inorganic constituents and impurities, Remsen for organic substances. Remsen also arranged for a Hopkins colleague, J. R. Duggan, to perform physiological experiments.[15]

The committee did not deny the use of glucose as an adulterant in

[13] Commissioner Green B. Raum to W. B. Rogers, April 27, 1882, in *Report on Glucose*, 7.

[14] *Ibid.*, 8, 32, appendix A; Hardee Chambliss, "Barker, George Frederick," *Dictionary of American Biography*, vol. 1, 661–62; Laurence P. Hall, "Gibbs, Oliver Wolcott," *ibid.*, vol. 7, 251–52; "William Henry Brewer," *National Cyclopedia of American Biography*, vol., 13, 561; Okun, *Fair Play in the Marketplace*, 229.

[15] *Report on Glucose*.

cane sugar and a substitute in other wares, but it minimized the extent of this problem and did not denominate such deception as fraud. With respect to health, the committee granted that "there may be . . . substances present in small quantities in the commercial products, and that these may be capable of producing injurious effects." But their analysts did not find contaminants which a few other chemists had publicized, like tin and copper, and found only the merest trace of sulfuric acid.[16]

Physiological tests performed at Johns Hopkins University were designed in awareness of conflicting German experiments with fermented potato sugar. Some scientists feeding this product to humans, cats, and dogs reported headaches, sweating, loss of appetite, and difficulties in breathing. Another experimenter did not get such ill effects. The academy committee tended to side with the latter scientist, doubting "whether there are injurious substances in potato-sugar." Whatever future tests with potato sugar might reveal, however, "it would not necessarily follow that the same is also true of maize-sugar." In any case, Duggan's eight experiments with glucose made from corn-starch sugar fermented into beer produced in himself and another person who drank it no ill effects. Though Duggan "repeatedly took huge quantities of the extracts, . . . his health continued excellent" throughout the two months the testing lasted. The committee could not say whether injury might result from continuous use of glucose over longer periods. But so far as Duggan's experiments revealed, "there was nothing whatever to indicate that the extracts contained anything injurious to health."[17]

This optimistic tone about glucose carried over into the committee's overall conclusions:

> First, that the manufacture of sugar from starch is a long-established industry, scientifically valuable and commercially important; second, that the processes which it employs at the present time are unobjectionable in their character, and leave the product uncontaminated; third, that the starch-sugar thus made and sent into commerce is of exceptional purity and uniformity of composition, and contains no injurious substances; and fourth, that though having at best only about two-thirds the sweetening power of cane-sugar, yet starch-sugar is in no way inferior to cane sugar in healthfulness, there being no evidence before the committee that maize-starch sugar, either in its normal condition or fermented, has

[16] *Ibid.*, 17–18, 24–25.
[17] *Ibid.*, 25–30.

any deleterious effect upon the system, even when taken in large quantities.[18]

Long before the academy committee submitted its final report, the glucose tax bill had expired in Congress, nor was it revived. The prestige of the academy, the lofty reputation of its committee members, the favorable flavor of their judgment, gave glucose a testimonial that protected its status in the marketplace. Chemists who had earlier been critical, now, to protect their professional standing, toned down their comments.[19] In due course the attack on the fraudulent use of glucose as an adulterant would be resumed. Meanwhile, interest intensified in challenging glucose's "twin brother."

Oleomargarine

A shortage of edible oils in Europe had led to the invention of oleomargarine, a war had popularized its use, and another Napoleon had been interested in the new product. Hippolyte Mège-Mouriés, a French food chemist, following in the steps of his own mentor, who had sought to find a butter substitute, patented margarine in 1869. His researches had been conducted on the royal farm in Vincennes, owned by Emperor Napoleon III, who personally pushed the quest for a bread spread less expensive than butter and possessed of longer keeping qualities. Just before the outbreak of the Franco-Prussian War, Mège began manufacture of his *beurre économique* in a Parisian suburb, and just after the war the National Council of Health officially recognized the new product as an article of trade, stipulating that it must be marketed as margarine and not as butter.[20]

---

[18] *Ibid.*, 31–32.

[19] Okun, *Fair Play in the Marketplace*, 230–32.

[20] The discussion of the invention of oleomargarine and its introduction into the United States is based on Martha C. Howard, "The Margarine Industry in the United States: Its Development under Legislative Control" (Columbia University dissertation, 1951); Earl W. Hayter, *The Troubled Farmer, 1850–1900: Rural Adjustment to Industrialism* (DeKalb, IL, 1968); W. R. Pabst, Jr., *Butter and Oleomargarine: An Analysis of Competing Commodities* (New York, 1937); Edward Wiest, *The Butter Industry in the United States: An Economic Study of Butter and Oleomargarine* (New York, 1916); J. H. van Stuyvenberg, ed., *Margarine: An Economic, Social and Scientific History, 1869–1969* (Toronto, 1969); S. R. Riepma, *The Story of Margarine* (Washington, 1970); Henry C. Bannard, "The Oleomargarine Law: A Study in Congressional Politics," *Political Science Quarterly* 2 (1887), 545–57; and Department of Agriculture, Division of Chemistry, *Foods and Food Adulterants: Dairy Products*, Bulletin 13, part 1 (Washington, 1887). In this government document a translated text of the Mège patent is cited, 10–12. The substance of this section in a somewhat different form was presented as the Fielding H. Garrison Lecture at the 1979 annual meeting of the

In fabricating his margarine, Mège believed he had produced artificially what cows accomplished naturally. Experiments in feeding milk cows persuaded him that butterfat was the cow's body fat transformed by internal chemical processes. So Mège sought to digest beef suet with pepsin or the chopped-up stomachs of cattle. Then he heated and pressed the oil out of this mass. The oil he churned with the finely chopped udders of cows or the equivalent organs of hogs or ewes, adding carbonate of soda to enhance emulsion, and coloring and salting to make the final product resemble butter.[21]

Mège soon sold his trade secrets and foreign patent rights to buyers in a number of nations. The United States Dairy Company of New York City acquired the Mège patent rights and set up a subsidiary concern called Commercial Manufacturing Company, Consolidated, which began making oleomargarine in 1876. In 1873 another New York concern had begun manufacture, using a different process. From 1871 onward, many American inventors appeared at the Patent Office with plans for butter substitutes. Some 180 patents were applied for and thirty-four granted prior to 1886.[22]

Francis K. Thurber and his brother became leading distributors of oleomargarine made according to the Mège patent, and it seems likely that Thurber held a controlling interest in the United States Dairy Company. This concern and its subsidiary went frequently to court seeking to halt infringers of their patent. Beginning in the first year of manufacture, the two companies employed Charles Chandler as an expert witness in these cases. The chemist argued that oleomargarine was identical with butter, produced by a means superior to that of the cow and dairy. Indeed, butter experts found it almost impossible to tell the true from the false, and chemists could do so only after extensive tests.[23]

From the start, dairymen felt uneasy and angry about the new competition. Agricultural depression, striking in the 1870s, continued into the early 1880s. Farm organizations, like the Grange and the Farmers' Alliances, sprang up to press for the agrarian point of view. Among them were cooperatives, which had become especially strong in dairying. While depression hurt farmers in all parts of the country, eastern farmers, particularly those who made butter and cheese, suffered se-

---

American Association for the History of Medicine and was published in the *Bulletin of the History of Medicine* 53 (1979), 392–414.

[21] Department of Agriculture, Division of Chemistry, *Foods and Food Adulterants: Dairy Products*, 9–12; Hayter, *The Troubled Farmer*, 62–63; Wiest, *The Butter Industry*, 215–18.

[22] *Ibid.*, 218; Hayter, *The Troubled Farmer*, 63; Okun, *Fair Play in the Marketplace*, 252; "Oleomargarine—How It Is Made," *Scientific American* n.s. 42 (1880), 255, 258–59.

[23] Okun, *Fair Play in the Marketplace*, 252–53.

verely, as production of these commodities expanded in the Midwest. Sorely beset, eastern dairymen settled on oleomargarine as the cause of their troubles.[24]

The dairymen's mood was converted into state regulatory law, first in 1877 in New York and Pennsylvania, the two eastern states where dairying was strongest, and then in a score of other states.[25] The laws decreed honest labeling but did not create the legions of inspectors necessary to assure enforcement. In New York state, where the controversy became most heated, dairy interests sought more rigorous laws, for a time stymied by the lobbying of Commercial Manufacturing, in which Thurber and Chandler played prominent roles. In 1884, however, New York enacted a law forbidding the manufacture and sale of butter substitutes; the state's highest court quickly declared it unconstitutional. In 1885 another New York law, this one upheld by the state courts, permitted dairy-interest enforcers to prohibit butter-colored oleomargarine; only white or a color other than yellow was legal.[26]

Meanwhile, a major new threat arose to challenge both dairymen and margarine producers using the Mège patent. Beginning in the early 1880s, the giants of Packingtown, first Gustavus Swift, then Philip Armour and other Chicago packers, entered the oleomargarine market in a massive way.[27] No patents governed their operations, and they simplified production procedures compared with Mège's methods. What lured them was the desire to make profitable use of everything but the pig's squeal. A deodorizing process had been developed to convert leaf lard into so-called "neutral" pork fat, tasteless enough to blend into a butter substitute. More beef fat was also available to be exploited, because a change in public taste—the desire for corn-fed beef—had led to fatter cattle. This fat, removed during slaughtering, was washed in water, cooled in ice, minced by machinery. After settling, the skimmed fat was pressed through cloth to separate the stiffer stearine from the lighter oleo oil. The oil was churned with milk or cream or both, and sometimes, to make a higher grade, with some creamery butter. Butterine, the variant name preferred by the packers, resulted. Processed beef

[24] Howard, "The Margarine Industry," 27–31; Hayter, *The Troubled Farmer*, 61–81.

[25] *Ibid.*, 278; Wiest, *The Butter Industry*, 241–47; *NY Times*, May 31, 1886.

[26] Okun, *Fair Play in the Marketplace*, chap. 11, gives a play-by-play account of the contest in New York.

[27] Senate Committee on Agriculture, *Testimony Taken Before the Committee . . . in Regard to the Manufacture and Sale of Imitation Dairy Products*, 49 Cong. 1 ses., Senate Misc. Doc. 131, (1886), 103, 146, 224–27, 253–55; Okun, *Fair Play in the Marketplace*, 270–71; Louise Carroll Wade, *Chicago's Pride: The Stockyards, Packingtown, and Environs in the Nineteenth Century* (Urbana, IL, 1987), 102–3.

fat, especially in winter, lacked "the peculiar stickiness . . . of butter" that gave it spreadability, requiring at that season a greater admixture of lard.[28] Formulas differed and varied: the formula for a good grade might be composed of 40 percent neutral lard, 20 percent oleo oil from beef fat, 25 percent butter, and 15 percent milk. For reasons of cost, vegetable oils from cottonseed and sesame seed sometimes took the place of part of the neutral lard. Manufacturers packed their product for delivery clear down to the retail level in tubs shaped like those traditionally used for butter.[29] Consumer cartons did not appear until the twentieth century.

The aggressive marketing of butterine, sold at a price that Francis Thurber could not match, posed a grave threat to Commercial Manufacturing. Court contests charging patent infringement failed, and the company was forced to discontinue production of oleomargarine, at least for the domestic market. Thurber publicly announced in 1885 that his wholesale firm would never again sell oleomargarine. He reknit his ties with agrarian groups with whom earlier he had sought to restrain monopolistic practices of railroads. Thurber resumed efforts to achieve national legislation embodying his conservative approach, both to rein in the butterine from Packingtown and to curb excesses and hazards in the marketing of all foods and drugs.[30]

Oleomargarine had been before the Congress since 1880. In the aftermath of Congressman Beale's report on adulteration, reflecting Angell's brash attack on margarine, John R. Thomas, a representative from Illinois, had introduced a bill to tax oleomargarine ten cents a pound.[31] In the same month, Commercial Manufacturing Company, sensing danger, had invited members of the House Committee on Agriculture to New York City, to inspect the factory and to be wined and dined at Delmonico's.[32] Thomas's bill received no attention in the Forty-sixth Congress, and he reintroduced it in the Forty-seventh. This time short hearings were held.[33]

[28] Senate Committee on Agriculture, *Testimony . . . in Regard to . . . Imitation Dairy Products*, 53, 104; Warren Miller, *Cong. Record*, 49 Cong. 1 ses., 7073.

[29] *Ibid.*, 5052, 7074; Howard, "The Margarine Industry," 20.

[30] Okun, *Fair Play in the Marketplace*, 271–79, 291–92; Lee Benson, *Merchants, Farmers & Railroads: Railroad Regulation and New York Politics* (Cambridge, MA, 1955), 104–14.

[31] *The Manufacture of Articles of Human Food and Drink*; H.R. 5962, *Cong. Record*, 46 Cong. 2 ses., 2755; *Biographical Directory of the American Congress* (1971), 1806.

[32] Okun, *Fair Play in the Marketplace*, 261–62.

[33] H.R. 142, *Cong. Record*, 47 Cong. 1 ses., 93; *Remarks of Hon. James R. Thomas of Illinois*, Hearings before the Subcommittee on Changes in the Laws, House Committee on Ways and Means, 47 Cong. 1 ses., February 10, 1882 (Washington, 1882); *Oleomargarine*,

Thomas testified that complaints against artificial butter were arising all over the country. Petitions bearing eighteen thousand names of butter producers had reached Congress urging enactment of his bill. He admitted that the goal of his proposed measure was not to raise revenue, but to safeguard the public health. "It would seem that Americans delight in being defrauded," Thomas said sadly, "and that they go yawping around with their mouths open, seeking to be taken in." Thomas's remarks were buttressed by an upstate New York representative, Ferris Jacobs. State laws had not worked, he argued, and "the dairy business seems to be in danger of extinction, unless relief is afforded by legislation."[34]

Before the full Committee on Ways and Means, oleomargarine makers got their innings through testimony given by a medical professor from Rochester, L. B. Arnold. He insisted margarine was "quite as valuable as butter from the cow," and cited Chandler and other scientists acclaiming oleomargarine's wholesomeness. Arnold denied that manufacturers sold margarine as butter, though retailers might sometimes do so. Congress should hold off from interfering in this legitimate business.[35]

Congressman Jacobs offered rebuttal in behalf of butter. Denying oleomargarine's legitimacy, he condemned the Thurber brothers as "kings in the empire of . . . spurious compounds." The margarine industry that "fattens on fraud," Jacobs insisted, "surely has no moral claim upon the tenderness and consideration of Congress." The consumer "hears the praises of the product of the French patent, but he longs for the fruits of God's patent, the pure spring water, the sweet grasses, and the lowing herd." To protect that consumer, as well as the honest farmer who could not interrupt his toil to lobby in Washington, the tax should become law.[36]

The Ways and Means Committee agreed that relief requested by the butter-producing regions of the country should be granted, and sent to the House a revised version of the bill. Twice, however, efforts to get that chamber to consider it met with rebuff. Nor did a number of other bills in the Forty-seventh and Forty-eighth Congresses make any progress.[37]

Hearings before the Committee on Ways and Means in Relation to House Bill 142, April 25 [and May 9], 1882, 47 Cong. 1 ses. (Washington, 1882).

[34] *Remarks of Hon. James R. Thomas*, 1–5.

[35] *Oleomargarine*, 1–14.

[36] *Ibid.*, 22–25.

[37] *Manufacture and Sale of Oleomargarine* [to accompany H.R. 6685], 47 Cong. 1 ses., House Report 1529; *Cong. Record*, 47 Cong. 1 ses., 1584, 3019. Other bills in the Forty-

Increasing frustration on the state level and burgeoning butterine sales from Chicago intensified political pressure to the degree that the Forty-ninth Congress could sidestep the issue no longer. In February 1886 friends of butter from twenty-six states convened in New York City, the delegates representing state agricultural officials, agriculture and dairy societies, and city mercantile exchanges. Francis Thurber, now out of the margarine market, took the most prominent part in the gathering. Whereas Mège margarine had been wholesome, he argued, the Chicago fabrication was neither wholesome nor safe. A federal tax of ten cents a pound would elevate its price to the point that no retailer would be tempted to sell it as butter. A committee of five, including Thurber, was chosen by the convention to formulate a bill and urge it upon Congress. They did their work swiftly, and a Pennsylvania congressman introduced the bill into the House.[38]

In April, after hearings, the House Agriculture Committee presented a substitute bill embodying the main thrust of the New York convention's proposal. The committee chose to disregard a report from the Judiciary Committee that the power to tax could not properly be used "merely to strike down a product or an industry." In late May and early June, the battle of butter versus oleomargarine engrossed House members through nine straight days of debate, the first major consideration given by either House of Congress to a pure-food issue. At the end of this extended debate, H.R. 8328 received approval. The Senate Committee on Agriculture and Forestry, chaired by a friend of Thurber's, Warner Miller of New York, held lively hearings. After four days of debate in mid-July, the Senate passed the House bill, amended so as to moderate its constraints on oleomargarine. Because the session neared its end, the House, after another day of debate, reluctantly accepted the Senate amendments.[39] President Grover Cleveland, although doubting the wisdom of key features of the bill, nonetheless signed it into law.[40]

In its contentious consideration of oleomargarine, during the spring

---

seventh Congress were H.R. 188, 2144, and 4090, and in the Forty-eighth Congress, H.R. 1995, 2421, 6708, 6709, 7166. The Congress was showered with petitions favoring control of oleomargarine.

[38] *Cong. Record*, 49 Cong. 1 ses., 4865; *NY Times*, February 19, 1886; Senate Committee on Agriculture, *Testimony . . . in Regard to . . . Imitation Dairy Products*, 238; Okun, *Fair Play in the Marketplace*, 278–80. William L. Scott of Pennsylvania introduced H.R. 6570 on March 8, 1886: *Cong. Record*, 49 Cong. 1 ses., 2193.

[39] *Cong. Record*, 49 Cong. 1 ses.; Committee on the Judiciary, *Adulteration of Food*, 49 Cong. 1 ses., House Report 1880; Okun, *Fair Play in the Marketplace*, 278–80. The House Committee on Agriculture made a report: *Illegal Sale of Imitations of Dairy Products*, 49 Cong. 1 ses., House Report 2028.

[40] *Cong. Record*, 49 Cong. 1 ses., 7919.

and summer of 1886, Congress confronted matters of vested interest, weighed concerns of public health, pondered issues of governmental authority, and probed the myths that enshrined the meaning of the American national experience.

Participants in the debate recognized both its significance and its strangeness. William Hatch of Missouri, in charge of the House bill, termed the controversy "the most remarkable parliamentary contest that has been on this floor for many years."[41] Miller, in charge of the Senate bill, confessed that it constituted "a new species of legislation, . . . but the exigencies of this case seem so great that this body can not afford to ignore them."[42] That very novelty led a South Carolina senator to condemn the bill for embodying "the most flagrant, unblushing disregard of the principles of the Constitution that has ever been introduced into the Congress."[43] Thus both sides agreed they wrestled with fundamentals. "No debate I have listened to," said a West Virginia representative, "has been marked by more frequent recurrence to those first principles which are supposed to be sound and safe guides in all legislation."[44] Traditional alliances fell apart. Never before, asserted a congressman from Arkansas, has a bill

> brought together so many heretofore supposed inconsistent, antagonistic, and hostile elements: . . . the free-trader standing side by side with the pig-iron protectionist, the advocate of the greatest amount of liberty . . . hugged breast to breast . . . with the advocate of . . . blue laws and sumptuary legislation.[45]

If a bomb had blown up all the old citadels of power, scattering adherents to the ends of the earth, and had each arisen speaking the "new doctrine given by this measure, confusion could not have been more completely confounded." A Chicago opponent of the bill expressed wonder that high tariff Republicans could unite with antitariff Democrats "to destroy capital and depress labor in one manufacturing branch in order to revive . . . the drooping dairy interests."[46]

Friends of the dairymen invoked an agrarian myth dating from classical Rome, employed repeatedly through the centuries when economic change threatened dislocations in society.[47] Americans had revived it in

---

[41] *Ibid.*, 5201.

[42] *Ibid.*, 7073.

[43] Matthew Butler, *ibid.*, 7149.

[44] William Wilson, *ibid.*, 5178.

[45] Poindexter Dunn, *ibid.*, 4917–18.

[46] Ransom Dunham, *ibid.*, 7398. See also comment by Joseph McKenna, 5166.

[47] Howard Mumford Jones, *O Strange New World* (New York, 1964), 227–65; William

the days of Revolution, and now during the three weeks of congressional debate on the oleomargarine bill, the myth undergirded the case for butter against its "greasy counterfeit."[48]

The farmer has "a primal right" to redress of his grievances, said William Scott of Pennsylvania, the congressman who had introduced the bill, because he is the source of the nation's strength, stability, patriotism, and morality.[49] "He suffers hardships in his battles with nature, but his struggles are the struggles of peace; he is always law-abiding and never fractious." Men of this stamp in a "country . . . distinctively adapted to agricultural pursuits" had speedily achieved "magnificent results." "From the standpoint of economics," added Robert M. La-Follette of Wisconsin, "the interests of agriculture are the interests of this Government."[50]

Seth Milliken of Maine called agriculture "the very father and mother of all industries," the source of even the city's manhood.

> The strong man comes from the country, where, bred in the pure air, he acquires strength and vigor. He comes to the city, but in its turmoils and cares and interests he exhausts his manhood and his strength. He can not reproduce himself. The country that sent him must send another in his place.[51]

The year 1886 witnessed violent turmoil between capital and labor. "The farmers," Milliken believed, "are the conservative force of the country, to be relied upon in [such] times of excitement which threaten the good order and safety of society." While "bloody collisions" rocked the cities, "the thinking, reflecting, intelligent, patriotic farmers" must be given support. It had been farmers, Senator William Evarts pointedly observed, who two decades earlier had borne "the brunt of war" to "save the Republic."[52]

Farmers were home owners, LaFollette noted. "Such homes, no matter how humble, are pledges of the perpetuity of the nation." LaFollette proclaimed how vital dairying had become for the security of the home itself. Income from milk and butter, for many farmers, made the difference between breaking even and falling behind. Other congressmen argued the crucial importance of manure from the dairy herd as fertilizer

---

D. Little, " 'Virtue and Liberty': An Inquiry into the Role of the Agrarian Myth in the Rhetoric of the American Revolutionary Era," *South Atlantic Quarterly* 77 (1978), 14–38.

[48] Thomas Palmer, *Cong. Record*, 49 Cong. 1 ses., 7088.

[49] *Ibid.*, 4865–66.

[50] *Ibid.*, appendix 225.

[51] *Ibid.*, 5042.

[52] *Ibid.*, 7193.

for the fields of grain, although the word "manure" was not permitted to besmirch the *Congressional Record*, euphemisms always being employed.[53]

LaFollette, speaking during his first term as a member of the Congress, did not, in a long and powerful oration, let the word "oleomargarine" besmirch the *Record* either. It posed too great a threat to the farmer, too massive an evil to society, even to name.

Choosing a health simile, LaFollette termed butter's competitor "pitiless as a plague. It wants only one thing: it wants your money—it does not care for your life." "Here is a villainous device," charged the Wisconsin congressman, "for making money lawlessly and subtilely eating the heart out of an industry which is to the Government what blood is to the body."[54]

Some of butter's champions granted that the depression in agriculture owed something to "the dullness of the times"[55] and to the challenge American exports were meeting in Europe as a result of construction of the Suez Canal and the invention of steam power, which "brought the wheat fields and the cheap labor of the Indies into serious competition with the enterprise of our own country."[56] However, spokesmen for butter sought by rhetoric and statistics to make oleomargarine assume the major blame for present woes and threatened doom. In less than a decade, they asserted, oleomargarine had replaced a fifth of the butter sold in the domestic market, and exports of butter had declined almost by half in five years, while exports of margarine had doubled.[57] A major part of this export disaster, it was argued, resulted from Europe's legitimate suspicion that much of what passed for butter going overseas was oleomargarine. Profiting from this suspicion, Canadian firms bought butter cheap in Boston and sold it dear in Europe as butter made in the Dominion.[58]

Demoralization in the butter market had tumbled the value of the nation's herds, brought bankruptcy to creameries, forced sheriff's sales of farms, and produced in rural New England a feeling of depression which, a witness before the Senate Agriculture Committee asserted, resembled that "of a community seized with a contagious disease from

[53] *Ibid.*, appendix 225, 2028, 7088.

[54] *Ibid.*, appendix 223–26.

[55] Warner Miller, *ibid.*, 7080.

[56] William Scott, *ibid.*, 4867.

[57] *Ibid.*, and Stephen Millard, *ibid.*, 4855.

[58] William W. Grout, *ibid.*, 4933; Senate Committee on Agriculture, *Testimony . . . in Regard to . . . Imitation Dairy Products*, 27.

which they think there is no possible escape."[59] The proud American yeomanry faced the fate of brutalized Irish tenants.[60] The despairing farmer would be turned "into the street a vagabond and a tramp," soon to appear "in the front ranks of some labor agitation."[61] "Profitable agriculture," insisted Michigan Senator Thomas Palmer, constituted "the foundation and reliance of the system of government and civilization."[62] If a "foreign assailant" should attack such a "vital part" of the nation, "no time would be lost before beating to arms for its defense." If dairying broke down, Senator Miller predicted, "you break down the whole country with it."[63] When bankrupt farms passed into the hands of capitalists, democracy tottered and "aristocracy or . . . monarchy" loomed.

Who were the villains in this imminent tragedy? Congressman Hugh Price of Wisconsin called them "the scalpers of the city, . . . fat, sleek, kid-gloved gentry who manipulate boards of trade," who already had cornered pork, lard, wheat, oats, corn, and butter and soon would "try to get a corner on salvation."[64] "I would sooner trust a Winnebago Indian with a jug of whiskey," Price told the House, "as trust to the Chicago Board of Trade any question relating to the interests of the farmer." Other friends of the farmer aimed their animosity more directly at the Chicago manufacturers of oleomargarine, operating under "the black flag of organized piracy."[65] Five or six men monopolized slaughtering and soon would dominate margarine production.[66] One man in a single factory could make more margarine than all of the butter that all of New York's farmers could produce. "This is a fight," one witness testified, "between 7,500,000 agriculturists and a score and a half of capitalists . . . who would see the world sink if they could get a golden canoe to float to heaven in."[67]

Oleomargarine's champions sought to ridicule and explode the farm-

[59] *Cong. Record*, 49 Cong. 1 ses.: William Scott, 4866; David B. Henderson, 4908; Milo White, 4939; Warner Miller, 7079, 7081; Senate Committee on Agriculture, *Testimony . . . in Regard to . . . Imitation Dairy Products*, 7–8 and 27–28. The cited witness was S. P. Hibbard, a Boston butter and cheese commission merchant.

[60] Warner Miller, *Cong. Record*, 49 Cong. 1 ses., 7081.

[61] William Grout, *ibid.*, 4933.

[62] *Ibid.*, 7086.

[63] *Ibid.*, 7081.

[64] *Ibid.*, 4928–30.

[65] F. K. Moreland, counsel for the American Agricultural and Dairy Association, Senate Committee on Agriculture, *Testimony . . . in Regard to . . . Imitation Dairy Products*, 237. See also testimony of G. W. Martin, *ibid.*, 31–34, who introduced an anti-Semitic note, referring to the New York oleomargarine makers as Jews.

[66] Warner Miller, *Cong. Record*, 49 Cong. 1 ses., 7081.

[67] R. M. Littler, Senate Committee on Agriculture, *Testimony . . . in Regard to . . . Imitation Dairy Products*, 134.

er's mighty myth. As with the golden calf in the days of Moses, jeered a Chicagoan, farmers strove to erect "an altar . . . for the worship of the dairy cow."[68] "This is a campaign," asserted Packingtown's representative in the Congress, "made out of a farmer's panic."[69] Butter spokesmen might proclaim agriculture's unanimity behind that product. But, in truth, opponents of the bill insisted, thousands of farmers in the South and West condemned the measure, realizing it would injure their interests.[70] This was especially true of farmers who raised cotton, wheat, corn, and hogs and cattle for meat. "Why," queried a Delaware senator, "should we protect the udder of the cow at the expense of her ribs?"[71] Dairy farmers, their opponents charged, distorted the economics of the situation. Everything except gold was cheap, and dairymen should not blame oleomargarine for the results of a stagnant economy.[72] Butter prices, in fact, had held steadier than those of other agricultural products.[73]

Oleomargarine's friends, moreover, pitted against the yeoman farmer's ancient and sacred status the imperatives of advancing technology. "Can Congress prohibit men of science from making new discoveries?" asked "Pig Iron" Kelley of Pennsylvania.[74] "The march of improvement lays a heavy hand upon some industries and builds up others," testified a member of the Chicago Live Stock Exchange.[75] "Paths of commerce change and vast cities go into decay. . . . Such has been the history of the world. . . . The dairyman is only having his share of the burden of civilization." Senator Zebulon Vance of North Carolina expanded on this theme:

> If now every time that science makes an improvement in our condition, or adds anything to the common comforts and support and civilization of mankind, the industry which is supplanted by that improvement has to be supported and carried along by public taxation, . . . had we not better abandon all attempts to promote sci-

[68] Irus Coy of the Chicago Live Stock Exchange, *ibid.*, 181.

[69] Ransom Dunham, *Cong. Record*, 49 Cong. 1 ses., 7938.

[70] Richard Coke, *ibid.*, 7085. The oleomargarine controversy helped prevent farmers from developing a united front. See H. Clarence Nixon, "The Cleavage within the Farmers' Alliance Movement," *Miss Val Hist Rev* 15 (1928), 22–33.

[71] George Gray, *Cong. Record*, 49 Cong. 1 ses., 7130.

[72] George D. Tillman, *ibid.*, 5124.

[73] Peter Collier, formerly chemist of the Department of Agriculture, Senate Committee on Agriculture, *Testimony . . . in Regard to . . . Imitation Dairy Products*, 183–85.

[74] William D. Kelley, *Cong. Record*, 49 Cong. 1 ses., 4898.

[75] Elmer Washburn, Senate Committee on Agriculture, *Testimony . . . in Regard to . . . Imitation Dairy Products*, 192.

ence and be done with it? . . . If we carry our dead with us we shall travel neither far nor fast.[76]

Oleomargarine made of good materials, insisted its supporters, was better than butter. This invention, so beneficial to the poorer classes, observed a South Carolina congressman, constituted not "the first instance where art surpassed nature."[77] Charles Chandler, testifying before the Senate Committee on Agriculture, persisted in taking Mège's stance, that oleomargarine was butter, made by a safe new process.[78] Chandler and Thurber had reacted differently to the mass marketing of butterine by Chicago packers. Whereas Thurber had stopped selling margarine and favored a regulatory law, Chandler had been retained by the packers and opposed the tax bill. Before the Senate committee he compared the dairyman's frightened fight against margarine with earlier futile battles against technological advance—the opposition by those using woad as a dye to the introduction of indigo, by the providers of wood and charcoal against the use of soft coal.

Butter's champions did not let these arguments go unanswered. Dairymen had no complaints about "the beneficent gifts of science," observed Senator Palmer, but took proper umbrage at the sorry substitute falsely masquerading as the real thing.[79] Oleomargarine was not a "legitimate industry," insisted Representative Hatch, but rather "the monumental fraud of the nineteenth century."[80] Even if the margarine interests could come chemically close to butter, noted Senator Miller, it did not follow that the manufactured article was as pure and wholesome as nature's product.[81] "I do not think," he analogized, "that because they are chemically alike any sensible man would . . . feed his horse with the cellulose obtained from sawdust . . . [in preference to] the cellulose obtained from blue grass or fine clover." In testifying before the Senate committee, D. E. Salmon, chief of the Bureau of Animal Industry of the Department of Agriculture, introduced a sober tone that would echo far into the future.[82] A new invention like oleomargarine, he warned, "which introduces a radical change into the manufacture of an article of

[76] *Cong. Record*, 49 Cong. 1 ses., 7129–30.

[77] George D. Tillman, *ibid.*, 5123.

[78] Senate Committee on Agriculture, *Testimony . . . in Regard to . . . Imitation Dairy Products*, 67–80; Okun, *Fair Play in the Marketplace*, 277–78, 281–82.

[79] *Cong. Record*, 49 Cong. 1 ses., 7086.

[80] *Ibid.*, 5202.

[81] *Ibid.*, 7078.

[82] Senate Committee on Agriculture, *Testimony . . . in Regard to . . . Imitation Dairy Products*, 217.

food which goes upon the table of every family in the land" might produce an unexpected and "remarkable effect upon the public health."

Oleomargarine's impact upon the public health provided the most dramatic issues in the great debate. Butter's champions termed margarine a "midnight assassin"[83] responsible for numerous deaths, a broad range of diseases, and burgeoning national dyspepsia. Filthy fats, assorted poisons, and "the Lord only knows what"[84] became transformed by chemical legerdemain into a "counterfeit masquerading in the stolen livery of the very industry it . . . [sought] to overthrow."[85]

Margarine's very birth, observed Senator Palmer, occurred during the siege of Paris, "when horse-flesh was made palatable by hunger and patriotism, when house pets were sold in the markets for food, when rats were devoured by the gaunt and garbage fought for by the starving."[86] This grim atmosphere of its origins had clung to margarine ever since. Armour's caldron in Chicago reminded an Iowa congressman of the witches' caldron in *Macbeth*.[87] "It has reached the point in the history of our country," he said, "where the city scavenger butters your bread." Witnesses at a House committee had asserted that "dead horses, dead cows, and even dead dogs, when they had been shot for hydrophobia," were rendered into what was sold as " 'pure' oleo oil."

The filthy fat allegation received frequent reiteration. Senators cited the testimony of Dr. Thomas Taylor, Department of Agriculture microscopist, who suggested that margarine factories might be the destination for hogs dead from cholera or from a diet of distillery swill.[88] Eastern butchers expressed the belief that their fly-blown waste fat found its way into oleomargarine. As a result of its raw ingredients, charged a North Carolina congressman, margarine was the sort of carrion that only jackals and turkey buzzards reveled in. If a bill should become law requiring the exposure of oleomargarine's true identity, "the overfastidious hod-carrier, street sweep, . . . [or] bootblack will thenceforth give" stores where margarine is sold "a wide berth, or hold his nose while passing."[89]

[83] Albert J. Hopkins, *Cong. Record*, 49 Cong. 1 ses., 4868.

[84] Stephen C. Millard, *ibid.*, 4894.

[85] William Grout, *ibid.*, 4933.

[86] Thomas Palmer, *ibid.*, 7086. See Gerald Carson, "The Siege of Paris," *Natural History* 86 (October 1977), 69–77.

[87] David Henderson, *Cong. Record*, 49 Cong. 1 ses., 4905.

[88] Warner Miller, *ibid.*, 7087–88, referring to testimony in Senate Committee on Agriculture, *Testimony . . . in Regard to . . . Imitation Dairy Products*, 30, 45–46, 128, 133, 154, 220.

[89] Wharton Green, *Cong. Record*, 49 Cong. 1 ses., 4968.

Such scurrilous accusations margarine's friends called "simply absurd."[90]

"You do not think," a senator asked the president of the Stevens Institute of Technology, that "you could make good oleomargarine out of a dead cat or dog?"[91]

"I will stake my reputation," Dr. Henry Morton replied, "that it could not be done." "An ounce of stale fat put into a ton of good fresh fat," he explained, "will spoil the whole."

Spokesmen for the leading margarine manufacturers also insisted that, unless the fat used was fresh, it was "utterly worthless."[92] "What is perfectly good on the side of a beefsteak," said a Boston scientist, "is perfectly good when it is melted out and mixed with salt and milk."[93]

Butter's friends continued skeptical. Even grant that filthy fats might be eliminated, argued Congressman William Grout of Vermont, that did not mean the course of civilization should be reversed so that Americans ceased to be "a butter-eating people, . . . taking a step backward toward the raw tallow and lard which were the delight of our Saxon ancestors in the forests of Germany."[94] But margarine posed threats other than those related to the freshness of its fat. Repeatedly, from the initial House report throughout the entire debate, members of the Congress pointed to poisons listed in patents for making oleomargarine, including strong acids and alkalis that might be presumed to deodorize stale and noxious fats.[95] Such ingredients in "bastard butter," asserted Representative Grout, made it "the mystery of mysteries—a far profounder mystery than hash or sausage."[96]

Charles O'Ferrall, a Virginia congressman, agreed. The poor man's cheap food should not introduce "its lurking disease to his children."

Yes, "cheap food!" The stomachs of pigs, sheep, and calves reduced by acids, and then bromo-chloralum used to destroy the smell and prevent detection of the putrid mass. . . . Yes, "cheap food" in the form of an apothecary's shop in the poor man's stomach![97]

Oleomargarine manufacturers and their scientist allies heatedly rejected the charge that poisonous and corrosive chemicals threatened the

[90] Henry Morton, Senate Committee on Agriculture, *Testimony . . . in Regard to . . . Imitation Dairy Products*, 60.

[91] *Ibid.*

[92] George H. Webster of Armour & Co., *ibid.*, 113.

[93] Ransom Dunham, *Cong. Record*, 49 Cong. 1 ses., 7400, citing James F. Babcock, Boston milk inspector, from his testimony before the Senate committee, 89.

[94] *Cong. Record*, 49 Cong. 1 ses., 4933.

[95] *Ibid.*, e.g., 4868, 4894, 4905, 4938, 5047–78, 7187.

[96] *Ibid.*, 4932–33.

[97] *Ibid.*, 4921.

national digestion. Chemist James Babcock, enforcer of Boston's food and milk laws, before the Senate committee went down the list of powerful agents named in patents, denying that nitric acid, sugar of lead, sulfate of lime, castor oil, and chlorate of potash were used in the making of margarine as commonly practiced or had been detected by chemical analysis.[98] Chandler ridiculed a rumor that workmen in oleomargarine plants had lost their toenails because of nitric acid.[99] It was proverbial that Patent Office files were filled with the wild fancies of fools. No patents governed the way oleomargarine was then being made, testified a Kansas City cattle raiser, and no poisons were used, only "a few simple and natural true butter ingredients, which are none the less so because they come from the animal in another form."[100] The industry submitted affidavits to the same effect, stating that of the fifty alleged dangerous ingredients cited from the patents in the House report "only three are ever used, and those so changed and improved in character from what the report would lead the public to believe that they practically make the whole list a falsehood."[101]

Not fully persuaded by such protestations, butter's champions leveled yet another major health charge against oleomargarine. The "cheap, nasty grease" harbored threatening germs and parasites.[102] A Minnesota congressman cited a scientist at his state university who, in viewing margarine under the microscope, found living organisms, spores, mold, hair, bristles, and portions of worms.[103] Any person who ate "so promiscuous and lively a mixture," the professor averred, ran not only physical but also moral risks. Department of Agriculture analyses were cited to similar effect.[104] Tuberculosis and trichinosis were among the animal diseases thought transferable to man through margarine. Dr. Salmon testified that the heat used in preparing oleomargarine did not reach a height lethal to bacteria and parasites.[105] Congressman Grout spoke shudderingly of plunging a knife blade into margarine and feeling "the wiggling kick of a million animalcules."[106] In real truth, margarine's opponents kept insisting, the consumer had no protection whatsoever against either oleo's hazard or its fraud. "The four senses which God has

---

[98] Senate Committee on Agriculture, *Testimony . . . in Regard to . . . Imitation Dairy Products*, 96–97.

[99] *Ibid.*, 68.

[100] Howard M. Holden, *ibid.*, 199.

[101] *Ibid.*, 224–27.

[102] R. M. Littler, *ibid.*, 133.

[103] Milo White, *Cong. Record*, 49 Cong. 1 ses., 4939.

[104] Warner Miller, *ibid.*, 7195–96, 7077.

[105] Senate Committee on Agriculture, *Testimony . . . in Regard to . . . Imitation Dairy Products*, 213.

[106] *Cong. Record*, 49 Cong. 1 ses., 5083.

given us," bemoaned Representative Lewis Beach of New York, "are completely baffled," nor did the family dining table come equipped with either microscope or reagents for chemical analysis.[107] A North Carolina representative challenged "doubting Thomases" about margarine's danger to authorize medical inquiry into their own ultimate deaths, insisting that the coroner's verdict in most cases might well read "died of bogus butter."[108]

If margarine were as lethal as its enemies proclaimed, countered its supporters, why had not the nation's graveyards required enlarging?[109] Where might be found a single tombstone inscribed "Dead from oleomargarine?"[110] Indeed, did there exist even one authenticated instance of a consumer having been made ill from artificial butter? Promargarine scientists—termed knaves and asses by the butter forces[111]—argued that only chemists and physiologists devoid of standing in their professions and paid for their testimony denied oleomargarine's wholesomeness.[112] There is irony in the fact that Charles Chandler, who himself received large fees from butterine makers, should level this charge against his opponents.

In truth, argued oleomargarine's supporters, their product surpassed most grades of butter on the market.[113] Margarine possessed preservative characteristics superior to those of butter, especially in hot weather. Compared with the cleanliness of oleomargarine factories, the milking of cows and the churning of butter throughout rural America went on in a much riskier bacterial environment.[114] Dr. Morton thought the chance of contracting tuberculosis from butter much higher than from margarine. Nor did butter bought by the consumer often comport with the idyllic pastoral scene painted by rural congressmen. Sometimes, suggested a Pennsylvania congressman, butter was adulterated with beets, carrots, and potatoes, and often foul rancid butter underwent deodorizing before reaching the consumer's bread.[115] Farm dairies, moreover, bought oleo oil from Packingtown to supplement cream from the cow.

Dairymen practiced even worse hypocrisy, charged margarine's

[107] *Ibid.*, 4910.

[108] Wharton J. Green, *ibid.*, 4968.

[109] George Tillman, *ibid.*, 4920.

[110] Thomas M. Browne, *ibid.*, 4982.

[111] William Hatch, *ibid.*, 5203.

[112] Charles F. Chandler, Senate Committee on Agriculture, *Testimony . . . in Regard to . . . Imitation Dairy Products*, 78.

[113] James B. Beck and John J. Ingalls, *Cong. Record*, 49 Cong. 1 ses., 7137, 7194.

[114] Senate Committee on Agriculture, *Testimony . . . in Regard to . . . Imitation Dairy Products*, 64.

[115] Andrew G. Curtin, *Cong. Record*, 49 Cong. 1 ses., 4896–97.

champions. While condemning producers of oleomargarine for coloring their product, butter makers themselves resorted to dyes. This charge provoked a color controversy that not only daubed the 1886 debate but tinted decades of future conflict.[116] To the dairy forces, the dyeing of oleomargarine, naturally "a pure dead white," to resemble butter constituted prima facie proof of fraud.[117] Senator Palmer said sadly:

> By the use of [the dye] a[nna]tto, . . . [oleomargarine] is tinted with the rich, golden, buttercup hue which has served as the trademark of the choicest product of the herd since that memorable and fruitful day described in Genesis xviii, where Abraham received the messengers of the Lord on the Plains of Mamre: "And he took butter and milk and the calf which he had dressed and set it before them; and he stood by them under the tree, and they did eat."[118]

To force margarine to retain its primal whiteness, or to assume some color that distinguished it from butter, seemed to foes of fraud sound policy. At the Agriculture Committee hearings, Senator Henry Blair of New Hampshire repeatedly urged this solution on promargarine witnesses.[119] Why not, he queried, color oleomargarine red or violet or chocolate? Then all but "blind men" would be protected from dishonesty. Such a step, margarine's supporters responded, would utterly destroy its value. Said Dr. Chandler, "We all want to spread our bread with yellow fat; we do not want to spread it with red fat."[120] Coloring margarine pink or blue or black, declared Dr. Babcock, "would excite a prejudice against it in the minds of everybody."[121] These witnesses, however, could not persuade Blair that his proposal was unsound. "You may take all the other colors of the rainbow," he remarked, "but let butter have its pre-empted color."[122]

What, though, was butter's true color? Oleomargarine's friends posed this query in an effort to embarrass their opponents. Dependent on the

[116] The Senate committee hearings furnished the main forum for the color conflict in 1886. Led by New York, some states were to pass laws requiring either that no color be added to margarine sold within their borders or that it be tinted pink. See Howard, "The Margarine Industry," 41; Hayter, *The Troubled Farmer*, 73.

[117] Warner Miller, Senate Committee on Agriculture, *Testimony . . . in Regard to . . . Imitation Dairy Products*, 101.

[118] *Cong. Record*, 49 Cong. 1 ses., 7086.

[119] Senate Committee on Agriculture, *Testimony . . . in Regard to . . . Imitation Dairy Products*, 61–62, 76–77, 93–95, 101, 172.

[120] *Ibid.*, 78.

[121] *Ibid.*, 94.

[122] *Ibid.*, 95.

diet of cows, butter churned from cream might, especially in winter, decline from a rich buttercup hue to almost white.[123] In late years, a Chicago exporter told the Senate committee, the coloring of margarine had forced most creamery operators into dyeing their product. "We now find them going to State legislatures and asking them to prohibit us from using the very article that we have forced into such general use among them." In all justice, he added, margarine makers should insist that butter makers must use a different color from the yellow, which the margarine trade had "brought into general use."

On the Senate floor, John Ingalls of Kansas twitted Warner Miller of New York by reading the label of a commercial butter dye, guaranteed to impart to "white butter a beautiful dandelion color."[124] Ingalls dilated so contemptuously on the "bucolic honesty" of rural dairymen that he quite roused Miller's ire. Ingalls's performance reminded the New Yorker of "a man standing in a wagon auctioning off . . . bogus jewelry, [or] offering to the people some elixir of life." Equal bitterness during the debate occurred on only a few other occasions when northern congressmen, irked by southern opposition to the bill, waved the bloody shirt.[125] An Iowan, changing the axis, announced that "the Western country demands and will have protection—by argument if need be, but by war if necessary." When challenged he retreated, saying he meant a battle not of arms but of "intellectual weapons."[126]

The bill before Congress had nothing to do with margarine's color, although the nation had by no means seen the last of that matter. Margarine's foes had determined that the best way to end fraud and—agrarians hoped—to eliminate butter's competitor completely was through taxation.[127] Besides an annual fee levied on every manufacturer, wholesale dealer, and retailer of margarine, the bill required manufacturers to pay a tax of ten cents a pound. Accurately branded wooden tubs bearing excise stamps took the margarine to the retailer, who was required to sell the product in wooden or paper packages labeled "oleomargarine." Violators faced heavy fines. Despite the House Judiciary Committee's contrary opinion, the taxing power seemed the safest constitutional route to travel. As the House report put it, the federal power to levy taxes was too well established to require argument, and such taxes need not be assessed for revenue only, but might also be levied to achieve

[123] H. W. Hinshaw, *ibid.*, 256–57.
[124] *Cong. Record*, 49 Cong. I ses., 7149–51.
[125] *Ibid.*, 4902, 4966, 7076.
[126] David Henderson, *ibid.*, 4969.
[127] House Committee on Agriculture, *Illegal Sale of Imitations of Dairy Products*.

general welfare purposes, as the Supreme Court had decreed.[128] "It has been held legal to tax playing-cards, proprietary medicines, perfumery, distilled spirits, tobacco and cigars," said Abraham Parker of New York. "Why is oleomargarine sacred? Why may we tax manufactured whiskey and not tax manufactured butter?"[129]

To that question opponents had several answers. The federal government, at the time of the debate, found itself in the unusual and embarrassing position of having a surplus of revenue over expenditures.[130] So, foes of the bill argued, a new tax on oleomargarine was surely inexpedient. Indeed, a move had already gained ground, supported by both major political parties, to cut the excise taxes left over from the war.[131] In any case, why should licensing fees for a wholesome food be set at many times the rate existing for liquor and tobacco?[132]

The central argument with which critics opposed taxing margarine rested, as had the Judiciary Committee's report, on the bill's alleged unconstitutionality. The measure, argued Senator Richard Coke of Texas, proposed a "wrongful and fraudulent use of the taxing power," not sanctioned by the Constitution because it improperly sought to control intrastate business.[133] Even the key Supreme Court decision relied on by the bill's sponsors, asserted a representative from Georgia, did not apply, for in it the court had made plain that the taxing power could not be used for ends inconsistent with those given to Congress by the Constitution.[134] And taxation did not constitute the true purpose of the proposed legislation. That goal was simply to eliminate oleomargarine.[135] Such a purpose prostituted the taxing power. It was a "monstrous" theory, charged Nathaniel Hammond of Georgia, that proposed taxation as the weapon to let one Yankee industry destroy another.[136] Such constitutional doctrine, a South Carolina senator said, approached the abolitionist infamy which had termed that sacred document "a covenant with death and an agreement with hell."[137]

Grant that oleomargarine might be constitutionally taxed, argued strict constructionists, then behold the fearful future. "No precedent so

---

[128] *Ibid.* The Supreme Court case cited was Veazie Bank v. Fenno, 8 Wallace 533.

[129] *Cong. Record*, 49 Cong. 1 ses., 5078.

[130] *Ibid.*, 4897–98, 5339, 5343, 7070, 7084.

[131] *Ibid.*, 4916, 7130–32, 7186, 7200.

[132] Elmer Washburn, Senate Committee on Agriculture, *Testimony . . . in Regard to . . . Imitation Dairy Products*, 191.

[133] Richard Coke, *Cong. Record*, 49 Cong. 1 ses., 7083–86.

[134] Nathaniel J. Hammond, *ibid.*, 4869.

[135] John H. Reagan and Isham G. Harris, *ibid.*, 4870, 7133.

[136] *Ibid.*, 4895–96, 4869.

[137] Matthew C. Butler, *ibid.*, 7148.

vicious" as this bill, if it should become law, said Senator Coke, will have "ever been placed on our statute-book."[138] It ends the free market of supply and demand and initiates interest-group politics. Beet-sugar forces will beseech Congress for a tax on cane, wheat growers for a tax on corn, horse raisers for a tax on mules. Someday someone may even seek a tax on natural gas. "If we once . . . take charge of everything that is fraudulent and injurious to the public health," asked Senator Vance, "where shall we stop?"[139] Congress might have to control the New England fishing industry, which turns Canadian red herring into French sardines, keep kaolin out of candy, chicory out of coffee, and ban the sale of green apples and watermelons. Congress might even be called upon, predicted another congressman, to tax all foods eaten above a level deemed desirable for health.[140]

It was in countering such mainly southern charges that northern congressmen sometimes felt tempted to rekindle sectional antagonism. William Hepburn of Iowa once spoke of John Reagan of Texas as a man who could "in the morning take an oath to support the Constitution and before night begin to plot against its integrity and seek to overthrow it."[141] In the main, however, butter's champions presented oleomargarine as a new kind of problem of such urgency and magnitude as to overwhelm earlier constitutional restraints. The obstructionism of strict constructionists exasperated them. Congressman Price asserted:

> If a hostile band of Indians was on its way to the capital, and a measure was before the House to provide for the common defense, and you would appeal to . . . [Congressman Reagan] for a plan of safety, he would study the Constitution to learn his duty, until our several scalps would be found gracefully dangling from their savage belts.[142]

The states had tried to grapple with margarine's evils, the argument ran, and had utterly failed.[143] Only the federal government possessed the power to provide relief. "Desperate cases," said Senator Palmer, "require heroic treatment."[144] LaFollette in the House and Evarts in the

---

[138] *Ibid.*, 7085. Professors as well as members of the Congress could view the future with alarm from the perspective of the precedent of this bill. Bannard, "The Oleomargarine Law."

[139] *Cong. Record*, 49 Cong. 1 ses., 7129.

[140] Poindexter Dunn, *ibid.*, 4919.

[141] *Ibid.*, 4902.

[142] *Ibid.*, 4928.

[143] *Ibid.*, 4865, 4872, 4894, 4910, 5041, 5205, 7081.

[144] *Ibid.*, 7088.

Senate presented learned discourses on broad construction to defend the bill's constitutionality.[145] Even one southern member of the House, Wharton Green of North Carolina, thought elastic construction legitimate to benefit the poor, among whom he counted himself. "I am tired of having my guild construed into drudges," he remarked, and now when the farmer seeks "this poor modicum of relief . . . he is met with the hackneyed . . . cry of class legislation and constitutional infraction. Down with such sophistry; to the dogs with such quibbling."[146]

Grout of Vermont, gazing toward the future from a perspective contrary to that of strict constructionists, saw a differing vision:

> As our population becomes denser and our commercial rivalries sharper and our accumulated wealth greater, who can tell how this paternal authority of the National Government may be used to allay these rivalries, to check the greed of monopolies, to protect one State against the fraudulent products of another, and bring all departments of our domestic commerce, which is but the sum of our domestic industries into such relations with each other that each part shall contribute to the vigor of every other part and thus create a harmonious system.[147]

To the strict constructionist's dictum, "Congress is nobody's doctor,"[148] a dairyman could answer: "I have a high regard for the Constitution of the United States, but a much higher regard for my own." The Constitution would not suffer "one-tenth as much" by the bill's enactment, he added, as the public health would suffer if it were not passed.[149]

And passed the oleomargarine law finally was, although butter's more strident champions had been forced to give ground prior to victory.[150] The Senate cut the tax per pound on oleomargarine from ten cents to two. The main bloc of bitter-end opponents came from the South, concerned about both Constitution and cottonseed oil. Southern state representatives cast forty-nine of the seventy-five votes in the House against the bill, and eighteen of the twenty-four negative votes in the Senate. Only one southern senator, from Virginia, and fourteen southern rep-

[145] *Ibid.*, appendix 225–26 and 7192–93.

[146] *Ibid.*, 4967.

[147] *Ibid.*, 4935.

[148] Nathaniel Hammond, *ibid.*, 4869.

[149] F. K. Moreland, Senate Committee on Agriculture, *Testimony . . . in Regard to . . . Imitation Dairy Products*, 239.

[150] An act defining butter, also imposing a tax upon and regulating the manufacture, sale, importation, and exportation of oleomargarine: 24 U.S. Stat. 209 (August 2, 1886); Bannard, "The Oleomargarine Law."

resentatives voted to place a burden on margarine. Border states and metropolitan areas registered a split vote. Northern and western farm areas overwhelmingly supported the law.[151]

The 1886 debate served as a curtain raiser to a larger drama. "Fraud exists everywhere," Senator Charles Van Wyck of Nebraska asserted during the debate. "That is the misfortune at this time, and the question is how to reach it."[152] Although omnibus food bills had been before the Congress for nearly a decade, these had not yet been taken seriously. The oleomargarine debate did not make the wider adulteration issue a matter of immediate urgent concern, but it increased awareness both within the Congress and throughout the country. Moreover, that the margarine bill became law set a precedent that Congress could act to regulate foods. The structure of the debate set precedents too. When, several sessions later, Congress undertook to consider broad food bills with a fervor akin to that devoted to margarine, the themes of 1886— the farmer's and the consumer's welfare, fraud, health, constitutionality—echoed again through House and Senate chambers.

The strategy of 1886 also influenced the future. Butter's friends desired to tax oleomargarine, but they wanted agriculture committees, not committees on ways and means or finance or manufactures, to consider their bill.[153] The closest call for the butter interests came on a one-vote Senate victory that sent the bill to the Committee on Agriculture instead of to Finance, where it would have died of inaction. The Internal Revenue Service of the Treasury Department enforced the oleomargarine law, but it was to be the Division of Chemistry of the Department of Agriculture that would provide the solid information on which an eventual pure-food law would rest. Harvey Wiley's division first acquired an "apparatus for photomicrography" in the very year of the margarine law's enactment.[154] The next year Dr. Wiley published the first part of the Bureau of Chemistry's famous continuing Bulletin 13 on *Food and Food Adulterants*. Part 1 concerned *Dairy Products*, including artificial butter.[155] Wiley himself performed much of the research and drafted the document.

[151] Howard, "The Margarine Industry," 40.

[152] *Cong. Record*, 49 Cong. 1 ses., 7148.

[153] *Ibid.*, 2193, 5339–45. The vote is recorded on 5344.

[154] Harvey W. Wiley to Norman J. Coleman, undated letter printed in Department of Agriculture, Division of Chemistry, *Foods and Food Adulterants: Dairy Products*, 3.

[155] *Ibid.* In this bulletin, 17, Wiley acknowledged that as to oleomargarine's wholesomeness there existed "a wide difference of opinion." "It is undoubtedly true that a great deal of artificial butter has been thrown upon the market that has been carelessly made, and therefore harmful to health. On the other hand a butter substitute, made carefully out of the fat of a perfectly healthy bullock or swine, is not prejudicial to health."

While oleomargarine prompted the first intense interest in Congress in the pure-food cause, which then expanded to almost every other comestible, the law of 1886 did not settle the fate of the butter substitute. For the Gilded Age, oleomargarine had become a symbol of the artificial life that provoked in many Americans grave concern.[156] In *Life on the Mississippi*, Mark Twain reflected this unease in citing a conversation he had overheard on a riverboat between two breakfasting "miscreants," drummers from Cincinnati and New Orleans, who vended respectively oleomargarine passing as butter and cottonseed oil labeled as olive oil.

> "Now, as to this article," said Cincinnati, slashing into the ostensible butter and holding forward a slab of it on his knife-blade. . . . "You can't tell it from butter; by George, an *expert* can't! We supply most of the boats in the West; there's hardly a pound of butter on one of them. We are crawling right along—*jumping* right along is the word. We are going to have that entire trade. Yes, and the hotel trade, too. You are going to see the day pretty soon, when you can't find an ounce of butter to bless yourself with, in any hotel in the Mississippi and Ohio valleys, outside of the biggest cities. . . . And we can sell it so dirt-cheap that the whole country has *got* to take it. . . . Butter's had its *day*—and from this out, butter goes to the wall."[157]

As Dr. Salmon had testified, newly concocted articles of food might pose hazards to the public health.[158] Margarine had been marketed when the first stirrings of worry about the food supply were reaching public attention. The spotlight focused on oleomargarine partly because the challenged butter makers had the propaganda and political power to do so.[159] As Martha Howard surmised, "Margarine conceivably suffered for the sins of many other food products, as well as its own."[160] The suffering occasioned by the new law, however, did not amount to much.[161] Packers scarcely felt the licensing fees, and the two-cent per pound retail tax, instead of the ten cents proposed in the House bill, did not squelch margarine as its opponents had wished, even though the Internal Rev-

[156] Riepma, *The Story of Margarine*, 113.

[157] Mark Twain, *Life on the Mississippi* (New York, 1985; originally published 1883), chap. 39.

[158] Senate Committee on Agriculture, *Testimony . . . in Regard to . . . Imitation Dairy Products*, 219.

[159] Donna J. Wood, *Strategic Uses of Public Policy: Business and Government in the Progressive Era* (Marshfield, MA, 1986), 154–64, 179.

[160] Howard, "The Margarine Industry," 23.

[161] Okun, *Fair Play in the Marketplace*, 277–78, 281–82.

enue Service commissioner deemed regulations under the law "very explicit and severe."[162] Production declined, but only slightly. Butter's ardent friends, frustrated by their pyrrhic victory, maintained their antagonism. Be it "workingman's butter" or "greasy counterfeit," oleomargarine faced the future as source of the most continuous controversy of any single food.

[162] *NY Times*, August 29, 1886; Howard, "The Margarine Industry," 40–48; Riepma, *The Story of Margarine*, 114; *Cong. Record*, 49 Cong. 1 ses., 7088.

V

The Impact of Technology
on Diet and Dosing

The devil has got hold of the food supply of this country.
—SENATOR ALGERNON S. PADDOCK, 1892[1]

The Paddock Bill

The only comprehensive food and drug bill to pass one of the chambers of the Congress before the advent of the twentieth century received favorable consideration from the Senate in 1892. Otherwise, the broad bills steadily introduced from 1879 onward expired because of bureaucratic rivalry, the conflicting goals of competing economic interests, and lack of popular support.

The Treasury Department had responsibility for enforcing the drug importation act of 1848, an 1883 law modeled on the drug act that banned imports of adulterated tea,[2] and the oleomargarine statute. A comprehensive food and drug bill introduced into the Congress that passed the tea act would have given Treasury enforcement authority.[3] The National Board of Health, granted this power in earlier bills, had by now become moribund.[4] A new contender, however, was entering the lists, the Department of Agriculture, which had begun to take a special interest in the problem of adulteration.

When business interests in 1887 and 1888 sought to reinvigorate the campaign for a comprehensive national law, they blamed earlier lack of success partly on "departmental jealousies." The draft bill emerging from these pure-food assemblies sought to finesse this delicate question by leaving blank which department should administer the law. Otherwise, the text had been formulated by a slight reworking of the draft proposed by the National Board of Trade in 1879. This result was not surprising, since Francis Thurber and his close allies dominated the con-

---

[1] *Cong. Record*, 52 Cong. 2 ses., 1816.
[2] 22 U.S. Stat. 451 (March 3, 1883).
[3] House Report 634 on H.R. 4789, 47 Cong. 1 ses.
[4] Bruton, "The National Board of Health," 372–76.

ventions, composed of canners, brokers, grocers, trade journalists, and a few public-health officials, mainly from the East Coast, besides a sprinkling from the Midwest. Threats to the honest trader from the dishonest adulterator furnished the dominant tone. Despite this element of self-interest, observed the keynote speaker in 1887, H. Wharton Amerling, a Philadelphia lawyer, a pure-food campaign by businessmen must be considered "an unselfish movement, . . . for its foes as well as its friends shall receive its blessings."[5]

Several proposals for a law were duly introduced into the Fiftieth Congress, the most important by a Virginia congressman, William H. F. Lee, son of Robert E. Lee. The "most comprehensive" bill yet placed before the Congress, it contained several innovations destined to survive as parts of the 1906 law. The House Agriculture Committee report not only argued forcefully the need for a law, but specified the Department of Agriculture to enforce it. Adulteration had a grievous impact on the food producer, so the department concerned with agriculture was "best calculated to enforce proper rules." Moreover, departmental chemists had already made "considerable progress in the examination and analysis of foods and food adulterants." Agriculture also possessed expertise in the most pressing need of the hour, the development of an inspection system for meat products that would allay European alarm and protect American markets.[6]

The export crisis was too threatening to go unmet by legislation, but not sufficiently overwhelming to sweep a broad food and drug bill

[5] *Proceedings of the National Pure Food Convention, Held at Washington, Wednesday, January 19th, 1887* (New York, 1887); Okun, *Fair Play in the Marketplace*, 284–85. Amerling was president of the American Society for the Prevention of Adulteration of Foods, Drugs, Medicines, &c., and coeditor of the *Anti-Adulteration Journal*. I am indebted to the late Samuel X Radbill for a copy of the July 1889 issue of this newspaper. In 1887 and 1888 Thurber sought to rekindle the support of John Shaw Billings for a pure-food bill, but with no obvious success. Thurber to Billings, January 11, 1887, and January 11, 1888, John Shaw Billings Papers, New York Public Library (National Library of Medicine microfilms, courtesy of Wyndham Miles). Thurber's wholesale grocery business crashed in the panic of 1893, and he withdrew from the grocery field and studied law. See "Francis Beattie Thurber," *National Cyclopedia of American Biography*, vol. 22, 176.

[6] H.R. 10320 and 11266, *Cong. Rec.*, 50 Cong. 1 ses., 4888 and 7953, June 4 and August 25, 1888; *Adulterated Articles of Food, Drink, and Drugs*, House Report 3341, 50 Cong. 1 ses.; Lyman F. Kebler, "The Most Comprehensive Food and Drug Bill," *J Amer Pharm Assoc* 29 (1940), 505–8; *Biographical Directory of the American Congress* (1950), 1450; Richard Curtis Litman and Donald Saunders Litman, "Protection of the Consumer: The Congressional Battle for the Enactment of the First Federal Food and Drug Law in the United States," *Food, Drug, Cosmetic Law J* 37 (1982), 315–16. The Lee bill was the first to include the prohibition of misbranding, a concept borrowed from the British Merchandising Marks Act of 1887.

through the Congress. The Senate Committee on Agriculture and Forestry, considering such a bill in the Fifty-first Congress, "deemed [it] best" to split the matter of meat inspection from the more complicated problem of food and drug sophistication and misbranding, and thus "to formulate bills dealing with each issue separately."[7] A meat-inspection law was enacted in 1890, and the separation of meat from other foods for regulatory purposes has continued ever since.[8] This division, which seemed expedient to the Senate Agriculture Committee, did not mean that its chairman lacked enthusiasm for the pure-food cause. Indeed, Senator Algernon S. Paddock's convictions and shrewd generalship managed to maneuver a food bill through the Senate. A later committee of the House considered Paddock's bill a landmark event in the congressional campaign to secure protection for the consuming public.[9]

Paddock, born in Glens Falls, New York, had dropped out of Hamilton College as a senior to teach school and read law. In 1857 he moved to the frontier town of Omaha, where he was admitted to the bar. A friend of William H. Seward, Paddock returned to New York in 1860 to campaign for Abraham Lincoln. For his services to the victorious Republican party, Paddock received the secretaryship of the Nebraska Territory. In 1875 the legislature of the state of Nebraska elected Paddock to the Senate, where in time he became chairman of the Committee on Agriculture. This post permitted him to work diligently in behalf of farmers, whose discontent was rising as their incomes fell. Paddock sought changes in railroad rates to aid the farmer, offered a bill to restrict abuses by middlemen in the grain business, favored meat inspection in the interests of both the range-cattle industry and consumers, and led the fight for a pure-food law.[10]

Like the House Agriculture Committee in an earlier session, the majority of Paddock's Senate committee believed that the Department of Agriculture should be charged with regulating foods and drugs. De-

[7] *Report to Accompany S. 3991*, 51 Cong. 1 ses., Senate Report 1366.

[8] On the meat-inspection acts, see chap. 6. Anderson, *The Health of a Nation*, 78, says that Secretary of Agriculture Jeremiah Rusk suggested dividing the bill. The lard interests simultaneously sought a law, similar to the oleomargarine statute, to protect their domestic and foreign markets from competition with compound lard, which was lard mixed with cheaper fats, especially cottonseed oil, but seldom labeled to show such modification. These efforts failed. See R. Alton Lee, *A History of Regulatory Taxation* (Lexington, KY, 1973), 30–37.

[9] *Pure Food*, 59 Cong. 1 ses., House Report 2118, part 1, 6.

[10] Allen LaVerne Shepherd, "Algernon Sidney Paddock: A Biography" (University of Nebraska master's thesis, 1967); W. E. Annin, "Algernon Sidney Paddock," in *Proceedings and Collections of the Nebraska State Historical Society*, 2nd series, vol. 5 (Lincoln, NE, 1902), 186–98. These sources were called to my attention by William C. Pratt.

partment scientists had carried on investigations and acquired the experience needed for the kind of enforcement that would restore consumer confidence in the food supply and thus aid the farmer. National control had become "imperative," because only nine states had enacted any laws at all, and even this state authority had been severely circumscribed by recent Supreme Court decisions. The gravity of adulteration became ever more evident. The committee cited state reports, federal bulletins, and Hassall's English studies. The senators asserted:

> Science has been called upon in the interests of honesty to trace and detect the frauds of scientific dishonesty, and the microscope, test tube, retort, and chemical reagent have opened to view the grave and growing consequences of a greed for gain which is assailing the public health, affecting the pocket of the consumer, and undermining what is so aptly denominated . . . as the very foundation of trade, namely, "Faith in commercial integrity."[11]

Paddock's food bill, passed over in both sessions of the Fifty-first Congress, received in the Fifty-second Congress extensive debate. Thousands of petitions, from urban boards of trade, state legislatures, the National Farmers' Alliance, the National Colored Farmers' Alliance, women's leagues, and individual citizens, enhanced the bill's stature in senatorial consideration. The enactment of the meat-inspection measure, Paddock argued, "cleared the way entirely" for the pure-food bill, assuring its constitutionality. States-rights senators, most of them from the South, disagreed and repeated their arguments in opposing the oleomargarine bill. They also viewed with alarm the "spies and informers" who would "cover this country" should the bill become law. There were "too many Pinkertons" already, without enacting this "Trojan horse with a bellyful of inspectors and other employees to open our gates" for political mischief. The Department of Agriculture would blanket the nation with high-paid officials "to watch the depots, to watch every crossing of every railroad, to watch the crossing of States lines, of every river, of every wagon, to watch every man upon horseback or in a buggy who may carry an article from one State into another."[12]

Paddock, who himself carried the burden of debate favorable to the bill, sought to dispel such nightmarish visions. The Division of Chem-

---

[11] *Report to Accompany S. 3991*, 51 Cong. 1 ses., Senate Report 1366, 8. The key Supreme Court decision was Leisy v. Hardin, 135 U.S. 100.

[12] Senate 1 was introduced on December 10, 1891, *Cong. Record*, 52 Cong. 1 ses., 22. Paddock spoke in behalf of his bill, 1367; senatorial critics included James H. Berry of Arkansas, 1808, and William B. Bate of Tennessee, 1371.

istry in the Department of Agriculture was "as nearly nonpartisan in its work as such an institution can be under our system, . . . purely a scientific force." Moreover, the law's purposes could be accomplished at modest cost. The United States, of all nations in the civilized world, Paddock asserted, was the only one lacking a broad general law. This law would "minimize . . . [an] appalling evil." Paddock devised his own grim vision of what might lie ahead:

> Take heed when the people demand bread that you continue not to give them a stone, lest the angry waves of popular discontent . . . engulf forever all that we most greatly value—our free institutions, and all the glories and hopes of our great Republic.[13]

In the amending process before the final vote, Paddock accepted a suggestion from Senator John T. Morgan of Alabama that would remain with successive bills until enactment of a law. In addition to criminal penalties imposed upon adulterators, Morgan proposed, the bill should permit actions aimed at seizing and condemning adulterated articles themselves. There was precedent for such a borrowing from admiralty proceedings in the law that permitted the government to seize importations of obscene literature. The Senate accepted this amendment and then, on March 14, 1892, without a roll-call vote, passed the food and drug bill. In the House of Representatives, opponents kept the bill from coming to a vote. So once again the hopes of pure-food advocates had been frustrated. Despite the numerous petitions, public opinion had not been exercised enough to stir the House to action. A decade elapsed before the Congress again exhibited the degree of interest in the pure-food cause that Algernon Paddock had stimulated in the Senate.[14]

One observer, whose own prospects were closely interwoven with the fate of Paddock's bill, bemoaned failure of the public to press for the bill's passage. "To be cheated, fooled, bamboozled, cajoled, deceived, pettifogged, demagogued, hypnotized, manicured and chiropodized," he wrote, "are privileges dear to us all. Woe be to that paternalism in government which shall attempt to deprive us of these inalienable rights." P. T. Barnum was correct in believing that "Americans like to be humbugged," concluded Harvey Washington Wiley.[15]

[13] *Ibid.*, 1717, 1718, 1722, 1726. The laws of European countries against adulteration had recently been summarized for the benefit of Americans concerned with public health. Edgar Richards, "Certain Provisions of Continental Legislation concerning Food Adulteration," *American Public Health Reports* 15 (1889), 114–21.

[14] *Cong. Record*, 52 Cong. 1 ses., 1853, 1870; Anderson, *The Health of a Nation*, 80.

[15] Harvey W. Wiley, "The Adulteration of Food," *Journal of the Franklin Institute* 137 (1894), 266.

The Chief Chemist

Harvey Wiley, chief chemist of the Department of Agriculture, reacted with uncharacteristic gloom and cynicism to the neglect of the Paddock bill by the House of Representatives, because he had hoped fervently, and even expected, that the bill would pass. The chemist had aided the senator by suggesting improvements in the draft of his pure-food measure and by keeping Paddock informed about new developments on the adulteration front. Adulteration, indeed, was rapidly becoming Wiley's principal professional concern.[16]

Since his college days, Wiley had been interested in the relation of food to health. Born in 1844 in a log cabin on a southern Indiana farm, he had grown up eating whole wheat flour and unbolted corn meal. The atmosphere in the Wiley home was strictly religious in the Campbellite persuasion and also reformist on moral grounds: the family favored abolitionism, read *Uncle Tom's Cabin* as it came out serially in an antislavery paper, and supported Abraham Lincoln for the presidency. Wiley had gone from a log schoolhouse and home tutoring to Hanover College. He interrupted his education during 1864 for four months of military service in Tennessee as a corporal in an Indiana volunteer regiment. Studying the traditional curriculum, Wiley became well grounded in the classics and experienced in public speaking before student literary societies, and he took a sound course in chemistry. After graduating, he taught public school, spent a summer apprenticed to a Kentucky country doctor, and then went to Indianapolis to teach Greek and Latin in the preparatory department of Northwestern Christian University. Soon he was instructing in anatomy and physiology as well. Simultaneously he attended the newly opened Indiana Medical College, receiving his M.D. diploma in 1871. Deciding not to practice, Wiley taught scientific courses, especially chemistry, in quick succession at the Indianapolis public high school, the medical school that he had attended, again at Northwestern Christian, and finally, when it opened its doors in 1874, at the new agricultural and mechanical university established by Indiana at Purdue. The year before, he had spent less than six months of intensive study at Harvard, adding to his M.D. degree a B.S. in chemistry.[17]

Wiley taught chemistry at Purdue by placing great emphasis on laboratory experience. He became deeply interested in the advancing frontier of analytical chemistry, its methods and apparatus, and reported his

[16] Anderson, *The Health of a Nation*, 79–80. Wiley wrote his own account of his life in *An Autobiography* (Indianapolis, 1930).
[17] Anderson, *The Health of a Nation*, 6–11, 17.

own modest contributions at conventions of the American Association for the Advancement of Science. Wiley secured a leave of absence to visit the vital center of food chemistry: he sat in on lectures at German universities and, more important, spent time at the Imperial Health Office, observing the newest techniques for analyzing food and exposing adulterants. Back at Purdue, Wiley, by vote of the legislature, added to his professorship the title and responsibilities of state chemist. He put his increasing analytical talents to work exposing fraudulent adulteration of fertilizers. At the request of the state board of health, Wiley revealed the extent to which sugars and syrups were adulterated with glucose. In 1881 he published his first article and delivered his first paper on this theme.[18]

In *Popular Science Monthly*, Wiley described the use of glucose and grape sugar as adulterants. In his AAAS paper on mixed sugars, Wiley sounded a strong note for consumer protection against dishonesty in marketing.[19] His stance at the start of his career as an outspoken foe of adulteration remained essentially unchanged for the next two decades: adulterators were economic cheats who offended against morality, but their manipulations posed scant danger to health.

Wiley's growing reputation as a sugar chemist won him the promotion that took him from Purdue to the Department of Agriculture. The hope was rising, among both governmental officials and farmers, that sorghum cane, a crop introduced into America in the 1850s, might be made to yield enough sugar to eliminate the need for sugar imports. Wiley, as a youth, had harvested the first sorghum cane and extracted the first syrup in his region. At Purdue he raised several varieties of cane on the college farm and set up a small factory for extracting syrup. Wiley made speeches about his endeavors, displaying optimism about sorghum's future while not blinking either the technical difficulty of crystallizing sugar from cane or the only modest yield. To Commissioner of Agriculture George B. Loring, Wiley's views seemed more realistic than the extreme prosorghum stance of the department's chief chemist, Peter Collier, with whom Loring was also feuding on other grounds. In 1883 Loring summarily dismissed Collier and appointed Wiley to the post. This precipitous step upset cane growers and placed Wiley under a cloud of suspicion not dispelled for some years.[20]

Approaching the age of forty when he arrived in Washington, Wiley was tall, stocky, and striking in appearance. He had a rough-hewn oval face, with a prominent nose and slanting black eyes remarkable for their

[18] *Ibid.*, 18–23.
[19] *Ibid.*, 22–23; Wiley, "Glucose and Grape-Sugar."
[20] Anderson, *The Health of a Nation*, 23–30.

penetrating glance. His short but ample beard, his mustache, and his hair, already beginning to recede on top, were jet black. A bachelor, Wiley enjoyed sociability, making friends easily and possessing the gift of banter and colorful expression. These traits somewhat disguised his passionate dedication to his work and his convictions, his boundless energy, and his driving ambition.[21]

Sugar dominated the first decade of Wiley's career in Washington. Supported by the sugar industry, he presided over a number of sorghum and sugar beet experiments, but after ten years the nation had made no progress toward becoming independent of imports. Wiley's experiences had not been for naught. He had gained agility of maneuver in the bitter bureaucratic struggles of the nation's capital, learning how to use the support of the sugar interests in securing appropriations from congressional committees. Even had his success with sugar been greater, however, this interest did not provide him with a broad enough base of power during a period in which government bureaus concerned with science were developing the problem-solving method of confronting their tasks. Scientists favored long-term plans and flexibility of decision, but the lay public scorned "scientific pontiffs" and wanted science in government to grapple with urgent practical demands.[22]

Losing ground in competition with the Bureau of Animal Industry, the Division of Chemistry needed another mission besides sugar if it was to keep pace, indeed, if it was to avoid extinction. Other bureaus that the division had been serving were developing their own chemical competence. Soil analysis might have served such a purpose, but this did not capture Wiley's interest. Instead, he found salvation for his division and fame for himself in making the rising concern about food purity his own, applying his technical abilities to illuminating the problem and his political talents to achieving a protective law. Treasury had gained priority in food and drug regulation, but that department did not produce an official with Wiley's skills and zeal. Perhaps as early as 1888, certainly by the time of Paddock's bill, the conclusion seemed quite assured that, if a comprehensive measure should ever pass Congress, the Department of Agriculture would administer the act.[23]

---

[21] *Ibid.*, 16, 32–33, 82, 117–18, 243, 259; Edwin Björkman, "Our Debt to Dr. Wiley," *World's Work* 19 (1910), 12443.

[22] Anderson, *The Health of a Nation*, 30–66; Dupree, *Science in the Federal Government*, 176–77; George H. Daniels, "The Pure-Science Ideal and Democratic Culture," *Science* 156 (1967), 1699–1705.

[23] Dupree, *Science in the Federal Government*, 176–78. Jack High and Clayton Coppin conclude that Wiley's ambition to secure a law that he could administer sometimes dis-

Some attention to adulteration on the part of departmental officials preceded Wiley's arrival. In 1869 the commissioner's report had warned farmers about adulteration of fertilizers and feedstuffs. Wiley's predecessor had discovered some sophistication of butter, oleomargarine, and liquors, and the lead he found in powders used to color coffee berries caused him to recommend making dangerous adulterations a criminal offense. Wiley picked up this analytical task immediately. His first annual report asserted that virtually all maple syrups contained additions of cheaper syrups made from cane, beet, and particularly corn. He told too of investigations to find the most appropriate methods for analyzing milk and butter. The chief chemist reported to the AAAS analytical difficulties he had encountered in distinguishing between butter and oleomargarine. Wiley's studies expanded when Commissioner Norman J. Colman assumed office in 1885, for Colman's deep concern for the plight both of producers, whose markets for butter and maple syrup suffered because of adulteration, and of consumers who were cheated by such fraud, led him to give the problem higher priority. Colman's successor, Secretary Jeremiah Rusk, the first head of the Department of Agriculture to hold cabinet rank, gave Wiley equally strong support for his research into adulteration, as did members of Congress. Beginning with the appropriation act of 1889, funds were allocated specifically for continuing and expanding Wiley's work, a sum that through the years steadily if gradually increased. Even before this, Wiley had persuaded himself that the study of food adulteration should constitute the central purpose of his career; he hoped to publish the major authoritative treatise on this theme.[24]

In the year that the oleomargarine tax became law, Wiley purchased photomicrography apparatus to aid in his continuing research into dairy products. The next year, 1887, the chief chemist published his study of butter, oleomargarine, and milk. Thus began the division's famous Bulletin 13 on *Foods and Food Adulterants*, destined to continue through ten parts and 1,400 pages, issued over a span of sixteen years. The central purpose of the bulletin, Wiley announced in its first part, would be to discuss "the best methods of detecting" adulteration. Revelations as to the extent of adulteration, the chief chemist held, should be in the domain of state experiment stations and boards of health.[25]

---

torted his view of the facts. "Wiley, Whiskey, and Strategic Behavior: An Analysis of the Passage of the Pure Food Act," *Business History Review*, in press.

[24] Anderson, *The Health of a Nation*, 70–73; Weber, *The Bureau of Chemistry and Soils*, 15–19; Wiley, "American Butters and Their Adulterations," *Science* 2 (1883), 291–92; Wiley, "Butter," *ibid.*, 5 (1885), 339–40.

[25] Department of Agriculture, Division of Chemistry, Bulletin 13, *Foods and Food Adul-*

Most of Part 1 dealt with highly technical analytical questions regarding the physical and chemical properties of butter and oleomargarine and how to detect them. Wiley assessed the literature, criticizing inadequate techniques, and stressed the indispensability of the microscope and polarized light. The chief chemist set this specialized data within a broader framework. He summarized oleomargarine's history, listed American patents for butter substitutes, and included the text of the 1886 law. Citing testimony given to the Senate committee, as well as the general literature, Wiley discoursed on oleomargarine's "wholesomeness." Conceding "a wide difference of opinion," he gave his own moderate and balanced judgment. It was true that "a great deal" of "carelessly made" artificial butter had been marketed that posed a hazard to health. "On the other hand a butter substitute, made carefully out of the fat of a perfectly healthy bullock or swine, is not prejudicial to health." With respect to the comparative nutritive qualities, Wiley was not so certain. He granted that the nation's leading authority on nutrition, Wilbur O. Atwater of Wesleyan University, deemed butter and oleomargarine "of practically equal value" for supplying heat and muscular energy to the body. Granted an absence of experimental evidence demonstrating butter's superiority, Wiley rejoined, "it must not be forgotten that butter has a much more complex composition than lard or tallow or cottonseed oil; that it is a natural food, and doubtless possesses many digestive advantages which science has not yet been able to demonstrate."[26]

Here Harvey Wiley revealed a fundamental preference for the natural over the artificial that later prompted him to take some stands which, in retrospect, were scientifically wrong. In this instance he was right, anticipating that butter contained important ingredients, in contrast with the oleomargarine of the day, that his new microscope could not detect and that Atwater did not suspect.

The year 1887 also saw publication of Parts 2 and 3 of Bulletin 13, one treating spices and condiments, the other, fermented alcoholic beverages, malt liquors, wine, and cider. Neither was written by Wiley. Clifford Richardson, author of Part 2, summed up the experience with spices of Britain, Canada, the American states, and the Treasury Department, bolstered by Division of Chemistry analyses: adulteration was well-nigh universal, if rarely harmful. Detection was an extremely ar-

---

terants, part 1 (Washington, 1887), 3; Anderson, *The Health of a Nation*, 71. Analyses of various foods are discussed in the *Report of the Commissioner of Agriculture* for 1879, 77–79; 1884, 53–61; 1885, 11, 109–23; 1886, 277–302; 1887, 181–213; 1888, 234–49, and *Report of the Secretary of Agriculture* for 1889, 163–81, and 1890, 23–24.

[26] Division of Chemistry, Bulletin 13, *Foods and Food Adulterants*, part 1. Part 1 also contained a section on the artificial colors used in coloring oleomargarine.

duous task, impossible for the consumer. Thus, education could not solve the problem, although it was a necessary preliminary to the only true solution, a pure-food law. "Could only a portion of the unfortunate dislike for oleomargarine be directed toward spices," Richardson wrote, "the result would be that much wasted energy would be turned into a profitable channel."[27]

In Part 3's analysis of the adulteration of liquors, written by C. A. Crampton, the difficulties of detection again became a dominant theme. The "skillfulness" of wine adulterators had increased recently to such a degree that "all the knowledge and resourcefulness which chemical science" could muster still permitted a "large part" of the adulteration to escape discovery. Part 3 also introduced a new note into the range of Bulletin 13's considerations, pointing to the widespread use in wines and malt liquors of chemical preservatives, particularly salicylic acid, which had been synthesized in Europe just after midcentury. Little attention had been given so far in the United States to salicylic acid as a preservative. Granted its proper use in medicine, Crampton questioned its presence in "an article of daily consumption" and wondered "whether it would not be more prudent to forbid its use altogether." In any case, its presence must be made known to purchasers.

In the year that Parts 2 and 3 appeared, a time of rising concern among farmers about "compound lard," Harvey Wiley presented his first testimony on adulteration before a committee of Congress. The chief chemist reported that his division's analyses of lard marketed by the biggest firms in Packingtown, bearing such names as Prime Refined Family Lard, found a high proportion of the samples adulterated with cottonseed oil. Wiley repeated the charge two years later in Part 4 of Bulletin 13. He cited similar evidence presented in British courts from a nation upset by American commercial deceptions. As he earlier had defended oleomargarine's wholesomeness, so in Part 4 he termed lard's adulterants "fully as free from deleterious effects upon the system as hog grease itself." Nonetheless, adulteration defrauded the American consumer and threatened markets abroad. "Food products made in this country," Wiley insisted, must be required "to be labeled and sold under their true name."[28]

In Part 5, published the same year, the division confronted baking powders, a kitchen product already surrounded by controversy, a contention destined to expand so bitterly as to cast a continuing shadow

---

[27] *Ibid.*, parts 2 and 3 (Washington, 1887).

[28] *Counterfeit or Compounded Lard*, 50 Cong. 1 ses., House Report 3082; Division of Chemistry, Bulletin 13, *Foods and Food Adulterants*, part 4 (1889).

over prospects for securing a pure-food law. Crampton, the author of this work, deferred to physiologists and hygienists the claims and counterclaims about dangers inherent in the competing tartrate, phosphate, and alum varieties.[29]

During 1892, the year in which Paddock's bill passed the Senate only to be stymied in the House, Harvey Wiley's division issued two more segments of Bulletin 13. Part 6 concerned sugar, molasses, syrup, honey, and confections. Part 7 dealt with tea, coffee, and cocoa.[30]

Wiley wished to carry his antiadulteration message beyond the range of the technically minded who could comprehend the chemistry of Bulletin 13. The chief chemist wanted to give "the people and Congress . . . at least a general view of the evil." So, in 1889, with funds from the new special appropriation he employed a special agent to prepare a more popular publication. Alexander J. Wedderburn, the man he chose, had worked for the Virginia Grange and had edited *National Farm and Fireside*. Within a year Wedderburn had Bulletin 25 ready for publication, *A Popular Treatise on the Extent and Character of Food Adulteration*, mainly a compilation of state and municipal laws and reports, and the opinions of scientists and businessmen. The evidence, said Wedderburn, demonstrated "in the strongest manner" the need for a national law. Adulteration of foods was "generally and steadily increasing," having reached the proportion, perhaps, of 15 percent. Most adulteration was not injurious to health. Yet fraud hurt everyone and bore "most heavily on the uneducated and the poor." It harmed the husbandman, particularly jeopardizing his export market. Beyond mere fraud lay "poisonous adulterations" that had injured the health of many consumers and "frequently caused death."[31]

The Canned-Food Boom

In 1849 the first gold from the California mines to reach Boston arrived in an empty food can that had originally been filled in that same city. The gold rush helped popularize canned food. A convenient form for sustaining travelers to California during the long overland journey or the longer sea voyage, canned goods also found much use in the mining

[29] *Ibid.*, part 5 (Washington, 1889); Okun, *Fair Play in the Marketplace*, 232–38.

[30] Division of Chemistry, Bulletin 13, *Foods and Food Adulterants*, parts 6 and 7 (Washington, 1892); Anderson, *The Health of a Nation*, 73–74.

[31] *Ibid.*, 74–75; Alexander J. Wedderburn, *A Popular Treatise on the Extent and Character of Food Adulteration*, Division of Chemistry, Bulletin 25 (Washington, 1890). Two years later Wedderburn updated his report: *Special Report on the Extent and Character of Food Adulterations*, Division of Chemistry, Bulletin 32 (Washington, 1892).

camps. The American canning industry, at this point, was just three decades old. William Underwood, whose company processed the can that conveyed the gold to Boston, had reached that city in 1819, soon beginning the bottling of catsup, pickles, fruits, and jellies for the Latin American and Asian trade. Underwood used the processing techniques of the great French pioneer Nicolas Appert, who had won a prize for his innovation from the French government in Napoleon's time. The same year that Underwood arrived in Boston, another English immigrant, Thomas Kensett, began to bottle food in New York City. Six years later he got a patent for "preserving" food in "vessels of tin." Among the first foods canned by this first American commercial canner was salmon.[32]

The canning industry grew slowly until the Civil War, a small-scale handicraft operation afflicted with high spoilage rates, selling its luxury goods like lobsters and oysters to those who could afford them out of season and to those making long ocean voyages, to navies and captains of commerce. Neither in America nor in Europe had canned goods yet contributed significantly to the diet of the ordinary urban family. Centered first in Baltimore, Portland, Maine, and Oneida County, New York, canning spread westward in the 1860s to the Midwest and California. The Civil War boomed business. At or near the battlefront, many soldiers first encountered canned milk, canned meat, and a coffee extract in their rations, and other canned wares vended by sutlers. Gail Borden had first thought of condensing food when he heard of the starvation of the Donner party. Obsessed with the concept of condensation—preachers, Borden believed, should condense their sermons—he had patented his milk condensing process in 1856, and five years later had finished a new factory in Wassaic, New York, just in time to have it commandeered by the federal government. At war's end soldiers carried a new idea home.[33]

Wartime expansion led to a decline in quality. Some canneries deliberately marketed inferior goods with their weight overstated on labels. Despite this, after the war, canned meats, milk, fruit, and vegetables became a regular part of standard army rations. An expanding civilian

[32] Edward F. Keuchel, "The Development of the Canning Industry in New York State to 1960" (Cornell University dissertation, 1970), 21, 24; Keuchel, "Master of the Art of Canning: Baltimore, 1860–1900," *Maryland Historical Magazine* 67 (1971), 351–62; Earl Chapin May, *The Canning Clan: A Pageant of Pioneering Americans* (New York, 1938), 1, 9–13; Thomas McLachlan, "History of Food Processing," *Progress in Food and Nutrition Science* 1 (1975), 461–91.

[33] Keuchel, "The Development of the Canning Industry," 12, 25, 33; Bell I. Wiley, *The Life of Billy Yank* (Indianapolis, 1952), 224, 241–42; Joe B. Frantz, *Gail Borden, Dairyman to a Nation* (Norman, OK, 1951), 201–76; Daniel J. Boorstin, *The Americans: The Democratic Experience* (New York, 1973), 309–11; May, *The Canning Clan*, 175–77.

market opened up as well. Canning as an industry was first listed separately in the census of 1870. By that year thirty million cans of food were being processed annually. From that point to the end of the century the United States surpassed Europe to become world leader in canning for the urban masses. The nation's cities grew enormously, and the newly knit railroad network permitted rapid movement to population centers of fruits, vegetables, milk, and meats, so abundantly available, processed in canneries multiplying near the sources of raw products. The canning industry, observed the *New York Times* in 1886, had become "a world necessity." Without canned goods, sailors could not be fed and "exploration either of the desert or the poles would come to a full stop." Without such processed foods, life for the common man would be much more difficult.[34]

"All manner of food is canned," wrote two members of Harvey Wiley's staff in a new part of Bulletin 13, "and that at prices which place it within the reach of the humblest pockets." The reported continued:

> Preserved food has been a great democratic factor, and has nearly obliterated one of the old lines of demarcation between the poor and the wealthy. Vegetables out of season are no longer a luxury of the rich. The logger may to-day have a greater variety of food than could Queen Elizabeth have enjoyed with all the resources and wealth of England at her command. In the American grocery—pineapples from Singapore, salmon from British Columbia, fruit from California, peas from France, okra from Louisiana, sweet corn from New York, string beans from Scotland, mutton from Australia, sardines from Italy, stand side by side on the shelves.[35]

In canning, as elsewhere, American ingenuity was evident. Corn canning led off in mechanization, from automatic cutters, through gun cookers, to steam retorts, and on to a continuous corn-canning unit, steadily improved before the end of the century into an "Automatic Line." Peas, tomatoes, and other products followed corn. More ravenous factories forced the mechanization of harvesting and the development of new varieties of crops, peas, for example, that would ripen all at once in one field while other peas ripened later in a different field. Accelerating production put a strain upon the supply of hand-crafted cans. These tin-plated steel cylinders, cut with tinsmith's shears, their seams sealed and their tops and bottoms affixed with solder, had to be

[34] Keuchel, "The Development of the Canning Industry," 33–103; Marshall B. Davidson, *Life in America*, vol. 2 (Boston, 1951), 143; *NY Times*, March 14, 1886.

[35] Division of Chemistry, Bulletin 13, *Foods and Food Adulterants*, part 8, "Canned Vegetables," by K. P. McElroy and W. D. Bigelow (Washington, 1893), 1024.

filled through a cap hole an inch and a half across, which then was soldered shut. Tedious to make, difficult to fill, hazardous to fruit jammed through the narrow aperture, impossible to seal with certainty, cans posed canners a severe challenge. The introduction of mechanical solderers and cappers, however, so upset can craftsmen in the 1870s and 1880s that riots wracked the Baltimore and New York canning industry. This violence pushed canners to devise new machinery which would reduce total labor and permit that labor to operate at a lower level of skill than that of the troublesome craftsmen. In the early twentieth century the "open top" or "sanitary" can appeared, machine made, easy to fill, with ends crimped on, thus reducing soldering to the external seam of the cylinder. The old hand craftsmen, in fighting mechanization, warned the public that food packed in machine-made cans posed a threat to health. Thus an artificial reason for concern joined more legitimate causes for worry about foods invisible to the eye of the consumer.[36]

Raw vegetables, fruits, and meat generally were so cheap that no strong economic motive prompted the canner to adulterate. Adding water occurred frequently, however, and examples of ingenious deception now and then reached the press. Unripe regular plums, for example, could be canned and labeled as the more desirable greengage variety. The "tricksters" of the trade bought refuse, "half-spoiled berries, knotty peaches, stale corn, green tomatoes," canned them, and used labels as pretty as those borne by cans containing sound fruit and vegetables. When turkeys and chickens glutted the market, canners purchased them cheap and put them, even though tainted, into cans. A consumer vogue for white sweet corn led canners to compete with each other to achieve the whitest product, using sodium sulfite as a bleach. Adulteration of canned fruits and vegetables, however, presented less of a problem than did sophistication of spices, condiments, jellies, baking powders, syrups, tea, and olive oil.[37]

Cases of sickness attributed to canned food were publicized and led

[36] May, *The Canning Clan*, 39–44, 84–96; Keuchel, "The Development of the Canning Industry," 71, 143–49, 284; Keuchel, "Master of the Art of Canning," 357–61; Richard O. Cummings, *The American and His Food: A History of Food Habits in the United States* (Chicago, 1940), 68–69; Martin Brown and Peter Philips, "Craft Labor and Mechanization in Nineteenth-Century American Canning," *Journal of Economic History* 46 (1986), 743–56; Patrick W. O'Bannon, "Waves of Change: Mechanization in the Pacific Coast Canned-Salmon Industry, 1864–1914," *Technology and Culture* 28 (1987), 558–77.

[37] Keuchel, "The Development of the Canning Industry," 52, 83, 91–92; May, *The Canning Clan*, 47–48; *NY Times*, November 20, 1870, December 26, 1881; William K. Newton, "The Sanitary Control of the Food Supply," *Public Health Papers and Reports* 9 (1883), 158–59.

to debates about cause. Most tinplate was made from an alloy of tin and lead, the same metals forming the solder usually employed to seal the cans, although sometimes a liquid flux containing zinc chloride was used. Were salts formed by the action of organic acids in fruits and vegetables on these metals toxic enough in the quantities produced to make people sick? This controversy in one instance got into court. In 1886 New York food wholesaler Francis Thurber was sued for culpable negligence because of the alleged poisoning of a Brooklyn girl by zinc chloride flux used in soldering a can of tomatoes that Thurber had sold but not canned. After hearing experts testify on both sides of the issue, the jury gave the verdict to the defendant because the evidence did not seem conclusively to incriminate the solder.[38]

By 1893, when the "Canned Vegetables" section of Dr. Wiley's Bulletin 13 appeared, metals seemed to Division of Chemistry scientists a clear and present danger. Copper and zinc salts used to preserve the fresh green color of peas, beans, and other vegetables, when eaten over long periods, "must be regarded as at least prejudicial to health." Riskier still were the tin and lead in the plating on cans, and most hazardous the lead dissolved by food acids from the solder used to seal each can's seam and the hole in its top. The use of lead "where it is liable to come into contact with food," asserted the authors, is "the most dangerous from a toxicological point of view."[39]

Evidence to be revealed nearly a century later tended to confirm the Division of Chemistry's grave concern. Bones from the bodies of members of the lost expedition of Sir John Franklin, which in 1845 had sailed from England in search of the fabled Northwest Passage through Canada to the Orient, revealed "abnormally, perhaps fatally, high concentrations of lead." Lead from the heavily soldered cans in which the explorers carried food, found in a refuse dump, almost certainly was a factor in the disaster.[40]

Not toxic metals, other authorities argued, but "ptomaines" were the cause of food poisoning. In the 1870s an Italian scientist, Francesco Selmi, persuaded that sickness resulted from nitrogen compounds

[38] John North, "Canned Food as a Cause of Acute Poisoning," *Journal of the American Medical Association* 8 (1887), 32–35; Keuchel, "The Development of the Canning Industry," 78; *NY Times*, April 10, 1884, March 14, 1886; William A. Hammond, "Canned Tomatoes and Chloride of Zinc," *New York Medical Journal* 43 (1886), 370–72; Henry A. Riley, "Medico-legal Cases," *Medical and Surgical Reporter* 54 (1886), 454.

[39] Division of Chemistry, Bulletin 13, *Foods and Food Adulterants*, part 8, 1016–17, 1035–74.

[40] Bill Gilbert, "A Frozen Sailor Summons up a Tale of Heroism," *Smithsonian* 16 (June 1985), 116–30; John Carey, "Answers from an Icy Grave," *Newsweek* 104 (October 8, 1984), 89; "Buried in Ice," "Nova" television program from WGTV, Boston, 1988.

evolving during the putrefaction of food, introduced the term "ptomaines" to designate such compounds. American scientists accepted this explanation. A physician and chemist, John North, decrying the metallic salt theory, blamed shoddy canning for food spoilage, spoilage for "artificial alkaloids" or ptomaines, and ptomaines for illness.[41]

During the years that the ptomaine explanation was spreading, two concurrent revolutions in European science, among their multitude of consequences, portended a major refashioning of food processing. The bacteriological revolution introduced by Louis Pasteur and Robert Koch provided verifiable explanations for some food poisoning, which would in time vanquish the ptomaine theory. Pasteur himself had pointed the way, demonstrating that food decomposition resulted from a living organism he termed a "ferment."[42] The chemical revolution, surging from German dye industry research, added to the supply of chemicals that could serve as food preservatives before food processors sensed the implications of the germ theory for their industrial art.

Perhaps it was Lord Lister's practical application of Pasteur's early work that first gave the clue. In an article on "Food Preservation" in *Appleton's Annual Cyclopaedia* for 1882, the author pointed out that carbolic acid, used in antiseptic surgery, could not be used satisfactorily for preserving meat, because it destroyed the meat. Boracic acid, research in England and France had revealed, did not have this compelling disadvantage: meat, oysters, and poultry submerged in a water solution of this acid would maintain their freshness for a long time. Boracic acid was sometimes mixed, in various combinations, with borax, saltpeter, and cooking salt. Other preservative chemicals began to be employed, particularly salicylic acid, benzoic acid, and formaldehyde. Canners and bottlers who used these chemicals did not always realize that they were doing so. Trade-named preservatives came on the market, bearing no list of ingredients on their labels, but sold to food processors as safe. Preservaline was mostly salicylic acid; Freezine, sodium sulfite; and Freezem, a dilute solution of formaldehyde. American critics began to object to the use of preservatives, and some European countries banned a number of them. Most food processors, however, began to think preservatives well-nigh indispensable. The deterring of spoilage sharply reduced the number of cans that had to be discarded or reprocessed.[43]

[41] North, "Canned Food as a Cause of Acute Poisoning," 32–35.

[42] Arthur L. Hunt, "Canning and Preserving," Bureau of the Census, *Twelfth Census of the United States, 1900*, vol. 9, part 3, 463.

[43] McLachlan, "History of Food Processing," 461–91; "Food-Preservation," *Appleton's Annual Cyclopaedia* (New York, 1884), 315–16; Keuchel, "The Development of the Canning Industry," 162.

In the section of Bulletin 13 on canned vegetables, Wiley recognized the wide divergence of views as to the "wholesomeness or unwholesomeness" of added preservatives. The weight of opinion, he believed, pointed toward the need for caution. Granted that "these bodies in small quantities are not injurious to health, yet the continual use of them, even in small quantities, may finally become prejudicial." The inhibitory action of preservatives on microorganisms also suppressed digestive ferments. While the evidence might not warrant "absolute inhibition," Wiley concluded, the presence of preservatives in foods should be "marked upon the label of the can" to forewarn consumers and their physicians of the "danger which they may encounter."[44]

As preservatives retarded decomposition within can and bottle, so they postponed a proper confrontation by the American canning trade with the realities of their processing environment as seen from the perspective of the new bacteriology. Not until the closing years of the nineteenth century did crises produce the first tentative explorations, and systematic concern began only after 1910.[45]

In 1894 the superintendent of a pea-canning plant in Manitowoc, Wisconsin, who slept above the cannery warehouse, had his slumbers interrupted by the sound of exploding cans. Foul odors assailed his nostrils, and he discovered that the bombardment had plastered peas over the warehouse walls and ceiling. The company president suggested seeking help from the University of Wisconsin. Aid came in the person of a young assistant professor of bacteriology, Harry L. Russell, who had observed Koch in Berlin and spent a while at the Pasteur Institute in Paris. In Manitowoc, looking through his microscope, Russell found the cans of peas filled with bacteria and said they had not been cooked enough. He inserted some of the offending bacteria into a sound can of peas, which two days later exploded. Russell recommended longer processing under higher pressure to destroy the bacteria without ruining the quality of the peas.[46]

[44] The quotations are from Wiley's introduction to Division of Chemistry, Bulletin 13, *Foods and Food Adulterants*, part 8, 1016. McElroy and Bigelow discussed the preservatives they discovered in their inquiry, 1029–35.

[45] May, *The Canning Clan*, 159.

[46] *Ibid.*, 31–38; Keuchel, "The Development of the Canning Industry," 123–26; H. L. Russell, "Gaseous Fermentations in the Canning Industry," in Agriculture Experiment Station of the University of Wisconsin, *Twelfth Annual Report* (Madison, [1895?]), 227–31. Armour became the first American meat-packing plant to employ a chemist, in 1884, to help fight a suit brought against the company alleging violation of the Mège patent in making oleomargarine. Howard, "The Margarine Industry," 21. But chemists had very little influence in the canning industry until 1909. H. A. Baker, "The Canning Industry—

More extensive and more amply publicized were the studies of two Massachusetts Institute of Technology bacteriologists beginning in 1896. Samuel C. Prescott and W. Lyman Underwood—a descendant of the canning pioneer—began by showing that specific microorganisms caused the spoilage of canned clams and lobsters. They went on to discover the bacteria responsible for souring corn, and, like Russell, they inquired into canned-pea spoilage. In articles and in addresses before canners' conventions, Prescott and Underwood explained their discoveries, preached a gospel of cleanliness, and gave counsel on temperatures and time periods conducive to satisfactory results. The first general book on the bacteriology of canning was published in 1899, but the dispersed and fragmented industry was not yet able to absorb and apply widely such bacteriological lessons. The most heated debate over preservatives still lay ahead, a necessary prelude to full acceptance of bacteriology's meaning for canning operations.[47]

Harvey Wiley would play a stellar role in the preservation debate. His concern raised by the research for Bulletin 13, Wiley remained dubious of the value of chemical preservatives, except under unusual circumstances, and became increasingly worried about potential hazards to those who ingested them. Before a decade had passed, Wiley determined to put his opinions to the test in a scientific way.[48]

Drug Manufacturing and Prescribing

The bacteriological revolution did not receive ready acceptance in American medicine. While a new breed of physiologists, bacteriologists, and physicians welcomed the new science pioneered in Europe, the generality of American practitioners seemed as reluctant as the canners to absorb the revolution's full thrust. Most doctors resisted its practical consequences for surgery and delayed even longer before accepting its relevance to other aspects of medical practice. As for the chemical revolution, physicians welcomed new drugs it made available, while not forsaking entirely old drugs long in use.[49]

Some Accomplishments and Opportunities along Technical Lines," *Journal of Industrial and Engineering Chemistry* 10 (1918), 69.

[47] Keuchel, "The Development of the Canning Industry," 126–42; May, *The Canning Clan*, 98–105; Edward Wiley Duckwall, *Bacteriology: Applied to the Canning and Preserving of Food Products* (Baltimore, 1899); H. A. Baker, "The Canning Industry—Some Accomplishments and Opportunities along Technical Lines," 69–71; Samuel C. Prescott, "Antiseptics and Their Use in the Preservation of Food," *Technology Quarterly* 15 (1902), 335–42.

[48] See chap. 6 on Wiley's "Poison Squad" experiments.

[49] Donald E. Konold, *A History of American Medical Ethics, 1847–1912* (Madison, WI, 1962), 35–38; Jonathan Michael Liebenau, "Medical Science and Medical Industry, 1890–

Even before the bacteriological revolution, however, a more scientific perspective had begun among leading American physicians, a point of view that slowly permeated practice throughout the country. John Harley Warner has described it as a third wave. The first dominant position, the rationalistic dogma of Benjamin Rush with its heroic depletive therapy had gradually yielded to a skeptical empiricism accompanied by a heavy-dosing stimulative therapy. Beginning in the 1860s the third therapeutic movement began and thereafter accelerated, a new rationalism based on more careful observation and some laboratory experimentation. Diseases came to seem more specific, less ready to transform themselves into other entities. The aim of practice shifted from an effort to restore the balance that represented a patient's unique natural condition to an attempt to correct measurable abnormalities accompanying disease—high temperature, rapid pulse, high blood pressure, faster respiration—by restoring them to fixed norms that characterized people generally. The earlier polypharmacy slowly yielded to a regimen of fewer and more narrowly targeted drugs that could influence individual bodily systems. In this transition the physician's "principal therapeutic task" shifted from "the emphasis on the exercise of judgment to that on the application of knowledge."[50]

The supportive therapy of the middle period continued as the new more carefully aimed medications came into wider use, and traditional medicines retained favor with revised rationales for their employment. "Drugging," William G. Rothstein asserts, "continued to be the watchword of American medicine in the second half of the century." Strong medicines were prescribed to restore normality, including antipyretics, analgesics, and stimulants.[51]

To reduce fever, bloodletting was supplanted by a sequence of drugs. First came two vegetable poisons, aconite and *veratrum viride*, which acted on the heart; then quinine, cheap enough by the 1870s and 1880s to play the role of virtual panacea. The chemical search in England for a synthetic quinine led in 1856 to the serendipitous discovery of the first aniline dye. In the 1880s there reached America from Germany the first pharmaceutical fruits of dye industry research, coal-tar antipyretics and analgesics. The first of these, antipyrine, received enthusiastic American

---

1929: A Study of Pharmaceutical Manufacturing in Philadelphia" (University of Pennsylvania dissertation, 1981), 94. Liebenau's revised dissertation was published as *Medical Science and Medical Industry: The Formation of the American Pharmaceutical Industry* (Baltimore, 1987).

[50] Warner, *The Therapeutic Perspective*, 7, 235–83, quotation at 7.

[51] *Ibid.*; Konold, *A History of American Medical Ethics*, 30–35; Rothstein, *American Physicians in the Nineteenth Century*, 177–97, quotation at 187.

welcome. Then came acetanilide and phenacetin. A German chemist, Carl Duisberg, deliberately fabricated phenacetin from a dye by-product to possess a structure similar to that of acetanilide. This achievement was one of the few successes encouraging a hope among some European pharmacologists that links existed between chemical structure and physiological response, so that therapeutics might be placed upon a completely rational basis. This hope turned out to be a mirage, and, in any case, few American physicians who prescribed phenacetin were aware of it. The early coal-tar antipyretics, beset by serious side-effects, became overshadowed at the very end of the century by a safer substitute, also a patented product from Germany, aspirin.[52]

The analgesic properties of this sequence of German drugs brought them rising prominence in the 1890s in part because the chief analgesic prescribed by American physicians had come under increasing attack. "Opium," an American physician wrote in 1889, "is the most conspicuous article in the pharmacopeia." Employed for many purposes besides relief from pain, opium served in American medical practice—noted an 1888 commentator—as "the great panacea and cure-all."[53] Introduction in the 1850s of the hypodermic injection method of administering morphine spurred opium's popularity, and between 1860 and 1910 the amount of opium imported expanded at almost treble the rate of population growth. The trauma of the Civil War also was an important factor in the increasing use of morphine. Modern comprehension of the risk of opium addiction began in the 1860s, but, even so, many physicians continued to regard this serious problem with indifference. Toward the close of the century, however, addiction acquired a patina of abhorrence, for, added to health misfortune came a wave of moral revulsion.[54] In such an atmosphere, physicians slacked off on prescribing opium, turning to cocaine, heralded as nonaddictive, to the German chemical analgesics, and to chemical hypnotics, also from Germany, like chloral hydrate.[55]

Stimulants or tonics continued to be a much-prescribed category in

[52] Warner, *The Therapeutic Perspective*, 227–31; Rothstein, *American Physicians in the Nineteenth Century*, 189–90; John Parascandola, "Structure-Activity Relationships—The Early Mirage," *Pharm Hist* 17 (1971), 3–10; L. F. Haber, *The Chemical Industry during the Nineteenth Century* (Oxford, 1958), 132–35; Haber, *The Chemical Industry* (Oxford, 1971), 17, 33; Aaron Ihde, *The Development of Modern Chemistry* (New York, 1964), 455–63.

[53] Rothstein, *American Physicians in the Nineteenth Century*, 190–94.

[54] Glenn Sonnedecker, *Emergence of the Concept of Opium Addiction* (Madison, WI, 1963), 16–20; David F. Musto, *The American Disease: Origins of Narcotic Control* (New Haven, CT, 1973), 1–13; David T. Courtwright, *Dark Paradise: Opiate Addiction in America before 1940* (Cambridge, MA, 1982), 2–3, 42–61.

[55] Rothstein, *American Physicians in the Nineteenth Century*, 193–94.

the physician's armamentarium, to improve pulse, breathing, appetite, and digestion. Quinine played this among its several therapeutic roles, and later strychnine was so used. The most widely recommended and prescribed tonic, however, and, Rothstein suggests, "probably the most important medicinal agent of the second half of the century," was beverage alcohol. Even the rising temperance movement had scant impact on this cardinal aspect of therapeutics. The germ theory could be (falsely) applied to bolster the use of whiskey and brandy in therapy. Since alcohol acted as a germicide *in vitro*, it might be presumed to kill bacteria—*in vivo*.[56]

American physicians, however, had not yet generally accepted the germ theory. Their workaday world centered on treating illness, not on explaining it. Few American researchers engaged in bacteriological studies. The results of the European pioneers were not initially unambiguous. Disillusionment as well as success marked bacteriology's trail, as with the demonstration that Koch had been wrong in his triumphant 1890 announcement of a cure for tuberculosis. Even when antitoxins began to appear, sickness caused by the horse-serum base blighted the joy with which they were received. Nonetheless, it was the success of diphtheria antitoxin, introduced in 1894, that began to give bacteriology the practicality in American general practice that it had acquired a decade earlier in surgery. Prodded by public-health officials and the eager demand of patients, skeptics in the medical profession began to give way as the twentieth century began.[57]

American firms began to manufacture the new immunologic products soon after their European discovery, although Germany kept the world, including the United States, largely reliant on her supply of patented coal-tar medicinals until the First World War. Nonetheless, by 1900 a native American pharmaceutical industry had become firmly established, and the drugs prescribed by physicians in the second half of the nineteenth century were both more machine-made and better standardized than drugs prescribed earlier. Not that serious problems did not exist.[58]

Providing alkaloids like morphine, quinine, and strychnine—pharmacists and chemists had isolated some thirty by 1835—became the main

[56] *Ibid.*, 194–97.

[57] *Ibid.*, 253–81; Phyllis Allen Richmond, "American Attitudes toward the Germ Theory of Disease (1860–1880)," *Journal of the History of Medicine and Allied Sciences* 9 (1954), 428–54.

[58] Glenn Sonnedecker, "The Rise of Drug Manufacture in America," *Emory University Quarterly* 21 (1965), 73–87; Williams Haynes, *American Chemical Industry, A History*, 6 vols. (New York, 1945–54), vol. 1, 302–34.

business for the first wave of American pharmaceutical firms, evolving from pharmacies in Philadelphia in the 1820s and 1830s. Military requirements during the Civil War had expanded such manufacturing, especially in Edward R. Squibb's Brooklyn plant. Many other companies were launched in the years following the war, spurred by chemical and technological advances. The standardization of drugs by means of chemical tests began in the 1870s, supplemented by biological assays at the end of the century. Guidebook for the state of the art, the *United States Pharmacopoeia* embodied for the first time in its 1882 revision a modern outlook, providing detailed tests for establishing the identity and purity of many drugs. Such precision would help not only the pharmacist but the responsible manufacturer. Some manufacturers themselves took part in this scientific task of standardization and strove to market products of consistently dependable quality. Dr. Squibb, for instance, sought to improve the purity of ether and chloroform used for anesthesia, as well as to standardize numerous drugs taken by mouth. During the same decades that canners devised mass-production techniques, so too did pharmaceutical producers. Machines were borrowed from other industries—mixers from bakers, centrifugal devices from launderers, sugar-coating pans from confectioners, vacuum stills from whiskey makers, pill compressors from bullet molders, tube-filling mechanisms from paint-and-color manufacturers. Such revamped machines were attached to steam turbine, diesel engine, or electric motor, and set to work making potions, pills, and plasters.[59]

Manufacturers took over from pharmacists the preparation of the old galenicals, especially in fluid extract form, boasting that they could provide a standardized product. Parke, Davis & Company, beginning with ergot, took important steps toward standardizing botanicals. By the late 1880s the G. D. Searle catalog listed for sale 400 fluid extracts, 150 elixirs, 100 syrups, 75 powdered extracts, 25 tinctures, and other drug forms, asserting uniformity of potency and action. While German industry might hold supremacy in new synthetic drugs, American companies like Parke, Davis searched the world for new crude drugs from which to make fluid extracts. Since at best fluid extracts were unstable, industry sought to improve dosage constancy by introducing solid dosage forms.

[59] Aaron J. Ihde, *The Development of Modern Chemistry*, 167; Edward Kremers and George Urdang, *History of Pharmacy* (Philadelphia, 1940), 265–67; Sonnedecker, "The Rise of Drug Manufacture in America"; Glenn Sonnedecker and George Urdang, "Legalization of Drug Standards under State Laws in the United States of America," *Food, Drug, Cosmetic Law J* 8 (1953), 743; Mahoney, *The Merchants of Life*; Frank O. Taylor, "Forty-Five Years of Manufacturing Pharmacy," *J Amer Pharm Assoc* 4 (1915), 468–81; Liebenau, "Medical Science and Medical Industry."

Eli Lilly coated pills with gelatin, then developed a gelatin capsule; William E. Upjohn devised a pill that would crumble easily, releasing its medication, unlike some older pills that went through the body undissolved; Wallace C. Abbott put alkaloids in tablets. In 1890 the value of pharmaceutical preparations—not counting "patent medicines"—made in the United States, while worth less than half that of fertilizers manufactured, were valued at half again as much as the production of explosives. Placing great stress on the drug makers' success in "masking or altogether obliterating the unpleasant properties of drugs," commentators in the report of the 1890 census termed the pharmaceutical industry one "of great commercial importance."[60]

Through the nineteenth century, Jonathan M. Liebenau argues, pharmaceutical manufacturers were little more than "drug compounders." Near century's end, the industry adopted medical science as a "veneer . . . increasingly useful in the promotion of products, but its tenets were not firmly held." By the mid-1890s, however, a few of the larger firms had established some sort of laboratory. These were not devoted to research in the European sense, nor were innovation and product development their primary purpose. Initially these laboratories centered on standardizing the quantity and quality of traditional drugs.[61]

In a few laboratories, more ambitious projects began to germinate. Parke, Davis, observing a trend toward increased emphasis on pharmacology in medical education, added bacteriologists to its staff to produce diphtheria antitoxin. These scientists began to standardize drugs by physiological assay as distinct from chemical assay. Smith Kline and Company brought a pharmacist trained at the University of Michigan to set up an analytical laboratory in 1893. Lyman F. Kebler began by analyzing the goods purchased from suppliers to make sure they were up to the mark. Shortly the laboratory acquired a role in the production of elixirs, extracts, and tinctures. Kebler strove diligently to enhance the laboratory's status, cooperating with scientists in other departments, expanding his own staff, and contributing to the pharmacological literature. When the time came for Harvey Wiley to expand his own domain by paying greater attention to drugs, Kebler was recommended to the chief chemist as being "worth to you twice any other man." Kebler went

[60] David L. Cowen, "The Role of the Pharmaceutical Industry," in Blake, ed., *Safeguarding the Public*, 72–73; Mahoney, *The Merchants of Life*, 53, 71, 86, 117, 133; Taylor, "Forty-Five Years of Manufacturing Pharmacy," 470–72; Henry Bower and Henry Pemberton, Jr., "Chemicals and Allied Products," in Bureau of Census, *Eleventh Census of the United States, 1890*, vol. 6, part 3, 279.

[61] Liebenau, "Medical Science and Medical Industry," 4, 104, 114; Liebenau, "Scientific Ambitions: The Pharmaceutical Industry, 1900–1920," *Pharm Hist* 27 (1985), 3–11.

to work in Washington in 1903.[62] Despite pioneering steps made by the pharmaceutical industry in the 1890s, industrial laboratories devoted to serious pharmaceutical research in the modern sense lay at least three decades in the future.[63]

Besides marketing their elegant preparations of established pharmacopoeial drugs, American pharmaceutical manufacturers brought out their own specialties, usually mixtures given distinctive names and promoted with the badges of proprietorship. Such ventures seemed almost indispensable to business success, a physician observed, because profits from the sale of pharmacopoeial products alone were slim indeed. Eli Lilly, for example, found ample sales for its Succus Alterans, a complicated vegetable formula secured in 1883 from an Alabama physician, which gained a popular reputation for relieving rheumatism and curing syphilis. There were hundreds more.[64]

Unhappy as sophisticated physicians might be about some specialties issued by even the most reputable pharmaceutical companies, the specialty field presented an even grimmer face. Countless pseudoethical specialties of no therapeutic merit quickly appeared, promoted to physicians with exactly the same methods employed by pharmaceutical houses. The names had a scientific ring—Syrup of the Hypophosphites, Extract of Pinus Canadensis, Lithiated Hydrangea. The ordinary busy physician, not well trained in the materia medica in any case, often fell victim to such disingenuous promotions. The pseudoethicals, warned a Philadelphia physician in 1892, were "iniquitous" and "dangerous": the sick patient "certainly deserves better than to be handed over to the mercies of . . . [such an] unholy crew."[65]

Harvey Wiley and his Division of Chemistry had not yet turned their attention to the adulteration of drugs. Other critics pointed out that some of the same problems persisted that had led to the 1848 law aimed

[62] Cowen, "The Role of the Pharmaceutical Industry," 75; Taylor, "Forty-Five Years of Manufacturing Pharmacy," 474; Liebenau, "Medical Science and Medical Industry," 105–7; Charles H. Fuchsman, "Lyman Frederic Kebler," in Wyndham D. Miles, ed., *American Chemists and Chemical Engineers* (Washington, 1976), 266–67; Anderson, *The Health of a Nation*, 103.

[63] Max Tishler, "Role of the Drug House in Biological and Medical Research," *Bulletin of the New York Academy of Medicine* 35 (1959), 592–93.

[64] H. Bert Ellis, "Necessity for a National Bureau of Medicines and Foods," *Bulletin of the American Academy of Medicine* 6 (1903), 486–87; Mahoney, *The Merchants of Life*, 86, 135, 147; Roscoe Collins Clark, *Threescore Years and Ten: A Narrative of the First Seventy Years of Eli Lilly and Company, 1876–1946* (Chicago, 1946), 33–34.

[65] Young, *The Toadstool Millionaires*, 159–61, 206–8; Solomon Solis Cohen, "Shall Physicians Become Sales-Agents for Patent Medicines?" Philadelphia County Med. Soc., *Proceedings* 13 (1892), 215.

at curbing adulterated importations. During 1882 and 1883, the Massachusetts State Board of Health surveyed the quality of drugs, most of them the more important articles of the *United States Pharmacopoeia*. Forty-one percent examined fell below official standards. Whereas powdered opium came off well, laudanum made from it fell considerably below proper strength. Cinchona bark did not prove to be uniformly reliable, and galenical preparations from the bark revealed uncertain alkaloidal strength. Quinine salts showed adulteration with milk sugar. Jalap and potassium iodide also came off badly. Nor did the immediate future present a brighter prospect. Despite efforts at standardization, the fluid-extract field showed great variability in the amount of alkaloidal principle in solution. German synthetics revealed sophistication. "Who would care to make use of [the patented and expensive] phenacetin," a physician asked his colleagues, "knowing that it might be adulterated with 90 percent [of cheaper, unpatented] acetanilid?"[66]

As the century drew toward its close, therefore, much about the medicines dispensed and prescribed by American physicians warranted criticism. Even though notable advances had been made in standardizing drugs, adulteration still ran rife. Moreover, both the revisers of the *United States Pharmacopoeia* and the makers of drugs had been preoccupied with questions of purity, to the neglect of efficacy. The question of the therapeutic utility of medications, posed earlier by Oliver Wendell Holmes, arose anew in a more probing form. It was easy enough for the leading scientific physicians to condemn pseudo-specialties. Even ethical specialties of reputable drug manufacturers, reminiscent of earlier days of polypharmacy, came under attack. More important, as experimental pharmacology and physiology developed, the curative strength of main pillars in the traditional materia medica seemed to crumble. William Osler coined a dozen aphorisms to express his disdain for the prevailing confidence in the utility of most drugs being widely prescribed. A president of the American Medical Association opined that, except for quinine in treating malaria and mercury for syphilis, drugs were "valueless as cures." Such judgments presaged, at least among the intellectual elite of American medicine, a tendency toward therapeutic nihilism more insistent and sweeping than the earlier skepticism expressed by Holmes when he considered foisting mankind's drugs upon the fishes.[67]

[66] B. F. Davenport, "Quality of Some of the Pharmacopoeial Drugs in Common Use," *Boston Med and Surg J* 112 (1885), 500–501; Ellis, "Necessity for a National Bureau," 486–87.

[67] Melvin P. Earles, "Commentary," in Blake, ed., *Safeguarding the Public*, 38–40, 43; William B. Bean, *Sir William Osler Aphorisms* (New York, 1950), 102, 118; Harvey Cushing,

Agricultural Chemists

Foods lacked what drugs possessed, a single volume prepared by experts and periodically revised defining standards of strength, quality, and purity, and providing detailed tests by which a sample might be examined to determine whether it conformed. The 1848 drug import law had established a multiple-pharmacopoeial standard. Various state pharmacy acts and food and drug statutes had written the standards of the *United States Pharmacopoeia* into law. Major food and drug bills introduced into the Congress had proposed doing the same. No equivalent to the USP existed for foods.[68]

In the mid-1890s a serious effort to remedy this deficiency got under way, a self-imposed task launched by the organization of official chemists on the payrolls of the several states. The movement to create food standards blended with a renewal of the campaign, dormant since the House of Representatives had failed to consider Senator Paddock's bill, to put a national food and drug law on the statute books. The insistence of the chemists revived congressional interest. Central figure in both campaigns, for standard making and for seeking a law, was Harvey Wiley, once a state chemist himself. In the course of these endeavors within the Association of Official Agricultural Chemists, Wiley established himself beyond question as the generalissimo of the pure-food coalition to press for passage of a law.

Connecticut established the first agricultural experiment station in 1875, followed by a number of other states acting on their own initiative. In 1887 Congress enacted the Hatch Act, providing annual grants, the first important federal step in the direction of aiding scientific research and development in states and universities. This spurred the other states to set up experiment stations. The movement arose from the zeal of a generation of young chemists, coming back from their German training. Imbued with a missionary fervor, they were determined to increase agricultural productivity and thus spur the nation's health, morality, and stature. A strictly academic career required so much effort in the classroom that no time was left for research, nor was research much valued by college administrators. Foresighted men, like Evan Pugh of Pennsyl-

The Life of Sir William Osler, vol. 2 (Oxford, 1925), 180; Maurice B. Strauss, ed., *Familiar Medical Quotations* (Boston, 1968), 125; James G. Burrow, "The Prescription-Drug Policies of the American Medical Association in the Progressive Era," in Blake, ed., *Safeguarding the Public*, 112. Harry F. Dowling in 1970 retrospectively evaluated the drugs in use at the start of the twentieth century in *Medicines for Man: The Development, Regulation, and Use of Prescription Drugs* (New York, 1970), 18.

[68] Sonnedecker and Urdang, "Legalization of Drug Standards under State Laws," 741–60.

vania and Samuel W. Johnson of Connecticut, saw experiment stations as necessary adjuncts of the new agricultural colleges that were being established, also with federal aid. Johnson played the role of prime lobbyist in securing the Connecticut station, became its chemist, and simultaneously received a professorship at Yale.[69]

Farmers favored the creation of agricultural experiment stations, eager to accept the chemists' promises of help. During the 1870s and 1880s, when most of the stations came into existence, the most pressing problem for which farmers wanted a chemical solution concerned fertilizers. Heavy promotion by manufacturers of artificial fertilizers had made their use seem desirable, particularly on soil long-tilled, in competition with more fertile soil farther west. So much time elapsed between fertilizing crops and harvesting them, however, that fraud ran rampant. Farmers believed that experiment stations, by analyzing fertilizers, might curb this evil. Laws were passed aimed at keeping manufacturers honest through accurate labeling.[70]

State chemists employed their analytical skills at exposing other products in which chemistry had been employed to cheat farmers: barn paints, veterinary drugs, feedstuffs. Improvements in commercial animal feed resulting from this exposure led Wiley to remark that if you wanted to be well nourished you should be a hog. Problems with fertilizer, however, the initial product of state chemists' analytical concern, led to the founding of an organization.[71]

A lack of uniformity in the analyses of fertilizers had provoked great disputation. "The condition of analytical work," as Wiley put it, "may be truly described as chaotic." The use of German, French, and English models for determining nitrogen, potash, and phosphoric acid in fertilizers led to divergent results. Moreover, the chemist of the seller might reach a conclusion different from that obtained by the buyer's chemist, which might in turn not coincide with conflicting analyses of official chemists from two adjoining states. Initiative to end this wrangling

[69] Rosenberg, *No Other Gods*, 153–72; Margaret W. Rossiter, *The Emergence of Agricultural Science: Justus Liebig and the Americans, 1840–1880* (New Haven, CT, 1975), 127–76; Louis I. Kuslan, "Samuel William Johnson," in Miles, ed., *American Chemists and Chemical Engineers*, 249–50.

[70] Rosenberg, *No Other Gods*, 155, 170; Hayter, *The Troubled Farmer*, 305; William Horwitz, "The Role of the A.O.A.C. in the Passage of the Food and Drugs Act of 1906," *Food, Drug, Cosmetic Law J* 11 (1956), 77–85.

[71] Charles W. Crawford, "The A.O.A.C. As an Aid to Food and Drug Regulation," *Journal of the Association of Official Agricultural Chemists* 35 (1952), 36; Hayter, *The Troubled Farmer*, 39–59; Rossiter, *The Emergence of Agricultural Science*, 149–71; Alan I Marcus, "Setting the Standards: Fertilizers, State Chemists, and Early National Commercial Regulation, 1880–1887," *Agricultural History* 61 (1987), 47–73.

came from a Georgia chemist, H. J. Redding, who persuaded the state commissioner of agriculture, J. T. Henderson, to call a meeting to confront the problem. Three assemblies were held in 1880 and 1881, to which commercial as well as governmental chemists were invited. At the third meeting, a serious dispute arose: the men from commerce charged that the methods desired by the men from government would do them serious injustice. The official chemists stood firm. In 1884 they formed themselves into the Association of Official Agricultural Chemists (AOAC), welcoming commercial chemists to their discussions but denying them a vote on establishing the methods of analyzing fertilizers by which their products would be assayed under state laws. Besides agreeing to such uniformity of methods among the states, the new association pledged to work for uniform fertilizer legislation. The first two bulletins issued by the AOAC dealt only with methods for analyzing fertilizers.[72]

Harvey Wiley, a founding father of the AOAC, quickly secured for the infant organization the Department of Agriculture's patronage. The proceedings of the meetings and official analytical methods agreed upon appeared as bulletins of the Division of Chemistry. Wiley's vision of the AOAC's purpose extended far beyond fertilizer. When the commissioner of agriculture addressed the organization's meeting in 1886, he expressed hope that the association would expand its work to setting standards for human foods and to detecting adulteration. Wiley echoed these sentiments the next year, speaking as second president of the AOAC, persuading the membership to change the constitution so as to undertake such expanded goals. This address came just as the first part of Bulletin 13 was headed for the press, a work the state chemists came to rely on as a sourcebook of authentic data. The next year Wiley made the first report the AOAC had heard on human food, concerned with butter and butter substitutes. In 1897 Willard D. Bigelow, Wiley's chief aide, presented a tentative report on methods for determining food adulterants. That same year the AOAC created a committee, which Wiley chaired, to establish standards for pure foods, so that a proper line could be drawn between the normal and the inferior or adulterated. Soon a more complex and sophisticated referee system was set up, supported by Department of Agriculture funds. In 1901 the AOAC accepted from its committee and adopted seventeen reports setting forth provisional methods for the analysis of foods. Seven of the seventeen had been prepared by Division

---

[72] *Ibid.*; Rossiter, *The Emergence of Agricultural Science*, 149–71; W. B. White, "A.O.A.C. Methods of Analysis," *Food, Drug, Cosmetic Law Quarterly* 1 (1946), 442–56, Wiley cited on 443.

of Chemistry chemists. The steady pace of these events demonstrated that the official chemists of the nation, first formally united by fertilizer, had found their major focus in food. In 1902 Congress took cognizance of the AOAC committee, authorizing its members to serve as advisers to the secretary of agriculture. Had the Congress remained constant in this determination, the AOAC standards might have acquired an official stature for foods that pharmacopoeial standards represented for drugs.[73]

In the meantime, the AOAC had revived interest in the languishing pure-food campaign. In 1895 the president of the association, Henry A. Huston, a former student of Wiley who succeeded his mentor at Purdue, addressed this theme eloquently, leading to the appointment of a committee on food legislation that Wiley chaired. Two years later the committee urged the membership to endorse the principle of a general law, specifically recommending reintroduction of the Paddock bill that had passed the Senate. The AOAC approved the committee's suggestions and conveyed the text to both houses of the Congress. At the end of 1897, Marriott Brosius of Pennsylvania introduced H.R. 5441 in the House of Representatives.[74]

[73] *Ibid.*; Anderson, *The Health of a Nation*, 68–69, 122–23; Horwitz, "The Role of the A.O.A.C.," 77–85; Henry A. Lepper, "The Evolution of Food Standards and the Role of the A.O.A.C.," *Food, Drug, Cosmetic Law J* 8 (1953), 133–47; Bureau of Chemistry, Bulletin 65, *Provisional Methods for the Analysis of Foods Adopted by the AOAC, 1901.*

[74] Anderson, *The Health of a Nation*, 123; *Cong. Record*, 55 Cong. 2 ses., 304 (December 18, 1897).

VI

Initiative for a Law Resumed

This great country [must] take its proper place among civilized nations and protect its citizens, as well as its hogs and cattle against disease.
— FRANK HUME, chairman of Local Call Committee, National Pure Food and Drug Congress, 1898[1]

The Pure-Food Congresses

The bill introduced on December 18, 1897, by Marriott Brosius of Pennsylvania conveyed to the Fifty-fifth Congress regulatory ideas from the Association of Official Agricultural Chemists committee, chaired by Harvey Wiley. Rooted in the Paddock bill, the AOAC draft was expanded to include cosmetics and a broader definition of drugs. The Paddock bill's stipulation that only a "knowingly" illegal act was actionable did not now appear. The bill authorized the secretary of agriculture to call upon the AOAC to fix food standards that would possess authority before the courts.[2]

The toughening of the bill worried businessmen, even those anxious for enactment of a national law, and no doubt contributed to the large and diversified attendance at a new National Pure Food and Drug Congress held in Washington in 1898. Prime mover was temperamental agricultural journalist Alexander J. Wedderburn, now master of the Virginia State Grange, who earlier had prepared popular versions of the Division of Chemistry's adulteration studies. He now made Wiley chairman of the assembly's advisory committee, but relations between the two men proved thorny. Wedderburn may have been prompted in part by ambition, hoping that his role as convener of such a congress would elevate him to the pinnacle of leadership in the pure-food cause. In a magazine he launched as soon as the congress ended, he touted himself

[1] *Journal of Proceedings of the National Pure Food and Drug Congress Held in Columbian University Hall, Washington, D.C., March 2, 3, 4, and 5, 1898* (Washington, 1898), 4. This document is number 12 in Pamphlet Volume 4,021, History of Medicine Division, National Library of Medicine, Bethesda, MD.

[2] H.R. 5441, *Cong. Record*, 55 Cong. 2 ses., 304; "Brosius, Marriott," *Biographical Directory of the American Congress* (1971), 645; Anderson, *The Health of a Nation*, 123–24.

as the most zealous and faithful champion of that cause, who, even when "left to battle alone . . . never lost heart, and never for a moment turned from the path." If Wedderburn strove to defeat Wiley for leadership of the crusade, he failed. At the congress itself, Wiley outmaneuvered Wedderburn and enhanced his own stature.[3]

In any case, the time was ripe for the kind of gathering Wedderburn launched. Since the effort a decade earlier to assemble elements of the private sector in behalf of public control over food and drugs, conditions had worsened. The nation had suffered another depression, which hurt both farmers and food processors. An important competitive ploy had always been depreciation of quality. This tactic now saw increased and more clever use, with soaring employment of chemical preservatives to hedge against spoilage of dubious raw products in processed bottle or can. "That people can do such things and look into their neighbor's countenances [sic] without a downcast eye and a shamed face," Congressman Brosius observed before the pure-food congress, "shows the virulency of the moral poison and the extent of its diffusion in the commercial community." Reputable food processors would be compelled to imitate the adulterators or "to quit business." Added to the burden of shady competitors on the respectable was the new series of state food and drug laws that had been recently enacted. The latter-day adulterator, according to a Senate report, possessed an intimate knowledge of these laws and "skill in evading" them. The law-abiding processor faced increasing confusion, as state laws and decisions of regulators conflicted, making compliance ever more costly. A federal law, as the Senate report put it, had become "imperative."[4]

So thought almost all delegates meeting in Columbian University Hall in March 1898, while war sentiment was intensifying after the sinking of the *Maine*. Wedderburn and his coplanners had cast a wide net in issuing invitations. Each state and territorial governor was asked to appoint ten delegates from among agriculturists and members of the food and drug trades. All relevant federal departments and bureaus, as well as state and local public health and food and drug agencies, were represented. Farm groups sent delegates, as did the AOAC. Especially significant was the attendance of spokesmen from national professional societies and trade associations. The American Chemical Society and the American Pharmaceutical Association had participants, and so did millers and brewers, makers of butter and makers of candy, fishers and bee-

---

[3] *Pure Food, A Monthly Magazine* 1 (May 1898), 1–2 (this first issue of the magazine, edited by Wedderburn, probably was the only one published); Anderson, *The Health of a Nation*, 124–26.

[4] *Journal of Proceedings of the National Pure Food and Drug Congress . . . 1898*, 9; *Adulteration, Misbranding, and Imitation of Foods, Etc.*, 55 Cong. 3 ses., Senate Report 1488, 2–3.

keepers, wholesale and retail grocers, even the National Peace Congress and the Women's Christian Temperance Union (WCTU). A reception given for delegates at the White House by President William McKinley enhanced the prestige of the convention.[5]

A prominent role played by trade and professional association representatives at the National Pure Food and Drug Congress of 1898—and at its successors of 1899 and 1900—characterized the campaign for a national pure-food law as part of a broader movement in the interrelations between American economic endeavor and government. A rising new middle class of businessmen and professionals, as Robert Wiebe has described the scene, had assumed increasing authority in American life, each trade and profession well-organized for action in a national organization possessing great esprit de corps. Such groups shared an abhorrence of the chaotic economic scene, but activity within the private sector did not seem capable of achieving the shared vision of an economy marked by order, stability, and efficiency. So the new middle class increasingly turned to the national government for help.[6]

The three hundred delegates who met in Washington heard orators expounding the familiar reasons for a national law: the consumer's welfare; the economic security of the honest producer, processor, and exporter; the sanctity of morals. Congressman Brosius, in stirring oratory, stressed all these themes. Born in the rich farming county of Lancaster, Brosius knew that malfeasance with processed foods harmed his constituency. "Adulteration of food products results in the cheapening of the products of the farm," he told the Congress, "and every farmer should engage in this crusade against a system of commercial piracy which thus robs both producer and consumer, . . . the common enemy of all mankind, the scourge of all."[7]

Brosius had fought through almost the entire Civil War, receiving a battlefield commission for bravery and a seriously impaired right arm. He was stirred anew to patriot sentiments by the war with Spain, and he saw between that military challenge and the pure-food fight a palpable connection. "The war that invites our devotion and patriotism just now," he told the assembled delegates, "is the war upon impure food. In this holy war every man shall put on his armor and keep it on until we make merry music at the funeral and dance on the grave of the last food pirate in the land."[8]

The bill that Brosius had introduced he deemed imperfect, "a rough

---

[5] *Journal of Proceedings of the National Pure Food and Drug Congress . . . 1898*, 17–23, 32.

[6] Robert H. Wiebe, *The Search for Order, 1877–1920* (New York, 1967).

[7] *Journal of Proceedings of the National Pure Food and Drug Congress . . . 1898*, 7–10.

[8] *Ibid.*; *Pure Food* 1 (1898), 17; "Brosius, Marriott," *Biographical Directory of the American Congress* (1971), 645.

draft," needing amendments. He urged the convention "to make the measure as satisfactory to diverse views as you can," then to return home and build sentiment for the enactment of "this much needed measure."[9]

Wiley, keenly aware of his audience, gave an address moderate in tone, playing down dangers from adulterated food but showing by vivid exhibit its widespread scope—grape juice laced with salicylic acid, glucose passed off as honey, artificial colors used for dyeing preserved meats, "coffee berries" that had never seen a coffee tree. He declared his opposition to prohibitory measures so long as all food products were accurately labeled. "What we want," he said, "is that the farmer may get an honest market and the consumer may get what he thinks he is buying."[10]

In the forum of the congress more radical sentiments received expression. A group called the Vital Friends proposed abolishing all canned goods, but the resolutions committee sidetracked this and other extreme opinions.[11] Main focus of the meeting centered on the Brosius bill. While the need for a national law was manifest, achieving agreement over exact terms posed a stupendous challenge. Wiley ably led the committee on legislation. Amazingly a virtual consensus was reached. Wedderburn summed up the situation for a later House committee:

When this great body of representatives gathered, . . . they took . . . [the pending] bill word by word, in the [legislative] committee, and stayed there for hours, into midnight, and part of the next day. [The entire assembly then] had the warmest kind of a fight, and yet they got together, all the diversified interests, the great wholesalers on one side and the retailers on the other, the scientist here and the consumer there. All urged one single thing, and that was to secure legislation.[12]

The text agreed upon moved the bill away from an agricultural scientist's ideal in the businessman's direction. A strong majority of the congress agreed with the president of the District of Columbia commissioners that, while the public should be protected, every care should be taken to "avoid unnecessary annoyance to legitimate manufacturers." The "most serious shortcoming" of the Brosius bill, as the brewers' spokesman assessed it, lay in the standard-setting clause: this crucial re-

[9] *Journal of Proceedings of the National Pure Food and Drug Congress . . . 1898*, 7–10.

[10] *Ibid.*, 12–16.

[11] *Ibid.*, 33–34.

[12] *Ibid.*, 27, 41–43; *Hearings before the Committee on Interstate and Foreign Commerce of the House of Representatives on The Pure-Food Bills . . .* , 57 Cong. 1 ses. (Washington, 1902), 630.

sponsibility should not be left to the AOAC's discretion, nor to that of the secretary of agriculture. On this point a compromise was worked out that represented the pure-food congress's major modification of the Brosius bill. The secretary must consult, not only the AOAC, but also chemists chosen by the American Chemical Society and government physicians selected by the president. This board of experts, in considering standards, must secure input from representatives of industry.[13]

Other changes occurred at the behest of various groups: the protection of trade formulas, desired by food processors; the relaxing of the adulteration definition for candy, desired by confectioners; and the restricting of the drug definition to exclude proprietary medicines, desired by drug-trade interests. The revamped text accepted by this disparate and voluntary body was duly introduced into the national Congress.[14]

The degree of harmony achieved in 1898 did not last through the 1899 and 1900 sessions of the pure-food congress. Trade rivalries, muted in the first session, later led to bitter jousting for advantage that could not be reconciled, especially on the part of dairy and oleomargarine interests and the producers of alum and cream-of-tartar baking powders.[15] At the 1900 gathering, groups worried about Wiley as future enforcer made a strong effort to define administrative aspects of a proposed bill so as to exclude the chief chemist. "The fewer [such gatherings] which meet hereafter the better," Wiley wrote. Henceforth the art of compromise reverted to the halls of Congress.[16]

The very convening of the pure-food congresses, nonetheless, revealed a rising awareness among concerned businessmen that a national food and drug law might be both useful and inevitable. The 1890s had brought turbulence to the domestic marketplace, partly because of economic crises, partly because the varying provisions of state laws made it increasingly difficult to package products for sale throughout the coun-

[13] The text of the Brosius bill as revised at the pure-food congress is printed in the *Journal of Proceedings*, 34–39. The speeches of Commissioner John W. Ross and Gallus Thoman of the United States Brewers' Association appear in *ibid.*, 6–7 and 27–30.

[14] Anderson, *The Health of a Nation*, 125; *Pure Food* 1 (1898), 63. The new Brosius bill became H.R. 9154, introduced March 15, 1898, *Cong. Record*, 55 Cong. 2 ses., 2844. The same bill was presented in the Senate by Charles J. Faulkner of West Virginia as S. 4144, *ibid.*, 2854.

[15] Donna J. Wood, *Strategic Uses of Public Policy*, 154–73.

[16] Anderson, *The Health of a Nation*, 126–27, 132–33; *Report of the Proceedings of the Second Annual Convention of the National Pure Food and Drug Congress* (Washington, 1899); *Memorial from the National Pure Food and Drug Congress*, 55 Cong. 2 ses., Senate Doc. 233; *Adulterated and Misbranded Food, Drugs, and Drinks*, 55 Cong. 3 ses., Senate Doc. 167. The second National Pure Food and Drug Congress had an even broader representation of trade groups than the first, including the Proprietary Association.

try. National marketing seemed to demand a national law. That law should be framed, each segment of the food and drug industries realized, so as to give it as much competitive advantage as adroit lobbying could achieve. Moreover, as Ilyse D. Barkan has suggested, key industries must delay the enactment of that law until they had sold off in foreign markets goods that would be taboo when a pure-food law should go into force. Yet, among the diverse elements of the complex coalition that would eventually bring enactment of a food and drug law, producers of food, beverages, and drugs preceded consumers in anticipating, even in desiring, that law's eventual arrival.[17]

Trichinous Pork and "Embalmed Beef"

In the meantime, while no omnibus pure-food bill made progress in the Congress, two events lifted the pure-food issue a notch or two in public attention and concern. The "embalmed beef" scandals of the Spanish-American War generated a flurry of intense worry about the nation's meat supply. This soon subsided but proved to be an important memory when revived by even more shocking events seven years later. Of equal or greater significance, a senator new to the pure-food campaign, William E. Mason of Illinois, conducted the most extensive hearings the adulteration issue had yet been given.

Skepticism about the quality of American meat had long existed, and European exploitation of such fears had provoked the meat-inspection laws of 1890 and 1891. American agricultural exports doubled in the 1870s, due to severe crop failures in Europe, increasing productivity on American farms, and the ingenuity of meat packers. Gustavus F. Swift and Philip D. Armour, arriving in Chicago in 1875, became pioneers in both the packing process and in distribution. Moving "disassembly" lines were devised, involving specialization of labor, so that it took 157 men engaged in seventy-eight separate processes to take apart a steer. Refrigerator cars and cold-storage warehouses became central to distribution systems enabling urban Americans to buy cheap chilled beef. When the home market could not absorb all that Packingtown's increasing efficiency could provide, overseas exports expanded. Swift made twenty transatlantic crossings to arrange for such European sales. Prices

[17] Wood, *Strategic Uses of Public Policy*; Ilyse D. Barkan, "Industry Invites Regulation: The Passage of the Pure Food and Drug Act of 1906," *American Journal of Public Health* 75 (1985), 18–26. Citing federal statistics, Barkan shows a staggered pattern of dumping goods between 1902 and 1906 which, she presumes, "may reflect coordinated efforts to disguise the practice," 23–24.

fell, so that the poor in Germany could eat more pork, and the poor in Britain more beef, than they earlier could afford.[18]

Such competition worried European farmers, especially when their own crop conditions improved, and a free market for American agricultural imports seemed unfair to European industrialists, faced with American protective tariffs on manufactured goods. Economic arguments for restricting American meat imports might be politically unwise: such barriers would increase food costs for the poor. Restraints based on health arguments seemed more palatable.[19]

Beginning in 1879 a wave of embargoes swept across Europe, supported by a spate of scare stories about trichinae and cholera in American hogs and pleuropneumonia in cattle. The acting British consul in Philadelphia, for example, in a report to his foreign office, told of a Kansan who had fallen ill with trichinosis:

> Worms were in his flesh by the million, being scraped and squeezed from the pores of his skin. They are felt creeping through his flesh and are literally eating up his substance. The disease is thought to have been contracted by eating sausages.[20]

Trichinae had first been discovered in pork by an American physician in 1846 and were demonstrated to be the cause of human disease by German scientists in 1860. An outbreak of trichinosis in Germany, blamed on American pork, aided agrarian forces in securing a ban, staunchly supported by Chancellor Otto von Bismarck. Besides Germany, Italy, Portugal, Greece, Spain, France, Austria-Hungary, Turkey, Rumania, and Denmark excluded American pork products entirely or in part. Although Britain did not forsake free trade, imports of American meat fell sharply.[21]

---

[18] Louis L. Snyder, "The American-German Pork Dispute, 1879–1891," *Journal of Modern History* 17 (1945), 16–28; John L. Gignilliat, "Pigs, Politics, and Protection: The European Boycott of American Pork," *Agricultural History* 35 (1961), 3–12; Bingham Duncan, *Whitelaw Reid: Journalist, Politician, Diplomat* (Athens, GA, 1975), 139–46; Boorstin, *The Americans: The Democratic Experience*, 316–22; Alfred D. Chandler, Jr., *The Visible Hand: The Managerial Revolution in American Business* (Cambridge, MA, 1977), 299–302, 391–402; Wade, *Chicago's Pride: The Stockyards, Packingtown, and Environs in the Nineteenth Century*; Suellen Hoy and Walter Nugent, "The German-American Pork War: Protectionism and Public Health in the Late Nineteenth Century," in press.

[19] Hoy and Nugent, *ibid.*, argue persuasively that, for Germany, health concerns predominated over economic considerations. This view is contrary to American opinion at the time and to most scholarship since.

[20] *Times*, London, February 19, 1881, cited in Gignilliat, "Pigs, Politics, and Protection," 5.

[21] Benjamin Schwartz, "Trichinosis in Swine and Its Relationship to Public Health,"

A decade of delicate diplomacy ending in inspection laws was needed to reverse this economic blow. Initially such laws, although urged by American consuls abroad and favored by livestock producers, did not appeal to packers and exporters, who objected to the expense and feared intrusion of government into their operations. Packers preferred the weapon of tariff retaliation, anathema to low-tariff livestock producers. Nor did many animal scientists believe that European criticism warranted a major governmental attack on diseases of livestock. They considered European charges of threats to health exaggerated, even specious, masking economic concerns. If Germans would sensibly cook their pork, as Americans did, trichinosis would cease to be a problem. Two governmental investigations—although without microscopic examination—exonerated American pork. The American stance was well stated by Whitelaw Reid, minister to France, who noted that in the United States, which consumed more pork than any other nation, total deaths from trichinosis since the discovery of that disease did not equal the annual death rate from strokes of lightning. In 1890 Dr. D. E. Salmon, chief of the Bureau of Animal Industry, could still say: "I doubt very much if the people of this country are quite ready to have sanitary laws applied to the eradication of swine diseases."[22]

A bill to give American meat a clean bill of health so as to protect exports had been before the Congress since 1884. By 1890 Congress was ready to enact a law that combined inspection with the threat of vigorous tariff retaliation. Congressmen did not believe that American pork conveyed trichinae overseas, but they recognized that lifting of the European bans would expand annual exports by $50 million. A select committee of five senators from cattle-raising states also was moved by the opinions of stockmen, echoing that printed in the *Breeder's Gazette*:

> It has been clearly demonstrated that . . . [through increasing exports] lies a way of escape for the harassed cattle-feeders from the clutches of Packingtown, if only some Moses would arise who possesses the ability and determination to so order affairs as to open the doors of European ports to the unrestricted entrance of our cattle even as he of Biblical history did make a dry path through the waters of the Red Sea.

The Senate committee believed that federal inspection would "inspire [such] confidence."[23]

Annual Report of the Board of Regents of the Smithsonian Institution, 1939 (Washington, 1940), 413–15; Snyder, "The American-German Pork Dispute," 19.

[22] Gignilliat, "Pigs, Politics, and Protection," with Salmon cited, 11; Reid cited in *Cong. Record*, 51 Cong. 1 ses., 8889–90 (August 20, 1890).

[23] *Inspection of Meats for Exportation, Etc.*, 51 Cong. 1 ses., House Report 1792; *Inspection*

The 1890 law forbade export or import of infected cattle and the export of unwholesome meat, authorizing the "careful inspection" of pork destined for export. This was recognized as meaning microscopic examination to detect trichinae. The law gave greater attention, however, to imports than to exports, especially banning livestock diseased or exposed to infection, but also barring "any adulterated or unwholesome food or drug or any vinous, spirituous or malt liquors, adulterated or mixed with any poisonous or noxious chemical drug or other ingredient injurious to health." To protect American exports against "unjust discriminations" by other nations, the president was given the authority to counter such hostile acts by excluding from American shores selected exports sent by an offending country.[24]

When foreign nations protested that the inspection did not include the condition of the hog at time of slaughter, Congress in 1891 considerably expanded the law. Mandatory antemortem inspection was decreed for all live cattle, hogs, and sheep. Carcasses and products intended for export also must be inspected. The law authorized inspection of meat in interstate commerce, although funds did not permit implementation of these provisions. The law permitted but did not require postmortem inspection, at the discretion of the secretary of agriculture, a function that the Bureau of Animal Industry nonetheless began promptly to perform. Representatives from European states came to observe American procedures, and shortly restraints on the acceptance of pork abroad were abandoned or relaxed. Sales soared, by 1895 reaching their preembargo high.[25]

Germany had eliminated its ban only after an American threat to place a duty on sugar, and the imperial action did not bind individual German states within the empire. In an effort to assure themselves of avoiding trichinosis while continuing to eat raw pork, Germans, through their

---

of Live Cattle and Beef Products, 57 Cong. 1 ses., House Report 2985; Select Committee on the Transportation and Sale of Meat Products, *Report*, 51 Cong. 1 ses., Senate Report 829, 30, 31, *Breeder's Gazette*, April 2, 1890, cited at 30. To this report is attached *Testimony Taken by the Select Committee* . . . (Washington, 1889). George G. Vest of Missouri chaired the Select Committee.

[24] An act providing for an inspection of meats for exportation, prohibiting the importation of adulterated articles of food or drink, and authorizing the President to make proclamations in certain cases, and for other purposes. 26 U.S. Stat. 414, August 30, 1890.

[25] An act to provide for the inspection of live cattle, hogs, and the carcasses and products thereof which are the subjects of interstate commerce, and for other purposes: 26 U.S. Stat. 1089, March 3, 1891. A further tightening of the law came in 1895 as part of the act making appropriations for the Department of Agriculture: 28 U.S. Stat. 727, March 2, 1895. *Inspection of Live Cattle and Beef Products*, 1; A. D. Melvin, "The Federal Meat-Inspection Service," in Bureau of Animal Industry, *Twenty-Third Annual Report, 1906* (Washington, 1908), 75.

local governments, set up an extensive network of microscopists, an in-spectional army, in fact, larger in number than the entire enlisted ranks of the United States Army at the outbreak of the Spanish-American War. The German states insisted on reinspecting imported American pork, charging such high fees as virtually to price it out of the market. Renewed charges arose that German cases of trichinosis were being traced to American pork. Such allegations seemed deliberately to chal-lenge American competence in microscopic technology.

The United States countered the new threat by sending to Berlin in 1898, as agricultural and scientific attaché, a gifted young zoologist, Charles Wardell Stiles. Schooled in Germany and acquainted with a number of that nation's leading scientists, Stiles also had great talent as a diplomat. Microscope in hand, Stiles traveled to places where news-papers reported trouble with allegedly trichinous pork. Everywhere he went, he collected information and evaluated the legions of local pork microscopists. Stiles discovered indubitable weak spots in the American export system, the shipping of small quantities of fresh uncured pork and of soft sausage, which might harbor trichinae. He also found loop-holes in the German customs system through which uninspected pork, although marked with inspection stamps, might filter. These inadequa-cies Stiles brought to the attention of both American and German au-thorities.

Germany's central charge, however, Stiles insisted, could be refuted absolutely. Germany's own most distinguished scientists, he noted, in-cluding Rudolf Virchow, had not been able to link any cases of trichi-nosis with American pork. German microscopic inspection, moreover, fell far short of what might be expected of the world's leading scientific nation, marred by the carelessness of many part-time and badly trained inspectors and by their antiquated and damaged microscopes. German inspection endeavors, Stiles asserted, fell far behind in accuracy and ef-ficiency the work of the young women microscopists employed by the Bureau of Animal Industry, who in the Chicago packing plants used American-made instruments especially adapted for trichinae inspection. "If the German Government desires to protect the German sausage-makers and hog-raisers against American competition," Stiles and the American ambassador urged, "a method may be adopted which will not be a scientifically unwarranted reflection, liable to injure American trade with other nations." Germany did soon pass a bill increasing central over local authority for meat inspection. Although protectionist in tone, the measure did not use a health rationale to support discrimination against American pork.[26]

[26] Gignilliat, "Pigs, Politics, and Protection," 10; James H. Cassedy, "Applied Micros-

While Stiles labored to clear pork from overseas aspersions, the reputation of American beef suffered a domestic blow. Indeed, beef came to bear the brunt of dissatisfactions that developed among soldiers and their families during the Spanish-American War. War was declared in April 1898, and the small regular army, rapidly expanded by volunteers, was sent to southern camps, awaiting transport to Cuba, under blockade by the American fleet. When tropical rains subsided, an expeditionary force of some seventeen thousand men sailed in mid-June from Tampa, disembarking east of Santiago. On July 1 two major battles were fought and won. Threatened now from both land and sea, the Spanish fleet, in trying to escape from Santiago harbor, met destruction. This naval encounter ended the war, although the army stayed on in Cuba into August, suffering some nine times as many deaths from disease as from casualties in battle. In almost no way had the army been prepared for war. Its supply and medical services proved especially ill-equipped for campaigning in a tropical clime.[27]

In early August, on the day after the troops had been ordered home from Cuba, the mother of a soldier wrote a letter to President McKinley. She had been reading in the newspapers stories reporting soldier complaints about the bad beef they had been provided. "We are living under a generous Government," the mother wrote, "with a good, kind man at its head willing to give the Army the best possible, and yet thieving corporations will give the boys the worst."[28]

McKinley also had been reading newspaper articles criticizing army sanitation and food. A midterm election loomed, and the president saw fit to appoint a special commission, headed by General Grenville M. Dodge, to investigate the wartime conduct of the War Department. In February 1899, because of testimony given before the Dodge commission, McKinley established a new court of inquiry, headed by Major-General James F. Wade, to probe particularly the by now sensational problem of army beef.[29]

---

copy and American Pork Diplomacy: Charles Wardell Stiles in Germany 1898–1899," *Isis* 62 (1971), 4–20.

[27] William Addleman Ganoe, *The History of the United States Army*, rev. ed. (New York, 1942), 371–85, 391–94; Edward F. Keuchel, "Chemicals and Meat: The Embalmed Beef Scandal of the Spanish-American War," *Bull Hist Med* 48 (1974), 249–64.

[28] Exhibit 18, *Food Furnished by Subsistence Department to Troops in the Field*, 56 Cong. 1 ses., Senate Doc. 270, (1898).

[29] Keuchel, "Chemicals and Meat," 249–64; H. Wayne Morgan, *William McKinley and His America* (Syracuse, NY, 1963), 425–26. *Report of the Commission Appointed by the President to Investigate the Conduct of the War Department in the War with Spain*, 56 Cong. 1 ses., Senate Doc. 221, the Dodge report, consists of eight volumes, the first seven of which, including verbatim testimony, are paginated consecutively. The Wade court report was

Most shocking was a charge made by the commanding general of the army, Major General Nelson A. Miles, before the Dodge commission. It was he who coined the startling term "embalmed beef." Miles liked the old way of supplying armies with beef, "driven on the hoof and slaughtered as it was required by the troops." He opposed the plan for this war, an adaptation of the Swift and Armour overseas marketing system, reliance on beef that was refrigerated or canned. The former, Miles testified, had been marred by "some serious defect."

> There was sent to Porto Rico 337 tons of what was known as, or called, refrigerated beef, which you might call embalmed beef, and there was also sent 198,508 pounds of what is known as canned fresh beef, which was condemned . . . by nearly every officer whose commands used it.[30]

Miles confessed ignorance of what "secret" ingredient might have been injected to "embalm" the beef, but sought to buttress this scandalous word with a letter from an army officer, a Pittsburgh physician. At Tampa, Major W. H. Daly had observed a quarter of beef hanging in the sun above the deck of an army transport. Despite the heat, the meat remained untainted after sixty hours of exposure. Only the use of "deleterious preservatives" would possibly permit this. Later, in Puerto Rico, Daly secured a ton of refrigerated beef from a commissary. He continued:

> It looked well but had an odor similar to that of a dead human after being injected with preservatives, and it tasted when cooked like decomposed boric acid, while after standing a day . . . it became so bitter, nauseous, and unpalatable as to be quite impossible to use.

Daly threw the meat into the ocean.[31]

A traditionalist as well as a vainglorious, frustrated, and spiteful man, General Miles may have lashed out so furiously at "embalmed beef" partly to counter his enemies in the military and political administrations. He may have been moved as well by bitter remembrances of how he and his troops had been humiliated in Chicago's stockyards in 1894 while seeking to maintain order during the Pullman strike.[32]

---

published in three consecutively paginated volumes as *Food Furnished by Subsistence Department.*

[30] General Miles's testimony before the Dodge commission appears in *Report of the Commission Appointed by the President*, 3240–64, 3795–98. The "embalmed beef" allegation appears on 3256.

[31] *Ibid.*

[32] Louise Carroll Wade, "Hell Hath No Fury Like a General Scorned: Nelson A. Miles,

The commissary-general effectively denied Miles's implied charge that he had bought poisoned beef, but used such abusive language in his testimony that he was court-martialed and suspended from rank and duty. The mystery of the sunstruck carcass in Tampa was dispelled by the Wade court. In fact that beef, as part of a private experiment, had been preserved not with injected chemicals but with sulfur fumes. The commissary department, however, had no official connection with the experiment, and no contracts for meat treated in this way had ever been made.[33]

The Wade court determined that refrigerated beef sold by the big packers was essentially sound. Poor handling, slow transport, inadequate sanitation, lack of ice, and tardy construction of cold-storage facilities in Cuba combined to produce serious problems. Harvey Wiley, who examined samples of refrigerated beef sent to him packed in ice from southern camps, told the commissions he found no evidence of chemical preservatives. He stated his belief that failure to provide troops a balanced diet played some role in soldier sickness:

> The human stomach does not tolerate the recurrence of the same article of food daily very well, and its continued ingestion as a ration might produce a feeling of nausea or distaste in the person eating it, just as a person can not eat a quail every day for thirty days in succession, although for one day, with a bottle of wine, it is a very palatable ration.

As to beef, Wiley pointed out that fresh meat spoiled quickly in a hot climate, attacked by microorganisms that produced ptomaines causing nausea and malaise.[34]

Canned beef when opened in the tropics, Wiley observed, was subject to like vicissitudes. He and his chief aide, W. D. Bigelow, testing cans of beef furnished by the army for all major preservative chemicals, found none but salt. Intended merely as part of the travel ration, canned beef had too often, served cold, been the mainstay of soldier diets, with only occasional variety, for weeks on end. Testimony given by representatives of the packers made clear that only the poorest quality of beef went into cans. Dozens of soldiers told both investigating commissions and inquiring reporters how stringy, gristly, and nauseating they found the

---

the Pullman Strike, and the Beef Scandal of 1898," *Illinois Historical Journal* 79 (1986), 162–84.

[33] Keuchel, "Chemicals and Meat," 253–56.

[34] *Ibid.*, 253–64. The cited testimony from Wiley appears in *Food Furnished by Subsistence Department*, 1681–89; the results of his analyses of beef appeared in *Report of the Commission Appointed by the President*, 854–62.

fare. They readily transferred General Miles's sobering adjective from the refrigerated beef to which it had been applied to beef in the can.[35]

Carl Sandburg remembered his meals aboard a transport ship:

> We were divided into messes of eight men for rations. A tin of "Red Horse" would be handed to one man who opened it. He put it to his nose, smelled of it, wrinkled up his face, and took a spit. Then that tin of "Red Horse" was thrown overboard for any of the fishes of the Atlantic Ocean who might like it. . . . What we called "Red Horse" soon had all our country scandalized with its new name of "Embalmed Beef." It *was* embalmed. We buried it at sea because it was so duly embalmed with all flavor of life and every suck of nourishment gone from it though having nevertheless a putridity of odor more pungent than ever reaches the nostrils from a properly embalmed cadaver.[36]

Theodore Roosevelt, aboard a similar transport bound for Cuba, en route to his heralded march up San Juan Hill, found his volunteer Rough Riders disdaining canned roast beef. He challenged a red-haired Kentuckian in the act of throwing his meat away.

"I can't eat the canned meat," the soldier said.

"If you are a baby," Lieutenant Colonel Roosevelt countered, "you had better not have come to the war. Eat it and be a man."

The Kentuckian tried to obey the order, but vomited.

Roosevelt thought for a while that only volunteers were having such troubles, but then learned that the regular cavalry hated canned beef too.

"I had by that time," Roosevelt—now governor of New York—told the Wade court, "tried to eat some of it myself when I was hungry, and found that I could not." It was "slimey . . . stringy and coarse, . . . like a bundle of fibers." The great majority of men, after trying canned beef for two or three days, got indigestion. After that, "hardly any of them would touch the meat, even if they were hungry."

When Roosevelt returned to the United States, he was surprised to find a debate raging over canned beef. In Cuba no such debate occurred because of lack of an affirmative side. Roosevelt summed up:

> I never, in the cavalry division, or in the few infantrymen with whom I came in contact, from the generals down to the privates,

---

[35] Keuchel, "Chemicals and Meat," 257–59; Anderson, *The Health of a Nation*, 128. Examples of soldier testimony appear in *Food Furnished by Subsistence Department*.

[36] Carl Sandburg, *Always the Young Stranger* (New York, 1952), 417. Edward Keuchel has suggested that "Red Horse" was likely corned beef.

heard anybody speak of the canned roast beef when they did not take it as a matter of course that it was a bad ration.[37]

At the height of the controversy, newspapers, citing the colorful soldier criticism, likened the furor to the Dreyfus affair in France, a challenge to the integrity of the nation's institutions. The packinghouses, nonetheless, survived the scrutiny of the Dodge and Wade investigations. Unpalatable the canned roast beef may have been when packed, but it was not poisoned with preservatives, being, indeed, identical with the canned beef sold in the civilian market. The meat gained its evil reputation with the troops mainly because of the heat, dirt, and germs of camp and battlefield conditions. Food took some of the blame for the main cause of military mortality, typhoid fever, which affected 90 percent of the army's regiments and assailed 20 percent of the troops. This state of affairs Dr. Walter Reed presented persuasively to the Dodge commission.[38]

Regardless of the facts, the embalmed-beef story received widespread credence because of its plausibility, as part of a broader pattern of wartime bungling. Moreover, the investigating boards made clear that federal inspection of packinghouses was limited to examination of animals just before and after killing to detect disease or serious injury. Inspection did not legally cover sanitation, nor, except by courtesy, include surveillance of canning operations. Further, the condemnation of beef for the troops, shocking in itself, also expanded growing public concern about pure-food issues. The most extreme charges were disproved by the investigating commissions, but doubts lingered on. Few Americans, certainly not Theodore Roosevelt, forgot "embalmed beef."[39]

Harvey Wiley, in the wake of the excitement, pushed to completion Part 10 of Bulletin 13 examining canned meats. His investigation found more to compliment than to criticize. Nonetheless, some 6 percent of the samples the Bureau tested contained chemical preservatives. Also, costly cans labeled "potted chicken" consisted almost completely of pork or beef.[40]

---

[37] *Food Furnished by Subsistence Department*, 1100–107.

[38] *Ibid.*, 734; Keuchel, "Chemicals and Meat," 260–64; *Food Furnished by Subsistence Department*, 635–37; Walter Reed, Victor C. Vaughan, and Edward O. Shakespeare, *Report on the Origin and Spread of Typhoid Fever in the U.S. Military Camps during the Spanish War of 1898*, vol. 1 (Washington, 1904), 656–76.

[39] Keuchel, "Chemicals and Meat," 263–64; *Food Furnished by Subsistence Department*, 635–37.

[40] Bureau of Chemistry, Bulletin 13, *Foods and Food Adulterants*, part 10 (Washington, 1902); Anderson, *The Health of a Nation*, 128.

The Mason Hearings

While the Wade court was midstream in its two-month inquiry into the state of beef sent to the army, another investigation of the nation's food began. Pursuant to a Senate resolution, the Committee on Manufactures, chaired by William E. Mason of Illinois, sat for fifty-one days of hearings in Washington, Chicago, and New York, listening to the testimony of 196 witnesses. The committee also collected hundreds of food samples and sent staff members to observe processing plants, warehouses, markets, and stores in eastern and midwestern states. Never before had a committee of the Congress taken such a detailed and widespread look at food problems. Nor had congressional curiosity about the issue hitherto provoked so much public interest. At least, so Harvey Wiley decided, judging by the torrent of press clippings that flowed in from the agency to which he had subscribed. Moreover, among the hundreds of clippings, "not a single one," Wiley told Mason, "has not commended the action of the committee."[41]

Wiley had been elated at Mason's venturesomeness. For the several previous years, as the chemist later recalled, "Pure food bills in the Senate had been regularly committed to the Committee on Manufactures, much as an infant would be left to starve in a barren room." Mason was a maverick who seemed truly interested. A Chicago lawyer and opponent of the political machine controlling the city, Mason had recently come to the Senate after service in the House. A religious man, sympathetic to the underdog, he had no qualms about opposing popular causes or about championing not yet popular ones. No member of the Congress, except perhaps Paddock, had yet expended so much concentrated energy on the pure-food crusade.[42]

The senator secured Secretary James Wilson's permission to make Wiley scientific adviser to the committee. In this capacity the chemist analyzed 428 food samples, helped question witnesses, and himself testified at length, giving a highly dramatic and much reported performance. Wiley also drafted the bill, based on earlier ones, that Mason introduced into the Senate. "I think if there is any one man in this country," Mason said on the Senate floor, "who deserves great credit for trying to furnish the facts for the benefit of the people of this country, that man is Harvey Washington Wiley."[43]

The Mason hearings surveyed the entire gamut of the nation's diet,

[41] *Adulteration of Food Products*, 56 Cong. 1 ses., Senate Report 516, 587, 653.

[42] Wiley, *An Autobiography*, 224; L. Ethan Ellis, "Mason, William Ernest," *Dictionary of American Biography*, vol. 12, 379.

[43] S. 2426, *Cong. Record*, 56 Cong. 1 ses., 4963.

assessing the extent of adulteration, noting recent changes in its pattern, exposing areas of conflict in opinion, wrestling with remedies. Wiley, mainly responsible for the overview, continued to regard adulteration conservatively, believing the proportion of it modest, the dangers small: "I might go to a store to-day," he testified, "and buy 100 food articles at random, ... ordinary staple food—and scarcely 5 percent would be adulterated." In spices and ground coffee, the percentage would rise much higher, as would be the case with food products made for selling to the poor. Other witnesses wondered if adulteration was not increasing. So thought the chemist charged with enforcing the food provisions of the Connecticut law, blaming for the rise "business competition and the demand for cheap goods and the necessity for utilizing waste products."[44]

Salients of improvement were noted, one of them the manufacture of confectionery. Within the last decade, Wiley observed, poisonous mineral and aniline dyes had been virtually banished from candy. The Confectioners' Association took credit for the change, wrought by publicity and state legislation. More work remained to be done. Perhaps a third of the confectionery still being sold, a shoddy product, came from pans on little stoves in back-alley basements.[45]

Many traditional abuses continued, like the diluting of honey with glucose, while new evidences of ingenuity appeared, like the cheapening of ground ginger with fragments of tarred rope. Wiley described blatant fraud employed in the labeling of imported wines. A dealer inquired of one of Wiley's aides what distinguished label he wanted affixed to his bottles of claret, offering "to take Chateau Lafitte, Burgundy, and Bordeaux all out of the same cask and label them to suit."[46]

Some adulterations critics deemed dangerous. Condensed skimmed milk, pretending to be whole milk, posed a subtle hazard to babies, noted C.S.N. Hallberg, a professor at the Chicago College of Pharmacy, because it lacked the butterfat that mothers counted upon. Victor C. Vaughan, dean of medicine at the University of Michigan, agreed: children subjected to such a deception might "suffer just as much as if a poison had been administered." Poisons were being directly administered in food through certain coloring materials and preservatives. Almost all injurious adulterations, Wiley testified, fell into these two classes.[47]

---

[44] *Adulteration of Food Products*, 41–42, 583–87 (Wiley), 448 (Edward H. Jenkins of Connecticut).

[45] *Ibid.*, 30–31 (Wiley), 304–5 (Charles F. Gunther), 309–12 (M. Shields).

[46] *Ibid.*, 14, 40, 117, 396.

[47] *Ibid.*, 82 (Hallberg), 201 (Vaughan), 41 (Wiley). Henry Sewall, "Vaughan, Victor

As to colors, both the older metallic salts and the newer coal-tar compounds presented worrisome problems. Both Wiley and Russell H. Chittenden, director of the Sheffield Scientific School at Yale, explained how copper and zinc salts caused canned peas and beans to retain their pristine greenness. Chittenden thought the practice should be prohibited, but Wiley would not go so far. Healthy stomachs, he thought, could stand the small amounts of copper and zinc required "without suffering any discomfiture, and do it repeatedly." He himself enjoyed eating preserved green peas. "Many people, on the other hand," Wiley acknowledged, "they do hurt, and the least possible amount upsets the digestion." To prevent fraud and protect the susceptible, the presence of metallic salts must be declared upon the label. Wiley gave it as his prescription: "Regulated but not prohibited."[48]

As to aniline dyes, committee witnesses were cognizant of danger but uncertain about its scope. Some dyes seemed quite safe, others were slightly toxic, while a few might pose grave risks. When a former manufacturer of oleomargarine denied the presence of aniline coloring in that product, both Wiley and a Chicago teacher of chemistry, Marc Delafontaine, offered quick challenge. His analyses showed, the teacher said, a sweeping shift in the coloring of oleo from annatto to aniline during the past year. Many other foods as well revealed a recent marked swing from vegetable to coal-tar coloring matters. Cheap jellies, skimmed milk, meat preservatives, flavoring extracts, catsup, and mustard, all must be included on such a list. Soda-water syrups, examined by James C. Duff in New York, revealed the sweetening base to be saccharin and the coloring aniline dye.[49]

Preservatives sparked sharp clashes of opinion before the Mason committee. Like coal-tar colors, chemical preservatives had come increasingly into use, seemingly necessary, as Delafontaine put it, "to keep . . . food products fit to eat" in a day when "the consumer lives farther from the maker or the farmer." Salicylic acid had been the most-used antiseptic, according to Albert B. Prescott, dean of pharmacy at the University of Michigan, while borax and formaldehyde were growing in importance. Often a fancy trade name disguised a preservative's true nature. The Wisconsin food chemist A. S. Mitchell, testifying in Chicago, brought to the witness chair examples of Freezine, Rosaline, and Preservaline he had bought on the way to the hearing. Such products, he

Clarence," *Dictionary of American Biography*, vol. 19, 236–37; Leigh C. Anderson, "Victor Clarence Vaughan," in Miles, ed., *American Chemists and Chemical Engineers*, 484–85.

[48] *Adulteration of Food Products*, 41–42 (Wiley), 425 (Chittenden).

[49] *Ibid.*, 223 (George M. Sterne), 31–32 (Wiley), 229 (Delafontaine), 498 (Duff), 115, 128, 132, 180, 198–99, 249, 448, 475 (other comments on aniline dyes).

said, were put in milk, cream, candy, sausage, hamburger steak, fish, and bulk oysters. Their makers recommended them for "almost every conceivable food that will spoil, and . . . as being harmless, and, as a greater temptation, for almost utter impossibility of detection by chemists."[50]

Mitchell did not think such products harmless, nor did Wiley. The chief chemist explained: "There is no preservative which paralyzes the ferments which create decay that does not at the same time paralyze to an equal degree the ferments that produce digestion." Therefore, such chemicals were "not fit to enter the stomach."[51] The committee subpoenaed Albert Heller, a Chicago manufacturer of commercial preservatives, who offered a spirited defense. Rather than poisoning, he insisted, they promoted health. Freezine, a 6 percent formaldehyde solution for preserving milk, ice cream, and cream puffs, Heller called "not only perfectly harmless, but . . . positively healthful, and especially so with infants." It could cut the death rate from cholera infantum by 70 percent. In any case, he asserted, the amount of formaldehyde getting into milk from Freezine was too tiny to be called an adulterant. Freezem was a powder for mixing with ground meat, mainly sodium sulfite. Heller denied using salicylic acid, while admitting the presence of boric acid in some of his products. There was no harm in that, he said. Boric acid, salt, and saltpeter, used in curing hams and bacon, actually embalmed the meat. "I wish to say," Heller told the committee, "that every one of us eats embalmed meat—and we know it and like it and continue to like it."[52]

Other witnesses defended preservatives, especially borax. That so many champions praised this preservative signified a concerted campaign by the borax interests. The use of borax had begun in 1875, Robert T. Lunham, a pork packer, testified, when the English had objected to American cured bacon and ham as too salty. By using less salt and a little borax, the problem had been solved. A sprinkling of borax kept bacon from getting slimy in transit and was washed off upon arrival overseas. Borax posed no greater threat to health than salt did, said Frank Billings, a Chicago physician. Refrigeration stood first among preservation methods, but when that could not be used there was "no question whatever that we must use some preservative." A Rush Medical College chemistry professor, Walter S. Haines, agreed: the risk from ptomaines outweighed that from antiseptics a thousand to one.[53]

Professor Chittenden, who had conducted many experiments with

[50] *Ibid.*, 232 (Delafontaine), 195 (Prescott), 111–14 (Mitchell).

[51] *Ibid.*, 44.

[52] *Ibid.*, 149–50, 171–82.

[53] *Ibid.*, 239–42 (Robert T. Lunham), 244–45 (Billings), 283–85 (Haines).

borax and boracic acid, found that in small amounts these antiseptics "produce[d] no measureable effect that could be spoken of as deleterious." Yet he remained cautious. Some occasions and some products might require preservatives, but all products containing them should announce their presence and amount. This posture was close to that of Wiley. He too accepted a role for "innocent preservatives," those properly used in products that most especially required them, like grape juice and catsup, and always acknowledged on the label. Products like Freezine and Preservaline aroused the chief chemist's ire: "The trouble with these is the fraud upon the public by using . . . a very cheap substance, under a name that the people don't know, and selling it for an immense profit." Preservatives should be used only under their proper names.[54] The disputation persuaded one witness that not nearly enough was known about the physiological effects of antiseptic chemicals. Much more experimentation was needed. All preservatives posed some hazard, and chemists must ascertain "the degree of toxicity . . . of the new antiseptics and within what limits they may be allowed, or whether they, or any of them, should be absolutely excluded by laws."[55]

Two other controversies that surfaced during the Mason committee hearings rivaled in bitterness the dispute over preservatives. The old war between butter and oleomargarine, aggravated rather than settled by the 1886 law, seemed about to burst into a new national battle. C. Y. Knight, secretary of the National Dairy Union, told the committee that deceptive retail sales of margarine for butter had doubled since 1886, so that the dairy interests intended to seek from Congress a law quintupling the oleomargarine tax. Margarine dealers denied dishonesty and defended their product's identity. "Butterine," testified a manufacturer, "is as distinct from butter as wool is from cotton or steel from iron. We consider that our product is a product of the advanced age."[56]

Equally contentious before Mason's committee were spokesmen for the two main wings of the baking-powder industry, those relying respectively on cream of tartar and on alum.[57] Charges and countercharges by major business groups posed problems not only for the common citizen, reading his newspaper, but also for members of Congress concerned about a food law. Achieving compromises that would permit passage of a bill proved as difficult in legislative chambers as in the private halls of pure-food congresses.

In fact, both the butter-oleomargarine and the baking-powder con-

[54] *Ibid.*, 418–22 (Chittenden), 45–46, 184 (Wiley).
[55] *Ibid.*, 232–33 (Delafontaine).
[56] *Ibid.*, 137–49 (Knight), 151–66 (various dealers), 314–21 (Henry C. Pirrung of Ohio).
[57] *Ibid.*, 87–89, 531–43, 548–68, 592–626; Wood, *Strategic Uses of Public Policy*, 164–73.

flicts provided reasons for stalemate in the Fifty-sixth Congress. Dairy-men, angry at Wiley's assertions of oleomargarine's wholesomeness, sponsored a bill that would keep regulatory responsibility out of his hands. The alum baking powder interests made their weight felt more secretly. Nor did Senator Mason's maverick status help forward the cause. Rivalry between Senate committees led to sharp words on the floor. In the House the Brosius bill, although reported and pressed for by Secretary Wilson, failed to receive consideration. A long battle lay yet ahead.[58]

[58] Anderson, *The Health of a Nation*, 131–36; *Cong. Record*, 56 Cong. 1 ses., 3006, 4969–70; *The Adulteration, Misbranding, and Imitation of Foods, Etc.*, 56 Cong. 1 ses., House Report 1426. The Brosius bill was H.R. 9677, *Cong. Record*, 3006. Several oleomargarine bills were introduced in the Fifty-sixth Congress, First Session, the most important of which was H.R. 3177, which in the Second Session passed the House but not the Senate.

VII

Progress toward a Law

We have experimented with a much greater number of subjects and for a much longer period of time than any of the similar experiments that have heretofore been conducted. We have thus, to this extent, eliminated more completely the errors due to imperfect observation, imperfect control and idiosyncrasy.
—HARVEY W. WILEY, 1904[1]

The New Century

On December 18, 1902, the House of Representatives passed a pure food and drug bill, the first such broad measure to be approved by either chamber of the Congress since the Paddock bill had received Senate sanction ten years before. Pure-food advocates dared to hope that their crusade neared successful termination. However, more than three years of frustration yet faced Harvey Wiley and his allies. Victory, they came to realize, would require increased public concern and support. "Public sentiment in favor of the bill," asserted the editor of the *American Grocer*, "needs to be crystalized and centralized, and its influence brought to bear upon Congress."[2]

As Wiley intensified efforts to fuse his diverse allies into a more effective pressure and propaganda group, and to mobilize public opinion for a pure-food law, the ambient climate of the dawning century came to his aid. While he sallied forth from Washington to lecture in behalf of his cause, Wiley launched, in the basement of his own building, a scientific experiment. To his mixed distress and gratitude, newspaper reports of it burst beyond the bounds of science so as to bolster his propagandizing for a law.

The arrival of the twentieth century had been greeted with widespread public excitement. In the stocktaking of what the old century had meant, and in the projections of what the new century might bring,

---

[1] Wiley, "Methods of Studying the Effects of Preservatives and Other Substances Added to Foods upon Health and Digestion," *J Franklin Inst* 157 (1904), 168.

[2] H.R. 3109, *Cong. Record*, 57 Cong. 2 ses., 433–58; editor Frank Barrett cited in Anderson, *The Health of a Nation*, 146.

146

science held a prominent place.[3] Science and technology, accelerating in pace during the nineteenth century, had blessed the nation with a treasure trove of practical advantages and promised fascinating and useful new wonders. "One of the great changes of the Progressive Era," Hunter Dupree has noted, "was a wider appreciation of the use of science in the public interest." The public gradually came to perceive that the national government could and must deal with matters in which science and public safety impinged, especially in the realm of health. Here even the national interest was involved. Health, a valuable American asset, lay subject to extravagant waste.[4]

Later in the decade the economist Irving Fisher sought to quantify health's value to the nation. "If," he wrote, "we appraise each life lost at only $1,700 and each year's average earnings for adults at only $700, the economic gain to be obtained from preventing preventable disease, measured in dollars, exceeds one and a half billions." Fisher saw the future as bright:

> The world is gradually awakening to the fact of its own improvability. Hygiene, the youngest of the biological studies, has repudiated the outworn doctrine that mortality is fatality, and must exact a regular and inevitable sacrifice at the present rate year after year. Instead of this fatalistic creed we now have the assurance of Pasteur that "It is within the power of man to rid himself of every parasitic disease."[5]

A major means of disease prevention emerged at the turn of the century, vaccines and antitoxins, and when frightening difficulties arose the federal government intervened. Emil von Behring had discovered in 1890 that immunity to diphtheria could be induced by injecting into the human body antitoxins developed in animals that had been inoculated with diphtheria toxins. The serum could also ameliorate the disease in patients already ill. Emile Roux, one of Pasteur's associates, in 1894 announced the increase of antitoxin supply by producing it in horses. The next year Hermann Biggs and William H. Park of the New York City Bacteriological Laboratory began to make, test, and use the antitoxin. Their careful venturesomeness in employing it in mass immunization campaigns won praise from Koch himself. Public-health laboratories in

[3] Mark Sullivan, *Our Times*, 6 vols. (New York, 1926–35), vol. 1, 362–72.

[4] Dupree, *Science in the Federal Government*, 271–301, quotation at 291; Shryock, *The Development of Modern Medicine*, 317, 401–5; Irving Fisher, *Report on National Vitality, Its Wastes and Conservation* (Bulletin 30 of the Committee of One Hundred on National Health: Washington, 1909).

[5] *Ibid.*, 14, 109, 119.

other cities and states began to follow New York City's example, spurred on by demonstrations provided by scientists at the United States Hygienic Laboratory in Washington. Pharmaceutical firms soon joined in manufacturing such biological products.[6]

In October and November 1901 disaster struck. Thirteen children died in St. Louis after having been inoculated with diphtheria antitoxin contaminated with tetanus bacillus. The antitoxin had been made by the St. Louis Board of Health from a horse that had contracted tetanus. A committee of inquiry blamed the board's consulting bacteriologist, under whose auspices the antitoxin had been prepared. He had known of the horse's illness, and yet had failed to destroy the contaminated serum, some of which had been inadvertently bottled. The bacteriologist was discharged. The board of health terminated antitoxin manufacture. A similar episode, killing nine children, occurred in Camden, New Jersey.[7]

Widely publicized, these tragedies precipitated calls for remedial action. Opposition on the part of fringe groups to scientific research and new modes of medical practice was then at one of its perennial peaks, and the *Journal of the American Medical Association* warned that "anti-vaccinationists, anti-vivisectionists, 'christian scientists', and crotchety persons in general" would use the St. Louis situation for "evil purposes." Such a threat and the need for assurances of public protection seemed to demand the enactment of a federal law. This spirit coincided with the desire of the major private scientifically based vaccine manufacturers to curb competition from smaller unsanitary laboratories.[8]

The deed was quickly done. The Medical Society of the District of Columbia, with the concurrence of the Hygienic Laboratory of the Public Health Service, proposed a law regulating the production and sale of biologics. The commissioners of the District of Columbia drafted the bill and transmitted it to appropriate congressional committees. With very little discussion and no publicity, the measure sped through Congress and received President Theodore Roosevelt's signature.[9]

The swift enactment of the Biologics Control Act contrasted with the

[6] Ramunas A. Kondratas, "The Biologics Control Act of 1902," in James Harvey Young, ed., *The Early Years of Federal Food and Drug Control* (Madison, WI, 1982), 6–12; Duffy, *A History of Public Health in New York City, 1866–1966*, 91–111; Victoria A. Harden, *Inventing the NIH: Federal Biomedical Research Policy, 1887–1937* (Baltimore, 1986), 27–29.

[7] Kondratas, "The Biologics Control Act of 1902," 14–16; Liebenau, "Medical Science and Medical Industry," 238–51.

[8] "Tetanus from Anti-diphtheria Serum," *J Amer Med Assoc* 37 (1901), 1255; Simon Flexner and James Thomas Flexner, *William Henry Welch and the Heroic Age of American Medicine* (New York, 1941), 254–62; Liebenau, "Medical Science and Medical Industry," 254.

[9] 32 U.S. Stat. 728 (July 1, 1902); Kondratas, "The Biologics Control Act of 1902," 16–17; 21–24.

laggard pace of a general food and drug law. Two factors help explain this. When compared with the long-established, complex processing of foods and manufacture of drugs, the biologics industry was new, small, and simple, with many of its units still in the public sector. Further, deviance from the strictest precautions, as the St. Louis case proved, might precipitate tragedy. Thus, major makers of vaccines and antitoxins lobbied for the law, which protected them as well as the public. No segments of the infant industry openly opposed the bill.[10]

Ease of enactment was reflected in strictness of provisions. The law licensed establishments engaged in preparing and selling in interstate or foreign commerce viruses, serums, toxins, and antitoxins. The law banned from the marketplace biologic wares not made by a licensed firm and not displaying the manufacturer's name and license number and an expiration date beyond which the product might not be fully effective. Regulations governing licensing were to be made by a three-man board, the surgeon general of the army, the surgeon general of the navy, and the supervising surgeon general of the Marine Hospital Service, with the concurrence of the Treasury Department. The Public Health Service could inspect the premises of biologics manufacturers. Violations of the regulations could bring fines and imprisonment.[11]

The Biologics Control Act was merely one of a host of events early in the new century that led a later scholar to assert that "it would be difficult to exaggerate the impact that the idea of preventable death had on Americans during the Progressive era."[12] This sentiment, when sufficiently aroused, would help move a food and drug bill into law.

The very concept of "health" became redefined during the Progressive years, losing much of the static and passive tone of the late nineteenth century as a mere absence of disease. Now many observers recalculated the human energy quotient upward, making it virtually boundless, and urged activity in pursuit of a useful purpose as the surest path to happy health. Theodore Roosevelt lauded "the strenuous life," and Walter Lippmann exalted "mastery" over "drift."[13] Such a gospel formed a facet of broader preventive medicine. Many persons of Progressive temper

[10] *Ibid.*, 16–17; Liebenau, "Medical Science and Medical Industry," 254.

[11] Kondratas, "The Biologics Control Act of 1902," 16–27; Liebenau, "Medical Science and Medical Industry," 255–56.

[12] Barbara Sicherman, "The New Mission of the Doctor: Redefining Health and Health Care in the Progressive Era, 1900–1917," in William R. Rogers and David Barnard, eds., *Nourishing the Humanistic in Medicine: Interactions with the Social Sciences* (Pittsburgh, 1979), 96.

[13] *Ibid.*, 95–124; Anita Clair Fellman and Michael Fellman, *Making Sense of Self: Medical Advice Literature in Late Nineteenth-Century America* (Philadelphia, 1981).

found a useful purpose in proposing environmental changes, to be wrought by private organizations or by legislatures at all levels, that would permit a healthier life for everyone.

This spirit and the new knowledge about disease transmission brought increased urgency to cleaning up city water and milk supplies and sewage disposal, to improving slum housing, to changing the environments in which children and women labored, and to viewing all these matters in a more statistical way. The federal government set up the Yellow Fever Board in Cuba in 1900 under Walter Reed, which proved the mosquito's role as vector in yellow-fever transmission. Beginning in 1902 Congress began to upgrade and enlarge the Hygienic Laboratory of the Marine Hospital Service, converting it into the Public Health Service. A permanent Census Bureau was established in 1902, giving "demography a stable place in the government."[14]

Expanding knowledge of tuberculosis, the leading cause of mortality, led to the sanatorium movement and to widespread prevention campaigns. In 1904 a new type of voluntary health organization, the National Tuberculosis Association, was formed, in which both physicians and laymen participated.[15] Shortly, similar associations sprang up to combat infant mortality, mental illness, and venereal disease.

New discoveries in bacteriology, parasitology, and immunology brought immense change to the medical profession. The Johns Hopkins Medical School, established in 1893, and other medical colleges attached to leading universities modeled themselves on the most advanced European institutions. The gulf widened between these schools, committed to the new scientific discoveries, and proprietary schools with neither resources nor teachers fitted for the new day. The American Medical Association sought to reform itself; however much elitism and desire to eliminate competition might mark its motives, the AMA wielded the yardstick of the new medical science in measuring medical training, hospitals, and other institutions in the accreditation processes.[16]

[14] Judith Walzer Leavitt, *The Healthiest City: Milwaukee and the Politics of Public Health Reform* (Princeton, 1982); Bean, *Walter Reed*, 95–154; Bess Furman, *A Profile of the United States Public Health Service, 1798–1948* (Bethesda, MD, 1973), 248–50; Liebenau, "Medical Science and Medical Industry," 256–58; Harden, *Inventing the NIH*, 16–20; Dupree, *Science in the Federal Government*, 279.

[15] Richard Harrison Shryock, *National Tuberculosis Association, 1904–1954* (New York, 1957).

[16] James Bordley III and A. McGehee Harvey, *Two Centuries of American Medicine, 1776–1976* (Philadelphia, 1976), 129–86, 327–52; Kaufman, *American Medical Education*, 143–79; Starr, *The Transformation of American Medicine*, 112–44, 162–79; Shryock, *The Development of Modern Medicine*, 336–55.

Fredrick Accum's *A Treatise on the Adulterations of Food*, published in London in 1820 and soon pirated in Philadelphia, has been called "the origin of the modern pure food movement." The ominous symbolism on the book's cover forecast recurrent popular concern about the condition of the food supply. Reproduced from the collections of the Library of Congress.

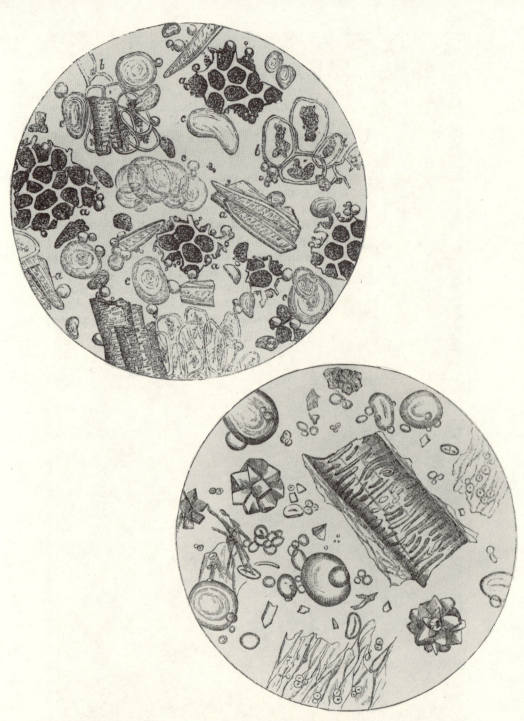

A food, coffee, adulterated with chicory and roasted wheat (top), and a drug, rhubarb, adulterated with wheat flour (bottom). These wood engravings made from drawings sketched as seen through a microscope illustrated the writings of Arthur Hill Hassall, whose exposures helped secure the British Adulteration Act of 1860. First published in the *Lancet*, these engravings come from Hassall's *Food and Its Adulteration* (London, 1855), 171, and *Adulterations Detected* (London, 1857), 677, in the collections of the National Library of Medicine.

Frank Leslie's Illustrated Newspaper exposed the hazards of the New York City milk supply in 1858. A dying cow, fed on distillery swill, continues being milked. In Brooklyn distillery milk is being adulterated with water. From vol. 5, pp. 368–369, reproduced from the Florida State University Library collections.

"One Day's Churning" in the manufacture of oleomargarine in the United States using the patented process of the French inventor, Hippolyte Mège-Mouriés. From *Scientific American* n.s. 42 (1880), 355, in the collections of the Robert W. Woodruff Library, Emory University.

Harvey W. Wiley, chief chemist of the Department of Agriculture, dining at the "hygienic table" with members of the "Poison Squad" during his experiments testing food preservatives for safety. Courtesy of the Food and Drug Administration.

Harvey Wiley weighing food on his balance that will be consumed by members of the "Poison Squad." Courtesy of the Food and Drug Administration.

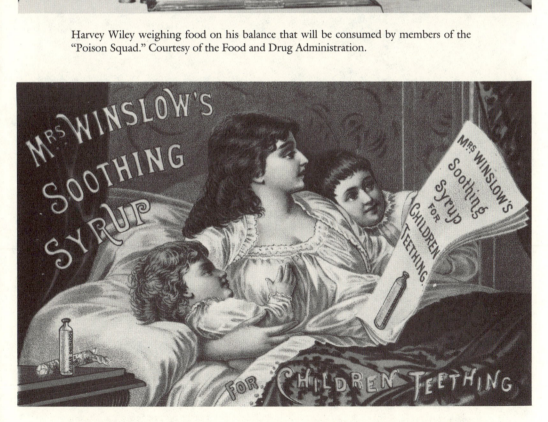

Mrs. Winslow's Soothing Syrup, a sugar syrup containing morphine sulfate, quieted crying babies and killed some of them. This nostrum became a major target of patent-medicine critics. This late-nineteenth-century trade card is in the collection of Edward C. Atwater, Rochester, New York.

Upton Sinclair's novel, *The Jungle*, published in 1906 without illustrations, so disturbed the public with his charges about the foul condition in the Chicago packinghouses that the sale of meat fell by half. A motion picture version made seven years later—with Sinclair playing the role of socialist agitator—was promoted by this large poster. From the Upton Sinclair Archives, courtesy of the Lilly Library, Indiana University, Bloomington, Indiana.

"DOCTORING" HAMS

Another of the garish colored posters for the movie version of *The Jungle*, featuring Sinclair's castigation of the packers for their chemical manipulation of meat products. From the Upton Sinclair Archives, courtesy of the Lilly Library, Indiana University, Bloomington, Indiana.

The reaction to Sinclair's *The Jungle* forced President Theodore Roosevelt to investigate Packingtown and to play a leading role in getting a compromise law through the Congress making meat inspection more rigorous. This cartoon from the Utica *Saturday Globe*, entitled "A nauseating job, but it must be done," was reprinted in *Review of Reviews* 3 (1906), 8, in the collections of the Robert W. Woodruff Library, Emory University.

The new science helped elevate the medical profession's prestige with the public, even though that new knowledge, paradoxically, made perceptive leaders of the profession aware that most medications long prescribed had been given patients in vain. Richard Cabot of the Massachusetts General Hospital adjudged that drugs and surgery cured only eight or nine out of some 215 diseases. Rev. Frederick T. Gates, perusing the pages of William Osler's textbook of medicine, found so few truly curative drugs mentioned that he determined John D. Rockefeller should finance a research center to do something drastic about the situation. The Rockefeller Institute for Medical Research, established in 1901, and the Carnegie Institution in 1902, revealed that private philanthropy shared the general public's confidence that medical science offered future dividends in better health.[17]

The "Poison Squad"

Testifying at a House committee hearing in March 1902, Harvey Wiley repeated an opinion he had frequently expressed before: "Legislation has no right to prescribe what food a man shall eat." He added:

> Personally, I have never gone so far as my associates in the pure-food congress and other movements relating to injurious substances in foods. I have always been of the opinion, and still am, . . . that it is entirely sufficient to place upon a food label the nature of any substance which has been added . . . and leave to the consumer himself and his physician the determination of whether or not that substance is injurious to him.[18]

Consumer and physician should suspect the most hazard, however, Wiley observed, in the field of preservatives. Modern chemical preservatives contrasted with historic ones like salt, sugar, vinegar, and wood smoke, in that most were without taste or odor in the dosages used, so consumers ate them unawares. "The most . . . dangerous of the deleterious substances in foods" were those "added to prevent decay." Admit-

---

[17] Sicherman, "The New Mission of the Doctor," 97–99; Flexner and Flexner, *William Henry Welch and the Heroic Age of American Medicine*, 269–78.

[18] Department of Agriculture, *Report of the Chief of the Division of Chemistry for 1893* (Washington, 1894), 193; *Hearings before the Committee on Interstate and Foreign Commerce of the House of Representatives on The Pure Food Bills*, 57 Cong. 1 ses. [March 11–24, 1902] (Washington, 1902), 225, 229, 262–63; Harvey W. Wiley, *Influence of Food Preservatives and Artificial Colors on Digestion and Health*, Department of Agriculture, Bureau of Chemistry, Bulletin 84 (Washington, 1904–1908), vol. 1, 7–8.

tedly, few impartial and competent studies had as yet been made of the effect of such preservatives on health.

Although Wiley believed that the burden of proof of safety should be borne by the advocates of preservatives, he had hoped for some time to make such tests himself. At his request, in 1902 Congress allotted him $5,000 for such research. Doubtless Congress wanted to buttress recently enacted legislation requiring inspection of imported foods and rejection of adulterated shipments. Adulteration, including the presence of preservatives, was defined in such varying ways by nations that more facts were needed as a regulatory baseline. The chief chemist began to work out his experimental plan.[19]

The book of Daniel, Wiley asserted, contained the earliest recorded food experiment, wherein the royal fare of Babylon was tested against a simple diet of vegetables and water. As in Daniel's day, Wiley chose to conduct his tests with men, not animals. Animals and men differed as to digestion; moreover, human beings could describe their symptoms. Unlike Daniel, Wiley did not use a separate control group in his experiments, although he came to be criticized for not doing so. Instead, he made each participant his own control. In testing a preservative, the young men eating at Wiley's "hygienic table" in the basement of the Bureau of Chemistry building dined for a ten-day "fore period" without the preservative included in their diet, during which an effort was made to determine the amount of food required to keep body weight constant and to establish normal metabolism. Then followed the "preservative period," during which the subjects received the chemical daily, increasing steadily, through a span of just over a month. During an "after period" the preservative was stopped, but observations and chemical analyses continued.[20]

The first trials began in December 1902. Wiley had chosen a dozen young men from a larger group of volunteers who had responded to his appeal to aid the cause of science and to get free meals. He selected "young, robust fellows" who might be expected to have "maximum re-

[19] Department of Agriculture, *Report of the Chemist for 1899* (Washington, 1899), 40; Wiley, "Methods of Studying the Effects of Preservatives and Other Substances Added to Foods upon Health and Digestion," *J Franklin Inst* 157 (1904), 161–78; Wiley, *An Autobiography*, 215–16; 26 U.S. Stat. 296 (1902). Recent summaries of Wiley's "Poison Squad" experiments include James Harvey Young, "The Science of Morals and Metabolism: Catsup and Benzoate of Soda," *J Hist Med Allied Sci* 23 (1968), 86–104; Wallace F. Janssen, "The Squad That Ate Poison," *FDA Consumer* 15 (December 1981–January 1982), 6–11; and R. Douglas Hart, "The Poison Squad," *Timeline* 2 (February–March 1985), 64–70.

[20] Wiley, *Influence of Food Preservatives*, vol. 1, 7–31; Wiley, "Methods of Studying the Effects of Preservatives"; J. C. Thresh, review of Wiley, *Influence of Food Preservatives and Artifical Colours on Digestion and Health*, vol. 4, in *Analyst* 33 (1908), 486–87.

sistance to deleterious effects of adulterated foods." Most were "engaged in scientific pursuits," working for low pay in the Department of Agriculture or attending medical school. They pledged themselves to eat nothing but "hygienic table" fare, to provide Wiley daily with all their bodily excretions for analysis, and to exempt the Department of Agriculture and all of its employees from responsibility for any illness or accident that might result. The recruits devised a slogan: "Only the brave can eat the fare."[21]

In planning his tests, Wiley believed he had done so "with an open mind and in a most conservative way." He studied the scientific literature but found little relevant, and he talked with officials at the Imperial Board of Health in Berlin who had conducted an experiment with borax on two human subjects. Wiley chose twelve participants, thinking a group this size large enough to counter the problem of individual idiosyncrasies. He would have been glad to have had a larger squad, but this would have made the analytical work impossible. As it was, his dozen volunteers represented, he believed, the largest group that had ever been used in a similar experiment, and his trials were to run for a longer time than previous ones.[22]

Wiley launched his chemical testing with borax and boracic acid. After the discovery of an abundant source in California lake beds, borax had become "probably the most important of the commonly used preservatives." In examining sixty-seven samples of commercial antiseptics advertised to prevent food decay, the Bureau of Chemistry had found that thirty-three contained borax. Besides being the most widely used, borax was, in Wiley's judgment, the "least objectionable" preservative, the safest with which to begin his trials. Germany, however, deemed borax dangerous and banned imports of American foods containing it, another reason for testing borax first. The healthy volunteers ate simple, wholesome meals prepared by an expert cook certified by the Civil Service Commission. Only foods of the best quality, mostly fresh, were served. Some canned soups, fruits, and vegetables entered the menus, always from the same canning batch and devoid of preservatives. All

[21] Wiley, *Influence of Food Preservatives*, vol. 1, 10–13; Department of Agriculture, *Report of the Secretary of Agriculture, 1903* (Washington, 1903), 172–76; Wiley, *An Autobiography*, 216; Janssen, "The Squad That Ate Poison"; Fred B. Linton, "Federal Food and Drug Laws—Leaders Who Achieved Their Enactment and Enforcement," *Food, Drug, Cosmetic Law Q* 4 (1949), 453; Thomas Swann Harding, *Two Blades of Grass: A History of Scientific Development in the U.S. Department of Agriculture* (Norman, OK, 1947), 47–48.

[22] Wiley, "Methods of Studying the Effects of Preservatives"; Wiley, *Influence of Food Preservatives*, vol. 1, 8–17; "Experiments in Food Preservation Conducted by the Department of Agriculture," *Scientific American* n.s. 88 (1903), 336, 338.

meat was ground before serving. Coffee and tea were permitted, but no alcoholic beverages. For the sake of morale, Wiley arranged his schedule so that he joined his "boys" for most of his own meals.[23]

The squad's routine proved most demanding. Each member recorded his weight, temperature, and pulse rate before each meal, and then noted what he had eaten. He carried a satchel wherever he went with containers for urine and feces to be delivered daily to the chemists. Physicians from the Public Health and Marine Hospital Service conducted comprehensive medical examinations every week. Volunteers were enjoined to report any symptoms that might be attributed to preservatives.[24]

The food and excretions were analyzed, using Association of Official Agricultural Chemists methods, to determine the major indicators deemed significant by nutritional tenets of the day—water, nitrogen, phosphorus, fat, and the heat of combustion as reckoned by calories. Excretions were tested for boric acid to detect how much borax accumulated in the system. Special tests sought to discover if borax might be eliminated in perspiration and exhalation. Blood tests for hemoglobin content were occasionally performed. Wiley himself often took a turn in the laboratory.[25]

After the "fore period," the first borax was given the volunteers in powdered form mixed in butter. A key commercial use for borax was to conceal the rancidity of stale butter. Quickly, however, the volunteers found out which item on their menu contained the preservative. They began to eat less butter. Wiley then tried milk, meat, and coffee as vehicles, with similar consequences. He then ended efforts at concealment and put the preservative in capsules. Dissolution tests revealed that, when taken in the middle of a meal, capsules would quickly release their contents into the digesting food, and, in the case of borax, without discomfort. Henceforth, diets were not skewed by suspicion of particular foods. Capsules remained standard throughout the rest of the five years of Wiley's preservative trials.[26]

At the start of the "preservative period," small amounts of borax were given, an approximation of the quantity that an average American diet

[23] Haynes, *American Chemical Industry*, vol. 1, 323; Janssen, "The Squad That Ate Poison"; *Hearings before the Committee on Interstate and Foreign Commerce of the House of Representatives on The Pure Food Bills*, 57 Cong. 1 ses., 229–30; Anderson, *The Health of a Nation*, 142; Wiley, "Methods of Studying the Effects of Preservatives."

[24] Wiley, *Influence of Food Preservatives*, vol. 1, 18–21.

[25] Wiley, "Methods of Studying the Effects of Preservatives"; Wiley, *Influence of Food Preservatives*, vol. 1, 19–26; Janssen, "The Squad That Ate Poison."

[26] Wiley, *Influence of Food Preservatives*, vol. 1, 29–30.

might contain. Dosage levels then increased "so as to reach, if possible the limit of toleration . . . by each individual." The range ran from half a gram daily at the beginning to five grams at the end. As the level of borax dosage rose, evidence of trouble determined by chemical analyses and physical examinations seemed less ominous than did symptoms described by the human guinea pigs. Appetites declined, accompanied by feelings of fullness, discomfort, and occasional stomach pain. Dull and stubborn headaches plagued the young men. At a level of three grams of borax a day, most of them could go about their regular duties, but a dosage of four to five grams daily produced "inability to perform work of any kind."[27]

These conclusions Wiley published in 1904 in the first part of Bulletin 84, *Influence of Food Preservatives and Artificial Colors on Digestion and Health*. The bulletin contained a wealth of laboriously compiled statistics reflecting the results of chemical analyses. It included also Wiley's extrapolation from the data and his conclusions concerning this particular experiment. Granted that the maximum amount of borax an American consumer would likely absorb—one-quarter gram a day—would fall far below the levels taken by the hardy volunteers, even this quantity overburdened the kidneys. Borax, Wiley asserted, modifying his earlier more tolerant posture, should be banned from food. Bad in itself, borax was only one of many preservatives in use. The sum total of preservatives in the diet posed a great hazard to public health. One could not be allowed and others barred. All must be treated alike. So none should be used. Granted that preservatives might protect consumers from hazards of food spoilage, and that unusual circumstances might require their use, as on long sea journeys and in remote places like mines and logging camps. However, preservatives should have no place in foods sold in the general market. Let processors prevent ptomaine poisoning by packing prime raw food in clean plants.[28]

As a shifting group of volunteers swallowed capsules of other preservatives at the hygienic table, borax came to seem, by comparison, mild. Salicylic acid and salicylates, sulfurous acids and sulfites, benzoic acids and benzoates, formaldehyde, all appeared more threatening. So Wiley did not relax his stern conclusion. "I would be in favor," he conceded before a House committee hearing in 1906, "of putting benzoic acid in a little salt-cellar, the same as is used for salt and pepper, and letting the people use it if they want to." But no preservatives should be

[27] *Ibid.*, 244–55.
[28] *Ibid.*, vol. 1; *Pure Food: Hearings before the Committee on Interstate and Foreign Commerce on the Pure Food Bills*, 59 Cong. 1 ses. [February 13–27, 1906] (Washington, 1906), 237–319.

added to processed foods. To this conviction, Wiley testified, "I was converted by my own investigations."[29]

Wiley explained his early experiments as he expanded his oratorical orbit to urge the need for a national pure-food law. He found a growing audience interested and concerned. That a dozen young men should deliberately dose themselves with chemicals, running risks of harming their health, perhaps putting their very lives in jeopardy, caught the public's morbid fancy. Distorted press reports exaggerated dangers and magnified alarm.[30]

One reporter in particular, George Rothwell Brown of the *Washington Post*, started the ball rolling. While the trials were still in the planning stage, Brown reported Wiley's objectives straightforwardly, although with a humorous slant. Science, during these years, seemed as much a theme for levity in the press as for sober scrutiny. Wiley worried that Brown's reporting might make his experiment seem ridiculous. He protested to Brown's editor to no avail. Secretary Wilson ordered the chief chemist to cut off contact with journalists. Brown, however, found loopholes that let his coverage continue. Although watchmen had orders to ban Brown from the building, he took to interviewing the cook through an open basement window. Wiley, upon the counsel of some of his staff, reversed himself. Since reports from the experimental table, fact or fiction, seemed certain to continue, the chief chemist took reporters into his confidence, giving them facts ready for release and trusting them not to reveal prematurely other things he told them. Wiley maintained a close camaraderie with journalists through the remainder of his career. During these early days of his hygienic table they termed him, not without admiration, "Old Borax."[31]

Reporter Brown gave to Wiley's volunteers the name of "Poison Squad," and this label stuck. It embodied the journalist's slant on the experiments, that they were dangerous, as well as humorous, a perspective adopted by other reporters and by the general public. A Supreme Court justice, speaking at a public dinner, jested about the "Poison

[29] Wiley, *Influence of Food Preservatives*, vols. 2–4; *Pure Food*, 59 Cong. 1 ses., 252, 272. The sodium benzoate experiments are discussed in more detail in Young, "The Morals of Metabolism."

[30] Wiley, "Methods of Studying the Effects of Preservatives"; Anderson, *The Health of a Nation*, 158.

[31] *Ibid.*, 151–52; Linton, "Federal Food and Drug Law—Leaders," 453–56; Wiley, *An Autobiography*, 216–17; "Experiments in Food Preservatives Conducted by the Department of Agriculture," 336, 338. The press gave a humorous slant to Charles Wardell Stiles's discovery of the hookworm in the South during the same month Brown was treating with levity Wiley's experiments. See John Ettling, *The Germ of Laziness: Rockefeller Philanthropy and Public Health in the New South* (Cambridge, MA, 1981), 35–38.

Squad." Songs—one entitled "They'll Never Look the Same"—paid tribute to the squad from the minstrel stage. Newspaper stories proliferated. "My poison-squad laboratory," Wiley later asserted, "became the most highly advertised boarding-house in the world." Wiley objected to the "Poison Squad" tag, and to often incorrect or exaggerated reporting. Yet he himself sometimes jestingly engaged in similar banter.[32]

The chief chemist was well aware that publicity about the fate of the "Poison Squad," even the exaggeration of danger, could serve his goals. An ever larger audience was becoming converted. When science, as represented by Wiley's experiments, could seem to demonstrate that adulteration went beyond cheating to palpable hazard, then both the public and their representatives in Congress became more interested in the campaign for a national law.[33]

Continuing Contest in the Congress

Legislatively, the pure-food issue received a great deal more discussion during the Fifty-seventh and Fifty-eighth Congresses than it had hitherto been accorded, but by 1905 a law seemed no nearer to enactment. Twice the House passed a bill. Twice the Senate, although engaging in extensive debate, refused to bring the measure to a vote.

Harvey Wiley continued his role as star witness at hearings before committees of both houses, as well as recruiter of other witnesses favoring a respectable law. Working closely with congressmen who had the bills in charge, Wiley sought to strengthen these proposed statutes at points he thought weak, to preserve their integrity against debilitating amendments, and yet to modify them in ways he deemed not too damaging so as to shift elements of industry from opposition to support. More adamant foes of the mainline bill framed their own competing measures, which Wiley criticized line by line. However, it was not by alternative proposals or by criticisms of the House-enacted bills that key senators shut off action, but by parliamentary tactics. A coalition of Republican conservatives, opposed not only to a pure-food bill of any rigor but to virtually all statutes regulating business, possessed the power, without being flagrantly obvious about it, to prevent a pure-food bill from being considered.[34]

In March 1902 concurrent sessions of the House Committee on In-

[32] Wiley, *An Autobiography*, 216–19; "Methods of Studying the Effects of Preservatives," 163; Anderson, *The Health of a Nation*, 151.

[33] Barkan, "Industry Invites Regulation," 22; Wood, *Strategic Uses of Public Policy*, 73–82.

[34] Anderson, *The Health of a Nation*, discusses events in the Fifty-seventh and Fifty-eighth Congresses, 137–71.

terstate and Foreign Commerce, chaired by William P. Hepburn, and the Senate Committee on Manufactures, chaired by Porter J. Mc-Cumber, who had succeeded Mason in this role, held hearings on various pure-food bills.[35] Most attention was given in the hearings to the proposal representing the views of food interests centered in Chicago, who held that the bill in the Paddock and Brosius tradition would ruin their businesses. Because of the unfairly bad press glucose had received, argued Frank H. Madden, representing the Wholesale Grocers of Chicago, the public would cease to buy products containing that sweetener should a law be enacted requiring ingredient labeling. At least 98 percent of the "thinking public," Madden asserted, deemed glucose "something vile and unfit for food." He admitted that 95 percent of the jelly consumed in the nation was made from glucose and the skins and cores of apples, although labeled strawberry or raspberry or whatever other flavor the processor chose to call it. This cheap, wholesome food did not deserve disparaging by physicians and chemists, who were "always discovering bugaboos," many of which were merely products of their own imaginations.[36]

Spokesmen for a trade organization making catsup, pickles, and preserves and for the National Association of Retail Grocers agreed with Madden and urged the passage of the bill embodying their ideas, sponsored by Representatives James R. Mann of Illinois and John B. Corliss of Michigan and by Senator Shelby M. Cullom of Illinois. The bill banned poisonous ingredients from foods in quantities that were harmful, but permitted safe ingredients to go unnamed on labels. Wiley would have no role in enforcement, and the secretary of agriculture only a tenuous authority. Nor did the measure cover medicines at all.[37]

This "shilly-shally" draft of a law—as an opponent called it—drew Wiley's masterful rebuttal. At the hearings the chief chemist analyzed the bill's inadequacies with devastating lucidity, seasoning his logic with wit, irony, indignation, and consummate showmanship. Wiley described himself as an early champion of glucose, which he deemed "a wholesome food, . . . not in any sense prejudicial to health." Nor was glucose a fraud, so long as maker, seller, and consumer all knew about its use. Showing the House committee glasses of pure crab-apple, currant, and quince jelly, made from perfect fruit and sugar, Wiley com-

---

[35] *Hearings before the Committee on Interstate and Foreign Commerce of the House of Representatives on The Pure Food Bills,* 57 Cong. 1 ses. [March 11–24, 1902]; Senate hearings are included in *Adulteration, Etc., of Foods, Etc.,* 57 Cong. 1 ses. [March 13–17, 1902], Senate Report 972.

[36] House *Hearings . . . on the Pure Food Bills,* 70–92.

[37] *Ibid.,* 14–63. Cullom's bill was S. 2987, Mann's H.R. 9352, and Corliss's H.R. 12348.

pared them with similar-appearing jelly made from apple scraps, glucose, and artificial colors. He then displayed swaths of woolen cloth dyed with colors extracted from such jellies. The chief chemist also held up a jar of strawberry preserves, "a mass of glucose" containing eleven or twelve strawberries. The berries, he noted, "are hardly shaking hands with each other, they are so far apart."[38]

Again, Wiley played down the dangers of adulteration. Some glucose might contain arsenic residues. Preservatives might pose hazards, as yet untested. The burden of proof that coal-tar colors, in the quantities used in foods, did no harm rested upon food processors. A worse danger than the threat to health posed by adulteration, however, was the menace to morality. Wiley elaborated:

> The evils of fraud are not confined to money alone. They are far-reaching. They are demoralizing. They put a premium on deceit. . . . No man can continually deceive his customer and retain that high moral sense which is the very soul of trade. The consumer may not be much out of pocket because of the cheapness of the articles purchased, but the manufacturers and dealers will soon be out of conscience.[39]

Under prevailing circumstances, Wiley asked rhetorically, quoting Tennyson, "Who but a fool would have faith in a tradesman's ware or his word." The Mann-Corliss-Cullom bill he considered "the most vicious piece of proposed legislation" he had ever read. Machiavelli himself might have had a hand in its drafting. Should it become law, the strong state laws would be repealed, and the labors of pure-food advocates through a quarter of a century would be undone. Consumers would "be left to the mercy of the mixer, the compounder, and the preserver."[40]

The bill may have been more bluff than serious proposal, but Wiley's skillful performance demolished it. No House or Senate committee member gave it his vote, thus shifting the focus of attention back to the mainline measure. Brosius was gone, killed in a home accident, and Wil-

[38] *Adulteration, Etc., of Foods, Etc.*, 67 (Hooper Coyne), 100–125 (Wiley); House *Hearings . . . on the Pure Food Bills*, 176–278. Among those writing to the committee in favor of Mann's version was Francis Thurber, 609.

[39] House *Hearings . . . on the Pure Food Bills*, 228–30, 257, 266. Wiley's strong stress on morality, illustrated in these quotations, is one reason Robert M. Crunden includes the chief chemist among his "ministers of reform" and gives the Food and Drugs Act of 1906 a prominent place among the progressives' moral-minded accomplishments. See Crunden, *Ministers of Reform: The Progressives' Achievement in American Civilization, 1889–1920* (New York, 1982). See chap. 12 below.

[40] *Adulteration, Etc., of Foods, Etc.*, 117–18; House *Hearings . . . on the Pure Food Bills*, 252.

liam Hepburn had become leader of the pure-food cause in the House. An Iowa lawyer, who had raised a cavalry company at the start of the Civil War and become its colonel, Hepburn had served three terms in Congress during the 1880s and had returned in 1892, destined to serve eight terms more. He now chaired the Committee on Interstate and Foreign Commerce and introduced the bill representing Brosius's final handicraft. Henry C. Hansbrough of North Dakota proposed the bill in the Senate. Even some trade groups that had championed the Mann-Corliss-Cullom measure came to support the Hepburn-Hansbrough bill. But other strong, trade pressure-groups held out, including the National Association of Retail Grocers and the cream-of-tartar baking-powder interests, which had ties with powerful senators. Even the National Association of State Dairy and Food Departments preferred an alternate course.[41]

Through the first session of the Fifty-seventh Congress, with leaders of both houses showing scant interest in the bill, it remained in a state of what Wiley called "innocuous desuetude." The efforts by Senator McCumber, a lawyer from North Dakota, to arouse the Senate to action seemed to spark next to no response. "Most evil in its potency," McCumber warned his colleagues, was the "growing tendency of the public to look upon commercial fraud as a legitimate means to business success." He saw the enactment of a pure-food law as "the first great step the Government has ever taken to establish and insure a standard of national honor, and integrity, and truthfulness in the commercial relations of its people." The pursuit of pure food went far beyond the people's health and purse. "It affects the manhood of the American people," McCumber believed, "their honesty, their truthfulness, their sincerity, their ideals. It affects all that makes or tends to make a nation great and powerful." These echoes of lofty sentiments that had been expressed in the oleomargarine debate of 1886 did not now move members of the Senate. Nelson W. Aldrich of Rhode Island, stalwart Republican, blocked McCumber's final effort to get the pure-food bill considered. Rumor had it that the major cream-of-tartar baking-powder company had influenced Aldrich's stand. The House of Representatives did not even debate the bill.[42]

[41] Anderson, *The Health of a Nation*, 136–38; "Hepburn, William Peters" and "Hansbrough, Henry Clay," *Biographical Directory of the American Congress* (1950), 1264, 1301–2; Louis Bernard Schmidt, "Hepburn, William Peters," *Dictionary of American Biography*, vol. 8, 568–69.

[42] Anderson, *The Health of a Nation*, 141–42; "McCumber, Porter James," *Biographical Directory of the American Congress* (1971), 1369; *Cong. Record*, 57 Cong. 1 ses., 4659–60, 7376. Hepburn's bill was H.R. 3109, Hansbrough's S. 3342. McCumber later introduced a revised bill, S. 6303.

Although action was stalled on the main track, progress occurred on the sidings. During the session Congress did enact several secondary bills that were to influence the major pure-food campaign. In the act appropriating funds for the Department of Agriculture, Congress repeated an authorization made two years earlier, permitting Wiley to investigate preservatives and colors "to determine their relation to digestion and to health," and this time provided adequate funds. Promptly, Wiley assembled his "Poison Squad" and began to feed boracic acid to its members.[43]

The appropriations act also authorized the secretary of agriculture, in collaboration with the Association of Official Agricultural Chemists and other experts he might choose, to set standards of purity for foods and to define adulterations, "for the guidance of the officials of the various States and of courts of justice."[44] The matter of standards had been one of the most thorny issues all along, the problem that excited the most interest during the pure-food congresses. Wiley and his cohorts ideally wanted precise standards of food purity set by the secretary of agriculture with the advice of the best experts, and desired these standards to have an official status, so that state—and eventually federal—regulators, going to court, could have an easy burden of proof: to demonstrate merely that the offending article deviated from the standard and thus violated the law. At the other extreme, food processors engaged in dubious practices wanted no standard-setting mechanism at all. If a law must come, that law should require regulators to prove adulteration anew, with no standards to go by, in each separate litigation. If standards must come, those standards should be advisory only and not binding upon the courts, and should be defined with industry input and not solely by such zealots as Wiley and his AOAC friends who would dominate the secretary of agriculture. Even many more responsible food processors tended to distrust Wiley as standard maker. Rigorous standards, they feared, would provide an entering wedge for more massive bureaucratic burdens to follow.[45]

Congressman Ezekiel S. Candler of Mississippi inquired of his House colleagues:

If . . . [the secretary of agriculture] is going to fix the standard of the food product, how long will it be before he will say what kind of clothing we shall wear in summer or in winter, what kind of

[43] Anderson, *The Health of a Nation*, 142; 32 U.S. Stat. 296.
[44] *Ibid.*
[45] Alexander J. Wedderburn testimony, 87, and Wiley on history of standard setting, 143–50, in *Adulteration, Etc., of Foods, Etc.*

horse you shall drive, . . . how you shall run your farm, how long your laborers shall work, or what you shall not pay them?[46]

Having secured such a generally favorable standard-setting mechanism in the appropriations act, Wiley was more willing to compromise on this matter in the developing omnibus bill. Secretary Wilson, in consultation with the AOAC, proceeded to use his appropriations act authority and in 1903 issued a circular proclaiming the initial standards set.[47]

Another special food law enacted in the first session of the Fifty-seventh Congress also influenced the pure-food campaign. Dairy farmers were so intent on securing tighter restrictions on oleomargarine that they were indifferent, if not hostile, to the food and drug bill. In 1902 their long lobbying succeeded. Led by Henry C. Adams, Wisconsin dairy and food commissioner, who had just been elected to the House, Congress quintupled the tax per pound on oleomargarine and added other burdens to butter's competitor. This goal accomplished, dairy interests looked with greater favor on broader food reform.[48]

In the second session, Hepburn managed to get the pure-food bill before the House for full debate. Southern congressmen, opposing it on constitutional grounds, reiterated arguments made during the first oleomargarine controversy. William C. Adamson of Georgia held that it was "utterly unnecessary to burden" the federal government "with little police matters all the local communities can better attend to," and, if the attempt were made, "a pestilential lot of spies, meddlers, and informers" would make the government "a great deal more impure than any food or drink any people ever consumed."[49]

Adamson alluded to Wiley's newly initiated "Poison Squad" experiments. While the Georgian believed the chief chemist to be "an excellent and amiable gentleman and an able scientist," he viewed modern experimental methods with distrust:

After science has done its best or its worst, after all the laboratories have exhausted themselves, in the last analysis it will be proved that

[46] *Cong. Record,* 57 Cong. 2 ses., 447.

[47] *Pure Food,* 59 Cong. 2 ses., House Report 2118, part 2, 18–19; Bureau of Chemistry, Department of Agriculture, *Food Definitions and Standards; Prepared by Committee on Food Standards, Association of Official Agricultural Chemists* (Washington, 1903).

[48] 32 U.S. Stat. 193 (May 9, 1902); Eric E. Lampard, *The Rise of the Dairy Industry in Wisconsin: A Study in Agricultural Change, 1820–1920* (Madison, WI, 1963), 262–63; "Adams, Henry Cullen," *Biographical Directory of the American Congress* (1950), 762; Howard, "The Margarine Industry," 109–17.

[49] The House debate and vote appear in *Cong. Record,* 57 Cong. 2 ses., 437–58.

the old ladies in the home, the housewives, the old cook who used the elbow grease to mix the dough to make the bread—not last year's wasp nests which we have now and which is called bread— knew more about the subject than all science and all scientists.

The Georgia congressman denied "a real and genuine upheaval originating from the people and demanding action" from the Congress on the pure-food theme. Instead, "one class of businessmen" seemed to be "trying to crush out another." As if to demonstrate this charge, Augustus Peabody Gardner of Massachusetts, son-in-law of Henry Cabot Lodge, followed Adamson to the floor to defend Gloucester's boneless codfish industry. To preserve this piscine product, boracic acid had to be externally applied. Wiley's "pure and impure experiments with 12 young men," just launched, were raising a question about this preservative. Congress should await the result of these tests, Gardner insisted, before enacting a law. Even if borax should be less than the perfect preservative, it might be needed to maintain on the market an inexpensive staple in the diet of the poor. Hunger might harm health more than did adulterated food. "People are willing to eat foods—like fish balls for Sunday breakfast—realizing they may not be perfectly pure." Gardner sought to exempt dried codfish from the purview of a national law by offering an amendment, promptly rejected by the House.

Hepburn defended the pure-food bill with eloquence and force. He was aided by other representatives, like Charles R. Schirm of Maryland, who painted a dismal picture of the nation's food supply. "Fortunes are being built up," Schirm said, "upon the wrecks of human bodies." The American dining room he termed "a chamber of horrors." A large majority of House members seemed to share this sentiment. When the pure-food bill came to a vote on December 19, 1902, it passed seventy-two to twenty-one.

The Senate, however, would not give the House bill consideration. Wiley personally pleaded with powerful senators to let the measure come to a vote. McCumber removed from the House version several provisions, like that authorizing the secretary of agriculture to fix food standards, that had aroused particular controversy. He assured the Senate that he had found no opposition to the bill as it then stood. Again and again he sought consideration, always thwarted by objections. "It seems to me," he told his colleagues late in the session, "we ought to have, in the course of two years, one hour or two hours in which to consider a bill that has been the first one on the calendar during all that length of time. . . . All I desire is to have an honest hearing for the bill." On March 3, 1903, the day before the session ended, McCumber managed to get a vote on the issue of considering his bill. He lost thirty-two to twenty-eight.[50]

Only on a minor front did pure food advance during the congressional session. Since 1899 the secretary of agriculture had been granted the authority to inspect imports reaching the nation's shores and to designate those posing a hazard to health. Thereupon the secretary of the treasury would forbid their delivery. In 1903 Congress intensified the rigor of import scrutiny. Two new categories were made taboo: foods bearing false labeling, and those forbidden or restricted in sale within the nation from which they had been shipped. To carry out his enlarged responsibilities Wiley expanded the Bureau of Chemistry staff, setting up branches at the port cities of San Francisco, New York, Boston, Philadelphia, New Orleans, and Chicago. High standards were set, but enforcement began by being deliberately lenient, especially as to misbranding by first offenders. Nonetheless, foreign exporters quickly learned the lesson that Wiley meant business. The United States ceased to be a dumping ground for shoddy foods and liquors sent from abroad. No importer took one of the bureau's restrictive decisions to court.[51]

American food processors and whiskey rectifiers also had an opportunity to observe Wiley as regulator. His rigorous rules and firm stance with respect to imports evoked an image of how the chief chemist would perform should he be charged with enforcing a national law. Wiley's comments on preservatives, as his "Poison Squad" experiments proceeded, and the lofty level of food standards promulgated by the secretary of agriculture further gave elements of industry concern. In both open and undercover ways they intensified their opposition to any food law Wiley might administer.

Superficially, the Fifty-eighth Congress, which met in three sessions between November 1903 and March 1905, seemed to treat the pure-food issue very like the Fifty-seventh Congress had done. Committees of both houses held new hearings, in which Wiley again played the most prominent role. The House debated the issue briefly and politely, the only "wrangle" related to the constitutional question, then promptly voted, passing the bill 201 to 68. The Senate gave pure food scanty debate, the senators in charge of the bill trying over and over again to secure for it consideration, always in vain.[52]

[50] *Ibid.*, 1724–26, 2647, 2966–67; Anderson, *The Health of a Nation*, 144–47.

[51] *Ibid.*, 145–46, 152–54; 30 U.S. Stat. 951 (1899); 32 U.S. Stat. 1157 (1903); "Report of the Chemist," *Annual Report of the Department of Agriculture, 1904* (Washington, 1904), 209–10; *ibid., 1905,* 499.

[52] *Hearings before the Committee on Interstate and Foreign Commerce of the House of Representatives on the Pure-Food Bills H.R. 5077 and 6295,* House Committee on Interstate and

Yet things had changed. Pure food inched upward as a national priority, because of publicity about the "Poison Squad," the expanded speechmaking and lobbying by Wiley and his allies, and the growing fervor of a Progressive spirit abroad in the land. Wiley's wooing and willingness to compromise had won over some dissident members of the National Association of State Dairy and Food Departments and a contingent of the food processors who had opposed the mainline bill at the 1902 hearings.[53] At the same time, speeches by Wiley and other champions of reform, drafted in a growing mood of confidence about chances for victory, sometimes took on a timbre of shrillness that worried elements of industry. Some modifications in the pure-food bill, made in the same hopeful spirit, increased its potential for regulatory rigor and intensified opposition. The Senate hearings of 1904 revealed more harshness and bitterness than had marked those of two years before.

Especially fearful and angry was the first witness at the February hearings of the Senate committee, Warwick Massey Hough. A shrewd, forceful, and unrelenting advocate, Hough, a St. Louis lawyer, spoke for the interests of the National Wholesale Liquor Dealers' Association, which included most of the distillers and wholesalers of blended or rectified bourbon whiskey.[54]

At about the same time that agitation for a national pure-food law had begun, whiskey made from corn replaced rye whiskey as the American favorite. The industry soared in importance as an object of governmental concern because a tax on whiskey, levied during the Civil War, became an increasingly significant source of governmental funds. Over half the total federal income between 1876 and 1904 came from the tax on drinking alcohol. The bourbon business split into two sharply antag-

---

Foreign Commerce, 58 Cong. 2 ses. (Washington, 1904); *Hearings before the Committee on Manufactures of the United States Senate on Bill (S. 198) . . . and the Bill (H.R. 6295)*, 58 Cong. 2 ses. (Washington, 1904); *Cong. Record*, 58 Cong. 1 ses., 178, 495; 2 ses., 791, 849, 878–900, 924–40 (passage of bill in House, 940), 958, 2848, 5695, 5818; 3 ses., 64, 126–29, 195–98, 261–64, 363, 784, 3754–55, 3845–49, 3943–44. James B. Clark of Missouri used the word "wrangle," *Cong. Record*, 58 Cong. 2 ses., 937. The House vote passing the bill was not recorded. A preliminary vote on January 20, 1904, gave some indication of the chamber's sentiment, and party lines held quite firm at this stage. On a vote to restore a more rigorous version of the bill, which passed 145 to 126, only five Republicans voted nay and only nine Democrats—one from the South—voted yea. *Cong. Record*, 58 Cong. 2 ses., 939.

[53] Wiley to Congressman Hepburn, December 3, 1903, and Wiley to Congressman James R. Mann, January 7, 1904, in *Hearings . . . on the Pure-Food Bills H.R. 5077 and 6295*, 42–45.

[54] This first session of the Senate committee hearing first was published in *Adulteration of Foods, Etc.*, 58 Cong. 2 ses., Senate Report 1209, Hough's testimony at 38–52, 62–64.

onistic wings. Bourbon distillers, centered mainly in Kentucky, Pennsylvania, Maryland, and Virginia, produced straight whiskey in their stills, which went on the market after a period of aging in wood. The blenders or rectifiers, whose plants were located principally in Illinois, Indiana, and Ohio, mixed a smaller amount of aged bourbon with a greater amount of grain spirits—ethyl alcohol—and added coloring and flavoring ingredients, producing a cheaper product, although the labels of blended and straight whiskeys did not make the differences between them clear. In 1896 a congressional committee concluded that about fifty times as much straight bourbon was being sold to rectifiers for mixing purposes as was being sold to consumers "in its original integrity." The next year Congress passed a Bottled-in-Bond Act, providing for bottling of bourbon in distilleries under governmental supervision, a fact affirmed to potential customers by the affixing of a green stamp. Legally the stamp indicated only that taxes had been paid, but the straight-whiskey makers promoted the stamp as a guarantee of quality. The battle between distillers and blenders raged on. Rectified whiskey dominated the marketplace, outselling straight whiskey by a ratio of more than three to one. Warwick Hough and those whom he represented did not want provisions to creep into a pure-food bill that would endanger the economic position of blended whiskey.[55]

Wiley recognized the blenders' political might. As compromiser, seeking to reduce opposition to the pure-food bill that might prove decisive, the chief chemist bargained with Hough and agreed to an amendment that would bar the need for any additional marks on whiskeys already branded by the Bureau of Internal Revenue. The House committee did not accept this proviso, however, and passed the bill in a form that Hough believed threatened the rectifiers. He came to the Senate hearings in a resentful mood. The clause in the House bill that would require mixtures and blends to be "labeled, branded, or tagged so as to show the character and constituents thereof" Hough considered ominous. He and Wiley had met again, Hough told the Senate committee. Wiley had sought to explain why the House committee had not accepted his compromise suggestion, and the two had agreed on a new amendment to the same effect, which would remove from the bill the requirement for a detailed label description of each component of a compound or blend. Hough was willing to use the word "blend" on

---

[55] Gerald Carson, *The Social History of Bourbon: An Unhurried Account of Our Star-Spangled American Drink* (New York, 1963), 87–89, 95–96, 129, 150–51, 165–70. High and Coppin, "Wiley, Whiskey, and Strategic Behavior," suggest that aging of distilled whiskey in barrels, the type covered by the Bottled-in-Bond Act, was a newer process than that used to produce rectified whiskey, and that the latter contained less poisonous fusel oil.

labels. Any greater precision, he argued, would expose valuable trade secrets. He also feared that the standard for drugs included in the bill, that they must conform to definitions in the *United States Pharmacopoeia*, might be unfairly used to discriminate against rectified whiskey.[56]

Hough then attacked the distillers of straight whiskey and their product, turning the Senate committee into a new forum for an old debate. Nothing a blender put in his product, Hough insisted, could be so "deleterious and dangerous" as the fusel oil in straight whiskey, which was "the worst poison on earth." Consisting chiefly of amyl and butyl alcohols, fusel oil was "absolutely destructive of every organ in a man's body." Therefore, applying the word "pure" to the product of the distiller's art turned out to be an absolute misnomer.[57]

If Wiley as compromiser had sought to placate Hough, Wiley as crusader abominated the blended product Hough represented. The natural, old-fashioned way of distilling appealed both to his fancy and to his palate. The chief chemist leagued with the distillers to plot ways of checkmating the blenders' stratagems. Some proponents of legislation thought that the contentious whiskey issue jeopardized enactment of a law and besought Wiley to work for exemption of alcoholic beverages from the bill's purview. Wiley resisted this temptation. He deemed blended whiskey so outrageously adulterated that it especially required regulation. Further, he recognized that a bill that neglected whiskey alone, among all food and drink, would lose the support of the increasingly influential temperance advocates. More fundamentally, the chief chemist believed in principle that a pure-food law must cover all products, with no exceptions.[58]

It was Wiley as crusader who saw to it that Hough was followed to the witness chair at the Senate committee hearing by the largest whiskey merchant in the nation, W. H. Thomas of Louisville. Taking a patronizing tone, Thomas termed Hough "a nice fellow, . . . a splendid fellow. . . . He wants to do what is right, but the people behind him want to destroy the old fashioned honest way of making whiskey." The whiskey that moonshiners sell, Thomas stated, "is more honestly made than what these compounders and blenders make." This fact, said Thomas, Hough knew full well, for he himself drank the straight whiskey that he as witness had disparaged. Indeed, he had been trying to make arrangements with Thomas to buy a supply.[59]

[56] *Adulterations of Foods, Etc.*, 38–52; Anderson, *The Health of a Nation*, 160; High and Coppin, "Wiley, Whiskey, and Strategic Behavior."
[57] *Adulteration of Foods, Etc.*, 48
[58] Anderson, *The Health of a Nation*, 168–69.
[59] *Adulteration of Foods, Etc.*, 53–57.

Wiley testified next, somewhat as compromiser but more ardently as crusader. Acknowledging his negotiated agreement with Hough, Wiley nonetheless avowed his sympathies with the distillers, who had been brought to the verge of ruin by competition from the compounders. The chief chemist countered Hough's charges of the dangers inherent in distilled whiskey because of fusel oil. Wiley explained the expensive aging process employed by distillers through which the fusel oil was converted by the action of natural oxidizing agents to harmless ethers that provided whiskey with its aroma and flavor. He then described the way in which rectifiers sought artificially to imitate the naturally aged product. The question, Wiley told the committee, was not which of the two whiskeys was more or less deleterious, but how to prevent deception. If the buyer knew that the bottle contained an artificially made compound with no deleterious additions, then the purpose of the bill had been accomplished.[60]

Not since the 1886 affray between butter and oleomargarine had such naked contesting between commercial competitors occurred as that between distillers and blenders at this committee hearing. The battling of opposing baking-powder factions had to recede into second place. Moreover, this 1904 whiskey confrontation constituted only the first round of a continuing fight that was to affect the fate of the pure-food law both before and after its enactment.

The other troubling issue that arose in the February 1904 Senate committee hearings concerned the definition of drugs. Unlike foods, from the very beginning of broad bills considered by the Congress, drugs—at least certain drugs—had been given a standard by legislative draftsmen. That standard was the venerable *Pharmacopoeia of the United States*, begun in 1820 and revised decennially by a committee of physicians and pharmacists. Even the 1848 law banning the importation of adulterated drugs had referred to the USP, as well as to several renowned European pharmacopoeias, as yardsticks by which to measure the quality of proffered imports. The 1879 Board of Trade draft law had recommended that a drug named in the USP be deemed adulterated if it differed "materially from the [USP] standard of strength, quality, or purity." Not all later bills included such a provision, but the USP standard came to be a recurring feature of mainline bills. Beginning in the 1880s, a number of state laws designated the USP a legal standard.[61]

By no means all medicines with which Americans were dosed received

[60] *Ibid.*, 57–61.
[61] Glenn Sonnedecker, "Drug Standards Become Official," in Young, ed., *The Early Years of Federal Food and Drug Control*, 28–30.

recognition in USP pages. The National Board of Trade model, borrowing from the British law of 1875, had taken account of these less august drugs: non-USP drugs listed in other standard works would have to meet the tests set forth in those volumes. In any case, a drug would be considered adulterated "if its strength or purity fall below the professed standard under which it is sold." Almost exactly these same words appeared in the Paddock bill of 1892, which defined drugs as "all medicines for internal or external use."[62]

Such a broad definition covered proprietary medicines. Denying any widespread fraud or extensive use of injurious ingredients in their business, leading proprietors strongly objected to having their wares regulated by law. The Proprietary Association, formed in 1881, opposed formula disclosure bills introduced into Congress and state legislatures. When the pure-food congresses met in Washington, the Proprietary Association, supported by other drug industry groups, succeeded in restricting the coverage of drugs in the recommended draft law to those listed in the USP. Bills considered in the Fifty-sixth and Fifty-seventh Congresses embodied such a narrow definition, and, during committee hearings and floor debate, references to proprietary medicines could be numbered on the fingers of one hand.[63]

While pleased with their triumphs in state legislatures, the Proprietary Association foresaw trouble ahead. In 1899 the committee on legislation warned the membership that "the demand for Pure Food laws is growing every year, and sooner or later, in all of the States such laws are likely to be enacted." The association should have handy a reasonable bill, the committee suggested, to urge as a substitute for the "vicious and ill-considered measures" that were being introduced. In 1903 the Proprietary Association took new alarm. Harvey Wiley, after years of accepting a narrow drug definition in national pure-food bills, had made a speech proposing a broader definition, and insisting on stringent controls over proprietary medicines especially. "Such a law," the committee on legislation believed, "would practically destroy the sale of proprietary remedies in the United States."[64]

Wiley had always been a foe of quackery. As a boy he had distrusted a neighborhood malaria nostrum. As chief chemist in Washington he had assembled "bales of advertising of fraudulent remedies." His bureau had tested "lost manhood" treatments for the Post Office Department

[62] *Ibid.*; *Adulteration of Foods, Etc.*, 74; Young, *The Toadstool Millionaires*, 227.

[63] *Ibid.*, 107–8, 226–28, 233, 235.

[64] *Ibid.*, 226, 228–29; Harvey W. Wiley, "Drugs and Their Adulterations and Laws Relating Thereto," *Washington Medical Annals* 2 (1903), 205–28; Proprietary Association, *21st Annual Report* (New York, 1903), 52.

and had begun to investigate suspicious nostrums shipped in from abroad. Wiley's main interest and concern, however, had always been food. This had dominated the bureau's research and monopolized Wiley's public oratory. Now, in 1903, in adding his voice to those already criticizing nostrums, Wiley was giving the stamp of governmental approval to the critique and lending his prestige to the suggestion that patent medicines should be covered by a national law. His conversion was complete. While still giving food his top priority, Wiley spoke out against patent medicines again and again. Early in 1903 he set up a drug laboratory in the Bureau of Chemistry, which devoted increasing attention to the analysis of proprietary medicines.[65]

It is ironic, in view of all this, that the restoration of a broad definition of drugs to the mainline pure-food bill resulted not from Wiley's initiative, but from the urging of certain proprietary drug marketers themselves, who anticipated some trade advantage from the change. They appealed in 1903 to Senator McCumber, who acceded to their plea and added to the coverage of USP drugs in the draft bill "any substance intended to be used for the cure, mitigaton, or prevention of disease." Learning of this expansion, some drug association officials, upset at the prospects inherent in such a change, persuaded the original proponents to reverse themselves. A deluge of mail besought McCumber to return to the original limited definition of drugs. The pressure seemed so great as to jeopardize the bill's success, and McCumber expressed a willingness to yield to it. But Weldon B. Heyburn, a newly elected senator from Idaho who had replaced McCumber as chairman of the Committee on Manufactures, refused to retreat from the advanced position.[66]

More ironies surfaced at the Senate committee hearing. Fiercely opposed to the broadened drug definition in private, the Proprietary Association made an amazingly mild protest before the senators. The association's counsel, George L. Douglass, remarked that, if the labeling clause banning statements that were misleading in any particular should be extended to proprietary drugs, "it would give rise to controversies in every State and Territory of the Union." Doctors from different schools of medicine, Douglass noted, disputed about the therapeutic value of various drugs. McCumber obliged Douglass by saying that he interpreted the word "misleading" as applying to label statements about ingredients but not about curative claims.[67]

[65] Young, *The Toadstool Millionaires*, 233–34; Wiley, *An Autobiography*, 53, 205; Department of Agriculture, *Report of the Secretary of Agriculture, 1903*, iix, 189.

[66] Young, *The Toadstool Millionaires*, 235; *Adulteration of Foods, Etc.*, 72–73, 83–87. The proprietors who launched the change were not named.

[67] *Ibid.*, 98–100.

Douglass could criticize the expanded drug definition in merely moderate tones because he was bolstered by other witnesses giving similar testimony. The national trade associations of both wholesale and retail druggists objected to extending the bill's coverage beyond drugs listed in the usp. So likewise did a special committee on legislation of the American Pharmaceutical Association, the scientific wing of pharmacy, which sent a letter for the record.[68] Senator Heyburn noted the irony inherent in such unanimity:

It was with some surprise that I saw the high class of retail druggists who are here opposing the bill. . . . This question seems to me to be divided something like a drug store with its two sides—on one side the drugs from which prescriptions are compounded and where the scientific work of the druggist is done, on the other side the patent medicine department, to which you go and reach your hand up on the shelf and get the package and say, "Fifty cents, please." I may be wrong, but I can not understand why the retail druggist who represents the higher class of the business should be devoting so much attention to phases of this bill which can affect only the patent medicine proprietors.[69]

Testimony given did not quash Heyburn's surprise. Reasons for opposing the regulation of proprietary medicines were general and vague. "Druggists," asserted M. N. Kline, spokesman for the National Wholesale Druggists Association, "are afraid to endorse anything which . . . will yield no result except the fear and trembling . . . that they are going to be held up by . . . some inspector somewhere, and subjected to the ridicule of their neighbors." This had happened, Kline said, under some of the state laws.[70]

The broadened drug definition, according to the witnesses, was "disastrous," "a great and radical departure," which would stir up "mischief-makers" and "lead to innumerable annoyances without practically accomplishing anything of value for the community." The provision simply could not work, for manufacturers would continue to keep their proprietary formulas secret and thus not establish their own standards by which their medicines could be judged. Do not delay the enactment of the basic law, a representative of the National Association of Retail Druggists pleaded, by the inclusion of this onerous provision. "You can not build everything in a single day." If later on experience should reveal

[68] *Ibid.*, 67–98.
[69] *Ibid.*, 100.
[70] *Ibid.*, 87.

the need for buttressing amendments, retail druggists would support them.[71]

Despite the unanimity of drug-trade protest, Heyburn, after a close committee vote, kept the expanded drug definition in his bill. Nor had any concessions been made to the whiskey rectifiers. In the sporadic Senate debate during the third session of the Fifty-eighth Congress, neither proprietary drugs nor blended whiskey received a word of comment. Through thirteen months Senators Heyburn and McCumber sought to get their bill considered. "There never was a time," Heyburn told his colleagues during the last week of the session, "when the demand of the people from one end of the country to the other was so imperative for such legislation as it is to-day." But every effort was blocked by parliamentary maneuvers initiated by some of the most powerful Republican members of the Senate: Aldrich, Orville H. Pratt of Connecticut, and John C. Spooner of Wisconsin. Their expressed reasons for thwarting consideration of the bill were brief and categorical: it was "imperfect" and "ill-considered"; "full of manifest injustice"; in need of "revamping in the interest of the liberty of the citizen." Heyburn's last two efforts to get the Senate to take up the bill were cut off in midsentence.[72]

Behind the scenes both rectifiers and proprietary interests had been active. The blended-whiskey lobby raised a huge war chest, and Warwick Hough boasted of having defeated the bill. The Proprietary Association enlisted a major portion of the nation's press, for which patent-medicine advertising furnished a significant revenue source. Newspapermen penned editorials and personally lobbied members of the Senate. A further factor for congressional caution lay in the presidential election of 1904. One of the House proponents of pure food commented on this to Wiley:

> While there ought to be no politics in a bill of this character, still it is perfectly plain that if a law like this goes into effect and is enforced just before a Presidential election, so as to interfere with commercial business, it will have a very deleterious effect on the party in power.[73]

Wiley had engineered several unsuccessful attempts to enlist a public expression of support for the pure-food bill from the president who was to be reelected in 1904, Theodore Roosevelt. In this and other direc-

[71] *Ibid.*, 68–69, 76, 80, 85, 90.

[72] Anderson, *The Health of a Nation*, 162–63; *Cong. Record*, 58 Cong. 3 ses., 264, 3754–55, 3854, 3943–44.

[73] Anderson, *The Health of a Nation*, 163–64; James R. Mann to Wiley, cited *ibid.*, 164.

tions as well, despite his expanding efforts, Wiley had not been able to amass enough pressure on the Congress to outweigh that of the interests which opposed reform. Suppressing his disappointment at the failure of the Senate to act in the spring of 1905, the chief chemist rededicated himself to the task of creating a coalition with enough power to achieve victory.[74]

[74] *Ibid.*, 164–66; Young, *The Toadstool Millionaires*, 235–36.

VIII

Combining and Crusading for a Law

The campaign [for a pure-food law] needed leadership. By profession, position, and temperament, Wiley was able to supply it. His greatest contribution to the cause was not his scientific work, not his ability to dramatize the issue, but rather the inspired generalship he offered. . . . He kept, though not without defections, a strange alliance on the battle line and gave the captains on the congressional front the help they needed. He was the one individual who gave continuity to the struggle for pure food and drugs, the one leader who consistently saw the big picture. Wiley was in large part responsible for the fact that food and drug legislation came when it did and in the form that it did.

—OSCAR E. ANDERSON, JR.,
The Health of a Nation[1]

Dr. Wiley's Coalition

Before Wiley had moved from Purdue to Washington, segments of business had been interested in getting a law. From the start the goal of each industry had been to shape public policy to make it useful in tough competitive battles that continued to rage. As lobbying pressures modified proposed measures, some elements of business that had supported earlier versions became opponents, while other elements joined the proponents pushing for a law. The alum baking-powder interests, for example, outspoken champions of bills they thought would curb their cream-of-tartar competitors, became indifferent, if not hostile, in 1904 when this goal seemed unlikely to result from the bills before Congress. The broadening of the definition of "drug" likewise turned groups neutral to, if not supportive of, a national law into vigorous enemies. The more strenuously whiskey rectifiers fought pure-food bills, the more strongly distillers of straight whiskey lobbied for them.[2]

---

[1] Anderson, *The Health of a Nation*, 196.
[2] These attitudes are evident in Senate hearings included as part of *Adulteration of Foods, Etc.*, 58 Cong. 2 ses. (1904), Senate Report 1209. See also Donna J. Wood, "The Strategic

174

Wiley strove hard to preserve business support, knowing it indispensable to ultimate success. Thus, while not disguising his preference for straight whiskey, he helped Hough draft amendments that might satisfy the rectifiers. While becoming increasingly dubious of preservatives, Wiley aided Senator Lodge and Representative Gardner in preparing amendments that would protect the New England codfish industry. Even at the midnight hour, the chief chemist was to acquiesce in, even to urge, provisions that he opposed in principle but thought necessary to achieve the enactment of a generally satisfactory law. Yet as his "Poison Squad" experiments toughened his convictions, and as he gained the allegiance of influential nonbusiness groups, Wiley, while still supported by some elements of business, relied less upon businessmen than he once had done.[3]

In the final stages, major elements of business continued support for a law, recognizing that its time had come, while striving until the very end, with some success, to insert what more ardent reformers deemed crippling amendments. The growth in the strength of Wiley's public interest allies had made business groups more wary. Doubts about Wiley's policies as to preservatives and whiskey, should he become potentate enforcing a new law, bulked large among reasons for some cooling of food-industry ardor for a pure-food bill. One of the chief chemist's most faithful allies was Frank Barrett, editor of the *American Grocer*, the journal that Francis Thurber had taken over soon after its founding. Barrett kept warning Wiley that his more extreme stands and threatening language jeopardized food-industry support.[4]

Renewed intransigence became obvious in the Fifty-ninth Congress, which began in December 1905. The previous spring a broad range of processors had formed the National Food Manufacturers' Association, ostensibly to secure a "proper" law, one guaranteed to keep enforcement out of Wiley's hands. Congressman Hepburn, at a House hearing, asked the organization's secretary, Thomas E. Lannen, point blank whether its purpose was not to prevent legislation that prohibited preservatives. Though Lannen denied it, Hepburn was unconvinced. The association, he asserted, was a "fake organization" created solely for lobbying, its officers merely fund-gatherers from manufacturers using preservatives.

Use of Public Policy: Business Support for the 1906 Food and Drug Act," *Business History Review* 59 (1985), 422–27, and Wood, *Strategic Uses of Public Policy.*

[3] *Adulteration of Foods, Etc.*, 33, 39, 57–60; *Hearings before the Committee on Interstate and Foreign Commerce of the House of Representatives on The Pure Food Bills H.R. 3044, 4527, 7018, 12071, 13086, 13853 and 13859*, 59 Cong. 1 ses. [February 13–27, 1906], 118, 310; Wood, *Strategic Uses of Public Policy*; High, "Wiley, Whiskey, and Strategic Behavior."

[4] *Hearings . . . on The Pure Food Bills*, 4–68; Anderson, *The Health of a Nation*, 171.

The association sent witnesses to the House committee to praise preservatives. Their value in protecting the public, testified Dr. Robert C. Eccles, a Brooklyn chemist and physician, far transcended their danger. Ptomaine poisoning from processed food posed a much greater hazard to health, he insisted, than did the small amounts of preservative required to negate such risk. Certainly the body could absorb such minimal quantities of salicyclic or benzoic acid without harm. If continual use of poisons like tea, coffee, and peaches had been truly dangerous, then "the whole race would have been swept from the face of the earth long ago." In any case, such traditional preservatives as vinegar, Eccles reckoned, might be eight times as dangerous as the new mild acids. Other witnesses urged upon the Congress similar arguments in behalf of the some three hundred producers of fruit, vegetables, fish, jellies, condiments, and preservatives, who composed the National Food Manufacturers' Association.[5]

Wiley, a rebuttal witness at the House hearing, sought to puncture such fulsome praise of preservatives and to expose the weakened protection to the public inherent in the food manufacturers' bill. The chief chemist further made the point that not all food processors opposed the pure-food bill that he supported. Even with its more rigorous provisions, the mainline bill now had the backing of the nation's major canners. As Wiley explained it, he himself had won back their straying allegiance.[6]

A national trade association binding canners together was still being formed. In February 1906 two major regional associations, one mainly midwestern, the other northeastern, joined by individual canners from as far away as California, assembled in Atlantic City to confer about their problems. The divergent state laws and a bad press from court cases in the strictest states had hurt the canning business. Most canners feared further decline if Wiley should set strict standards under a national law. The president of the midwestern packers, A. C. Fraser, a Wisconsin pea canner who did not use preservatives, invited Wiley to make a speech, realizing full well how "hostile" was the convention climate. Wiley converted the episode into high drama at a House committee hearing.[7]

[5] *Hearings . . . on The Pure Food Bills*, 119–35, 137, 142–44. Members of the National Food Manufacturers' Association are listed in *Cong. Record*, 59 Cong. 1 ses., 2661. Senator Hernando DeSoto Money of Mississippi presented his ideas in an amendment to S. 88, the main bill, *Cong. Record*, 59 Cong. 1 ses., 1868, 2771–73, and Representative William A. Rodenberg of Illinois introduced his own bill, H.R. 13859.

[6] *Hearings . . . on The Pure Food Bills*, 237–360.

[7] Fraser's account of the episode appears in *ibid.*, 90–96, Wiley's account, 317–19. Fraser,

Fraser had met him at the railroad station, Wiley said, "very much frightened," doubting that Wiley should undertake the planned address. The canner feared for the chief chemist's safety.

"What is the matter?"

"Well, they say you are trying to ruin their business."

"I can not help what they say; I am trying to save their business." Even if they carried "guns in their hip pockets," he would make his speech. "I am not afraid to go before any American audience." Yet Wiley did ask Fraser to "have a back door nearby so I can get out" in case worse came to worst.

Fraser introduced Wiley to a hall packed with canners, food jobbers, and brokers. Wiley reported to the House committee:

> I told the canners exactly the truth, . . . that they, instead of helping their business by claiming right to put a coloring matter in their goods, were driving hundreds of thousands of American citizens away from the very stuff . . . [the canners] wanted to sell. . . . When the people find saccharin or coal tar sugar in one man's canned goods, they immediately jump to the conclusion that everybody is using it. . . . That one man who does [use] it injures the business of every man who does not. . . . I believe your product is one of the finest and best that can be offered to the American people and absolutely necessary to our welfare. . . . You [must] take the American people into your confidence, and . . . say to . . . [them], "There is absolutely nothing in the goods which we present you but what we say is in them"; and then instead of selling one can you will sell three before five years. But if you continue to try to deceive the American people, and to claim the right to use things that 95 percent of our people do not want you to use, your business is going to suffer.

Wiley could sense some relaxing of the tension. One member of the audience began to clap. Others posed questions, and the chief chemist answered them straight from the shoulder, then summing up: "You are honest business men. . . . Is there one man in this room that wants to take one dollar from an American citizen which, if that American citizen knew what he was selling him, he would not give?"

A long moment of silence reigned, and then—Wiley told the House committee—came "a tremendous outburst of applause." He had over-

---

a physician, had been responsible for getting bacteriologist H. L. Russell to investigate problems of pea spoilage in Wisconsin. See Keuchel, "The Development of the Canning Industry," 204.

come the canners' hostility, he believed, "simply because when the ethical principle is presented to the American people, the American people will respond." Wiley's fervent account of his encounter with the canners also provoked applause in the committee hearing room.[8]

The canners' convention had proceeded to adopt a resolution. In it they expressed their confidence that no form of food product marketed was "so pure and free from adulteration" as canned fruits and vegetables, asserted their conviction that the ending of adulteration would benefit both consumers and canners, objected to the conflict in state laws, and petitioned the Congress to enact a pure-food law both "stringent and capable of rigid enforcement."[9]

The conversion of the canners had come not so suddenly as in Wiley's dramatic account. Vegetable and fruit canners did not rely on preservatives nearly so much as did processors of jellies and meats. The two regional associations that the chief chemist addressed had met in Columbus a year earlier and had then sent the Congress a resolution favoring a national food law only slightly less urgent in tone than the 1906 version adopted after Wiley's appearance among them. His apprehensions of danger on that occasion seem excessive, or at least overdramatized at the House hearing.[10]

Later the National Food Manufacturers' Association sought to subvert Wiley's allies, converted or confirmed at the canners' assembly, achieving at least a degree of success. Most canners, however, remained wedded to the mainline bill. Wiley's staunchest supporters in food processing seem to have been elements of the retail grocery trade and food processors striving to avoid preservatives by using top grade raw materials under sanitary conditions. These two groups were represented in the committee of six that importuned President Roosevelt in February 1905 to take a public stand favoring a strong pure-food law. A. B. Fallinger came from the National Association of Retail Grocers, and Sebastian Mueller was an official of the H. J. Heinz Company.[11]

Another sector from which Wiley won allies posed nearly as many problems as did the ranks of business. Such difficulties might, at first

---

[8] *Hearings . . . on The Pure Food Bills*, 319.

[9] *Ibid.*, 93.

[10] Keuchel, "The Development of the Canning Industry," 202–7; Arthur I. Judge, "The Development of the Present National Organization[,] The National Canners' Association," in Arthur I. Judge, ed., *A History of the Canning Industry by Its Most Prominent Men* (Baltimore, 1914), 68–75.

[11] *Cong. Record*, 59 Cong. 1 ses., 2760; Sullivan, *Our Times*, vol. 2, 530. Henry Heinz himself was perhaps the most outspoken and unwavering supporter of a strong law in the food processing industry. See Robert C. Alberts, *The Good Provider: H. J. Heinz and His 57 Varieties* (Boston, 1973), 171–76.

glance, seem paradoxical, for it might be assumed that officials who ran food and drug control programs in the several states would be counted among Wiley's early and faithful supporters. Not so. The members of the National Association of State Dairy and Food Departments, organized in 1897, proved to be a varied lot. Political appointees, thus attuned to the economic circumstances of their states, the commissioners had perspectives that ranged from a high degree of friendliness toward food processors to a zeal for severe controls that surpassed Wiley's own. Princes in their own fiefdoms, some state officials may also have been jealous of Wiley's rising stature and fearful of the impact of a national law.[12]

The national association had sent delegates to the pure-food congresses at the end of the nineteenth century, but their 1898 convention ended in a tie vote on a resolution favoring a national law. For the next several years the convention did resolve in favor of a national law, but the majority, led by officials from Ohio and Illinois, opposed the mainline bill in Congress, preferring instead a proposal that kept enforcement authority out of Wiley's hands.[13]

Prime mover in bringing the organization of state commissioners into the alliance espousing the Hepburn bill was a vigorous young food and drug administrator from Kentucky, Robert McDowell Allen. Trained at the state college in Lexington as a chemist and at Transylvania in law, Allen had been appointed in 1901 secretary of food control by M. A. Scovell, director of the Agricultural Experiment Station and an admirer of Wiley. In 1902 Scovell sent Allen, then twenty-two, to Washington to meet the chief chemist, then fifty-seven. The two became friends, and in 1903, during Allen's seven-year tenure as secretary of the National Association of State Dairy and Food Departments, he arranged for Wiley to address the organization's convention. The chief chemist's explanations and general lobbying eased suspicions of him, and the convention resolved to urge the Congress to pass a pure-food bill. The motion did not mention the Hepburn bill, but neither did it specify an anti-Wiley alternative. Instead, it directed the association's executive committee to work toward enactment of a law. Under Allen's influence, the committee endorsed the major provisions Wiley favored. At the next year's convention, the state commissioners explicitly voted support for the Hepburn-McCumber bill.[14]

[12] *Hearings . . . on The Pure Food Bills*, 51, 211.

[13] Anderson, *The Health of a Nation*, 125, 131, 141, 146, 158.

[14] *Ibid.*, 158, 164–65; Wiley, *An Autobiography*, 176; Margaret Ripley Wolfe, "The Agricultural Experiment Station and Food and Drug Control: Another Look at Kentucky Progressivism, 1898–1916," *Filson Club History Quarterly* 49 (1975), 323–38.

A pure-food congress held jointly in St. Louis with the state commissioners' meeting was Allen's brainchild. Highly publicized, the congress featured lurid exhibitions of adulteration, brand names not omitted, and forthright speeches, three by Wiley himself. This increased public awareness of the pure-food issue but lost the pending bill some business support. Allen had secured financial backing for the congress from the straight-whiskey interests. Scovell chaired a committee considering whiskey that, despite Warwick Hough's testimony in behalf of the rectifiers, ruled that only straight whiskey could be considered pure.[15]

As the critical Fifty-ninth Congress loomed, Allen took the initiative, with Wiley's help, in lining up the committee to call upon the president to ask his support in securing a law. Allen himself headed the six-member group, which included two state food commissioners, Horace Ankeny of Ohio and J. B. Noble of Connecticut.[16]

In contrast with the state food commissioners, the state agricultural chemists had been unified in support of a rigorous bill throughout the final decade of effort that led to the law. The Association of Official Agricultural Chemists, indeed, had, in the mid-1890s, reinvigorated the lapsed consideration in Congress of the pure-food issue. In 1897 the AOAC had established a committee on food standards, with Wiley its initial chairman, which began work immediately, issuing its first formal report in 1900. Thus, this work was well advanced when the Congress in 1902, as part of the agricultural appropriations act, made this committee official advisers to the secretary of agriculture in setting food standards "for the guidance of various states and courts of justice." During the final years of effort to secure the law, the secretary issued circulars announcing standards for a wide range of foods, including grains, syrup, honey, wine, vinegar, fruit, salt, vegetable oils, and flavoring extracts.[17]

Beginning with the mainline House bill of 1899, the secretary of agriculture was given authority to establish standards. Bills differed as to

[15] Ibid., 331–32; Anderson, The Health of a Nation, 164–65; Sullivan, Our Times, vol. 2, 522–25; High and Coppin, "Wiley, Whiskey, and Strategic Behavior."

[16] Sullivan, Our Times, vol. 2, 530; Anderson, The Health of a Nation, 173; Hearings . . . on The Pure Food Bills, 203–4.

[17] Proceedings of the Fourteenth Annual Convention of the Association of Official Agricultural Chemists, . . . 1897, Department of Agriculture, Division of Chemistry, Bulletin 51 (Washington, 1898), 117–40; Proceedings of the Fifteenth Annual Convention of the Association of Official Agricultural Chemists, . . . 1898, Division of Chemistry, Bulletin 56 (Washington, 1899), 128–29; Proceedings of the Seventeenth Annual Convention of the Association of Official Agricultural Chemists, . . . 1900, Division of Chemistry Bulletin 62 (Washington, 1901), 146–48; Anderson, The Health of a Nation, 152–53; White, "AOAC Methods of Analysis," 331–32; Lepper, "The Evolution of Food Standards and the Role of the A.O.A.C.," 135–38.

whom he was required to consult, but the AOAC was almost always included. State chemists, paid in part with federal funds and not so vulnerable to political pressures as were state commissioners, naturally favored writing into a pure-food law the kind of standard-setting mechanisms in which they were engaged, and which had been given the stamp of official authority in the year-by-year appropriation acts.[18]

Some state food commissioners resented the monopoly that the state chemists had gained in advising on standards. The National Association of State Dairy and Food Departments formed its own standards committee in 1901, which criticized some of Secretary Wilson's standards, defined with AOAC help, as "faulty." Early in 1906 the association convention resolved to seek "harmony of action" between commissioners and chemists by asking Wilson to let the commissioners' standards committee share with the AOAC committee in making recommendations. The secretary replied that the appropriations act did not permit this, but he diplomatically invited the commissioners' committee to attend his next meeting with the AOAC committee. Tensions remained unresolved by the time the 1906 act received congressional approval.[19]

State chemists had pioneered in exposing fraud, and they continued such revelations. Sometimes their publications impressed both congressmen and public. Edwin F. Ladd of North Dakota serves as a stellar example. Born in Maine, trained at the Agricultural Experiment Station in Geneva, New York, Ladd went to North Dakota in 1890. His analyses showed processed foods to be more adulterated there than elsewhere, North Dakota serving as a dumping ground for shoddy products. Emphasizing health hazards less than the state's subservience to eastern economic interests, Ladd secured a strict pure-food law in 1901 and aroused support for its enforcement. When a traveling attorney for the National Biscuit Company asked him how a company could remain in business when confronted with such divergent state laws, Ladd "slammed his hands down angrily on the arms of his chair and said, 'By God, no east-

[18] *Ibid.*, 138–40. In the Fifty-sixth Congress, Brosius introduced H.R. 2561 on December 7, 1899, then later a revised version, H. R. 9677, which contained the standard-setting authority given to the secretary of agriculture. He was to exercise this power with the advice of a board composed of the department's chief chemist; the chairman of the AOAC food-standards committee; five physicians selected by the president, including one each from the medical departments of the army, the navy, and the Marine Hospital Service, and two at large; and five other experts selected by the secretary by reason of their "attainments in physiological chemistry, hygiene, commerce, and manufacture." See *Cong. Record*, 56 Cong. 1 ses., 151, 3006; *The Adulteration, Misbranding, and Imitation of Foods, Etc., in the District of Columbia, Etc.*, 56 Cong. 1 ses., House Report 1426 (1900), 4–5.

[19] *American Food Journal* 1 (February 15, 1906), 16; (March 15, 1906), 14–15; 2 (August 15, 1907), 14–15.

ern lawyer is going to tell me what we can eat out here in North Dakota!'" Ladd sent county newspapers details of adulteration, and his
stature rose when an association of eastern food processors sued him for
libel. The North Dakota poet laureate recast Ladd's chemical discoveries
in verse.

> There's aniline
> In the soup tureen
> And borax thick on the gay sardine.[20]

Ladd worked hand-in-glove with Wiley in the AOAC and, as state
commissioner, formed part of the left wing in the National Association
of State Dairy and Food Departments, which favored a stringent national law. At the St. Louis convention he gave, almost certainly at Allen's invitation, a sensational address on adulteration. In 1904 also Ladd
published a short article in a magazine called *What to Eat* containing
shocking evidence about what not to eat in North Dakota. A lot of what
passed for catsup turned out to be dyed pumpkin. Nor had Ladd found
a can labeled potted turkey or potted chicken to contain a "determinable
quantity" of either of these fowl.[21]

Such startling examples caught Porter McCumber's eye, and he cited
his state's food commissioner on the Senate floor. As R. James Kane has
observed, McCumber had taught himself the same lesson that Ladd had
learned, that the Populist conviction of a conspiracy among outside interests to do the farmer in continued to concern North Dakota rural
residents. Unlike Wiley, who blamed adulteration largely on fear and
the threat of competition, Ladd, when he spoke for home consumption,
alluded to greedy vested interests intent on subverting public well-
being. Although neither a Populist nor a Progressive, McCumber
shared Ladd's rhetoric of a clandestine conspiracy among the moneyed
interests, of which food adulteration was an especially egregious consequence.[22]

Indeed, in the twentieth-century climax of the effort to secure a pure-
food law, almost all the congressional leaders in that struggle came from
agricultural states west of the Mississippi River. Senator Henry Hans-

[20] R. James Kane, "Populism, Progressivism, and Pure Food," *Agric Hist* 38 (1964), 162–
64; Fred B. Linton, "Ladd of North Dakota," *Food, Drug, Cosmetic Law J* 7 (1952), 314–21;
William Cahn, *Out of the Cracker Barrel: The Nabisco Story from Animal Crackers to Zuzus*
(New York, 1969), 120.

[21] Ladd, "Adulterated Food Products and Food Studies," *North Dakota Agricultural Station Bulletin 63* (1904), 525–29; *What To Eat* article cited in *Cong. Record*, 58 Cong. 3 ses.,
261.

[22] *Ibid.*; Kane, "Populism, Progressivism, and Pure Food," 164–66.

brough also represented North Dakota. Senator Weldon B. Heyburn came from Idaho. William P. Hepburn, who carried the principal burden in the House, was an Iowan. None of these three had been Populists, nor were they in any thorough sense Progressives. On many economic issues they took conservative stands. Like Ladd, Kane suggests, these congressional leaders of the pure-food cause came from an area continuing to believe "that governmental agencies should be made available for the redressing of grievances springing out of economic injustice." The West harbored long nourished feelings of sectional frustration. The power of the industrial interests these westerners hated had little influence in their own state legislatures. Besides a sense of conviction and an awareness of the absence of political risk, the pure-food leaders from agrarian states realized that voters would think favorably of a campaign in behalf of consumers that was being so adamantly opposed in Congress by eastern Republicans. Nor did Great Plains legislators have to be concerned about opposition from whiskey rectifiers, patent-medicine makers, or proprietors of "bogus drug mills," since in the western territory such entrepreneurs were few and far between.[23]

When Ladd presented his diatribe against adulterators at the St. Louis pure-food congress, he sparked the interest of other groups distinctly different from provincial farmers of the west. Letters of commendation came from representatives of the General Federation of Women's Clubs and the National Consumers' League, organizations that were urban, middle-class, and national.[24]

In that same year, 1904, the president of the General Federation of Women's Clubs, which had been established in 1890, signaled a change in the focus of club women's interest. Speaking at the annual convention, Sarah Platt Decker informed the membership: "Dante is dead. He has been dead for several centuries, and I think it is time we dropped the study of his inferno and turned attention to our own." Henceforth, polite culture should be replaced by concern for problems plaguing women's contemporary everyday world.[25]

Throughout the nineteenth century, indeed, women had organized to seek through political pressure remedies for injustices they observed in the social order. Their efforts had been mainly local and aimed at abuses within the domestic sphere. By the early twentieth century, however, government had begun to assume some of the responsibilities that had traditionally been considered the domain of women's voluntary en-

[23] *Ibid.*, 166; *Chicago Tribune*, May 30, 1906.
[24] Kane, "Populism, Progressivism, and Pure Food," 164.
[25] Samuel P. Hays, *The Response to Industrialism, 1885–1914* (Chicago, 1957), 73.

deavor. Women recognized and supported this change. The food and drug campaign formed a central element in this trend, the "domestication of politics," the shifting of major policy obligations from the private to the public sector. During these crucial transition years, as Kathryn Kish Sklar has observed, "women's political culture matured and . . . entered the mainstream of American politics," as many women "experienced a congruence between the search for power over their own lives and their search for influence in society as a whole."[26]

In 1891 Senator Paddock had received a stirring memorial from the Women's National Industrial League urging "stringent" laws to protect working-class homes from debased foods and "vile" patent medicines. "In the household, even the bread purchased contains alum, inferior and musty flour, and often mashed potatoes and white sand." Mrs. Winslow's Soothing Syrup had "killed thousands of children," and other quack medicines had turned sane citizens into "idiots" confined to lunatic asylums. Seven years later, after the first pure-food congress, Alex Wedderburn had urged women to form "Pure Food Clubs in every neighborhood" to lobby the cause with their congressmen.[27]

Harvey Wiley added women's clubs to his lecture itineraries. His secretary later remembered her "boss," "attired in Prince Albert and a silk topper somewhat out of date because it had been purchased in dear old London," setting forth to give some women's group the latest news from the pure-food front. Early in 1903 Wiley had besought the president of the General Federation of Women's Clubs to get her membership and their male friends to deluge the Senate with letters demanding action on the food bill that had passed the House.[28]

The bachelor chief chemist could be patronizing about woman's role. "I fully realize," he wrote for publication, "the peculiar function of woman in social life. I know she is not intended by nature, by taste, nor by education, as a rule, to follow the pursuits which are reserved for men." However, Wiley could not see that woman was "to be excluded from a participation, in an organized way, in the great problems which look to the uplifting of man."[29]

[26] Paula Baker, "The Domestication of Politics: Women and American Political Society, 1780–1920," *American Historical Review* 89 (1984), 620–47; Kathryn Kish Sklar, "Organized Womanhood: Archival Sources on Women and Progressive Reform," *Journal of American History* 75 (1988), 176–83, quotations at 176 and 177; Rima D. Apple, *Mothers and Medicine: A Social History of Infant Feeding, 1890–1950* (Madison, WI, 1987), 98–99.

[27] *Memorial of the Woman's National Industrial League of America*, 51 Cong. 2 ses., Sen. Misc. Doc. 70; *Pure Food Mag* 1 (1898), 3.

[28] Anderson, *The Health of a Nation*, 145, 169, 170; Mary T. Read, "When We Were Very Young," *Food and Drug Review* 21 (January 1937), 5–7.

[29] *Annals of the American Academy of Political and Social Science* 28 (September 1906), 92–93.

In the pure-food cause the chief chemist found federation members "enthusiastic, hard working, persistent and effective," indeed, "the most efficient organization now existing." Their pure-food committee sought to educate the federation membership and women generally through making talks, presenting exhibits, and distributing literature. Wiley provided examples of adulterated food for the exhibits and prepared a popular bulletin, *Some Forms of Food Adulteration and Simple Methods for Their Detection*, which contained easily performed tests by which housewives could turn their own kitchens into laboratories. The committee also canvassed the condition of pure-food legislation in all the states and set their members at work to strengthen laws and intensify enforcement. The committee especially kept pressure on the national Congress by petitions and "incessant newspaper warfare" so as "to waken the public conscience to the ethical questions involved in this fight for the honest label." When critical votes neared, the pure-food committee triggered telegrams by each state federation president to every member of her state's delegation in the relevant chamber of the Congress.[30]

The most ardent and active federation champion of the pure-food cause had been converted by Wiley himself. In his endless round of speech making, the chief chemist had gone to Cranford, New Jersey, in 1903. Some weeks earlier Secretary Wilson had received a request from Alice Lakey, president of the Village Improvement Association, that he send someone to speak about pure food. Wiley's journey to Cranford proved significant both for his campaign and for Lakey's career. Trained as a concert singer, Lakey had been forced by ill health to forego this option, and she had come home to live with her father. Yet she had energy to spare. Wiley's speech raised her righteous indignation about adulteration and quickened her interest in a pure-food law. Moreover, Wiley as a person appealed to her as the type of leader in whose ranks she could enlist with enthusiasm. Armed with information and advice from the chief chemist, Lakey undertook to speak to women's groups all over the country. She made a quilt of flannels dyed with the same

---

[30] *Ibid.*, 82, 98–103; Mary I. Wood, *The History of the General Federation of Women's Clubs for the First Twenty-Two Years of Its Organization* (New York, 1912), 210–11, 216–17; Anderson, *The Health of a Nation*, 179; *Some Forms of Food Adulteration and Simple Methods for Their Detection*, Department of Agriculture, Bureau of Chemistry, Bulletin 100 (Washington, 1906). Simple home chemical tests for detecting some food adulterants had been published occasionally for some years, such as Thomas Hoskins's 1861 book, *What We Eat*. Spying out adulterants had also been an aspect of the popular microscopy craze. See "The Microscope and Its Marvels," *Littell Living Age* 28 (1851), 352; C. M. Force, "The Detection of Adulteration in Food," *American Monthly Microscopical Journal* 2 (1881), 1, 122, 161; 3 (1882), 1, 21; John Harley Warner, " 'Exploring the Inner Labyrinths of Creation': Popular Microscopy in Nineteenth-Century America," *Journal of the History of Medicine and Allied Sciences* 37 (1982), 25.

risky aniline colors used to brighten canned foods. She convinced the New Jersey State Federation of Women's Clubs to endorse the pure-food bill Wiley wished enacted. She persuaded the General Federation to create its pure-food committee. Lakey also carried her message to the National Consumers' League, and became chair of its food adulteration committee. It was Lakey who complimented Ladd on his St. Louis oration.[31]

Through her energy, enthusiasm, and ability, Lakey rose to a place among the inner circle of strategists in planning how to lobby most effectively for a law. Wiley kept her informed about the state of the campaign. When Robert Allen took his committee to seek President Roosevelt's open endorsement of the pure-food bill, Alice Lakey went along, the one woman among the committee's six members.[32]

Women other than federation members favored food legislation. The Women's Christian Temperance Union had sent delegates to the 1898 pure-food congress. Their interest in a law increased when, early in the new century, both medical and popular journals began to expose the unlabeled alcoholic content of "boozers" and "bracers," patent medicines that had an especially lively sale in areas "dry" by local option. Even the widely sold women's remedy, Lydia E. Pinkham's Vegetable Compound, contained 20.6 percent alcohol. Wiley regularly furnished information on Bureau of Chemistry analyses to Martha M. Allen, in charge of the WCTU campaign against alcoholic nostrums. The chief chemist's rejection of advice to remove control of liquor from the pure-food bill, in order to end the powerful lobbying by the rectifiers, owed something to his fear of losing WCTU support.[33]

In the final stages of the campaign, another female voice, notable among the ranks of women, spoke up urging the law's passage. Women should let the Congress know, said Jane Addams in Chicago, how determined they were to protect their families from adulterated food.[34]

If women, in the early years of the new century, had developed a network capable of bringing pressure on the Congress in behalf of a pure-food law, so too had a largely male professional group, America's

[31] Helen T. Finneran, "Lakey, Alice," in Edward T. James, Janet Wilson James, and Paul S. Boyer, eds., *Notable American Women, 1607–1950*, 3 vols. (Cambridge, MA, 1971), vol. 2, 360–61; Alice Lakey, "The Pure Food Law: What Has It Accomplished?" *Outlook* 88 (1908), 260–64; William D. McKenzie, "The Consumers' League and Its Work for Pure Food," *American Pure Food and Drug Journal*, undated clipping provided by Helen Finneran Ulibarri, 8–12; Anderson, *The Health of a Nation*, 169, 170, 179; Sullivan, *Our Times*, vol. 2, 521–22; Kane, "Populism, Progressivism, and Pure Food," 164; Maurice Natenberg, *The Legacy of Doctor Wiley* (Chicago, 1957), 35.

[32] Anderson, *The Health of a Nation*, 169, 170; Sullivan, *Our Times*, vol. 2, 530.

[33] Anderson, *The Health of a Nation*, 156, 179.

[34] *Ibid.*, 179.

physicians. Like Alice Lakey of the General Federation of Women's Clubs, a key figure in the revived American Medical Association worked hand-in-glove with Harvey Wiley.

Scientific and economic imperatives underlay the effort beginning in 1900 to transform the AMA. Founded in 1846, it had not been well attuned to its potential for service during the late nineteenth century. The organization had not assumed leadership in applying the consequences of the bacteriological revolution to either American medical education or practice. At the turn of the century, for every doctor entering the profession from a sound school, a score of others got their diplomas from transient proprietary ventures. As a result, competition grew keener and incomes remained low, during a period of constantly increasing inflation. Such a situation served the public health abominably.[35]

In this climate outright quackery flourished. Not only were physician critiques of over-the-counter nostrums infrequent, many doctors had themselves been converted by shrewd promoters into sales agents for the insidious pseudoethical preparations whose advertising flooded the columns of medical magazines, not excluding the *Journal of the American Medical Association*.[36]

On this front, occasional criticism had led AMA leaders to reform policy, but never altogether or for long. Publishing deficits led to relaxation in standards. In 1905 *JAMA* did not have as many disreputable ads as many medical journals harbored, but this was only faint praise. Out of some 250 journals, only a few could not be "bribed into defrauding their readers" by accepting specious advertising. Some journals were "owned openly or covertly" by the men who marketed pseudoethical specialties.[37]

In 1905 the American Medical Association revived its policy of barring

---

[35] Kaufman, *American Medical Education*, 84–85, 116–23; James G. Burrow, *AMA: Voice of American Medicine* (Baltimore: 1963), 8–11; Burrow, *Organized Medicine in the Progressive Era: The Move toward Monopoly* (Baltimore, 1977), 31–51; Starr, *The Social Transformation of American Medicine*, 84–85, 116–23; Kenneth M. Ludmerer, *Learning to Heal: The Development of American Medical Education* (New York, 1985), 3–101.

[36] Young, *The Toadstool Millionaires*, 159–61, 207. To judge by references in the *Index-Catalogue of the Library of the Surgeon-General's Office[,] United States Army* (First series, 16 vols., Washington, 1880–1895; Second series, 21 vols., 1896–1916; Third series, 10 vols., 1918–1932), physician critique in medical journals during the late nineteenth century aimed at the adulteration of foods and legitimate medicines was even less frequent than the rare condemnation of patent medicines. Sanitarians in public-health journals and state health officials in annual reports outdid physicians in the extent of such exposure. Examples of physician critique are G. F. Hanson, "Some Examples of Drug and Food Adulteration," *Pacific Medical Journal* 39 (1896), 545–50, and Lee K. Frankel, "Food Adulteration and the Pure Food Law," *J Franklin Inst* 143 (1897), 241–67.

[37] Young, *The Toadstool Millionaires*, 207–8; Burrow, *AMA*, 71–74.

nostrum advertising from the *Journal*, while mounting a forthright attack upon this unhealthy imposition upon both physicians and patients. In order to distinguish between "ethical" proprietaries of merit and worthless pseudoethicals, the AMA established a Council on Pharmacy and Chemistry to test such medicines. Those passing muster would be described in a forthcoming volume, *New and Nonofficial Remedies*. Those failing to make the grade would be exposed in *JAMA*'s pages. Harvey Wiley, in speaking to the AMA the year before, had made clear the value of distinguishing between meritorious and fraudulent proprietary remedies. Now he signed the council's statement of purpose when it was initially announced. Both he and his drug deputy, Lyman Kebler, served as council members, using Bureau of Chemistry laboratories to run some of the tests. Before long the new council also began to analyze and *JAMA* to report on patent medicines sold directly to the public.[38]

Housecleaning in the *Journal*'s advertising columns formed but one small part of an extensive rebuilding of AMA structure and revamping of policy. In 1901 the association adopted a new constitution, creating a House of Delegates composed of representatives of state societies, thus linking local and national concerns. Simultaneously, a campaign to remodel state and local societies began to strive for both improved public health and enhancement of the physician's status through political action. In the states, political pressure raised the bars of admission to the profession, reducing competititon and elevating quality. On the national level the AMA's effort to secure a federal Department of Health did not succeed. The profession's new political consciousness, however, and its well-organized machinery for making its weight felt, provided Harvey Wiley significant support in the pure-food and drug campaign.[39]

A Cincinnati gynecologist, Charles A. L. Reed, had served as AMA president during the remodeling of its structure, and it was Reed who chaired the association's Committee on Medical Legislation during the last two years of congressional consideration of the food and drug bill. Reed's three-man committee was tied in with a much larger national committee concerned with legislation, made up of delegates from state medical societies. The two together proved to be an efficient mechanism

---

[38] *Ibid.*, 74–75; "Council on Pharmacy and Chemistry," *J Amer Med Assoc* 44 (1905), 719–21; "Report of the Council on Pharmacy and Chemistry," *ibid.* 46 (1906), 896–97; J. H. Long, "Why the Work of the Council on Pharmacy and Chemistry is Necessary," *ibid.* 46 (1906), 1344–45; George H. Simmons, "The Commercial Domination of Therapeutics and the Movement for Reform," *ibid.* 48 (1907), 1645–53; Wiley, "Federal Control of Drugs," presented to AMA Materia Medica Section, June 7, 1904, in 1903-4-5 volume, Miscellaneous Papers, Bureau of Chemistry Records, RG 97, National Archives.

[39] Burrow, *Organized Medicine in the Progressive Era*, 14–28.

for conveying information about legislation from the scene of congressional action down to the grass roots, and also for triggering resolutions and letters to Congress from all parts of the nation.[40]

In 1904 the committeemen wielded their lobbying weapon in behalf of the Hepburn bill, which the House had passed but on which the Senate seemed disinclined to act. Delegates from the states wrote to Senator Heyburn and to representatives and senators from their districts and states, expressing interest in the pure-food bill. They also urged medical societies back home to pass resolutions and mail them to Heyburn, along with local clippings such resolutions might generate. Dr. Reed was cheered by the magnitude of the response. Physicians from twenty-seven states wrote favoring the bill, and Heyburn had the letters and petitions printed in a Senate document. On the Senate floor Heyburn referred to three thousand letters and hundreds of medical society petitions received during his vain effort to gain consideration for his measure.[41]

Through the disappointing remainder of the Fifty-eighth Congress, Reed kept in touch with Heyburn and Wiley. As the Fifty-ninth Congress neared, *JAMA*, while anticipating success for a pure-food law, noted: "We shall be compelled to put in sleepless nights to be sure the measure is not passed in emasculated and deformed shape." Reed promised Wiley to "do anything that we can to help the cause along," even offering to bring the entire membership of the AMA's national legislative council to a Senate hearing. When no hearing was scheduled, Reed sent a delegation to meet with Heyburn and assure him of the association's continuing support. *JAMA* kept doctors informed of the maneuvering.[42]

Wiley sensed another useful way in which the might of organized physicians could be brought to bear. When Robert Allen's committee saw President Roosevelt for the second time, in November 1905, Dr. Charles A. L. Reed went along.[43]

[40] Burrow, *AMA*, 54–62; *Adulteration or Misbranding of Foods or Drugs, Etc.*, Letters and Petitions . . . Urging the Passage of . . . H.R. 6295 . . . , 58 Cong. 2 ses., Senate Doc. 248 (1904).

[41] Burrow, *AMA*, 75–76; "Report of the Committee on Legislation," *J Amer Med Assoc* 42 (1904), 1577–79; *Adulteration or Misbranding of Foods or Drugs, Etc.*, 58 Cong. 2 ses., Senate Doc. 248; *Cong. Record*, 58 Cong. 3 ses., 128.

[42] Burrow, *AMA*, 76–78; "The Progress of Pure Food Laws," *J Amer Med Assoc* 45 (1905), 858; "The Pure Food Question," *ibid.* 1090; "National Legislative Council," *ibid.* 46 (1906), 210–15; Reed to Wiley, October 25, 1905, and George Simmons to Lewis S. McMurtry, October 16, 1905, Bureau of Chemistry, Incoming Correspondence, NA 97, National Archives.

[43] Sullivan, *Our Times*, vol. 2, 530.

Theodore Roosevelt had come home from the bad beef and the great glory of Cuba—this war has been called TR's "finest hour"—to the governorship of New York. Then, accepting the role of William McKinley's running mate, Roosevelt, both welcoming the vice presidency as stepping stone and fearing it as dead end, was rescued from the possible latter fate by McKinley's mad assassin.[44]

Soon after assuming the presidency, late in 1901, Roosevelt had occasion to get fiercely angry at Wiley for speaking out publicly against a policy the president favored. The chief chemist, as an expert on the nation's sugar production, was called to testify by a committee of the Congress. In forceful language Wiley asserted that plans for reduced duties on sugar from Cuba, which the president desired, would bring "the complete destruction" of American producers. Free Cuban sugar, the chief chemist told the committee, choosing an unfortunate metaphor, would eventuate in "rendering the patient unconscious, and probably producing immediate death, or at best leaving the patient with a clot on the brain, paralyzing at least half of his body, and making the sorry remainder of his life a burden to himself and his friends." Reminding Wiley of the president's proposal, one congressman asked the chief chemist, provoking general laughter, "Do you contemplate remaining in the Agricultural Department?" Indeed, Roosevelt, furious at Wiley's challenge, sought his dismissal, but Secretary Wilson kept this from happening. For the rest of his life, however, Wiley thought that this initial episode had put him in the president's bad graces. There were other likely reasons for their strained relations. From his college days, Roosevelt had held scientific research in some disdain. The president, who courted the press out of "an unquenchable craving for attention and deference," also may well have become irritated at Wiley's high favor among journalists and widespread publicity. Wiley's sister, upon meeting the editor of the *San Jose Mercury*, remarked that she had seen mention in its pages of her brother. The editor replied: "Why, Dr. Wiley is the greatest man in the U.S. & is almost as well known as Pres. Roosevelt."[45]

For several years Roosevelt took no observable notice of the intensi-

[44] John Blum, *The Republican Roosevelt*, 2nd ed. (Cambridge, MA, 1977), 2.

[45] Anderson, *The Health of a Nation*, 100–101; Wiley, *The History of a Crime against the Food Law* (Washington, 1929), 270–74; *Reciprocity with Cuba*, Hearings before Committee on Ways and Means, 57 Cong. 1 ses., House Doc. 535 (1902), 474–519, quotation at 503; John Milton Cooper, Jr., *The Warrior and the Priest: Woodrow Wilson and Theodore Roosevelt* (Cambridge, MA, 1983), 9, 28–29, 65, 69–70, quotation at 69; Elizabeth Corbett to Wiley, February 4, 1906, Harvey W. Wiley Papers, Manuscript Division, Library of Congress.

fying pure-food campaign. Perhaps, as Samuel Hopkins Adams surmised in retrospect, it had not yet become political enough for him to consider. What the president labored at, nonetheless, created an environment of crucial importance to the pure-food cause. He sought to establish his control over the Republican party, many of whose stalwart members viewed his ascendancy with great alarm. Roosevelt proceeded cautiously prior to his election in his own right in 1904. "I am no longer a political accident," he then said to his wife, and began to act more boldly, a masterful strategist at the profession of politics. He gradually developed his policies and unveiled his apologia for them.[46]

Fundamentally conservative, Roosevelt took for granted and sought to sustain the existing order of power and privilege in society. He embraced the benefits to the nation of the industrial revolution and found gigantic economic structures inevitable and useful. The power of trusts, however, permitted their managers to misbehave. When this occurred, although countervailing groups might offer opposition, only one agency possessed superior power to punish in the public interest. That was the national government, centering especially in the president himself. Such high-level policing would help achieve a "square deal" for all Americans, especially for farmers, laborers, and small businessmen who were straight-dealing, efficient, ingenious, industrious, and moral. Roosevelt, like Wiley, made his case in moral terms. "Every new social relation," the president said, "begets a new type of wrong-doing—of sin, to use an old-fashioned word—and many years always elapse before society is able to turn this sin into a crime which can be effectively punished by law." Roosevelt saw himself as occupying a wholesome middle ground between the "lunatic fringe" and the "selfish rich."[47]

The most sinful corporate giants of his time, Roosevelt believed, were railroad holding companies. Transportation, he said, lay at the root of all the industrial success of the preceding half century. Yet the railroad combines had not played fair for all shippers, conniving with industrial trusts—for example, the meat-packing companies—for secret lower rates. In 1902 Roosevelt initiated an antitrust case against the Northern Securities Company, a western railroad network formed the year before with J. P. Morgan's help, and two years later the Supreme Court reversed its stand, taken nine years earlier, that the Sherman Antitrust Act did not apply to holding companies, and validated the government's charges. This victory encouraged Roosevelt to launch cases against

[46] Interview with Samuel Hopkins Adams, April 5, 1955; Blum, *The Republican Roosevelt*, 37–107; Sullivan, *Our Times*, vol. 2, 460.

[47] Cooper, *The Warrior and the Priest*, xii, 33–34, 65–67, 83–84; Blum, *The Republican Roosevelt*, 60–61, 109.

other monopolies—including the "beef trust"—whose practices he deemed sinful.[48]

The president, however, desired a more continuous policing of monopolies, with more precise rules and powers, than individual court actions would accomplish. As a first major step, Roosevelt proposed that a new law be enacted giving rate-fixing and other powers over the railroads to the Interstate Commerce Commission. The president accorded top priority through two Congresses to converting this bill, managed in the House by William P. Hepburn, into law.[49]

Roosevelt had not yet achieved this significant victory when he sent his annual message to the Congress on December 5, 1905. Arguments urging enactment of the railroad legislation dominated the document. Other matters, however, received some attention: the need to economize in government, to achieve elasticity in the monetary system, to make elections honest, to place restrictions on immigration, to establish a national park at Yellowstone. Included also, sandwiched between discussions of the desirability of revising copyright law and the necessity of controlling smoke emission in the national capital—and occupying less space than either of these—came three sentences in which Roosevelt recommended passage of the food and drug bill.[50]

These sentences were the result of a year's activity. Senator Heyburn had written to Roosevelt a year before requesting the president to mention the bill in his annual message, but he had not done so. Then in February 1905 Robert Allen's committee had called upon the president. Roosevelt had listened sympathetically, promised to inquire into the situation, and invited the delegation to come back in the fall. Over the summer he had talked with Wiley, with the noted organic chemist Ira Remsen of the Johns Hopkins University, and with his own physician. When the committee returned in November, Roosevelt informed its members that he had made up his mind to recommend the pure-food bill's enactment in his message to Congress. He added that, because of the "stubborn opposition," it would take more than his request to get the bill passed.[51]

The next month, in one short paragraph in a message printing out to nearly a hundred book-sized pages, Roosevelt fulfilled his promise to

[48] *Ibid.*, 57–58, 119–21; Northern Securities Company v. United States, 193 U.S. 197 (1904).

[49] Blum, *The Republican Roosevelt*, 73–105; Cooper, *The Warrior and the Priest*, 79–80.

[50] Roosevelt, *Presidential Addresses and State Papers*, 4 vols. (New York, 1970), vols. 3 and 4, 560–658, reference to food and drug bill at 637.

[51] Anderson, *The Health of a Nation*, 166; Sullivan, *Our Times*, vol. 2, 530–31; *Hearings on The Pure Food Bills*, 58 Cong. 1 ses., 203–4.

the informal committee representing state food officials, elements of business, women's clubs, and the medical profession, which Allen and Wiley had organized. The president advised the new Fifty-ninth Congress:

> I recommend that a law be enacted to regulate interstate commerce in misbranded and adulterated foods, drinks, and drugs. Such law would protect legitimate manufacture and commerce, and would tend to secure the health and welfare of the consuming public. Traffic in foodstuffs which have been debased or adulterated so as to injure health or to deceive purchasers should be forbidden.[52]

The Muckrakers

"The Pure-Food bill was rarely regarded anywhere as a measure of the first importance until within the past year or so," editorialized the *Nation* in June 1906. "But when its history began to be printed as a capital illustration of the Senate's treasons, stratagems, and spoils, that body began to take notice."[53] That message had been conveyed in the nation's magazines.

The growing number of urban consumers, cut off from personal experience with the origins of their food, had turned for counsel on everyday purchases to magazine journalism, both in its reading matter and its advertising. During the 1890s established elite journals were joined by popular magazines selling for a dime. Enterprising publishers sought out and arranged for articles and stories entertainingly written and amply illustrated, which would appeal to urban middle-class readers. Circulation trebled in scarcely more than half a decade. Early in the new century some of these magazines began to sound a new alarming tone. They began to warn their readers about the dangers of adulteration, casting suspicion even on products recently advertised in their own columns. They also began to question the integrity of political leaders on all levels, charging corrupt alliances between businessmen and legislators. Such exposure eroded the trust that the middle class had developed in its economic and political institutions and made its members amenable to voices calling for reform. The leadership of American thought, observed the philosopher William James, was leaving the universities and entering the ten-cent magazines. The matter of food and drug safety

---

[52] Roosevelt, *Presidential Addresses and State Papers*, vol. 3 and 4, 637.
[53] "The Year of the Food Law," *Nation* 82 (1906), 522–23.

became a significant segment in the issue-oriented politics that came to flourish in such an atmosphere.[54]

To some journalists, analyzing the anatomy of corruption, the Senate itself seemed its very heart and soul. Senators were elected by state legislatures, subservient to powerful local economic interests and not immune to pressure from national trade associations and trusts. Thus senators, to keep their seats, had to be beholden to these influential forces. Senate rules let them pay their obligations often without being too obvious, but journalists, tracking the course of real power up the governmental ladder, found clues as to interests that individual senators served. In time, adding the separate cases of subservience together, reporters reached a shocking total, which David Graham Phillips designated with one word, "treason." His "The Treason of the Senate" series ran in *Cosmopolitan* from March to November 1906.[55]

Treason was too weak a word, Phillips told his readers, "to characterize the situation in which the Senate is the eager, resourceful, indefatigable agency of interests as hostile to the American people as any invading army could be, and vastly more dangerous." Phillips sought to substantiate this charge with the factual explicitness and elaborate personal profiles characteristic of reform journalism. He linked specific senators to the interests that controlled them, cited instances of subservience, explained how Republican and Democratic senators had formed a "merger" to work in behalf of business bosses. Henry Cabot Lodge, one of Roosevelt's long-time friends, Phillips described as "the familiar coarse type of machine politician, disguised by the robe of the 'Gentleman Scholar.' " Nelson W. Aldrich, once wholesale grocer, now leader of the Senate, Phillips spoke of as the interests' "right arm," "the organizer of this treason." Crushing the pure-food bill was only one of the "public plunderers' " sins.

The public responded with enthusiasm to this new sensation, but the president reacted with outrage to what he deemed a drastically distorted

[54] Barkan, "Industry Invites Regulation"; Louis Filler, *Crusaders for American Liberalism*, new ed. (Yellow Springs, OH, 1950); Cornelius C. Regier, *The Era of the Muckrakers* (Chapel Hill, NC, 1932); Harold S. Wilson, *McClure's Magazine and the Muckrakers* (Princeton, 1970); Christopher P. Wilson, "The Rhetoric of Consumption: Mass-Market Magazines and the Demise of the Gentle Reader, 1880–1920," in Richard Wightman Fox and T. J. Jackson Lears, eds., *The Culture of Consumption: Critical Essays in American History, 1880–1980* (New York, 1983), 39–64; Richard L. McCormick, *From Realignment to Reform: Political Change in New York State, 1893–1910* (Ithaca, NY, 1981), 252–55; Norman Hapgood, *The Changing Years* (New York, 1930), 63.

[55] The Phillips series was published as a book, *The Treason of the Senate* (Stanford, CA, n.d.). Filler, *Crusaders for American Liberalism*, 246–58; Regier, *The Era of the Muckrakers*, 110–13; Wilson, *McClure's Magazine*, 226.

depiction of his collaborators in the enterprise of governance. Letting in "light and air" through investigative reporting was well and good, but the president drew the line at "sewer gas." He likened such erring journalists to "the Man with the Muck-rake" in John Bunyan's *Pilgrim's Progress*, who rejected a "celestial crown" to continue raking to himself "the filth of the floor." The disparaging term "muckraker" stuck.[56]

Prior to Phillips's sweeping charge of treason, the Senate had been rebuked in a milder way for its obstructionism with regard to food and drug control. Two articles in *World's Work* carried the burden of this attack. In May 1905 Edward Lowry described "The Senate Plot against Pure Food," opening with an episode from a House committee hearing considering the bill. An unidentified man entered the chamber and asked to be heard.[57]

"Whom do you represent?" the committee chairman asked him.

"The people," the man replied.

"What people?" the chairman asked incredulously.

"The people of the United States."

As his committee colleagues laughed, the chairman informed the uninvited visitor: "I am sorry that we can't spare you any time. We have a number of gentlemen here representing special interests affecting this bill, and we must devote what time we have to them."

Those special interests, Lowry went on, had chosen to stop the food and drug bill in the Senate, and this explained why twenty years of agitation had come to naught. On this measure of such great concern to the nation's welfare the public had not yet been sufficiently aroused. The battling had been "a clash of private interests." Opposition to the bill had been "masked," had "never come out into the open." Lowry sought to remove the disguise, to link obstructing senators with their interests. Lodge represented Massachusetts, which sold hake packed as codfish. Maine's senators wanted to protect that state's sardines, labeled as imported from France. New Jersey's senators supported canners who packed fruit with preservatives. Lowry could not explain the Senate leader's opposition: "just why Senator Aldrich held . . . [the bill] up this winter no one seems to know."

Aldrich's obstructionism, however, seemed clear to Henry Beach Needham, whose "Senate of Special Interests" preceded Phillips's first "treason" article by a month. After describing a very rare Senate speech

---

[56] Roosevelt, "Muck-rakers," in William Griffith, ed., *The Roosevelt Policy* (New York, 1919), 367–68; Filler, *Crusaders for American Liberalism*, 25–53.

[57] Edward Lowry, "The Senate Plot against Pure Food," *World's Work* 10 (1905), 6215–17.

by the Rhode Island senator, in which he condemned the pure-food bill as a threat to American liberty, Needham explained:

> The Senate knew that the wholesale grocers were strongly opposed to the bill, because, if it became law, they could not make two gallons or two pounds out of one gallon or one pound. The Senate knew that Senator Aldrich got his start in life in the wholesale grocery business. The Senate knew that ex-grocer Aldrich still retains an interest in a wholesale grocery in Providence. But senatorial courtesy would not permit Senator McCumber [in defending the bill] to speak of these things.

Like Lowry, Needham sought to link other senators with the special interests that determined their opposition to the bill, paying special heed to whiskey rectifiers. He explained in detail "tricks of the legislative game" by which obstructionists could win without revealing their hands.[58]

Despite their stance, so typical of muckraking journalism, neither Lowry nor Needham approached the white-hot searing flame of Phillips's rhetoric. Moderate as they were, these articles must have been those later credited by the *Nation* with turning the Senate toward action. Nor in their discussions of the food, drink, and drug industries, allegedly controlling the policy of certain senators, did these reporters get very specific about sins against society. Both journalists contented themselves with a general description of adulteration. Indeed, although the food-processing industry had developed its trusts, the muckrakers neglected them—with one stellar exception, the beef trust.[59] Food trusts were smaller, less powerful, less dramatic in their evil-doing than the gigantic combinations in transportation and oil. Occasionally the malefactions of one of them might form part of a broader study, as the Royal Baking Powder Company was revealed playing a conniving role during exposure of corruption in Missouri.[60] Food combines, as power units, however, received almost no attention.

The minimal amount of reporting that treated the nation's food supply tended either to praise its variety, quality, and safety—a posture of antimuckraking—or to expose and condemn its adulteration, focusing on the food and barely mentioning the processor. Edwin Ladd represented the most agitated wing of such commentary. Harvey Wiley, publishing in *Public Opinion* on "Fraud in Food Manufacture" and "Decep-

---

[58] Henry Beach Needham, "Senate of Special Interests," *World's Work* II (1906), 7206–11.

[59] The beef trust is discussed in chap. 10 below.

[60] Regier, *The Era of the Muckrakers*, 85.

tion in Beverages," took a moderate and factual tone, as did Senator McCumber writing in the *Independent*, despite the title, "The Alarming Adulteration of Food and Drugs." Lay journalists only infrequently entered this analytical field.[61]

One province of the food and drug domain did come to be illuminated by genuine muckraking, and that was proprietary medicines. For generations the outright absurdity of most patent medicines had been subject to sporadic attack by alert physicians and pharmacists, with the revitalized AMA increasing the tempo. State chemists had analyzed nostrums and published the discouraging results. A few metropolitan dailies had launched anti-patent-medicine campaigns, but these were usually temporary or timid or both, a one-shot charge against a notorious quack whose competitors might be advertising in nearby columns. Some papers and magazines erected advertising entry barriers. In the nation's centennial year, *Harper's Weekly* had been too genteel to accept advertising for products causing abortions, raising the prolapsed uterus, or banishing venereal disease, but had run promises for the certain cure of asthma, cancer, cholera, consumption, diabetes, diphtheria, epilepsy, rheumatism, nervous ailments, and opium addiction. A few farm journals and popular science magazines not only banned all nostrum advertising, but campaigned against health quackery.[62]

A magazine catering to women readers, the *Ladies' Home Journal*, assumed in the 1890s an antinostrum stance. Its publisher, Cyrus H. K. Curtis, and his son-in-law, its editor, Edward Bok, banned all patent-medicine advertising from the *Journal's* pages. This proved to be no financial burden, for the special audience reached by the *Journal* during a period of the "feminization" of American purchasing made advertising easy to secure. Bok sometimes criticized nostrums, especially the bitters highly laced with unlabeled alcohol. Many subscribers had joined the revived temperance crusade, and WCTU leaders, less naive than they once had been, now knew that Hostetter's Bitters and Peruna could provide an unwitting or a secret tipple. Bok gave the fight against demon rum disguised as medicine a helping hand.[63]

[61] Kane, "Populism, Progressivism, and Pure Food," 161–66; "The Exaggeration of Food Adulteration," *Independent* 58 (1905), 49–51; Ladd, "Adulterated Food Products and Food Studies"; Wiley, "Fraud in Food Manufacture" and "Deception in Beverages," *Public Opinion* 38 (1905), 357–60, 437–39; McCumber, "The Alarming Adulteration of Food and Drugs," *Independent* 58 (1905), 28–33.

[62] Young, *The Toadstool Millionaires*, 58–74, 205–25; James Harvey Young, "*Harper's Weekly* on Health in America, 1876," *J Hist Med Allied Sci* 41 (1986), 169–71.

[63] Edward Bok, *A Man from Maine* (New York, 1923), 126; Bok, *The Americanization of Edward Bok* (New York, 1923), 340–43; Salme Harju Steinberg, *Reformer in the Marketplace* (Baton Rouge, LA, 1979), 98–106.

The *Journal*'s occasional criticisms became an intensive campaign in 1904, precipitated by an unfortunate mistake. In an editoral castigating "The 'Patent-Medicine' Curse," Bok, citing a Massachusetts State Board of Health report, listed the ingredients in Doctor Pierce's Favorite Prescription as alcohol, opium, and digitalis. The company, asserting that its medicine contained none of these drugs, charged libel and sought $200,000 in damages. Bok quickly found that the Massachusetts analysis was long out of date. Chemists he hired confirmed the Pierce contention. Bok printed a retraction, prepared for trial, and intensified his condemnation of the patent-medicine business.[64]

Hoping to find an old bottle of the Favorite Prescription in some backwater store that might confirm the Massachusetts document, Bok hired an investigator. Mark Sullivan, Harvard-trained journalist and lawyer, failed in his quest, and Bok lost the suit, the jury awarding Pierce $16,000. Bok kept Sullivan at work on an undercover probe of the patent-medicine business. Using assumed names, he advertised as if seeking to employ men skilled in different functions of the industry. He interviewed those who responded, the chemists who concocted formulas, the writers of advertising copy, the direct-mail specialists. Eager for better jobs, these men revealed secrets while boasting of their accomplishments. Sullivan thus learned that letters written by ailing men and women in response to advertisements were sold or rented to other proprietors, packaged in bundles according to disease. He bought packages and had them photographed. He also photographed the tombstone of Lydia E. Pinkham, who had died in 1883, although advertising for her Vegetable Compound gave the impression she was still alive and well and living in Lynn, replying to confiding letters from women readers. Bok cited an anonymous proprietor on the persuasiveness of advertising remedies for female complaints: "We can make . . . [women] feel more female troubles in a year than they would really have if they lived to be a hundred."[65]

Sullivan unearthed the "red clause" that proprietary advertisers had come to insist upon in their contracts with newspapers. He secured the minutes of a Proprietary Association meeting at which Frank J. Cheney, maker of Hall's Catarrh Cure, reported on the clause he had devised, requiring the cancellation of all advertising should the state in which the newspaper was located enact a law to restrict or prohibit the manufac-

---

[64] *Ladies' Home Journal* 21 (May 1904), 18, and (July 1904), 18; Bok, *Americanization*, 342–43.

[65] Mark Sullivan, *The Education of an American* (New York, 1938) 183–91; *Ladies' Home J* 21 (November 1904), 18; 22 (March 1905), 18; (April 1905), 20; (September 1905), 15; (January 1906), 14, 18; (February 1906), 23.

ture or sale of proprietaries. Cheney boasted of how he had used the clause in Illinois to energize newspapers into defeating a tax on patent medicines threatened by the legislature. Cheney's fellows learned the lesson quickly, and "muzzle-clauses" proliferated. Sullivan secured pictures of such contracts, and also of letters sent to the press by proprietary producers when danger threatened.[66]

The sensational story of his sleuthing Sullivan assembled in an article called "The Patent Medicine Conspiracy against the Freedom of the Press." Bok liked it but considered it too long and "legalistic" and offered it to Norman Hapgood, the sober, scholarly editor of *Collier's*. Hapgood published the article during November 1905. By this date *Collier's* was midstream in the most intensive campaign ever waged against patent medicines by an American popular magazine.[67]

The reporter Hapgood had set to work at preparing a full-scale exposé of quackery was Samuel Hopkins Adams, a writer perfectly suited to his assigned task. As an undergraduate at Hamilton College, Adams, before turning to journalism, had pursued a premedical course. He spent nine years perfecting his talents at crime reporting on the *New York Sun*. He then became a writer for *McClure's Magazine*, turning to his interest in medical science for subjects to report. Adams presented the current status of tuberculosis, yellow fever, typhoid fever, and surgical techniques. He revealed unusual sensitivity to problems on the expanding frontier of public health, including the way in which business often blocked protective measures that science had made available. While Adams performed yeoman's service in educating the middle class on these topics, he found his true metier when he turned to patent medicines.[68]

Ray Stannard Baker, a colleague at *McClure's*, first suggested that Adams prepare a series on proprietary remedies. The idea appealed to him, and he was weighing it when approached by Norman Hapgood. Adams owed first loyalty to S. S. McClure, but that capricious publisher was lukewarm to the idea. Hapgood was in dead earnest, so Adams signed a contract and went to work.[69]

---

[66] Sullivan, *The Education of an American*, 188–91; [Mark Sullivan], "The Patent Medicine Conspiracy against the Freedom of the Press," *Collier's* 36 (November 4, 1905), 13–16, 25.

[67] *Ibid.*; Bok, *Americanization*, 344; Sullivan, *The Education of an American*, 191–92.

[68] Hapgood, *The Changing Years*, 177–78; *Collier's* 34 (March 25, 1905), 8; 35 (April 22, 1905), 9, 27; *Hamilton Alumni Review*, January 1937; *Bookman* 21 (1905), 562–63; interview with Adams; James H. Cassedy, "Muckraking and Medicine: Samuel Hopkins Adams," *American Quarterly* 16 (1984), 85–99.

[69] Interview with Adams.

The buildup in *Collier's* for the Adams series lasted from April to October 1905. Week after week, in editorial, verse, and picture, Hapgood trained his guns on the nostrum target. E. W. Kemble drew "DEATH's LABORATORY," a skull with patent-medicine bottles for teeth. Hapgood described how the nation's most prestigious newspapers accepted disreputable ads, and surrounded his words with a border linking patent-medicine pitches with the mastheads of the papers in which they appeared. The rhymster Wallace Irwin exposed in doggerel the insidious Dr. Sharko, a cancer quack.[70]

Adams, meanwhile, collected and studied nostrum advertising. He bought bottles of the medicines advertised and had the contents analyzed by the professor who had taught him chemistry at Hamilton and by experts at a pharmaceutical laboratory. He sought counsel from state chemists and from specialists in medicine and pharmacy, asking if the ingredients discovered by analysis could fulfill the curative promises in the ads. Adams tracked down men and women who had testified to cures in advertising pages and got their stories firsthand. Nor was the busy reporter diffident about approaching proprietors themselves. An old German physician, Samuel D. Hartman, who marketed Peruna, so prominent a proprietary that babies were named for it, gave Adams ready welcome. Even after being warned that the planned article was certain to be critical, Hartman told the reporter almost everything.[71]

Not all proprietors proved so forthcoming. A group of remedy makers put private detectives on Adams's trail. One weekend, en route to a house party in Connecticut, Adams met in the station another invited guest, the wife of a close friend, and they rode together on the train. Soon Adams was warned to stop his investigations or his journey with another man's wife would be made public in an embarrassing way. Luckily the reporter knew the mayor of the city in which lived the proprietor chiefly responsible for Adams's shadowing. More luckily still, the mayor knew just the facts to squelch the blackmail threat. Recently the nostrum maker, surprised in a roadhouse room with another man's wife, had jumped from a window and broken a leg. Adams quietly let his awareness of this tale be known and proceeded with his work, no longer hounded by detectives.[72]

"A character inherited from a line of insurgent theologians," observed a *Collier's* colleague, "gave . . . [Adams] firm conviction in his beliefs." He "gloried in combat." Adams's amiable, indeed, aesthetic, appearance

---

[70] *Collier's* 35 (June 3, 1905), 5; (July 5), 12, 13, 22; Irwin, "A Testimonial," *ibid.* (July 22), 17.

[71] Interview with Adams.

[72] *Ibid.*

may have fooled patent-medicine proprietors into thinking him a less than worthy foe. The failed blackmail effort must have raised some doubts. Certainly all miscalculations ended when the first article in Adams's series appeared in *Collier's* on October 7, 1905, entitled "The Great American Fraud."[73]

Across the top of the first page stretched an illustration showing a hooded skull in front of patent-medicine bottles exuding noxious vapors. Sinewy serpents, often the nostrum maker's symbol of evil, had now turned coat and slithered among the vials. Adams then launched his attack:

> Gullible America will spend this year some seventy-five millions of dollars in the purchase of patent medicines. In consideration of this sum it will swallow huge quantities of alcohol, an appalling amount of opiates and narcotics, a wide assortment of varied drugs ranging from powerful and dangerous heart depressants to insidious liver stimulants; and, far in excess of all other ingredients, undiluted fraud. For fraud, exploited by the skilfulest of advertising bunco men, is the basis of the trade. Should the newspapers, the magazines, and the medical journals refuse their pages to this class of advertisements, the patent medicine business in five years would be as scandalously historic as the South Sea Bubble, and the nation would be the richer not only in lives and money, but in drunkards and drug-fiends saved.

Adams followed this introduction with a sweeping overview of what his series would present. He rebuked proprietors for trafficking on the fear of epidemics. Even the genial Dr. Hartman had been guilty of a "ghoulish exploitation" of Peruna during New Orleans's recent yellow-fever scourge. Adams described the throttling of press freedom inherent in the restraining clause in advertising contracts printed in red ink. He reproduced the contract offered by the Cheney Medicine Company to William Allen White's *Emporia Gazette*. Adams explained that nostrum testimonials could be easily gathered from gullible ignoramuses or secured through various pressures from people in public life. He observed that legislation, "the most obvious remedy," always made slow progress when business, with millions at stake, dug in its heels. At the last annual meeting of the Proprietary Association, Adams noted, a report stated that "the heaviest expenses" had been incurred "in legislative work."[74]

[73] Will Irwin, *The Making of a Reporter* (New York, 1942), 155; portraits in *American Magazine* 62 (1906), 225, and *Bookman* 21 (1905), 563.

[74] *Collier's* 36 (October 7, 1905), 14, 15, 29.

Adams followed his first general attack with the exposure of Peruna that he had predicted to its friendly proprietor. Peruna's alcoholic content, Adams discovered, ran about 28 percent, and a dollar bottle cost its producer—including the bottle—between fifteen and eighteen cents. As a remedy Peruna was promoted to cure nothing but catarrh, but in Hartman's pathology catarrh encompassed appendicitis, consumption, mumps, and female complaints. Adams reported on Peruna "alcoholics" he had met, at least one a member in good standing of the WCTU. Many of the nation's distinguished citizens who had given testimonials for Peruna served in the United States Congress.[75]

Next in the series came Liquozone, a nostrum trafficking on the public's wariness about germs, parading as a universal antiseptic. Yet analysis showed Liquozone to contain 99 percent water. The risks to the sick lay in relying on Liquozone instead of seeking proper medical treatment. The nostrum's proprietors named a long list of medical and charitable institutions at which their remedy was allegedly achieving success. Jane Addams's Hull House was only one such notable place which, never having used Liquozone, protested the false promotion.[76]

Exceeding fake antiseptics as a positive danger came "The Subtle Poisons." Because these nostrums were less transparent in their quackery than Peruna and Liquozone, even highly intelligent people fell prey. Catarrh powders containing cocaine and soothing syrups loaded with morphine composed a class of nostrums that created "enslaving appetites." Although not revealing the fact in his article, Adams knew firsthand about such nostrums' hazardous potential. Returning home from one of his trips, he found it touch and go as to whether his own mother had become addicted to a patent medicine containing an unlabeled narcotic. This was a "shameful trade," Adams charged, "that stupefies helpless babies and makes criminals of our young men and harlots of our young women." Nearly as dangerous were nostrums composed of acetanilide. These too could be habit forming and sometimes, because of a personal susceptibility or an overdose, could lead to death. Adams listed the names and addresses of twenty-two such victims. The symptoms of still-living victims of acetanilide also were grim. Adams cited a medical report: "Stomach increasingly irritable; skin a grayish or light purplish hue; palpitation and slight enlargement of the heart; blood discolored to a chocolate hue." Yet Orangeine, a widely sold acetanilide mixture, claimed that it would improve the blood and strengthen the heart.[77]

[75] Adams, "Peruna and the 'Bracers,' " *Collier's* 36 (October 28, 1905), 17–19.

[76] Adams, "Liquozone," *Collier's* 36 (November 18, 1905) 20–21.

[77] Adams, "The Subtle Poisons," *Collier's* 36 (December 2, 1905), 16–18; interview with Adams.

Next Adams addressed proprietors who were "Preying on the Incurables":

> There are being exploited in this country to-day more than one hundred cures for diseases that are absolutely beyond the reach of drugs. They are owned by men who know them to be swindles, and who in private conversation will almost always evade the direct statement that their nostrums will "cure" consumption, epilepsy, heart disease, and ailments of that nature.

Adams illustrated his article with "A Rogue's Gallery," a score of such ads clipped from two New York Sunday papers. These nostrums contained chloroform, opium, alcohol, and hashish, which well might hasten the course of the diseases they promised to subdue. In somber mood, Adams concluded:

> Every man who trades in this market, whether he pockets the profits of the maker, the purveyor, or the advertiser, takes toll of blood. He may not deceive himself here, for here the patent medicine business is nakedest, most cold-hearted. Relentless greed sets the trap, and death is partner in the enterprise.[78]

In February 1906 Samuel Hopkins Adams concluded his series on "The Great American Fraud." As he set to work on a new series exposing fake clinics, the AMA published his first series in a little book. Sales to the disturbed lay public mounted rapidly. No doubt existed that Adams's muckraking had expanded awareness of the nostrum evil and of the need for legislation to control it. As the Fifty-ninth Congress opened, that oft-banished measure had again been introduced.[79]

While gathering materials for his *Collier's* articles, Adams had gone to Washington to consult with Harvey Wiley. The two continued in close touch. As Congress considered the pure food and drug bill, Adams returned to the capital to lend his support to the chief chemist, who again strove to rally his allies so as to win the victory.[80]

[78] Adams, "Preying on the Incurables," *Collier's* 36 (January 13, 1906), 18–20.

[79] Adams, "The Fundamental Fakes," *Collier's* 36 (February 17, 1906), 22–24, 26, 28; Adams, *The Great American Fraud* (Chicago, 1906). The New York Academy of Medicine has five editions of this book issued from Chicago and New York between 1906 and 1912.

[80] Adams to Wiley, May 29, 1905, Wiley Papers, Library of Congress; Adams to Wiley, January 8, March 6, 10, 16, 20, 1906, Incoming Correspondence, Bureau of Chemistry, RG 97, National Archives; Wiley to Adams, March 26, 1906, Letterbook, *ibid.*

IX

Prelude to Victory

I am not so much exercised about these misbranded and so-called "poisonous" substances as some Senators are. . . . Of course, if we believed all that these scientists say, these young fellows in the Department of Agriculture, we would not dare breathe, eat, or drink. But I do not believe it.
—SENATOR JACOB H. GALLINGER
in the Senate, 1906[1]

I will show you . . . by experimental data which I will lay before you that if you put in foods the same quantity or less [of benzoate of soda] than the Lord puts in cranberries that you will produce a most distinct injury.
—HARVEY W. WILEY
before a House committee, 1906[2]

The Senate Acts

Collier's ran the final article in Samuel Hopkins Adams's stirring series on "The Great American Fraud" in its February 17, 1906, issue. By that date the House Committee on Interstate and Foreign Commerce had moved midway through a heated fortnight's hearing devoted to the pure-food cause. The Senate, deciding not to hold a hearing, stood on the eve of a major floor debate centered on its current version of a food and drug bill. One other major event took place in mid-February, although its crucial relevance to the legislative process did not become immediately apparent. The day after Adams's article appeared, Upton Sinclair published *The Jungle.*

On the second day of the Fifty-ninth Congress, the day after the reading of President Roosevelt's state of the union message, which included his brief endorsement of the pure-food cause, Senator Weldon Heyburn again introduced a bill. Its provisions were substantially the same as those of the McCumber bill in the previous Congress, although several modifications had been made to placate pockets of opposition. Proces-

[1] *Cong. Record,* 59 Cong. 1 ses., 1218.
[2] *Hearings . . . on The Pure Food Bills,* 59 Cong. 1 ses., 243.

sors leery of Dr. Wiley's alleged extremism were appeased by inclusion of Treasury and Commerce departments with Agriculture for regulation making. Retailers fearful of fines and jail were given immunity for selling violative packaged foods and drugs provided such sales were not "knowingly" made. Liquors were separated from foods because, as Heyburn put it, too many citizens did not regard the former as "a necessity."[3]

Heyburn and McCumber believed that the pure-food law's day had come at last. The problem had grown, said McCumber, until the value of adulterated and misbranded goods was "a sum sufficient to pay the entire expenses of the civil war," or "to pay the national debt three times over." The president had given his support. The press, especially the "leading magazines," had rallied round. "Has there ever been in the history of this country," Heyburn challenged his fellow senators, "a more universal demand for action upon the part of Congress than the demand that has gone up from one end of the country to the other in regard to legislation upon the pure-food question?"[4]

Nonetheless, through January 1906 and into February, the Idaho senator sought several times to get his colleagues to bring the matter to a vote, without success. The tried and true method of denial by parliamentary tactics still functioned. The opposition, however, recognized the changing climate. Maneuvering in virtual silence had been replaced by maneuvering plus open debate. Senators offered amendments to bring the bill more to their liking, an acknowledgement that the mainline measure would in due course pass. Intransigent senators repeated philosophical and constitutional reasons for opposition and offered once more a substitute that would satisfy industrial groups least reconciled to any law at all.[5]

In mid-February the break came. The progressive Indiana senator, Albert J. Beveridge, explained in retrospect what happened. "The Senate was in a jam," he wrote Mark Sullivan two decades after the event, "and public feeling had become intense. Aldrich [the Republican leader] came to me one afternoon and said: 'Tell Heyburn if he asks consideration for the Pure Food bill there will be no objection.'" Beveridge surmised that this yielding was a tactical step to gain some other advantage deemed by the "Old Guard" more important in their contest with liberal senators. Also, the president had appealed personally to Aldrich to withdraw his opposition. Beveridge believed that the conser-

[3] *Cong. Record*, 59 Cong. 1 ses., 140, 894–95. S. 88 was introduced on December 6, 1905.
[4] *Ibid.*, 1216, 1415, 1417.
[5] *Ibid.*, 1754–55, 2054.

vatives "counted on killing" the pure-food measure later in the House. He continued:

> So I went to Heyburn and told him to bring up the Pure Food bill instantly and the Old Guard would not block him. Heyburn could not believe it and said he was tired of being made a fool of by asking useless consideration which he had asked so many times before. However, I insisted, for I never knew Aldrich to promise anything that he did not make good. I told Heyburn there was no time to waste, and to act without any questions. I sat down beside him and told him that I would be responsible. Finally, about the middle of the afternoon, Heyburn got up.[6]

An agreement was reached to vote on February 21, and the sporadic discussion of earlier weeks was concluded with three days of intense debate and a series of last-minute compromises. McCumber pointed to the major opponents of the bill. Ranking first were the well-financed rectifiers, who, the North Dakota senator said, in ten minutes could fabricate what they billed as ten-year-old whiskey. They were supported by shoddy wine merchants, importers of adulterated olive oil, jelly makers who used glucose and aniline dyes, and promoters of "vile and fraudulent alleged remedies."[7]

Most of these trade groups supported the substitute bill introduced by Senator Hernando DeSoto Money of Mississippi. Money's bill, McCumber said, "would no more prohibit the introduction of fraudulent and spurious goods in any State than a sieve would hold water." The intent of its proponents, he held, was to block passage of a law if they could, and, if this effort failed, "to secure the enactment of a food law which would enable those manufacturers to enter those states out of which they would be kicked to-day."

Money's bill had come from the hand of the secretary of the National Food Manufacturers' Association. It openly reflected its sponsors' hostility to Wiley, placing enforcement in the Department of Commerce and Labor. Secretary of Agriculture Wilson, Money said, was "a very honorable, industrious, and indefatigable worker. . . . But the Secretary can be deceived as well as anybody else." Moreover, Money added:

> I can not understand why the Department of Agriculture, devoted to the product, the raw stuff and nothing else, should be invested

[6] Sullivan, *Our Times*, vol. 2, 533–34.

[7] Anderson, *The Health of a Nation*, 176; *Cong. Record*, 59 Cong. 1 ses., 1218–19, 1414, 2771–73.

with the authority and power to administer laws which relate to the transportation of manufactures. . . . It is incongruous.[8]

Money's bill covered only articles moving in interstate commerce; when foods or drugs reached their destination within a state, only state law applied. The bill also preempted to Congress the role of setting standards, not delegating this matter to the enforcers of the law. The standards proposed provided for a generous use of chemical preservatives and exempted proprietary medicines from any restraints whatever, inasmuch as only medicines listed in the *United States Pharmacopoeia* and the *National Formulary* (NF) would be covered by the law. Further, Money's bill embodied a major ploy of the whiskey rectifiers, who wanted natural poisons as well as "added" poisons covered. Thus, the blenders hoped, the allegedly poisonous fusel oil in distilled whiskey would be subject to attack. Even though Money's measure had no hope of passage, it provided the focus for the debate and a pressuring device toward compromises that would give regulated industries points of future advantage.[9]

Supplementing Senator Money's effort, three interest groups especially had senatorial champions seeking specific changes in the Heyburn-McCumber bill. Henry Cabot Lodge again arose to the defense of the codfish industry. He offered an amendment allowing a preservative externally applied if it could be removed by the consumer. The influential Joseph B. Foraker took up the cause of the rectifiers, a major industry in his home city of Cincinnati. Like Money, Foraker wanted all poisonous and deleterious ingredients, not just "added" ones, banned from liquors. He also sought to keep from liquor labeling descriptions which blenders might deem disparaging, by limiting the words that could be required to "blended," "rectified," or "vetted." For the first time in either house of Congress, proprietary medicines received significant attention in debate about pure drugs. Speaking in their defense, James A. Hemenway of Indiana also offered an amendment.[10]

Hemenway reflected the concerns of A. R. Beardsley, an Indiana state senator, an official of the Dr. Miles Medicine Company, and chief of publicity for the Proprietary Association. The Heyburn bill, Beardsley had advised Hemenway, might be interpreted so as to present the issue

[8] *Ibid.*, 2643–66.

[9] *Ibid.*, 137–44, 2656, 2771–73. The *National Formulary* had been first issued by pharmacists in 1888 mainly to continue the availability of formulas that had been excluded by the more rigorously scientific *United States Pharmacopoeia* of 1883. See Sonnedecker, *Kremers and Urdang's History of Pharmacy*, 275–76.

[10] *Cong. Record*, 59 Cong. 1 ses., 896, 1129–34, 2644, 2724–27.

of curative claims on proprietary medicine labels to the courts. This would mean seeking to "settle by . . . [government] chemical experts and in the Federal courts a class of questions about which medical men and schools of medicine have been at war for generations." Such a course would "precipitate endless controversies" all over the nation. The school of medicine that dominated the enforcing agency would be given an unfair advantage. "Does the Senator recognize," Hemenway asked Heyburn, "that a medicine which has cured a hundred persons might not cure the hundred and first one?" Then that uncured person might persuade the secretary of agriculture that the medicine "did not do what it was represented it would do, [and] the article becomes contraband." Hemenway sought a change in phraseology that would clearly ban control of therapeutic label claims.[11]

In challenging Hemenway's case, Heyburn and McCumber proved less effective than they might have been. They did not point out the vast distance separating the outright fraudulence of many patent-medicine label claims, about which all scientists agreed, from the honest differences of opinion among medical practitioners. The AMA pressured the Senate to control "worthless, dangerous and enslaving drugs." McCumber and Heyburn, however, did not assume such a rigorous stance, nor did they agree between themselves. Heyburn, while insisting that the law's main goal was "to compel the telling of the truth," seemed to suggest that proprietary remedies could bear therapeutic label claims if they also bore an accurate listing of ingredients. The promises should be less than categorical, a medicine described only as "a remedy for" a given disease, with the guarantee that it "will cure in some cases." McCumber was even less demanding than his Idaho colleague. He did not hold that the bill's phrasing forbade claims of "curative qualities." "I think," he said, "that it is aimed only at [an accurate listing of] the ingredients or substances."[12]

Considering the flexibility of the bill's two chief proponents, it is surprising that Hemenway did not seek greater change in the bill's phrasing than he did. The clause being debated termed a drug misbranded "if the package containing it, or its label, should bear any statement regarding the ingredients or the substances contained therein, which statement shall be false or misleading in any particular." Hemenway first sought to amend by replacing the words "ingredients or the substances" with "existence or nonexistence or the amount or purity of any ingredient or

[11] *Ibid.*, 2724; Anderson, *The Health of a Nation*, 176.
[12] *Cong. Record*, 59 Cong. 1 ses., 2721–25, 2748.

substance," then later accepted a lesser modification of the language proposed by McCumber.[13]

Heyburn and McCumber took a tolerant view also, despite the AMA's opposition, of another change in the drug provisions. Elements of the pharmaceutical industry desired a variation clause relating to USP and NF drugs that would permit their marketing at less than full official strength. The AMA condemned this policy forthrightly: "That there should be any but one grade, and that the highest grade of pharmaceutical preparations, is an idea . . . repugnant to every sense of honesty, decency, and common humanity." McCumber nonetheless acquiesced in a loosening of the language already granting variations, so that official preparations of one-half or other less-than-full strength would be legal, so long as the label made this plain.[14]

Heyburn and McCumber, while worried about the consequences of Lodge's codfish amendment, took pains to propitiate the influential Massachusetts senator, accepting his proposal in a slightly altered form. However, with respect to Foraker's principal effort to give whiskey rectifiers an advantage, the mainline bill's proponents stood firm, and the Ohio senator's amendment to have the law cover all and not just "added" poisons went down to defeat. McCumber did collaborate with Foraker on a secondary amendment to please the blenders, limiting the label designations that would be required to a choice of "blended," "rectified," or "mixed" whiskey.[15]

The major confrontation between the Heyburn and the Money bills came as scheduled on February 21. By a voice vote, Money's bill lost, then Heyburn's bill won approval, sixty-three to four, with twenty-two senators not voting. The nays represented opposition on constitutional grounds. Senators Foraker and Hemenway voted affirmatively. Aldrich abstained. Harvey Wiley, sitting with Robert Allen of Kentucky, watched the proceedings from the Senate gallery.[16]

During the course of the Senate debate, Wiley had done what he could to keep up the pressure, continuing to orchestrate efforts of the coalition of women, physicians, and food processors favorable to his version of a law. Especially important was AMA action, cued by Wiley, on the morning of the Senate vote. Charles A. L. Reed arranged to have a letter on every senator's desk urging passage of Heyburn's bill. The Idaho senator had Reed's letter read aloud and thus printed in the

---

[13] *Ibid.*, 2724.

[14] *Ibid.*, 2722–23, 2748, 2763; Glenn Sonnedecker, "Drug Standards Become Official," in Young, ed., *The Early Years of Federal Food and Drug Control*, 28–39.

[15] *Cong. Record*, 59 Cong. 1 ses., 2770–71.

[16] *Ibid.*, 2771–73; Anderson, *The Health of a Nation*, 180.

Congressional Record. Reed said that he spoke for over 2,000 county medical societies and 135,000 physicians in the nation.[17]

Wiley considered the Senate vote also a "victory of the women of this country," who gave the pure-food cause a broader base, less rooted in economic interest, than it had hitherto possessed. The president too, by speaking out in public and by pressuring Aldrich in private, had played a significant role. Other major legislation, especially the railroad rate bill, needed attention, and an election loomed. These may also have been factors in moving the Senate to act, after its years of delay. Wiley's biographer, Oscar E. Anderson, concludes his discussion of the Senate's favorable vote with a query: "Was it not simply that the Senate leadership was both aware of the trend of public sentiment and conscious that the pure-food bill was never likely to be offered in a form less objectionable to the interests that for long had been arrayed in opposition?"[18]

The House Committee Ponders

The pure food bill that Congressman William P. Hepburn had introduced in the House made fewer concessions to special interests than had Senator Heyburn's bill, and especially than the amended bill that had passed the Senate. That bill contained no standard-setting mechanism at all; such authority was vested entirely in the courts. In the House bill, the secretary of agriculture alone would have authority to make rules and regulations. He was specifically given the power to fix food standards, aided by the AOAC committee and such other specialists as he might choose to consult. Once determined, the standards were to guide officials enforcing the law and judges interpreting it. The secretary of agriculture, through the same mechanism, could determine the safety of preservatives and other food additives. The bill contained no "knowingly" clause that might make enforcement more difficult. All mixtures, compounds, combinations, imitations, and blends of foods—including liquors—had to reveal their character and constituents on their labels.

---

[17] *Ibid.*, 178–81; *Cong. Record*, 59 Cong. 1 ses., 2748. Between this decisive AMA action and a similar set of telegrams to members of the House of Representatives on the eve of that body's final vote in June, the association had undergone a crisis of uncertainty. This was inspired by Victor C. Vaughan's strong objections to the AMA *Journal*'s opposition to a committee of experts to advise the secretary of agriculture. The editor feared that the choice of such a committee might be influenced detrimentally by political pressures. For a fortnight the *Journal*'s prolaw voice was stilled, then it resumed. See *J Amer Med Assoc* 46 (1906), 901, 1036–37, 1209, 1966, 1860–61; Burrow, *AMA*, 78–83.

[18] Anderson, *The Health of a Nation*, 181.

In one significant way the House bill was less rigorous than the Senate counterpart: it did not provide for regulating patent medicines.[19]

When the House Commerce Committee began a fortnight of hearings on February 13, all concerned parties recognized that the chances for a pure-food bill's enactment had never before been so great. Midway through the hearings the Senate passed its bill. This atmosphere imparted to the testimony a forthrightness, even an acrimony, rarely matched during the previous quarter of a century. Debate on the Senate floor, moreover, had been at second hand, with political figures arguing the case for business and consumer interests. Before the House committee, business groups presented their own—sometimes conflicting—cases, with much bolstering testimony from scientific experts. So the debate, if tempestuous, also possessed an evidential quality. After spokesmen for business completed their ample say in criticism of his bill, Hepburn brought Harvey Wiley to the stand as final witness. Defending the bill in the public interest, Wiley sought to refute the arguments and evidence presented against it by the representatives of business, especially their scientific experts. By turns diplomatic and corrosive, countering alleged facts with data from his own experiments, maintaining a high moral tone, eloquent of word and flamboyant in demonstration, Wiley turned in one of the masterful performances of his career.[20]

Two major groups, both fearful of Wiley as would-be regulator, took the lead in condemning the Hepburn bill, the whiskey rectifiers and food processors anxious to continue using chemical preservatives. Warwick Hough, the blenders' attorney, repeated his stock arguments. Resorting to history, he stated that the original whiskey was a blended form; hence, blends should not be deprived by law of the full right to use the name "whiskey" without qualification. Hough did not want the "mixtures or compounds" clause to be applied to blends either to disparage them or to reveal the rectifiers' secrets. Straight whiskey, he reiterated, contained inherently poisonous ingredients absent from rectified whiskey, and should not be protected by the word "added" in the bill.[21]

The colorful Edmund W. Taylor, a distiller from Frankfurt, Kentucky, and spread-eagle orator of the old school, took the chair to

[19] *Ibid.*, 181–82; *Cong. Record*, 59 Cong. 1 ses., 202, 2756.

[20] *Hearings . . . on The Pure Food Bills*, 59 Cong. 1 ses.

[21] *Ibid.*, 96–115, 118. High and Coppin, "Wiley, Whiskey, and Strategic Behavior," conclude that Hough and the rectifiers had the better of the historical argument in their debate with the straight-whiskey distillers. Wiley urged crucial House members to attend the hearing to listen to Hough's testimony: H. C. Adams to Wiley and John Lamb to Wiley, February 5, 1906, Wiley Papers.

counter Hough's testimony. Colonel Taylor gave a differing version of history, wherein neutral spirits, the stock item in the blenders' product, did not deserve the designation "whiskey," as proven by such sources as the *United States Pharmacopoeia*, Internal Revenue Service rules, and a Kentucky state court of appeals. Yet "every single drop" of counterfeit whiskey, Taylor asserted, which composed 95 percent of what was sold for whiskey on the American market, was labeled as "genuine."[22]

The rectifiers, however, had not relied on Hough alone. They resorted to a ploy not uncommon in congressional considerations, bringing back a former member of that august body to help present their case. In this instance the witness was ex-Senator William E. Mason, who less than a decade earlier had presided over the first extended hearings given to a pure-food bill, with Wiley his principal aide. Now in 1906 Mason had no fault to find with his former ally, although he praised an alternate bill that Wiley deemed anathema. The bill, drafted by a strongly anti-food-law editor, almost certainly at the prompting of the rectifiers, had been introduced by William Lorimer of Illinois. This measure defined interstate commerce in the narrowest possible way, and set no national standards.[23]

The most extensive testimony at the hearing came from food manufacturers wanting to preserve preservatives, especially sodium benzoate. This "innocent" chemical, insisted a canner and pickle maker from Keokuk, Iowa, was "absolutely necessary to . . . [his] business." He feared that Dr. Wiley's "private opinion" of the preservative's harmfulness would, should Hepburn's bill become law, "ripen into his official opinion." In that case, "if the United States Government should sit down on my business," the Keokuk canner held, "I should kind of feel as though I was squashed."[24]

These points—the indispensability of sodium benzoate and the fear of Wiley's rulings—one wing of the food processing industry proceeded to elaborate more fully than ever before. Walter S. Williams, a Detroit manufacturer of pickles, preserves, and condiments, testified himself and brought scientists with well-known names to support his case. Williams held not only Wiley in suspicion, but also his associates in the AOAC, already at work helping the secretary of agriculture establish food standards. Some of those standards, like that for apple butter, Williams insisted, did not reflect the advanced state of the processing art. AOAC

[22] *Cong. Record*, 59 Cong. 1 ses., 165–88.
[23] *Ibid.*, 40–44; Anderson, *The Health of a Nation*, 182.
[24] William Ballinger, *Hearings . . . on The Pure Food Bills*, 4–9.

scientists did not give manufacturers "credit for any progress or any ingenuity."[25]

Wiley and his AOAC allies did not possess the special expertise required to evaluate the impact of chemicals upon the human body. So testified one of the scientists Williams had employed to investigate sodium benzoate. He was Victor C. Vaughan of the University of Michigan, who had made his views known before to committees of Congress. "Men who are engaged all their lives in assaying soils and estimating the value of fertilizers," Vaughan asserted, "are not fitted by education to determine the effect of anything on the human body." Any commission to study preservatives required the presence of a bacteriologist.[26] Although Wiley's "Poison Squad" experiments with sodium benzoate had not yet been published, Vaughan disagreed with the chief chemist's already announced conclusions in his boric acid report. He did not believe that Wiley's test had demonstrated harmfulness from this preservative when given in small amounts.

Another noted scientist employed by Williams concurred in Vaughan's judgment of Wiley's work. Such short-time trials, testified Edward Kremers, plant chemist from the University of Wisconsin, could not be conclusive. "While I am a respecter of science," Kremers told the House committee, "I believe in the selective capacity of man; I confess to having more confidence in man selecting in the course of centuries the right thing than the scientists pointing out the right way." Any "physiological test" conducted through only a few weeks or months could not convict an article of diet that had been "used for a long time without any apparent injurious effects." Such was the case with sodium benzoate, a constituent of the cranberry, used through the centuries not only as a food but as a folk remedy. The impact of the amount of sodium benzoate used in making catsup, Kremers held, would be "very trifling." [27]

Still another witness sought to make an even stronger case for this popular preservative. A physician and pharmacist, Robert C. Eccles of Brooklyn represented the National Food Manufacturers' Association. The threat to public health from food poisoning, he insisted, far outweighed the hazard of preservatives. Except for diseases transmitted by insect bites, germs conveyed by food caused the greatest amount of illness. This had been shown during the Spanish-American War, when the troops had suffered so severely from food infected by the feet of flies. "To preserve a food," therefore, Eccles asserted, was "to improve it and

[25] *Ibid.*, 9–23.
[26] *Ibid.*, 63–72.
[27] *Ibid.*, 26–40.

not to adulterate it." Formaldehyde in milk reduced infant mortality. When Brooklyn had banned preservatives in 1886, the death rate had soared immediately. When food could not be kept frozen, Eccles advised, the use of chemical preservatives—noted on labels—should be mandatory.[28]

Dr. Eccles favored the bill drafted by the secretary of the National Food Manufacturers' Association, the Money bill in the Senate, introduced in the House by William A. Rodenberg of Illinois, which would authorize the use of specified amounts of preservatives. The bill's author, Thomas E. Lannen, a former state food official, also testified in its behalf, and some of the sharpest exchanges of the hearing came between Lannen and Hepburn. The Iowa congressman charged Lannen's backers with being "simply a fake organization" of propreservative businessmen assembled to defeat the mainline bill. Lannen called this indictment "absolutely untrue" and countered with his own allegations. The Department of Agriculture had "exercise[d] arbitrary power," had denied "fair play" to the manufacturers Lannen represented, who had been converted into criminals in the public mind. Lannen sought to take a high and mighty tone with Hepburn. "I think as I am representing this association, which represents several billion dollars," Lannen began huffily at one point, "that this committee can very well listen." But an irritated Hepburn had had enough. He interrupted Lannen and cut him off.[29]

These industry witnesses wanted regulatory power kept from the hands of the secretary of agriculture, considered a pliant tool of the zealot Wiley. Congress itself, or at least some other federal department, should set standards, and, if a department had that power, manufacturers should be given the right to appeal controversial decisions to a board of scientists selected by the president or by the Congress.[30]

Wiley's view of things had been defended before he himself took the witness stand. Colonel Taylor, speaking for distillers, had supported the Hepburn bill. So too had A. C. Fraser, president of the Western Packers' Canned Goods Association. Robert Allen had denied allegations that many state food officials opposed Hepburn's bill and disliked the food standards set by the secretary of agriculture with AOAC counsel.[31]

Wiley sat in the hearing room day by day listening to his critics. When his turn came, the chief chemist counterattacked, seeking to refute both

[28] *Ibid.*, 119–24, 127–34.
[29] *Ibid.*, 137–64.
[30] *Ibid.*, 5, 23, 52.
[31] *Ibid.*, 91–95, 202–22, 227–37.

the main thrust and the specific details of his opponents' arguments.[32] While crediting contrary witnesses with sincerity, Wiley believed they had so misunderstood his "Poison Squad" experiments and so misinterpreted the scope and intent of the secretary of agriculture's standards as to conjure up "a demon of future dangers, . . . nothing more than a phantom of a perturbed imagination."[33]

The chief chemist regretted that he had been too busy to publish the results of his benzoate-of-soda experiment. Eleven of his twelve volunteers, he stated, had lost weight and had suffered stomach pains and nausea, even though the highest dosage level of preservative fed to them fell far below the amount that some packers wanted to put in foods. He asserted that the experimental evidence itself contradicted a psychological interpretation for the symptoms developed by the young diners. Even though the intent of his trials had been to reach merely the first intimations of danger, Wiley was certain that organs of excretion had suffered damage. "I had no demonstration of it," he told the congressmen, "because I could not kill the young men and examine the kidneys."[34]

Wiley credited his experiments with having changed his mind. "I formerly believed that certain preservatives could be used, as Dr. Vaughan believes now, simply by having the people notified on the label." That opinion rested on the judgments of scientists, Vaughan among them, whom the chief chemist had respected. After the hygienic table trials, however, Wiley observed, "I could not conscientiously, without doing violence to my deliberate judgment, urge that the addition of a preservative to food was harmless in any quantity." He agreed that, under severe circumstances of travel in unsettled places, he would sanction the use of preservatives. He would also be willing to put benzoic acid in shakers like salt and pepper and let people sprinkle it on their food if they so desired. However, he had become adamantly opposed to a steady forced diet of preservatives in processed foods for the American public.[35]

The cranberry argument did not persuade him otherwise. That the Lord had put sodium benzoate in natural foods did not justify man—as Kremers had asserted—in adding it during food processing. Quite the contrary, Wiley insisted. This chemical in cranberries and other products of nature put some burden on the human system. Increasing by

[32] Wiley's testimony, *ibid.*, 237–44; his supplementary report submitted to the committee, 344–409.

[33] *Ibid.*, 240.

[34] *Ibid.*, 281, 283.

[35] *Ibid.*, 240, 252, 272.

even "an infinitesimal amount" the preservative intake by eating catsup and other foods that might contain it would produce "a subtle injury which will tell in time." Damage that is not measurable is harmful nonetheless.[36]

Moreover, Wiley argued, processed foods posed greater threats than did the products of nature. "No chemist can ever imitate nature's combinations," he told the committee. "Synthetically, of everything made by man, almost nothing has the hygienic value of that made by nature." He would prefer to stick with "the normal food of man," food "prepared by the Creator and modified by the cook." Harmful consequences did "not occur to such a degree when nature puts deleterious substances in foods" as when man does. The Rodenberg bill would sanction large quantities of benzoic acid in processed foods, ten times as much as Kremers had found in cranberries.[37]

Wiley sharply attacked positions taken by the scientists who had given evidence. Riled by Vaughan's criticism of his researches because no bacteriologist formed part of the team, the chief chemist responded that "bacteriology . . . [had] nothing in the world to do with it." Wiley pointed out what he deemed other evidence of illogic in Vaughan's testimony, concluding waspishly, "I should think that a jury would be somewhat confused by expert testimony of this kind."[38]

The thrust of Dr. Eccles's key point was posed to Wiley by a committee member, James R. Mann of Illinois. Was not the question mainly one of balancing risks, to counter the hazard of ptomaine poisoning by "taking chances on slight poisons from preservatives?" Denying expertise on ptomaines but not denying the magnitude of their danger, Wiley avoided a direct answer to Mann's query at the hearing. In a document submitted to the committee immediately afterward, the chief chemist sought to counter Eccles's most telling point, that where preservatives had been banned, deaths from food poisoning increased. The Brooklyn physician and he had debated the point before, Wiley wrote, and the facts did not support Eccles, who credited preservatives for falling mortality that deservedly belonged to other causes. Dr. Eccles, Wiley concluded allegorically, would transform Hygeia, who would henceforth hold a flask of formaldehyde in one hand and a pail of preservatives in the other, breathe fumes of burning sulfur, and utter the warning: "Beware of the deadly poisons of pure food! Eat nothing that is not doped!"[39]

[36] *Ibid.*, 244–45.
[37] *Ibid.*, 243–44, 250–51, 369.
[38] *Ibid.*, 266, 270.
[39] *Ibid.*, 253, 355–60.

As part of the standard diet, Wiley insisted, preservatives in processed foods had no legitimate place. Sound raw materials, a clean manufacturing environment, proper procedures, and adequate containers rendered preservatives unnecessary, even for that most susceptible condiment, catsup. "All this difficulty about keeping catsup," Wiley told the committee, "is a phantom."[40]

If, however, the pressure to protect catsup with sodium benzoate and to ship codfish sprinkled with borax should prove to be irresistible, Wiley testified, he would suggest that they be specifically exempted by the law. That would be preferable to sanctioning a minimum preservative level for all processed foods, thus grafting "an unethical principle" onto the bill. The chief chemist would agree that doped catsup and codfish would present a hazard "infinitesimally small," but he would not accept the argument that, because the quantity of preservative was minimal, no danger existed.[41]

Wiley defended the role of the AOAC in standard setting, asserting that the only opponents of this effective mechanism were "enemies of this legislation." The chief chemist also expressed his approval of a board of experts to help the secretary of agriculture make his determinations. That proviso had been omitted from the latest House bill, Wiley averred, because of the objection that it would expand officialdom and increase expense. He did not believe such a concern justified. "Moral suasion" would prove to be so powerful after the law came into effect that not even one new inspector might be required. The chief chemist opposed, however, a board of review or appeal to reconsider the secretary's standards after they had been promulgated: "if you should admit the principle you would never come to any decision as long as anybody wanted to protest." The proper place to test the secretary's standards lay in the courts.[42]

Wiley sharply challenged his old foes, the rectifiers, at the hearing. Denying that he was a whiskey drinker, admitting to tasting it only in the line of duty, the chief chemist told the House committeemen that he had increased his knowledge during the past year, studying the subject for three months in Europe. He had seen true Scotch whiskey being made, solely from pure barley malt, properly fermented, then distilled in a pot still. Wiley doubted if a barrel of this pure product reached the United States. What crossed the ocean labeled Scotch had been adulterated with spirits made from American corn. Most so-called American

[40] *Ibid.*, 311–15.
[41] *Ibid.*, 310–11.
[42] *Ibid.*, 298–304, 342.

bourbon was similarly impure. "With regard to foods," Wiley explained, "I never used the word 'purity' except in one sense. A pure food is what it is represented to be. It has nothing to do with its wholesomeness at all." A pure food might be unwholesome, might even contain a poison. He had lately revised his opinion of fusel oil in distilled whiskey; it might be more dangerous than he once had thought. Nor did he charge rectifiers with deliberately adding to their mixtures ingredients that were injurious to health, although they might do so unwittingly. The difference between straight and rectified whiskey was "an ethical question." The nation's revenue laws termed every mixed whiskey a spurious imitation. "A man is entitled . . . to get the character, quality, and kind of material he asks for, and if you ask for whiskey you ought not to get a bottle of slush."[43]

Blended whiskey, Wiley maintained, "is insipid; it is tasteless; it has no character. It is like one of those beautiful painted forms that the milliner puts up and puts a gown on compared with a real girl." While they laughed at his witticism, Wiley swiftly mixed a blend before the committeemen's eyes. It was made of ethyl alcohol, water, caramel color, Scotch flavor, and an aging or beading oil that formed bright particles like those in aged straight whiskey. The chief chemist showed the committee a recipe book, then demonstrated that by changing the flavor he could as promptly produce bourbon, rye, or brandy.

Many Americans got their alcohol by an even more disguised route. This fact came out in hearings before the same House committee on a separate bill. The mainline House bill, unlike its Senate counterpart, did not contain a provision regulating proprietary medicines. Edwin Y. Webb, a representative from North Carolina, thought this a major omission and introduced a measure he hoped might be "engrafted in the pure food bill." Webb would require honest labeling, the names in English of all ingredients, the quantities of narcotics, chloral hydrate, and alcohol. Before the committee Webb praised *Collier's* for its "great service in exposing medicine frauds" and quoted Samuel Hopkins Adams's assertion "that more alcohol is consumed in the United States in patent medicines than is sold direct by regularly licensed dealers, not including ales and beer."[44]

Webb recited some of Adams's horror stories and described the devious methods by which proprietors were fighting legislation to control

[43] *Ibid.*, 322–40.

[44] *Hearings before the Committee on Interstate and Foreign Commerce of the House of Representatives on H.R. 13086, Requiring Shippers and Manufacturers of Medicine for Interstate Shipment to Label Said Medicine and Print Thereon the Ingredients Contained in Such Medicine*, 59 Cong. 1 ses. (Washington, 1906), 1–19.

them. The pressure of publicity, especially the Adams series, however, was making its weight felt in proprietary ranks. At its 1905 meeting, Webb said, the Proprietary Association had passed a resolution against narcotic nostrums. Two producers of patent medicines with large national markets had announced with considerable fanfare a retreat from secrecy, one to name all ingredients on its labels, the other to furnish complete formulas.

When the hearings concluded, Congressman Mann called Dr. Wiley to his office for a cut-and-paste session. With their eyes on the bill the Senate had passed, they revamped the Hepburn bill. A subcommittee and then the full committee made further changes. Mann, who was to bear responsibility for leading the fight for passage, reported the bill to the House on March 7 as a substitute for the Senate bill. Similar to bills that had passed in two previous Congresses, the new House bill took some account of Senate views. It extended the authority to make regulations beyond the secretary of agriculture to include the secretaries of the treasury and of commerce and labor. The bill also extended the consultants the secretary of agriculture could call on when deciding about the wholesomeness of preservatives and when fixing standards. Not only the AOAC food-standards committee, but also the Association of State Dairy and Food Departments committee might be asked for advice. The bill defined a board of experts the secretary was authorized to consult, when an interested party so requested, to aid him in arriving at a decision concerning the safety of a preservative. The House bill now followed the Senate version and held that no violator could be sent to prison unless he had "knowingly" committed an offense.[45]

The full committee disappointed Wiley in revising the draft he and Mann had worked out to govern whiskey, which denied rectifiers the right to use the word "blend." The presence of "harmless coloring and flavoring ingredients," the committee decreed, should not bar the liquor from being labeled with this word. Wiley was pleased, however, that Webb and the committee leadership won the insertion, for the first time in a House bill, of a patent medicine provision. The chief chemist, with Samuel Hopkins Adams's help, had worked on the phrasing, and its terms exceeded the Senate bill in rigor. Senator Heyburn's measure barred false and misleading claims only with respect to "constituent" ingredients, and it did not require the listing on labels of any ingredients. The House bill did not contain the limiting word "constituent." Moreover, medicine labels must specify "the quantity or proportion of

[45] Anderson, *The Heath of a Nation*, 185–87; *Pure Food*, House Report 2118, 59 Cong. 1 ses., parts 1 and 2; *Cong. Record*, 59 Cong. 1 ses., 3489, 3494, 8890–92.

any alcohol therein, or any opium, cocaine, or other poisonous substance which may be contained therein."[46]

On two previous occasions, the House had passed a pure-food measure, only to have the Senate bill prevented by parliamentary tactics from coming to a vote. This time it appeared as if the same game might be underway, with the roles of the two chambers reversed. The months crept by, and House managers could not gain consideration for their bill. Other more important business seemed always to take precedence. Wiley became discouraged. He wrote an ally: "The city has been full of lobbyists with plenty of money, indomitable energy and unceasing push, and it appears that they have the poor little food bill by the throat and are administering to the infant a lethal dose of soothing sirup." On one occasion, friends of pure food saw professional lobbyists opposed to the bill checking out from Washington hotels and journeying to their homes. A journalist was told by a Republican leader of the House that, because of pressure from large business interests, the leadership had decided to let the bill die for the session.[47]

This rumor may have been untrue. Mann himself later denied it, saying that Speaker Cannon had constantly assured him that "the pure-food bill would have its day in court." Yet when June came and legislative lethargy still persisted, Wiley abandoned hope. He had not heard from Mann or Hepburn for a long time. The bill's friends seemed stricken with apathy, its foes "filled with new vigor daily." The measure, Wiley wrote Robert Allen, appeared to be "completely suffocated"; "I do not see any chance that it will [pass]."[48]

If, however, death by inaction was the sentence intended for the pure-food bill by its foes, fate entered in to reverse the judgment. While the bill languished, a rising tide of public anxiety had followed publication of Upton Sinclair's novel, a current powerful enough to make the pure-food issue a matter of great national concern.

[46] Anderson, *The Health of a Nation*, 186.

[47] Sullivan, *Our Times*, vol. 2, 534; *Chicago Tribune*, May 30, 1906; *Cong. Record*, 59 Cong. 1 ses., 6464–67, 8836–37; Wiley to William Frear, April 7, 1906, History Office, Food and Drug Administration, Rockville, MD.

[48] *Cong. Record*, 59 Cong. 1 ses., 8889–95; Anderson, *The Health of a Nation*, 188.

X

The Jungle and the Meat-Inspection Amendments

> As for the other men, who worked in tank-rooms full of steam,
> and in some of which there were open vats near the level of the
> floor, their peculiar trouble was that they fell into the vats; and
> when they were fished out, there was never enough of them left
> to be worth exhibiting,—sometimes they would be overlooked
> for days, till all but the bones of them had gone out to the world
> as Durham's Pure Leaf Lard!
> —UPTON SINCLAIR, *The Jungle*[1]

A Socialist Novelist's Revelations about Packingtown

A recent and earnest recruit to the romantic socialism of the turn of the
century, Upton Sinclair was led to Chicago's Packingtown by the failure
of a strike in 1904. The workers had challenged the power of the meat-
packing barons, but had gone down to defeat. Sinclair had written a
manifesto for the leading socialist paper, *Appeal to Reason*, offering the
stricken strikers hope through joining the Socialist party. In response
he received letters begging him to come to Chicago to report on their
lives.[2]

[1] Upton Sinclair, *The Jungle* (New York, 1906), 117. A shorter version of this chapter
was published as "The Pig that Fell into the Privy: Upton Sinclair's *The Jungle* and the
Meat Inspection Amendments of 1906," *Bull Hist Med* 59 (1985), 467–80.

[2] Sinclair gave his own account of events prompted by *The Jungle* in several works,
including *The Brass Check* (Pasadena, CA, [1919]); *American Outpost* (Pasadena, CA, 1932);
and *The Autobiography of Upton Sinclair* (New York, 1962), and he discussed them with
several interviewers at Claremont Graduate School: Upton Sinclair, "Reminiscences
about Some of his Novels and about his Political Career" (Typescript, Oral History Program, Claremont Graduate School, Claremont, California, 1963). The main biographical
accounts are William Bloodworth, Jr., "The Early Years of Upton Sinclair: A Study in the
Development of a Progressive Christian Socialist" (University of Texas dissertation, 1972),
and Leon Harris, *Upton Sinclair: American Rebel* (New York, 1975). The vast Upton Sinclair Archives at the Lilly Library of Indiana University contain very little prior to 1907,
for in that year Sinclair's papers were burned in a fire that destroyed his cooperative living
venture, Helicon Hall, financed by royalties from *The Jungle*. Sinclair's influence on the

Then twenty-five, Sinclair had been trying to make a living by writing romantic novels, none of which had sold well. His latest, *Manassas*, set in the Civil War, had passionately denounced the evil of enforced black servitude. The editor of *Appeal to Reason* wrote Sinclair suggesting a sequel to his fictional account of the struggle over chattel slavery which would depict the emerging battle over wage slavery. When the editor advanced the impoverished author $500 for serial rights, Sinclair accepted with alacrity, determined to set his novel in Packingtown.[3]

Arriving in Chicago in October 1904, Sinclair spent seven weeks among the stockyard workers, spying on the grisly scene of their lives and labors. He was aided in making contacts with workers by a socialist newspaper editor, Algie Martin Simons, and a liberal reporter, Ernest Poole. Poole remembered Sinclair as he arrived, "a lad in a wide-brimmed hat, with loose-flowing tie and a wonderful warm expansive smile." What Sinclair soon saw took the smile from his face. "I went about, white-faced and thin," he later wrote, "partly from undernourishment, partly from horror." Leaders of the failed strike gave Sinclair valuable tips. "You can go anywhere in these huge plants," one of them told him, "you can see anything you want to see; all you have to do is wear old clothes and carry a dinner pail. . . . Everybody, including the bosses, will take you to be a working man."[4]

meat-inspection provisions of 1906 has received considerable attention from scholars. An early example is Mark Sullivan, *Our Times*, vol. 2, 471–83, 535–50. Recent accounts include Martin I. Fausold, "James W. Wadsworth, Sr. and the Meat Inspection Act of 1906," *New York History* 51 (1970), 42–61; Joel Arthur Tarr, *A Study in Boss Politics: William Lorimer of Chicago* (Urbana, IL, 1971), 152–63; Christine Scriabine, "Upton Sinclair and the Writing of *The Jungle*," *Chicago History* 10 (Spring 1981), 26–37; Robert M. Crunden, *Ministers of Reform: The Progressives' Achievement in American Civilization, 1889–1920*, 163–99; "USDA Government Inspected," in James West Davidson and Mark Hamilton Lytle, *After the Fact: The Art of Historical Detection* (New York, 1982); Suk Bong Suh, "Literature, Society, and Culture: Upton Sinclair and *The Jungle*" (University of Iowa dissertation, 1986); and Louise Carroll Wade, "Upton Sinclair and Packingtown," a paper presented at the 1986 meeting of the American Historical Association. The most thorough exploration of the political repercussions of the novel is John Braeman, "The Square Deal in Action: A Case Study in the Growth of the 'National Police Power,' " in John Braeman, Robert H. Bremner, and Everett Walters, eds., *Change and Continuity in Twentieth-Century America* (Columbus, OH, 1964), 35–80.

[3] Sinclair, *American Outpost*, 153–56; Sinclair, "Reminiscences"; Sinclair, "What Life Means to Me," *Cosmopolitan* 41 (1906), 593; Allen F. Davis, *Spearheads for Reform* (New York, 1967), 117–20.

[4] Sinclair, *American Outpost*, 153–56; Sinclair, "Reminiscences"; Kent and Gretchen Kreuter, *An American Dissenter: The Life of Algie Martin Simons, 1870–1950* (Lexington, KY, 1969), 76–81; Ernest Poole, *The Bridge: My Own Story* (New York, 1940), 92–96; Truman Frederick Keefer, *Ernest Poole* (New York, 1966), 30–32. Later Simons was to review *The Jungle*, calling it a "great novel" that in some ways "surpassed" Zola, and insisting on the

In a 1906 interview Sinclair said he had made only three visits to the yards, although he later claimed he had explored "every inch" of the large packing plants. In the evenings he met with exstrikers and added their stories to his own observations. He expanded his inquiries to others with some knowledge of the yards, talking with lawyers, doctors, nurses, policemen, politicians, real-estate agents, settlement-house workers. Sinclair was fortunate to meet another inquirer bent on a similar mission. Adolphe Smith, an English expert on abattoirs, had come with a commission from the British medical journal, the *Lancet*, to evaluate Packingtown. A socialist with deep concern for the quality of working-class life, Smith had examined insanitary conditions in much of the world. He favored government-owned packing plants and judged privately owned plants severely. Sharing a day of observation, Smith helped Sinclair understand what he was seeing and place it in perspective. The English journalist told the American author that he had never encountered "such complete indifference to sanitation and to human considerations." This judgment confirmed Sinclair's own impressions: "To me it was the most horrible thing I had seen in all my life."[5]

Toward the end of his Chicago stay, Sinclair had assembled factual data but had not yet conceived a fictional framework. Walking the streets one Sunday afternoon, he followed a bridal procession to the back room of a saloon and spent four hours watching the celebration. This heart-warming scene Sinclair converted into the powerful opening episode of his novel. The Lithuanian groom became Jurgis, the book's tragic hero, and the bride, modified to embody the character of the author's wife, became Ona, *The Jungle*'s ill-fated heroine. Sinclair had assembled some printed sources that helped him as he planned his book: Smith's *Lancet* articles, editor Simons's 1899 pamphlet entitled, *Packingtown*, and reporter Poole's article about a typical Lithuanian worker in the packing plants.[6]

---

truth of Sinclair's most shocking charges: "Packingtown, 'The Jungle' and Its Critics," *International Socialist Review* 6 (1905–1906), 312–14.

[5] Frederick Boyd Stevenson, "Sinclair, the Beef Trust Griller," *Wilshire's Magazine*, August 1906; Sinclair, "Reminiscences"; Our Special Sanitary Commissioner [Adolphe Smith], "Chicago, The Stockyards and Packing Town," *Lancet* 1 (January 7, 1905), 49–52, (January 14), 120–23, (January 21), 183–85, (January 28), 258–60; Wade, "Upton Sinclair and Packingtown"; Adolphe Smith and John Thompson, *Street Life in London* (New York, 1969; originally published 1877); Adolphe Smith, *Monaco and Monte Carlo* (Philadelphia, 1912), 5–6.

[6] Sinclair, "Reminiscences"; Wade, "Upton Sinclair and Packingtown"; Algie Martin Simons, *Packingtown* (Chicago, 1899); Kreuter, *An American Dissenter*, 70–71, 76–79; Antanas Kaztauskis [Ernest Poole], "From Lithuania to the Chicago Stockyards—An Autobiography," *Independent* 52 (1904), 241–48; Poole, *The Bridge*, 95.

Sinclair began to write on Christmas day of 1904 in a rural cabin near Princeton, New Jersey. "I wrote that book sometimes blinded with my own tears," he later said; "it was such a terrible story." He finished his manuscript the following summer. Meanwhile, beginning in February 1905, the early chapters had been serialized in *Appeal to Reason*. Macmillan, which had published *Manassas*, refused to publish the new novel when squeamish evaluators advised that the stark realism of slaughterhouse scenes would keep the book from selling. Praise for the manuscript from Jack London did not change the editors' minds. Sinclair was unwilling to make all the cuts Macmillan demanded. Four other publishers also insisted on what the author deemed emasculating changes.[7]

Doubleday, Page & Company, however, sensed market potential in Sinclair's exposé. Sinclair considerably revised the text as it had appeared in socialist publications. Doubleday sent proofs to the *Chicago Tribune* editor, who replied calling Sinclair's charges of Packingtown's delinquencies "a tissue of falsehoods." Sinclair persuaded the publisher to dispatch an independent investigator to Chicago. The lawyer reported that a packer's publicity agent had written the *Tribune*'s negative evaluation, and that Sinclair's revelations were essentially true. Amid a flurry of publicity, Doubleday, Page placed *The Jungle* before the American public on February 18, 1906.[8]

The stark, tragic lives of Packingtown's laborers—from the venality involved in getting jobs, through the long hours of grueling toil while work lasted, to the desperate insecurity when unemployment came—formed the central theme of Sinclair's novel, presented with anguished pathos through the story of Jurgis and Ona, their relatives, and their circle of immigrant friends. Packingtown's working environment *The Jungle* painted in darkest hue: the noisy turbulence of the cattle pens, the bloody squalor of the killing beds, the penetrating dampness of the chilling rooms, the dusty stench of the fertilizer plant, the fetid steaminess of the tank rooms.

As an inevitable, if secondary, part of his pattern, Sinclair depicted the impact of that environment and of the packers' pressure for profits upon the nation's meat supply. He described the casualness of govern-

[7] Sinclair, "Reminiscences"; Sinclair, *American Outpost*, 158; Sinclair, *The Brass Check*, 32–38; Harris, *Upton Sinclair*, 78–82. *The Jungle* appeared in *Appeal to Reason*, February 25–November 4, 1905, but was not completed, although the ending appeared in another Socialist publication, *One-Hoss Philosophy*: Ronald Gottesman, *Upton Sinclair: An Annotated Checklist* (Kent, OH, 1973), 30; Suh, "Literature, Society, and Culture," 129–30.

[8] *Ibid.*, 80–81; Upton Sinclair, "The Condemned-Meat Industry: A Reply to Mr. J. Ogden Armour," *Everybody's Magazine* 14 (1906), 608–16. Suh, "Literature, Society, and Culture," 137–63, analyzes in great detail the nature and intent of Sinclair's changes in the text.

ment inspectors, easily distracted when unfit carcasses, cattle that had just calved or had died from unknown causes on freight trains en route to the yards, came through the line. Hogs dead from cholera on the trains, Sinclair wrote, were sent on to a plant in Indiana and rendered into lard. Meat that had turned sour was rubbed with soda to remove the smell and sold to free-lunch counters. Spoiled hams were treated again with a stronger pickling compound or had the bone removed and the spoiled part burned out with a white-hot iron.[9]

The greatest deception and threat, Sinclair charged, came from meat that was canned or ground. Cattle killed for canning, "old . . . crippled . . . diseased," would take "a Dante or a Zola" to describe. What was advertised as "potted chicken" really contained pork and beef fat, tripe, and waste ends of veal; "deviled ham" consisted of similar ingredients, plus "the hard cartilaginous gullets of beef, after the tongue had been cut out." Sausage might be made from tubercular pork unfit for export, hams too badly spoiled to refurbish, and old sausage, "mouldy and white," returned from Europe where it had been rejected.[10] Sinclair wrote:

> There would [also] be meat [in sausage] that had tumbled out on the floor, in the dirt and sawdust, where the workers had tramped and spit uncounted billions of consumption germs. There would be meat stored in great piles in rooms; and the water from leaky roofs would drip over it, and thousands of rats would race about on it. It was too dark in these storage places to see well, but a man could run his hand over these piles of meat and sweep off handfuls of the dried dung of rats. These rats were nuisances, and the packers would put poisoned bread out for them; they would die, and then rats, bread and meat would go into the hoppers together.[11]

Packingtown products, Sinclair asserted, became contaminated in even more abhorrent ways. Sometimes workers fell into vats and were converted into lard.[12]

The stage had been set for such shocking charges to produce a national sensation. The "embalmed beef" scandal of the Spanish-American War lay near enough the surface of public memory for quick recall. Since the war the packers had garnered numerous new critical headlines on

[9] Sinclair, *The Jungle,* 42, 73–74, 114, 160–61.

[10] *Ibid.,* 114–15, 160–62.

[11] *Ibid.,* 161. Wade makes clear that Sinclair's stress on the spitting by tuberculous workers in the packing plants reached readers increasingly agitated by public campaigns aimed at this dread disease: "Upton Sinclair and Packingtown."

[12] Sinclair, *The Jungle,* 117. This episode Sinclair found in Simons's *Packingtown.*

economic grounds. For a quarter of a century meat processing had reigned as one of the nation's largest industries, with the giant Chicago-based packers, pressuring the railroads to give them rebates, constantly increasing the extent of their oligopolistic power. To muckraking journalists, all trusts endangered the populace, and the beef trust came to be seen as the most threatening of all.[13]

Charles Edward Russell, in a series of articles for *Everybody's Magazine* that ran from February through August 1905, called the beef trust "The Greatest Trust in the World." The Big Four packers wielded "a greater power than in the history of men has been exercised by king, emperor, or irresponsible oligarchy." Indeed, wrote Russell, the beef trust owned "politicians, legislators, and Congressmen."[14]

Russell did not intend to paint Armour, Swift, and their cohorts in colors of personal villainy, but to expose the harm that good men do. He posed the paradox of "crime and lawlessness" brought about by businessmen themselves virtuous. The leaders of the beef trust had "merely followed to its logical conclusion the idea of the survival of the fittest, the right of the strong to annihilate the weak." The system, not the individual, lay at fault, and for that system all Americans held moral responsibilty. More rigorous enforcement of antitrust legislation, including the punishment of individuals for corporate wrong-doing, Russell suggested, might save the republic.[15]

The trend, however, did not seem to be in that remedial direction. The packers had just formulated a new corporate entity, the National Packing Company. Russell read into this structure the cause behind a decline in prices paid to cattle producers and a simultaneous rise in prices charged to consumers of beef.[16] Consumers were easily aroused. No nation in the world except Australia had as high a per capita consumption of meat as did the United States, 179 pounds a year, 186 pounds if lard was included.[17]

---

[13] Mary Yeager, *Competition and Regulation: The Development of Oligopoly in the Meat Packing Industry* (Greenwich, CT, 1981); Chandler, *The Visible Hand*, 295, 299–302, 334, 349, 381, 391–402, 413–14, 463. The early history, up to 1893, of the yards is presented in Wade, *Chicago's Pride: The Stockyards, Packingtown, and Environs in the Nineteenth Century*.

[14] Charles Edward Russell, "The Greatest Trust in the World," *Everybody's Magazine* 12 (1905), 147–56, 291–300, 503–16, 643–54, 779–92, 13 (1905), 56–66, 217–27. The articles were immediately published in a book, *The Greatest Trust in the World* (New York, 1905), to which citations in the text refer, 3, 5, 34–44, 193–99.

[15] *Ibid.*, 89, 227–41.

[16] *Ibid.*, 13, 14, 105. Yeager, *Competition and Regulation*, analyzes the formation of the National Packing Company.

[17] These figures are as of 1900. A. D. Melvin, "The Federal Meat-Inspection Service," in

Public concern over advancing beef prices helped give the beef trust high priority on the list of trusts Theodore Roosevelt wanted to investigate and to restrain. The popular mood about a major issue always played a decisive part in the course Roosevelt chose to adopt. After several months of Justice Department probing, in May 1902 the government sought to enjoin the major packing companies from continuing a number of collusive practices like rigging bids for livestock and fixing retail meat prices, which allegedly violated the Sherman Antitrust Act. The courts awarded the government merely a pyrrhic victory. The packers saw quickly that, by treading carefully, they could continue their dominance in the meat marketplace. Journalistic critics and the informed public, however, were doubly aroused by the judicial contest: the government's charges had publicized the packers' iniquities, yet the courts' decisions had not really curtailed the beef barons' power.[18]

Roosevelt somewhat mistrusted the courts as agencies for curbing the trusts, and desired to bring greater antimonopoly initiative into the executive branch. Particularly he wanted to give more publicity to malefactions of great wealth. So he sought from Congress, and secured in 1903, a Bureau of Corporations in the Department of Commerce and Labor. This bureau, headed by James R. Garfield, son of the assassinated president, would study corporate practices and make abuses known. The beef trust, already deemed "evil" by the president, became the first object of the bureau's inquiry.[19]

The resulting document, in the words of a recent scholar, was "coldly analytical and cautious, . . . a model of objectivity and restraint." That the packers controlled prices so absolutely, as Charles Edward Russell had charged, seemed doubtful to the bureau. Nor did it side with popular opinion that the spread between cattle and beef prices in 1903 was unusually wide. Considering costs, the bureau concluded, beef prices were "reasonable." Consumers had no right to complain.[20]

Complain, however, they continued to do, not only about prices but now also about the bureau's lack of integrity and competence. "The public is not interested in tedious and voluminous reports," opined the *New York Sun*. "It wants to know why its steaks and its roasts cost more than they did a short time ago." Terming the report "preposterous," the *New York Press* urged Garfield to resign forthwith. Russell, outraged,

---

Department of Agriculture, Bureau of Animal Industry, *Twenty-Third Annual Report* (1908), 59 Cong. 2 ses., House Doc. 53, 65.

[18] Cooper, *The Warrior and the Priest*, 70; Yeager, *Competition and Regulation*, 181–85.

[19] *Ibid.*, 185–88; Arthur M. Johnson, "Theodore Roosevelt and the Bureau of Corporations," *Miss Val Hist Rev* 45 (1959), 571–90; Swift and Co. v. U.S., 196 U.S. 375 (1905).

[20] Yeager, *Competition and Regulation*, 187.

thought the bureau's findings filled with "gross inaccuracies and amazing misstatements."[21]

Worse yet was to come. Bureau of Corporations information that Roosevelt thought would help the court penalize packers for their misdeeds, instead got them off the hook. In the trial of the leading figures in the beef trust for having violated the terms of an earlier court injunction, the judge accepted defense interpretations and ruled that the bureau had secured information from the packers under what amounted to compulsion. Thus, under the Fifth Amendment, company officials could not be prosecuted for guilty actions they had admitted to bureau agents. This "immunity bath," as the attorney general dubbed the decision, upset both president and populace. To make things still worse, during the trial the government became convinced that the packers were bribing reporters to write slanted accounts. The judge's ruling came in March 1905, the month after publication of *The Jungle*. Both in the White House and in the public forum, the rising protest revealed a sudden change. Economic aggravations angered, but they did not equal the nausea and outrage produced by threats to diet and health.[22]

While economic issues had dominated attacks on the beef trust prior to *The Jungle*, hints of health concern had not been wholly absent. The campaign Harvey Wiley waged against preservatives included, but did not concentrate upon, canned meat, helping keep alive the trauma of "embalmed beef." Adolphe Smith's *Lancet* series, terming the packing plants of Chicago "truly Augean stables," warned that Americans might be "swallow[ing] trichinae wholesale" and tuberculosis germs as well. Smith preceded Sinclair in reporting allegations that some workers had met an "awful death" by falling into vats and being rendered into lard. An upstate New York butcher who had worked for the beef trust through forty years published a book focused entirely on threats to health posed by meat from Packingtown. The butcher's charges were expressed with an explicitness that rivaled Sinclair's own. Even Russell, toward the end of his long economic indictment of the packers, managed a brief mention of health hazards in their meats. Reminding readers of the Spanish-American War scandal, and referring to the *Lancet*'s "terrifying allegations," Russell called inspection laws "a jest" and al-

[21] *Ibid.*, 188; *New York Sun*, April 29, 1905, cited in Johnson, "Theodore Roosevelt and the Bureau of Corporations," 382; Russell, *The Greatest Trust in the World*, 142–72.

[22] Johnson, "Theodore Roosevelt and the Bureau of Corporations," 571–90; Yeager, *Competition and Regulation*, 189–90; Roosevelt to William Henry Moody, January 26, 1906, Theodore Roosevelt Papers, Library of Congress. Some letters from this collection cited in this chapter are included in Elting E. Morison, ed., *The Letters of Theodore Roosevelt*, 8 vols. (Cambridge, MA, 1951–1954), vol. 5.

luded vaguely to "dark secrets" of meat processing beyond the possibility of public viewing.[23]

None of these exposures produced public panic. Either foreign, obscure, or passing references in journalism with a basically different intent, these charges of dangers in the diet left the citizenry largely unmoved. So too did Sinclair's novel as serialized in a socialist newspaper. So too had Wiley's long campaign against all food adulteration as immoral and, with respect to preservatives, dangerous.

The Jungle as a book, however, spurred a mighty reaction in the body politic that, in four months, led to the enactment of two laws. As Sinclair throughout his long life never ceased saying, protecting the public diet had not been his intent. He had hoped to win converts to socialism. In that he mainly failed. His comparatively few pages on the unclean conditions in Packingtown and in its products were what upset the citizenry. In a famous remark, Sinclair himself summed up the situation: "I aimed at the public's heart, and by accident I hit it in the stomach."[24]

Several factors explain *The Jungle*'s rapid rise to notoriety. Doubleday, Page, for all their genteel worries about accepting the manuscript, engaged in extensive promotion, alerting readers to the book's charges about tainted meat. Page proofs were sent to leading newspapers throughout the country, with a release date, so that when Sinclair's novel came off the press, it received a barrage of shocked comment. Sinclair himself beat the drum for *The Jungle* from an informal office he set up in a New York hotel. The publisher liberally distributed publicity copies, not neglecting the president. Roosevelt also received the novel from James R. Garfield, Senator Alfred J. Beveridge of Indiana, and Upton Sinclair. Angry at the packers, disturbed by their attempts to bribe the press, frustrated by the failure of efforts to control them through the courts, the president read the book at once.[25]

Early reviews in middle-class magazines rejected Sinclair's socialist propaganda and considered the novel, as fiction, poor. "Its figures are

[23] Smith, "Chicago, The Stockyards and Packing Town," *Lancet* 1 (January 7, 1905), 50, (January 14), 122, (January 28), 259–60; Samuel Merwin, "The Private-Car Abuse," *Success Magazine* 8 (1905), 249–54; Herman Hirschauer, *The Dark Side of the Beef Trust* (Jamestown, NY, 1905); Russell, *The Greatest Trust in the World*, 211–13. Russell did write that "thousands of cows that never should be slaughtered are cut up for food."

[24] Sinclair, "What Life Means to Me," 594.

[25] Christopher P. Wilson, *The Labor of Words: Literary Professionalism in the Progressive Era* (Athens, GA, 1985), 137–39; Suh, "Literature, Society, and Culture," 283–86; Crunden, *Ministers of Reform*, 189; Braeman, "The Square Deal in Action," 45; Braeman, *Albert J. Beveridge: American Nationalist* (Chicago, 1971), 102. Isaac F. Marcosson, who engineered the promotion of *The Jungle* for Doubleday, Page, discusses his role in *Adventures in Interviewing* (New York, 1919), 280–89.

puppets," wrote the *Dial* reviewer, "its construction is chaotic, its style is turgid." *Outlook* accused Sinclair of excessive sensationalism. *Independent* judged that he had focused unduly on "what is abnormal, painful, decayed." Yet most commentators singled out bad meat for mention, suggesting—in the words of *Outlook*—that *The Jungle*, despite its fictional faults, would serve a useful purpose if it could lead to "more rigid inspection and more drastic regulation."[26]

The diseased meat theme unquestionably explained *The Jungle*'s soaring sales. Twenty-five thousand copies were bought in the first six weeks. Seven thousand copies, Sinclair noted, were sold on one day in June. During July and August *The Jungle* reigned as the nation's bestseller, in September passing the 100,000 mark. More than a million readers had read the novel, it was estimated, by the end of 1906. The book became an international sensation. A British edition appeared, reviewed by Winston Churchill, commented on by H. G. Wells and George Bernard Shaw. Translations were published in seventeen languages. The evils of Packingtown first denounced by the *Lancet*, editorialized that journal, and more recently criticized by Sinclair, "are now being re-echoed by the press of all countries."[27]

The packers did not suffer Sinclair's slings and arrows in silence. Ogden Armour, *The Jungle*'s author learned later, had wanted to sue Sinclair for libel, but officials of the firm persuaded the packer that the effort posed great risk. Sinclair had documents of state cases in which the company had pleaded guilty and paid fines for selling meats containing forbidden adulterants and preservatives. Instead, speaking for the trust, Armour published a ghost-written series of articles in the *Saturday Evening Post* seeking to counter "ignorantly or maliciously false statements." Government inspection served its intended purpose, Armour argued, and was not guilty of the weaknesses charged by critics. "In Armour & Co.'s business," its chief asserted flatly, *"not one atom of any condemned animal carcass finds its way, directly or indirectly, from any source, into any food product or food ingredient."*[28]

[26] William Morton Payne, "Recent Fiction," *Dial* 40 (1906), 262; "Socialist Fiction Pro and Con," *Public Opinion* 40 (1906), 476, 479–80; "A Group of Novels," *Outlook* 82 (1906), 758; "The Jungle," *Independent* 60 (1906), 740–41.
[27] Braeman, "The Square Deal in Action," 45; Harris, *Upton Sinclair*, 83; Sinclair, "What Life Means to Me," 591–95; "The Chicago Stockyards and the Meat Scandal," *Lancet* 2 (1906), 1626; Scriabine, "Upton Sinclair and the Writing of *The Jungle*," 31; Winston Spencer Churchill, "The Chicago Scandals: The Novel Which Is Making History," *P.T.O.*, June 16, 1906, 25–26, June 23, 1906, 65–66; H. G. Wells, *The Future in America: A Search After Realities* (New York, 1974; originally published 1906), 84, 118. Suh, "Literature, Society, and Culture," 303–7, 311–13, analyzes most fully *The Jungle*'s sales record.
[28] Eight articles under Armour's name appeared in the *Saturday Evening Post* during the

Armour's defense brought countercharges, the continuing debate expanding public concern. Sinclair took the lead in rebutting Armour, insisting in several articles that the packers' hygienic failings, which he had clothed in the guise of fiction, indeed were sordid fact. Other partisans joined Sinclair in refuting Armour: the former head of meat inspection for Chicago, who had been removed from office for taking his job seriously; a woman physician who practiced among Packingtown's workers; the lawyer sent out by Doubleday to check on the authenticity of Sinclair's charges. Writing in the Doubleday, Page magazine, *World's Work*, they all found Armour's rosy picture fallacious.[29]

Popular magazines also wielded the weapon of photojournalism. Sinclair's most shocking allegations could not be pictured, but the packers' vaunted disassembly line appeared as an abhorrent spectacle set on a stage of filth. Cattle were knocked on the head; hogs had their throats slit; blood ran deep in the killing beds. In dirty rooms some meat became canned beef, some filled sausage skins.[30]

The public voted in the marketplace, where Armour lost and Sinclair won. Another packer, Thomas E. Wilson, testifying before the House Committee on Agriculture, said that the sale of "fresh meats and manufactured products" had "apparently [been] cut in two." The president could empathize with the public: the crisis brought vividly to his mind the canned meat he had consumed in Cuba.[31]

Suspicious of the packers yet aware of their power in his party, sobered by Sinclair's allegations yet offended by his propaganda for socialism, Roosevelt began strenuously to seek further information that

---

first half of 1906, vol. 178, which were then collected in a book, *The Packers, the Private Car Lines, and the People* (Philadelphia, 1906). The quotation is from Armour, "The Packers and the People," *Sat Eve Post* 178 (March 10, 1906), 8. Sinclair, *The Brass Check*, 34–35; Sinclair, "Reminiscences"; Filler, *Crusaders for American Liberalism*, 166.

[29] Sinclair, "Is Chicago's Meat Clean?" *Collier's* 35 (April 22, 1905), 13–14; Sinclair, "The Condemned Meat Industry," *Everybody's* 14 (1906), 608–16; Sinclair, "Stockyard Secrets," *Collier's* 36 (March 24, 1906), 24; Sinclair, "Is *The Jungle* True?" *Independent* 60 (1906), 1129–33; Sinclair, "The Meat-Inspection Situation," *Collier's* 37 (June 16, 1906), 24, 26. The three articles by knowledgeable Chicagoans appeared in *World's Work*: W. K. Jacques, "A Picture of Meat Inspection," Caroline Hedges, "The Unhealthfulness of Packingtown," and Thomas H. McKee, "The Failure of Government Inspection," 12 (1906), 7491–7514. *Literary Digest* also paid close attention to the debate.

[30] *Current Literature* 41 (1906), 4–10; *Collier's* 37 (June 23, 1906), 14; photograph reproduced in Fausold, "James W. Wadsworth, Sr. and the Meat Inspection Act of 1906," 53.

[31] *Conditions in the Stock Yards*, Hearings before the Committee on Agriculture . . . on the So-called "Beveridge Amendment" to the Agricultural Appropriation Bill (H.R. 18,537), 59 Cong. 1 ses. (Washington, 1906), 75. Sinclair wrote that Roosevelt had told him how the meat crisis had caused him to remember the canned meat in Cuba: *American Outpost*, 167.

would let him determine where the truth lay. Immediately upon *The Jungle*'s publication, Secretary of Agriculture Wilson launched an investigation. To check on Sinclair's charges of inspection-service laxness, Wilson sent three of his key aides to Chicago—the department's top lawyer and the chiefs of inspection and of pathology in the Bureau of Animal Industry. The secretary simultaneously ordered inspectors to make sure that condemned carcasses were destroyed, and he tightened regulations governing sanitation in packing plants.[32]

In due course the department's report reached Roosevelt's desk, a detailed technical document, defensive in tone, followed shortly by a sequel seeking to refute specific charges made against the inspection system in *The Jungle*, the *Lancet*, and *World's Work*. Accusations against inspectors of neglect and corruption could be written off as "willful and deliberate misrepresentations." As to insanitation, a few bad instances had been deliberately exaggerated to make uncleanliness seem characteristic of the whole. Sinclair had been particularly guilty of such distortions.[33]

The president did not believe that the department's report, when it reached him in early April, provided "the clear, definite answers" to widespread criticisms of packer and inspector practices that he required. In any case, Roosevelt had not waited patiently for the department's verdict on its own employees. Sinclair had gone beyond giving his book to Roosevelt. The author, in a barrage of letters and telegrams to the president, insisted that official judgments could not be relied on, because the Department of Agriculture was part of the problem. Sinclair urged Roosevelt to check the facts by means of a secret independent investigator. This course seemed persuasive to the president, and he recommended it to Secretary Wilson, sending along Sinclair's letter. No "merely perfunctory investigation" would do, Roosevelt told the secretary. "I would like a first-class man to be appointed to meet Sinclair, as

---

[32] Braeman, "The Square Deal in Action," 47. The three investigators were solicitor George P. McCabe, pathologist John Mohler, and chief of inspectors R. P. Steddom. Garfield had told Roosevelt, as the president reported it to Sinclair, that the "conclusions" of *The Jungle* "were too pessimistic, but that there was very much of what you had done in which he absolutely sympathized with you." See Roosevelt to Sinclair, March 9, 1906, Roosevelt Papers. E. B. Miller, in "How Important was Upton Sinclair's *The Jungle* to Federal Meat Inspection Reform?" *Veterinary Heritage* 10 (February 1987), 3–25, makes clear how the inspection laws of the 1890s and new developments in science had improved the quality of education in veterinary medicine and the technical skill of federal inspectors.

[33] Committee Report to Secretary of Agriculture, April 3, 1906, and Supplemental Report of Department Committee, April 12, 1906, in Department of Agriculture, Bureau of Animal Industry, *Twenty-Third Annual Report*, 407–56; Braeman, "The Square Deal in Action," 49.

he suggests; get the names of witnesses, as he suggests; and then go to work in the industry, as he suggests." Keep the person chosen "absolutely secret," the president warned. Wilson thought the most suitable investigator might be the commissioner of labor, Charles P. Neill, a former political-economy professor at Catholic University who had earlier lived in the University of Chicago Settlement House near the packing yards at which Sinclair had eaten his meals while in the city. Neill had helped Roosevelt before on social-welfare questions. The president, after checking with Jane Addams, approved the suggestion. He paired with Neill a social worker from New York City, James B. Reynolds, who had a law degree and who had served as secretary to the New York mayor.[34]

The president invited Sinclair to come to Washington, where, as the young socialist remembered it, the two had "several conferences," including a White House lunch with part of the "tennis" cabinet. Roosevelt wanted Sinclair to go to Chicago with Neill and Reynolds to introduce them to his sources of information. Thinking himself too busy, Sinclair arranged at his own expense for two of his socialist friends to head west to arrange contacts for Roosevelt's commissioners. Ella Reeve Cohen had earlier written about Packingtown for Hearst, and now she returned, accompanied by a younger socialist, Richard Bloor, to gather information for Neill and Reynolds. Sinclair suggested that Ella and Richard pose as a married couple, and as a result the Bloor name "clung to" Ella for the rest of her life. Living with packinghouse workers, Sinclair's emissaries lined up a list of witnesses from whom they gained the impression that even Sinclair had underestimated the gravity of the packers' delinquencies. Ella Bloor concluded that "no words are adequate to paint the horrors of the packing houses."[35]

In her first report to Sinclair—which he quoted in a letter to the president—Ella Bloor noted deep suspicion among workers about the sincerity of the Neill-Reynolds mission. It had been planned as an under-

---

[34] *Ibid.*, 48–49; Roosevelt to Sinclair, March 9, 15, and 21, April 9, 11, and 13, May 29, June 2, 1906; Sinclair to Roosevelt, April 10 (two letters and a telegram) and 12, May 20, June 1, 1906, (Sinclair's early letters are referred to in Roosevelt's replies); Roosevelt to James Wilson, March 12 and 22, 1906, Roosevelt Papers; *Conditions in the Stock Yards* (Hearings), 140–41; Davis, *Spearheads for Reform*, 120–21; John J. Carey, "Reynolds, James B." in Walter I. Trattner, ed., *Biographical Dictionary of Social Welfare in America* (New York, 1986), 620–21.

[35] Roosevelt to Sinclair, March 9 and 15, 1906, Roosevelt Papers; Sinclair, *The Brass Check*, 39–40; Ella Reeve Bloor, *We Are Many* (New York, 1940), 82–91; *NY Times*, May 29, 1906; Ingrid Winther Scobie, "Bloor, Ella Reeve," in John A. Garraty, ed., *Dictionary of American Biography: Supplement Five* (New York, 1977), 69–71. Ella Reeve was destined to gain notoriety as the Communist "Mother" Bloor.

cover inquiry, but Neill's prominence made impossible the secrecy Sinclair thought indispensable. Men so well known could hardly be expected to prowl around incognito. The Chicago press announced the commissioners' arrival, and agents for each packer met them at the front door and accompanied them on their rounds. Thus Sinclair's secret informers dared not meet with Neill and Reynolds for fear of exposure. Indeed, workers with whom the Bloors talked believed the whole venture was intended to be a "whitewashing."[36]

This impression seemed substantiated by a front-page *Chicago Tribune* story on April 10, stating that the Department of Agriculture team had refuted Sinclair's charges against the packers and that Roosevelt would condemn *The Jungle* in a forthcoming speech. In great agitation, Sinclair both telegraphed and wrote the president. "I cannot believe," he said, "that you will allow falsehoods to be telegraphed to Chicago Tribune in your name and feel that I am entitled to vindication."[37]

Roosevelt took great pains to deny the *Tribune*'s allegations and to explain to Sinclair how the false dispatch probably came to be written. Throughout their association, indeed, the president treated the socialist writer with overt courtesy and sought to calm his outbursts of excited suspicion. It was a strange alliance. Sinclair recognized in Roosevelt the surest source of vindication for his own criticisms of the packers. Moreover, his association with the president, which had an air of conspiratorial scheming, must have been flattering to the young writer's ego. Yet Sinclair recurringly doubted Roosevelt's thorough fidelity to the cause, and when he did so, as in the *Tribune* instance, he let Roosevelt know. Sinclair also urged the president to keep in mind the grievances of workers as well as the stomachs of consumers.[38]

Roosevelt deplored Sinclair's socialism and became exasperated with his outbursts. Yet the president took time to compose a calm refutation of the author's socialist arguments, ending with a handwritten postscript: "But all this has nothing to do with the fact that the specific ills you point to, shall, if their existence be proved, and if I have the power, be eradicated." Roosevelt also reassured Sinclair that he had asked Neill "to give me a report upon the workers just as much as upon the meats," even though the president had authority to deal only with the latter. Further, Roosevelt told Sinclair that packer awareness of the Neill-Reynolds mission did not necessarily obviate a plan for a secret investi-

[36] Sinclair to Roosevelt, April 10, 1906, Roosevelt Papers; Suh, "Literature, Society, and Culture," 291; Braeman, "The Square Deal in Action," 48–52.

[37] *Ibid.*, 53; two letters and a telegram, Sinclair to Roosevelt, April 10, 1906, Roosevelt Papers.

[38] *Ibid.*; Roosevelt to Sinclair, April 11, 1906, Roosevelt Papers.

gation "by a special man to be put inside to find out the exact facts," a venture "that will doubtless take months."³⁹

While cooperating with Sinclair for the advantages it would provide in obtaining facts, Roosevelt was motivated always by the suspicion that *The Jungle* had grossly exaggerated, if not falsified. Sinclair could not have missed this point in the president's letters. Roosevelt kept urging him to avoid making "reckless statements" in public not sustained with proof. Another refrain recurred: "Really, Mr. Sinclair, you *must* keep your head." Impetuosity could not hasten the investigation. "I intend before I get through," Roosevelt wrote, "to be able to have authoritative reasons for saying 'proved,' or 'unproved,' or 'not susceptible of proof,' or 'probably true,' or 'probably untrue,' on each specific charge advanced against the packers." He would neither be hurried nor thwarted.⁴⁰

When Neill and Reynolds returned to Washington early in May from their two-and-a-half weeks in Chicago, they presented the president with an oral report on conditions in the stockyards, which he later summed up in the word "revolting." Sinclair hurried to Washington to talk with the commissioners, and what they told him gave him a sense of complete vindication. Despite the lack of secrecy, they had assembled enough facts to substantiate his principal charges. Only a few of his grisly details, like the rendering of workers into lard, remained undocumented. While Neill and Reynolds considered unproven the certainty of malfeasance by government inspectors, they granted that ample opportunity existed. Sinclair returned home hoping that Neill and Reynolds would rapidly write up and publish what they had learned, thus giving a sort of governmental sanction to *The Jungle*.⁴¹

A President's Negotiations about Meat

The plans of Theodore Roosevelt, however, differed from those of Upton Sinclair. By the time the president heard from his commissioners, his main goal had changed from revelation to legislation. He had begun to consider the threat of announcing to the nation the Neill-Reynolds discoveries as a valuable club to hold over the heads of packers to get

³⁹ Roosevelt to Owen Wister, April 27, 1906; Roosevelt to Sinclair, March 15, April 9 and 11, 1906, Roosevelt Papers. There is no evidence that such a secret investigation was undertaken.

⁴⁰ Roosevelt to Sinclair, April 11 and May 29, 1906, Roosevelt Papers.

⁴¹ Braeman, "The Square Deal in Action," 41; *Conditions in the Stockyards*, 59 Cong. 1 ses., House Doc. 873, consisting of the Message of the President to the Congress, June 4, 1906, transmitting the report by Reynolds and Neill, and the text of that report, "The Conditions of the Stock Yards of Chicago"; Sinclair, "Reminiscences"; Sinclair, *The Brass Check*, 40; *NY Times*, May 28 and 29, 1906.

them to acquiesce in a remedial law. The meat barons had made evident their fear of more bad publicity. A packer agent had besought Neill to keep silent, promising that reasonable suggestions for improvements would be promptly put into effect, after which a new investigation could be made. The commissioner had replied that he had no authorization "to make trades." Next, Louis F. Swift talked with the president, promising to correct inadequacies in the packing plants voluntarily if Roosevelt would prevent the commissioners' report from going to press. The president insisted that legislation was necessary.[42]

Even before *The Jungle*, Senator Beveridge had reached the same conclusion. In the process of transforming himself from a conservative to a progressive, Beveridge sensed that the pure-meat issue might advance his political fortunes. Publication of *The Jungle* confirmed him in this belief. With the encouragement and aid of Garfield, Beveridge began to work on the draft of a bill to mandate for the domestic market the laws of the 1890s enacted to reassure Europeans that American meat was safe. When the senator told the president what he was doing, Roosevelt answered, "Bully, but you'd better wait until Neill and Reynolds get back from Chicago." Beveridge had not known the president had sent them there. When they returned the Indiana senator added them to his counselors and continued drafting. At a dinner party Beveridge received a second surprise: he learned from Secretary Wilson that Solicitor George McCabe of Agriculture was also drawing up a bill. Desiring priority, Beveridge asked the president to tell Wilson to send the senator a copy of the bill. The secretary reluctantly complied. Beveridge preferred his own effort, but in his continuing revision he added Wilson and the chief of the Bureau of Animal Industry, A. D. Melvin, to his collaborators. On May 21, the day after completing his draft, Beveridge introduced the bill in the Senate.[43]

Beveridge's bill required the inspection of all cattle, sheep, swine, and goats whose meat was to be sold in interstate or foreign commerce. Carcasses found "unfit for human food" must be destroyed. Meat products and canned meats must also be inspected and dated. Such products found by inspectors "to be impure, unsound, composed of unhealthful ingredients, or . . . treated with . . . dyes or deleterious chemicals," must be destroyed. All meat and meat products crossing state lines must bear the mark "inspected and passed." Sanitary conditions in the packing houses came explicitly under the purview of the Department of Agriculture. To ensure enough inspectors and to protect them from recur-

---

[42] Braeman, "The Square Deal in Action," 53–54; Tarr, *A Study in Boss Politics*, 155; *Conditions in the Stockyards* (Hearings), 34–35, 95–99.

[43] Braeman, *Albert J. Beveridge*, 101–2; Braeman, "The Square Deal in Action," 54–55; Claude G. Bowers, *Beveridge and the Progressive Era* (Boston, 1932), 226–29.

rent economy drives in Congress, the bill provided for funding inspection not from annual appropriations of Congress, but from a fee fixed by the secretary of agriculture and levied on packers for every animal inspected.[44]

Beveridge was proud of his bill, both as a consumer protection measure and as an expression of national authority. The measure, he wrote in a letter, represented "THE MOST PRONOUNCED EXTENSION OF FEDERAL POWER IN EVERY DIRECTION EVER ENACTED."[45]

Beveridge's bill sent a new shock wave through packer ranks. Having been rebuffed in a direct appeal to the president, the meat barons sent their allies into battle. The costs of inspection under the Indiana senator's proposal, the packers told livestock raisers, would be passed on to them, putting greater pressure on their already threatened industry. This scare tactic worked. The American National Livestock Association provoked a barrage of letters and telegrams aimed at the White House, opposing both the bill and the release of Neill and Reynolds's findings. Two livestock leaders met with Roosevelt and told him of the packers' desire to sanitize their plants. Expressing sympathy for the livestock growers' plight, the president insisted on the need for the law. He bolstered his claim by having Neill summarize his Chicago findings for the cattle raisers and senators from their states.[46]

Four days after introducing his bill, Beveridge attached it as an amendment to the pending Agricultural Appropriation Act. Roosevelt renewed his threat to release the Neill and Reynolds report unless a satisfactory law was enacted. One of the cattlemen met with Beveridge, who refused to postpone his insistence upon a vote. The stockman phoned to Chicago for instructions. The packers, perhaps in some panic, more likely deciding that better terrain for a fight lay in the House, decided not to oppose Beveridge's effort. Without a dissenting vote, the amendment passed the Senate.[47]

The next day, cheered by the vote, the president pushed his campaign in a letter to James W. Wadsworth, chairman of the House Committee on Agriculture. Again he threatened to reveal the "hideous" conditions in the packing houses, discovered by Neill and Reynolds, unless a bill substantially like the Beveridge amendment promptly became law. Even the packers, Roosevelt asserted, would benefit by such a statute.[48]

Neither the packers, however, nor Representative Wadsworth, him-

[44] *Cong. Record*, 59 Cong. 1 ses., 7127, 7420–21; Braeman, *Albert J. Beveridge*, 102–3; Braeman, "The Square Deal in Action," 55–57.

[45] *Ibid.*, 57; Braeman, *Albert J. Beveridge*, 103.

[46] Braeman, "The Square Deal in Action," 58–59.

[47] *Ibid.*; *Cong. Record*, 59 Cong. 1 ses., 7420–21.

[48] Roosevelt to Wadsworth, May 26, 1906, Roosevelt Papers.

self a raiser of cattle in upstate New York, concurred with the president. Reversing their private promises to Roosevelt of voluntary reform, the beef barons denied publicly that anything serious was wrong. All criticisms were untrue. No new law was needed. The Beveridge amendment contained unnecessary impositions upon the industry. Dating cans would discourage purchasers, when in fact adequately canned meats remained safe for years. Dyes and preservatives enhanced rather than harmed canned meats and therefore should not be banned. Nor should packers be required to shoulder the cost of inspection. Even worse, Beveridge would place the packers at the complete mercy of the secretary of agriculture, who could approve the shutting down of a plant by an inspector because of alleged insanitary conditions, with no appeal to the courts permitted on substantive grounds. This provision unconstitutionally deprived the packers of their property without due process of law.[49]

As Louis Filler has made clear, the intransigent posture assumed by the packers related to power. Like Beveridge, they recognized in his bill the vast expansion of federal authority over what had hitherto been considered private and personal concerns. If they could, they wanted to thwart this thrust. The spokesman for the Chicago packers at the House hearing shortly to come, Thomas E. Wilson, general manager of Nelson Morris & Company, made this plain. The basic issue, he stated, was "our right to control our business."

> What we are opposed to and what we appeal to you gentlemen for protection against, is a bill that will put our business in the hands of theorists, chemists, sociologists, etc., and the management and control taken away from the men who have devoted their lives to the upbuilding and perfecting of this great American industry.[50]

The intrusion of government in their business initiated by a rigorous meat inspection law would be bad enough. The packers further feared that such a law might be a harbinger of worse to come, an expanding interference by government in relations between labor and management.

Despite the odds against them, the packers could count on strong factors in their favor. Close contacts with the press gave their defense massive publicity. Besides Chairman Wadsworth, they had other loyal

[49] Braeman, "The Square Deal in Action," 59–60; Fausold, "James W. Wadsworth, Sr. and the Meat Inspection Act," 42–61; *Conditions in the Stockyards* (Hearings), 5.

[50] Filler, "Progress and Progressivism," *American Journal of Economics and Sociology* 20 (1961), 296–97; *Conditions in the Stockyards* (Hearings), 5; Yeager, *Competition and Regulation*, 206–8.

allies on the House committee, especially William Lorimer of Chicago, so-called "blond boss" of Illinois. Stock growers deluged the president and the Congress with letters and telegrams condemning the Beveridge bill. Despite Roosevelt's characterizations, the discoveries by Neill and Reynolds, to judge by their conversation with cattle raisers, were less startling than the shocking extremes of *The Jungle*.[51]

Indeed, the two investigators had deliberately pursued a cautious course. They accepted leads from Sinclair and Ella Bloor and sought to check out such horror stories, but found them impossible to substantiate. "We did not use any single fact," Reynolds reported, "from that source." They rejected rumors and confined themselves to what they had seen with their own eyes.[52]

Bloor, suspicious of Neill and Reynolds from the start, irritated by their coolness in receiving her suggestions, expected them to "tone down" unpleasant observations. At this crucial juncture in the legislative process, she and Richard Bloor sought to agitate public sentiment by revealing to the *New York Times* some lurid episodes for which Roosevelt's inquirers had not been able to find hard evidence. One example involved a boy and later his father, both of whom had tumbled into vats and been rendered into lard.[53]

Upton Sinclair soon took a similar tack. The president had been ostentatiously keeping Neill and Reynolds's oral reports secret, hoping that judicious leaks plus the threat of publication might help pressure the Beveridge bill through the House. A conversation Neill had with House Speaker Joseph G. Cannon, who came from Illinois, had "horrified" him and won him over, at least temporarily, to support a strong bill. Roosevelt obviously hoped to expand this tactic. Even though he certainly recognized that his investigators' details might be less gaudy than some passages in *The Jungle*, the president realized that the world would regard them as fact, confirming the general tenor of Sinclair's charges. Publication, he wrote Sinclair, "would chiefly be of service to the apostles of sensationalism" and, by depressing meat sales even more, would injure "scores of thousands of stock-growers, ranchers, hired men, cowboys, farmers and farm hands all over this country, who have been guilty of no misconduct whatever."[54]

[51] Braeman, "The Square Deal in Action," 58; Tarr, *A Study in Boss Politics*, 155–63; Irving Dilliard, "Lorimer, William," in Harris E. Starr, ed., *Dictionary of American Biography: Supplement One* (New York, 1944), 511–12.

[52] *Conditions in the Stockyards* (House Doc. 873), 3; *Conditions in the Stockyards* (Hearings), 131, 150, 161; Roosevelt to Wadsworth, June 8, 1906, Roosevelt Papers.

[53] Bloor, *We Are Many*, 87; *NY Times*, May 29, 1906.

[54] *Ibid.*, May 28, 1906; Sinclair, "Reminiscences"; Fausold, "James W. Wadsworth, Sr. and the Meat Inspection Act," 47; Roosevelt to Sinclair, May 29, 1906, Roosevelt Papers.

Sinclair, however, sought to force the president's hand. The novelist held Neill and Reynolds's observations, heard from their own lips, in higher regard than did Ella Bloor. He expected their publication to vindicate his own critique, stamped with the imprimatur of the president. Moreover, he considered an aroused public opinion of greater import than enactment of a law. Like Bloor, Sinclair went to New York with his affidavits and observations and dictated through the night to stenographers at the *New York Times*. More important, he reported for publication what Neill and Reynolds had told him. He had written the president, Sinclair declared, insisting that the American people must be awakened to a sense of their own responsibility. Beveridge bill or no Beveridge bill, it would take the Neill-Reynolds report to produce this awakening. Compounding this pressure on Roosevelt, Sinclair telegraphed the minority leader in the House asking him to urge the president to release his investigators' probe of Packingtown's problems.[55]

Roosevelt replied to Sinclair's request, refraining from any show of wrath because Sinclair had let the cat out of the bag. "You are not bound to me," the president wrote, "by any agreement or understanding not to make public anything you see fit." Roosevelt chided Sinclair, however, for repeating in the *New York Times* "utterly reckless" and unproven statements. His own role, the president asserted, was "to see that nothing but the truth appears . . . and that it appears in such shape that practical results for good will follow."[56]

Sinclair's disclosure forced a change in presidential plans. On the same day that Roosevelt answered Sinclair's letter, he ordered Neill and Reynolds to put their report in writing within forty-eight hours. The president told a senator he would not publish the document unless forced to by congressional action. The House member to whom Sinclair had telegraphed introduced a resolution asking the president for the report.[57]

Meanwhile, Representatives Wadsworth and Lorimer revamped Beveridge's amendment to nullify the packers' chief objections. This step acknowledged the end of the packers' show of intransigence and their acquiescence in the inevitability, even the desirability, of a law if shaped to suit their desires. The cost of inspection would come from the public purse, not from fees levied on the packers. Inspection and dating of canned meat were cut from the bill. Larger quantities of preservatives

[55] *NY Times*, May 28 and 29, 1906. Sinclair later said he revealed the contents of the Neill-Reynolds report with their tacit acquiescence: *American Outpost*, 169–75.

[56] Roosevelt to Sinclair, May 29, 1906, Roosevelt Papers.

[57] *NY Times*, May 19, 1906; Representative John Sharp Williams of Mississippi introduced House Resolution 544 on May 29. *Cong. Record*, 59 Cong. 1 ses., 7647.

would be tolerated. The clause specifically banning the shipment of un-inspected meat in interstate commerce was eliminated. Even minor departmental rulings could be appealed by aggrieved packers to the federal courts. To Roosevelt and his advisers, the Wadsworth-Lorimer draft was a "sham bill" signifying disaster. "It seems to me," the president wrote the New York congressman, "that each change is for the worse and that in the aggregate they are ruinous, taking away *every particle of good* from the suggested Beveridge amendment."[58]

The time had come for the president to play his by now somewhat tattered trump. Only by provoking "an aroused public feeling," Roosevelt believed, could he possibly secure "a decent law." He sent the Neill-Reynolds report to Congress, with a message urging enactment of Beveridge's version of a law as indispensable to remedy the "revolting" conditions in Packingtown. Fees paid by packers must be the mode of financing, to avoid the constant danger of negating the law by cutting back congressional appropriations for its enforcement. The law, to be effective, insisted the president, must mandate inspection "from the hoof to the can."[59]

The eight-page Neill-Reynolds report struck both public and Congress as somewhat déjà vu. It made no new revelations and cited no incidents of dead workers contaminating the food supply. Nevertheless, the report's straightforward prose, describing what the two social workers had seen, even after frantic efforts by packing companies to clean up, had a sobering impact.[60]

The pavement in the yards, Neill and Reynolds stated, impossible to clean, was "slimy and malodorous when wet, yielding clouds of ill-smelling dust when dry." Buildings had been constructed with scant regard for light, ventilation, or toilets. "Nothing," the investigators wrote, "shows more strikingly the general indifference to matters of cleanliness and sanitation than do the privies for men and women," and they elaborated on this theme. Uncleanliness was universal. "Dirt, splinters, floor filth, and the expectoration of tuberculous . . . workers" abounded. Meat products processed in such an unhygienic environment posed a "constant menace to consumers' health."

In a passage soon to receive intense scrutiny, the social workers stated:

[58] Fausold, "James W. Wadsworth, Sr. and the Meat Inspection Act," 48–49; Tarr, *A Study in Boss Politics*, 155–63; Braeman, "The Square Deal in Action," 63; Roosevelt to Wadsworth, May 31, 1906, Roosevelt Papers.

[59] Roosevelt to Lyman Abbott, June 18, 1906, Roosevelt Papers; *Conditions in the Stockyards* (House Doc. 873).

[60] *Ibid.*; Tarr, *A Study in Boss Politics*, 155.

As an extreme example of the entire disregard on the part of employees of any notion of cleanliness in handling dressed meat, we saw a hog that had just been killed, cleaned, washed, and started on its way to the cooling room fall from the sliding rail to a dirty wooden floor and slide part way into a filthy men's privy. It was picked up by two employees, placed upon a truck, carried into the cooling room and hung up with other carcasses, no effort being made to clean it.

As Sinclair had desired, Neill and Reynolds also commented on working conditions in the plants. These were abominable. "The account book" governed all. Health and comfort received no consideration. "Even the ordinary decencies of life" were "completely ignored." Such circumstances led inevitably to "moral degradation."

Although more inspectors were required, the investigators observed, postmortem inspection seemed "carefully and conscientiously made." Inspection before slaughter possessed no value, they concluded, and offered opportunities for "undue advantage . . . by outside parties." Neill and Reynolds ended their short document with comments on needed legislation, all in harmony with the Beveridge amendment.[61]

In response to the president and his investigators, the packers chose the course of defiance. Ogden Armour rebuked Roosevelt for his "strong personal animus." Representative Lorimer, returning to Washington after a strategy session in Chicago, condemned the report as "a gross exaggeration of conditions." The principal packers labeled it slanderous. Worried at how the Beveridge bill would shift the balance of power against business, other industrial groups, including the National Association of Manufacturers, rallied to the packers' side. Such opposition by "great bodies of capitalists" in the cause of "class consciousness" angered the president.[62]

To argue their case in detail in the fairly friendly forum of the House Committee on Agriculture, the packers chose Thomas E. Wilson. Supported by sympathetic questions from packer allies, Wilson presented the packers as proponents of reasonable legislation, although dead set against Senator Beveridge's destructive draft. What Wilson favored, as the *New York Times* observed, distinctly resembled Wadsworth's pro-

[61] *Conditions in the Stockyards* (House Doc. 873).

[62] Fausold, "James W. Wadsworth, Sr. and the Meat Inspection Act," 50; Braeman, "The Square Deal in Action," 64–65; Roosevelt to Lyman Abbott, June 18, 1906, Roosevelt Papers. After NAM officers had begun their campaign against the Beveridge bill, however, the board of directors canceled the effort. Robert H. Wiebe, *Businessmen and Reform: A Study of the Progressive Movement* (Chicago, 1968; originally published 1962), 49.

posal. In Wilson's version of a proper bill, canned meats would bear no dates, no chemicals or dyes would be categorically banned, some unsound animals could still properly be used for food, and the secretary of agriculture would not have the final word on standards for sanitation. Wilson did not care how many inspectors might be added in packinghouses, he said, "provided we do not have to pay for them."[63]

The major thrust of Wilson's testimony lay in lambasting the report by Charles P. Neill and James B. Reynolds. They could be included, it was clear by implication, among the "sociologists" and "theorists" who would wrest control of the "great American [packing] industry" from the practical men who had given their lives to creating it. The sociologists' short stay in Chicago, Wilson insisted, could not equip them properly to give evidence on the basis of which Congress should legislate. Indeed, their careers and "fine sensibilities" led them astray in interpreting what they had seen. The "sight of blood and other offals" might well shock genteel observers into exaggerating conditions, whereas men with practical experience would recognize the inevitability of such gore in a packinghouse.[64]

Most of their criticisms struck Wilson as "unjust and unwarranted." He did not believe their charge that old canned meat was returned to packing plants, taken out of the cans, treated with chemicals, recanned, and returned to the marketplace. Nor did Wilson accept the assertion that stale meat scraps went into potted ham: the scraps were probably "pure and wholesome" shank meat, trimmed off and separately cured. If, Wilson asserted, Neill really saw men relieving themselves in slaughtering areas, it could not have happened in a major plant. Wilson further denied the blanket charge of an unhygienic environment:

> I do not believe the conditions are bad considering the nature of the work that is being done. We can not avoid handling the offal or the entrails, and they carry some odor with them. . . . I do not think that Doctor Neill would support their being perfumed.[65]

A key effort on Wilson's part to undercut Neill and Reynolds's credibility came in his challenge to their account of the pig that fell into the

[63] *Conditions in the Stockyards* (Hearings), 10, 14–15, 30, 56–57, 61, 89–90; *NY Times,* June 7, 1906.

[64] *Conditions in the Stockyards* (Hearings), 5, 6. Some citizens who favored stringent inspection were willing to admit that "slaughtering is not a *kid glove* business and blood bespattered men and floors do not necessarily indicate filth." C. E. Smith to George W. Norris, June 7, 1906, George W. Norris Papers, Manuscript Division, Library of Congress.

[65] *Conditions in the Stockyards* (Hearings), 5, 11, 22, 27, 42–43.

privy. Displaying photographs, Wilson argued that, even if a hog carcass had tumbled from the rail, no more than the feet could have gotten through the door into the toilet area. In any case, Wilson insisted, privy room floors were kept clean. The pig could not have become contaminated.[66]

Following Wilson's lead, propacker congressmen kept returning to this episode when Neill and Reynolds followed the packer to the witness chair. Neill was given Wilson's pictures to study, then asked if he could challenge the packer's assertion that the account of events in the report defied logistical possibilities.[67]

"How much of the hog went into the urinal?" asked Congressman Franklin E. Brooks of Colorado.

"Not very much," Neill replied. He held his hands nine inches to a foot apart. "There might have been only that much."

"Which end," asked Brooks, "the head or the foot?"

"The head end."

"The nose of the hog stuck into that hole?"

"I don't remember whether the head was on the carcass or not."

Tempers flared, as Neill was asked to give his memory of the incident in full detail. He did so, stressing that the hog fell at least partially into an "extremely filthy" water closet, and, without being cleaned, was carried off to the cooling room and hung with the other carcasses. The event, Neill insisted, revealed "an utter want of any conception of cleanliness on the part of the workers in that particular place."

"You say no effort was made to clean it?" chairman Wadsworth asked.

"None was made," replied Neill.

"Perhaps that was not the proper time to clean it."

"Yes; it had just passed the washing room, and instead of sending it back there they hung it up without doing anything about it. That was just exactly the impression it created upon me—"

"That was an impression?"

"And the room in which it was put had no water in it. There were quite a number of hogs there—"

"Do you really think that hog went into [a] can without being cleaned?"

"I do; yes," asserted Neill.

But Wadsworth had not yet done. In a few minutes he brought the discussion "back to that poor hog," indicating that the handling of this

[66] *Ibid.*, 27–28. The National Archives has no files of the House Committee on Agriculture for this session of Congress in which Wilson's photographs might have been found.

[67] *Ibid.*, 115–17, 119; Fausold, "James W. Wadsworth, Sr. and the Meat Inspection Act," 51–53.

episode involved "the credibility of the report," suggesting that Neill had been a "careless" observer, and subjecting him to more harassing. questions.[68]

Finally, Congressman Sydney Johnston Bowie of Alabama protested. In contrast with the "proper respect" shown Wilson, Neill was being handled "as if he were a culprit or as if he were being prosecuted."[69]

Lorimer asserted that he did not mean to be discourteous, but the Neill-Reynolds report was a document of "generalities," devoid of "specific statements made about any case . . . except the case of the pig that fell into the closet." "Everybody in the country has read that report," Lorimer continued. "The general opinion of the people . . . is that everything in the packing houses in Chicago is filthy, and that nothing coming from those packing houses is fit to be eaten. . . . Now, what I am aiming to do is to find out specifically the reasons on which this report is based."[70]

"The evidence that there was rubbish in there," Neill replied, "was evidence sufficient to satisfy what I consider two reasonable-minded men. . . . I did not prepare myself by specific notes of what everything was in the way of rubbish. I didn't say: 'Item, nail; item, piece of floor.' So I say six weeks later it is not quite fair to try to discredit my judgment because I can not remember the particular items that made up a particular lot of rubbish."

Neill himself protested his treatment by the propacker committee members. "I feel like a witness under cross-examination whose testimony is trying to be broken down."[71]

Reynolds had a similar, if somewhat less trying time, when his turn came to testify. Again the "unwashed" hog held center stage. Was the implication in the report that this hog ended up in a can of meat, Wadsworth wanted to know, a fact or an assumption? Reynolds denied that the report "absolutely" said that the hog had gotten into the can. "We saw no effort made to clean the hog," he asserted. Neill spoke up from the audience to insist that the inference could be fairly drawn that the hog had not been later cleaned, because it "became mixed with the general run of hogs, and there was practically no way to distinguish it from the others."[72]

Despite the badgering, the two investigators emerged with credibility intact. Members of the committee sympathetic to their cause and plight

[68] *Conditions in the Stockyards* (Hearings), 120–22.
[69] *Ibid.*, 125.
[70] *Ibid.*, 126.
[71] *Ibid.*, 128.
[72] *Ibid.*, 144–46, 163.

came to their defense when Wadsworth, Lorimer, and Brooks seemed to go beyond the proper bounds of questioning. Bowie, John Lamb of Virginia, Charles Russell Davis of Minnesota, and Henry C. Adams of Wisconsin played such helpful roles.[73] Neill and Reynolds's staunchness could be counted as an asset to the president in the process of compromise already begun, and in which Congressman Adams, a former food commissioner in his home state, would soon take a crucial part. The lateness of the session, the loyalty of the packers' congressional allies, and the uneasiness of the business community, however, tipped the balance of reconciliation away from Beveridge's tougher bill to favor Wadsworth's less stringent version.[74]

In contrast to his long aloofness from the pure-food issue, the president stood at the center of the compromising efforts to fashion a meat-inspection bill that both Senate and House would accept. His Cuban experiences, his continuing legal involvements with the beef trust, his moral judgments, the degree of public agitation, all impelled Roosevelt to desire prompt enactment of such a law. He recognized, as did Speaker Cannon, that the unity of the Republican party was at stake. Failure to achieve enough harmony to resolve this heated issue portended unfortunate political repercussions.[75]

Even before the House hearing, the president had sent Wadsworth a draft bill, retreating slightly from Beveridge's bill that had passed the Senate. Wadsworth, in turn, mildly modified his substitute, and this version, after the hearing and heated debate within the Committee on Agriculture, received approval by a close bipartisan vote of nine to seven. On June 14 this bill was reported to the House.[76]

The president was outraged. Wadsworth had made no genuine effort to reconcile differences, but had persisted in retaining provisions "so bad that in my opinion if they had been deliberately designed to prevent the remedying of the evils complained of they could not have been worse." The government would pay the inspection bill. Canned meat would not be dated. A delay in bringing inspectors under civil service would entrench patronage appointees sympathetic to the packers. The

[73] *Ibid.*, 125, 128; *Amendments to Agricultural Appropriations Bill*, 59 Cong. 1 ses., House Report 4935, parts 1 and 2. Upton Sinclair asserted that Wadsworth refused his request to testify before the committee: *The Brass Check*, 45.

[74] Fausold, "James W. Wadsworth, Sr. and the Meat Inspection Act," 53–55; Tarr, *A Study in Boss Politics*, 160–63; Braeman, "The Square Deal in Action," 63–73.

[75] *Ibid.*

[76] *Ibid.*, 66; Bowers, *Beveridge and the Progressive Era*, 231; Fausold, "James W. Wadsworth, Sr. and the Meat Inspection Act," 53; Tarr, *A Study in Boss Politics*, 160–63.

bill expanded the right of judicial review beyond procedural issues to every decision of substance, no matter how minor.[77]

"You are wrong, 'very, very wrong,'" Wadsworth replied, "in your attitude toward the Committee's Bill." It was "as perfect a piece of legislation, to carry into effect your own views on this question, as was ever prepared by a Committee of Congress."[78]

Cannon, while favoring Wadsworth's text, could not afford to have House and president at such explosive odds. The speaker journeyed down Pennsylvania Avenue to the White House, where he found Roosevelt also worried about the rift. They decided to place the responsibility for bridging the gap in the hands of Congressman Adams, whom Roosevelt considered "a square, honest, sensible fellow who knows his business and wants to do right." The same day Adams met with the president, Reynolds, and Solicitor McCabe, and revisions were agreed upon that Roosevelt believed would improve the House bill. The expansive court-review provision and the delay on introducing civil-service requirements were cut, and dating on cans was inserted. A compromise covered financing: inspection would be paid for with money appropriated by Congress, but if these funds proved insufficient, the secretary of agriculture would have standby authority to collect fees from the packers. Adams took the new draft to an informal meeting of the Committee on Agriculture and received its approval. Wadsworth and Lorimer, however, out of town for the weekend, did not attend.[79]

Cannon sought to curb the anger of the absentees when they returned, urging the need for amity with the White House. Roosevelt at the same time sought to persuade Beveridge that the new version was as satisfactory as his bill. "I am concerned with getting the result, not with the verbiage," the president said. Especially he wanted to avoid "an obstinate and wholly pointless fight about utterly trivial matters, or about matters as to which we may ultimately find ourselves forced to yield."[80]

The House Committee, with Speaker Cannon's blessing, made

[77] Braeman, "The Square Deal in Action," 67–69; *Conditions in the Stockyards* (Hearings), 272–74; Roosevelt to Wadsworth, June 15, 1906, Roosevelt Papers.

[78] Wadsworth to Roosevelt, June 15, 1906, cited in Braeman, "The Square Deal in Action," 69, and in Tarr, *A Study in Boss Politics*, 161.

[79] *Ibid.*; Braeman, "The Square Deal in Action," 68–70; Roosevelt to Cannon, June 16, 1906, and Roosevelt to Beveridge, June 16, 1906, Roosevelt Papers. Adams died soon after the enactment of the meat-inspection amendments. His papers at the Wisconsin State Historical Society contain no mention of his role in bringing about the compromise: Rima D. Apple to author, December 30, 1985.

[80] Braeman, "The Square Deal in Action," 71; Roosevelt to Beveridge, June 30, 1906, Roosevelt Papers.

changes in the White House draft Adams had helped devise. Excised was the secretary's standby authority to levy fees, but a permanent annual appropriation of $3 million for enforcement was added. Dating of cans disappeared again, but so too did the civil-service waiver. The committee agreed to eliminate the provision for court review, which the president so opposed, if the clause in the Senate amendment making the secretary of agriculture's judgment "final and conclusive" should also be struck out. Cannon took Roosevelt the newest revision, and, while not happy about the loss of dating for canned meats, the president gave his approval.[81]

Wadsworth brought the new bill before the House on June 19, explaining the changes. During brief debate, only one criticism was leveled at the measure. John Sharp Williams, House minority leader, believed that the packers, who had been "poisoning our wives and children," should be forced to foot the bill for meat inspection. Even he, however, supported the House committee version, admiring the compromise worked out by "the two gentlemen from New York," Wadsworth and Roosevelt. "We might quote Shakespeare's utterance," Williams added:

> Now is the glorious winter of our discontent
> Made glorious summer by these sons of New York.[82]

Before the day ended, the House passed the measure without a recorded vote. The high level of House harmony betokened certain conflict with the Senate.[83]

That tension became evident the next day. Beveridge and the chairman of the Senate Committee on Agriculture, Redfield Proctor of Vermont, both stood firm on the Senate version of the bill, including dating of cans and payment by packers. Pointing out that canned meat bought on contract from the packers by the British army required dates on the cans, Beveridge insisted that American consumers warranted the same protection. Porter McCumber of North Dakota wanted the month as well as the year to appear on the can, and Weldon Heyburn of Idaho desired the dating provision expanded to include carcasses.[84]

The chief challenge to Beveridge's bill came from Francis Warren of Wyoming, a large sheepherder and spokesman for the range-cattle in-

[81] Braeman, "The Square Deal in Action," 71–72; *Cong. Record*, 59 Cong. 1 ses., 8720–22; Roosevelt to Redfield Proctor, June 18, 1906, Roosevelt Papers.

[82] Fausold, "James W. Wadsworth, Sr. and the Meat Inspection Act," 55; *Cong. Record*, 59 Cong. 1 ses., 8720–29.

[83] *Ibid.*, 8728–29.

[84] *Ibid.*, 8763–70, 8878–90, and 9016–27 for the debate in the Senate; Braeman, *Albert J. Beveridge*, 108.

dustry. Denying that livestock growers sought to protect the packers' interests, indeed, acknowledging that the former had been brought close to ruin by the latter's pricing power, Warren insisted that inspection should be paid from taxes. Otherwise, packers would pass the cost along, piling one more intolerable burden on stock raisers' backs. The $3 million tax cost for controlling a $1 billion industry would amount to a "mere bagatelle." The government already paid for investigating the white fly, the brown-tailed gnat, and the bobtailed beetle. What was wrong, then, in charging the United States for inspecting the nation's "greatest industry"?[85]

Why, Beveridge asked Warren rhetorically in return, if the packers were sure to pass on their inspection fees to livestock growers, did they so bitterly oppose that feature of the bill? Beveridge, like Proctor, termed the fees no burden but rather an advantageous advertising expense. "These packers," said Proctor, "do a large amount of advertising, and certainly they do none that will yield such a tremendous return as this one of having the Government stamp on their products."[86]

Despite the fact that Roosevelt's compromising had not placed in the House bill Beveridge's two cherished provisions, the Indiana senator took pains to praise the president. The strengthening of Wadsworth's original impossible draft had resulted from "the courage, determination, and the absolutely unselfish devotion to the interest of the people of President Roosevelt."[87] Still, Beveridge stuck staunchly by can dating and packer fees, and the Senate sided with him, on June 23 instructing its conferees to insist upon the Beveridge amendment when they met with the House delegates. As the last week of the session wore on amidst "oppressive heat," while members of the Congress grew ever more "impatient" to conclude "this wearisome turmoil," Senate and House conferees met three times without avail. Proctor and his colleagues could not persuade Wadsworth and his colleagues to budge an inch. A proposed compromise on financing, Proctor told the Senate, "the House conferees positively refused to consider." An effort by the president through Speaker Cannon to get the House conferees to yield on the dating issue met the same flat denial.[88]

[85] *Cong. Record*, 59 Cong. 1 ses., 9018–19. Congressman George W. Norris held views similar to those of Senator Warren: enforcement must be "rigid" but government must pay the costs, because the law would benefit all the people, and because, should the costs be levied on the packers, they would pass them on to "the man who raised the steer." Norris to T. L. Jones, June 18, 1906, Norris Papers.

[86] *Cong. Record*, 59 Cong. 1 ses., 8763, 8765.

[87] *Ibid.*, 8766, 9021.

[88] *Ibid.*, 9027, 9376–78, 9565–75, 9655–61, 9664–65, 9752; Roosevelt to Cannon, June 26, 1906, Roosevelt Papers.

Once during the course of these events, the House engaged in a flurry of debate. Several members, led by John Lamb of Virginia and featuring William E. Humphrey of Washington, expressed their preference for Beveridge's bill, but by a vote of 157 to 51 the House reiterated support for Wadsworth's substitute. Wadsworth gave Lorimer the final word in the debate. Reminding the House of his own years of labor in Packing-town, he flatly denied that the packers had provided the public with "bad and unwholesome meat." Neill and Reynolds, Lorimer said, "men who never had any practical experience in anything," had prepared a report "not based on facts." Nor were they able to come up with facts when questioned by members of the House committee. Lorimer fore-bore mention of the pig that fell into the privy.[89]

Lorimer's self-righteous defense of the packers and belittling of the president's investigators contrasted sharply with the tone of Senate commentary, as members of that body acknowledged defeat on the dating and financing issues and, in order to get any law at all, yielded to the terms of the House. As House leaders listened from the gallery, senators bitterly acknowledged their displeasure. "I feel as though . . . I will go home like a licked dog," bemoaned Knute Nelson of Minnesota, "whipped by the packers and by the raisers of range cattle, . . . force[d] . . . to eat the canned goods whether they were made yesterday or whether they are as old as Methuselah." The law amounted to "a legislative abortion." McCumber summed up the results of the conflict: "We have met the enemy and we are theirs—indemnity, $3,000,000."[90]

Senator Proctor shared in this gloom, while hinting a hope that voters might take vengeance on the House victors. Yet he deemed it obvious "that the importance of this measure as a whole far outweighs any objections to these two items of detail." The "greater good" demanded the law's enactment. Beveridge took the same stance. Even without the two lost provisions, "the country" could be "congratulated upon getting a good deal better bill than any informed man had a right to expect under all circumstances at this session." In all reforms, the Indiana senator added, "everything at first proposed cannot be at first secured." Beveridge pledged himself to persevere in his efforts to complete the task he had begun.[91]

So the Senate grudgingly agreed to recede from its disagreement with the House substitute for the Beveridge amendment, the conference

[89] *Cong. Record*, 59 Cong. 1 ses., 9569–75.

[90] *Ibid.*, 9655–61.

[91] *Ibid.*, 9656–57. Beveridge fulfilled his pledge and introduced bills in the next two Congressional sessions to bolster the law, with no success. Bowers, *Beveridge and the Progressive Era*, 248–49, 266–67.

committee met a fourth time, and on the next to last day of the session both Houses accepted the result. On the final day the president signed the Agricultural Appropriations Act embodying the meat-inspection amendment.[92]

Roosevelt sent Beveridge the pen with which he had signed the law, plus praises for priority:

> You were the man who first called my attention to the abuses in the packing houses. You were the legislator who drafted the bill which in its substance now appears in the amendment to the agricultural bill, and which will enable us to put a complete stop to the wrong-doing complained of.[93]

The president did not send a similar letter to Upton Sinclair, nor later, when discussing the meat-inspection law in his autobiography, did Roosevelt mention the novelist. Sinclair had not figured by name in the congressional debate; only once did Senator Lodge refer to him obliquely, as "a man who wrote a book." A month after signing the law, the president, in a letter to William Allen White, explained his relationship with the socialist novelist. Sometimes in a movement, Roosevelt wrote, one must join with others of differing and wrong reasons for backing the venture.

> Thus in the beef packing business I found that Sinclair was of real use. I have an utter contempt for him. He is hysterical, unbalanced, and untruthful. Three-fourths of the things he said were absolute falsehoods. For some of the remainder there was only a basis of truth. Nevertheless, in this particular crisis he was of service to us, and yet I had to explain again and again to well-meaning people that I could not afford to disregard ugly things that had been found out simply because I did not like the man who had helped in finding them out.[94]

Sinclair came away from his encounter with the president disappointed and disillusioned. He had been less interested in a law that would reform Packingtown than in persuading Roosevelt to develop

---

[92] *Cong. Record*, 9664–65, 9752. The texts of the amendments are contained in *ibid.*, 9791–92, and in 34 U.S. Stat. chap. 3913, An Act Making Appropriations for the Department of Agriculture, 669–97. The meat-inspection provisions appear 674–79.

[93] Roosevelt to Beveridge, June 30, 1906, Roosevelt Papers.

[94] Roosevelt, *Theodore Roosevelt: An Autobiography* (New York, 1920), 443; *Cong. Record*, 59 Cong. 1 ses., 8769; Roosevelt to White, July 31, 1906, Roosevelt Papers. That Roosevelt had intended Sinclair as one of his targets in his "muck-rake" speech is apparent in a letter the president wrote to William Howard Taft, March 15, 1906, Roosevelt Papers.

genuine concern for the lot of stockyard workers. "But," Sinclair wrote in retrospect, "I tried in vain." *The Jungle*, he concluded, had "caused the whitewashing of some packing-house walls, and it furnished jobs for . . . lady-manicurists, but it left the wage-slaves in those huge brick packing-boxes exactly where they were before." He realized that he "had been made into a 'celebrity,' not because the public cared anything about the sufferings of . . . [the] workers, but simply because the public did not want to eat tubercular beef." As time passed, Sinclair came to view the law with greater tolerance and his own role with enhanced pride. In his *Autobiography*, published in 1962, he wrote: "I helped to clean up the yards and improve the country's meat supply."[95]

[95] Sinclair, *The Brass Check*, 47; Sinclair, *Autobiography*, 126.

XI

The Law Secured

It seems so strange that a good can only be accomplished after
a determined fight. I believe that if a movement was started to
abolish the kingdom of Satan that the usual mighty opposition
would at once arise, even in this House.
—REPRESENTATIVE JOSEPH GOULDEN
OF NEW YORK,
June 22, 1906[1]

The Food and Drugs Act of 1906

Debate on the pure-food bill began in the House of Representatives on
June 21, 1906, four months after the hearings before the Commerce
Committee had concluded. William Hepburn had shrewdly kept the
committee bill alive in May by linking it with two other measures, each
having some support, winning privileged status for all three.[2] Strict constructionists, led by William Adamson of Georgia, objected. The bill
should be called "pure foolishness" instead of "pure food," Adamson
said, adding derisively: "The Federal Government was not created for
the purpose of cutting your toe nails or corns."[3]

Whatever doubts existed about the food bill's fate in the Fifty-ninth
Congress vanished as public opinion reacted to the scandal in Packingtown. This crisis, observed the *Outlook*, blew "the smoldering fire into
flame"; moreover, of the meat bill and the food bill, the latter was "unquestionably the more important." Harvey Wiley agreed that agitation
over meat at last aroused public support for pure-food legislation.
House members concurred. James L. Slayden of Texas credited "hys-
teria provoked by a fiction writer's description of what he saw in Chicago" with furnishing the momentum. William H. Ryan of New York
insisted: "The people are demanding pure food."[4]

---

[1] *Cong. Record*, 59 Cong. 1 ses., 8979.

[2] *Ibid.*, 6464–69. The two other bills dealt with the penal code and immigration restric-
tion.

[3] *Ibid.*, 6465.

[4] "Against Poison and Fraud," *Outlook* 83 (1906), 490–97; Anderson, *The Health of a
Nation*, 195; *Cong. Record*, 59 Cong. 1 ses., 8987–88. Joseph A. Goulden and Henry M.

The president also recognized how public reaction to Packingtown's problems carried over into a concern about all processed food. Whereas in January, Roosevelt had not included the food bill in a list of the four or five measures he was "anxious" to have passed, he now added a hand-written postscript to a letter to Speaker Cannon: "I earnestly favor" passage of a pure-food law.[5]

Increasing the intensity of public support, reported the *Nation*, was use of the food bill by journalists as an example of the Senate's "treasons, stratagems, and spoils." Samuel Hopkins Adams's patent-medicine exposure struck some House members as especially influential. Slayden asserted that Adams deserved more credit than "any other single man in the country." Newspapers in New York, Washington, Chicago, Indianapolis, and Springfield, Massachusetts, took tougher editorial stances supporting a strong bill. Telegrams from what the *Nation* termed "militant constituents"—physicians and women especially—maintained House members' awareness of the far-flung extent of national concern. Wiley kept in constant touch with members charged with moving the bill through the House.[6]

The crucial vote came on June 20, when the Committee on Rules proposed that the House resolve itself into a Committee of the Whole to debate the pure-food bill for twelve hours, then report it back to the House for a final roll-call vote. The decisive approval of this proposal, 143 to 72, forecast final passage. Spirited discussion during the next three days, therefore, did not have at issue absolute victory or defeat. House members spoke for audiences in their home districts and sought to in-

Goldfogle of New York also related the agitation over meat to public support for the pure-food bill: *ibid.*, 8978, 8982.

[5] Roosevelt to George Otto Trevelyan, January 22, 1906; Roosevelt to Joseph Gurney Cannon, May 27, 1906, Roosevelt Papers.

[6] "The Year of Food Laws," *Nation* 82 (1906), 522–23; *Cong. Record*, 59 Cong. 1 ses., 8988; Samuel Hopkins Adams, "Curbing the Great American Fraud," *Collier's* 37 (July 21, 1906), 16–17; Anderson, *The Health of a Nation*, 190–96; Burrow, *AMA*, 80–81. Members of Congress may have detected the upsurge of public concern more from the press than from their constituent mail, except for the campaigns made by the AMA and by women's clubs. In the Papers of Representative George W. Norris of Nebraska, for example, who tended to retain such correspondence, for May and June 1906 there are seven telegrams and letters about the meat-inspection amendment, all favoring it, and only three letters about the food bill. A. Mansfield, M.D., conveys a resolution by the Nebraska State Medical Association House of Delegates urging the House not to weaken the bill that had passed the Senate (May 10); John B. Waldon, a wholesale grocer, favors a strong law (May 31); James F. Rourke, a canner, supports the food bill, except for the weights and measures provision (May 10). Norris hoped that the law would be quickly passed and objected to "filibustering tactics," especially repeated demands for yeas and nays, that were delaying the final decision. Norris to Nebraska Mercantile Company, June 4.

fluence the outcome of voting on amendments, which would determine the degree of rigor in the bill and of burden on various commercial interests.[7]

Hepburn, in charge of the most ardent probill forces, let James R. Mann of Illinois take the lead in speaking for the measure. Adamson of Georgia, directing the opposition, found irony in Mann's role. Once Adamson's ally, opposing the lineal ancestor of the present committee bill, Mann now led "the hosts of error." A short, stocky, bearded, beetle-browed lawyer and skillful parliamentarian, Mann enjoyed the role of handling bills on the House floor. A colleague once accused him of undertaking "not only to play Hamlet, but the fair Ophelia and the King and Queen and first gravedigger" as well. His managerial talents were impressively displayed in the final days leading to the food bill's passage.[8]

Other former foes had also abandoned opposition, among them Augustus Gardner of Massachusetts, whom the committee had "placated," complained Adamson, "by giving him codfish and beans." Indeed, the Georgian thought, the pulling and hauling of lobbyists had "secured changes without number and some without character." The bill had suffered such "mutilation" that "the shades of Statesman Brosius" would not recognize it.[9]

Aware of the depleted ranks of the bill's adversaries, and acknowledging defeat, Adamson nonetheless reiterated his adamant opposition. He objected to paying for burgeoning bureaucracy and "the attendant evils of spies and informers and pestiferous agents running around meddling with the business of the people." He raised suspicion of scientific specialists who would enforce the law: "I believe there are millions of old women, white and black, who know more about good victuals and good eating than my friend Doctor Wiley and all his apothecary shop." The Georgia congressman found a new analogy to express the absurdity of enacting such an unconstitutional law. "You may just as well get the traditional boy with his sore toe," Adamson said, and have "Congressman Mann speak about the horrible condition of that sore toe for two hours and say that the Congress ought to do something to cure that sore toe. It is just as logical and sensible and fully as constitutional."[10]

Mann, defending the committee version of the bill, gave a detailed, adroit presentation, greeted at its conclusion with "prolonged ap-

[7] *Cong. Record*, 59 Cong. 1 ses., 8836–37.

[8] *Ibid.*, 8955; L. Ethan Ellis, "Mann, James Robert," *Dictionary of American Biography*, vol. 12, 244–45.

[9] *Cong. Record*, 59 Cong. 1 ses., 8955.

[10] *Ibid.*, 8955–56.

plause." He summarized the range of adulterated wares in the market-place, and, borrowing Wiley's technique, displayed some items he described: cherries reddened with aniline dye, cottonseed oil parading as olive oil, pepper cheapened with ground olive pits, a dead bee floating in glucose labeled honey.[11] Definitions for pure products, Mann explained, needed to be precise so that a taboo against adulteration could be adequately enforced. The Senate bill contained no authorization for standard setting. The House bill placed this obligation upon the secretary of agriculture, to give guidance to officials administering the law and to courts enforcing it. Regarding the disputed problem of what counsel the secretary should seek in establishing standards, the House bill was generous, not restrictive. He would call upon the food standards committee of the Association of State Dairy and Food Departments and whatever other experts he might choose.[12] The secretary, aided by the same consultants, should also decide, Mann noted, "one of the great questions of the age," whether or not preservatives were wholesome. But the law would go further still. If any interested person requested it, the secretary would be obligated to get the opinions of five experts from different specialties, persons whose credentials would enable them to judge whether a given preservative was harmful.[13]

On the hotly disputed issue between whiskey interests, Mann said, the House committee "did not take a decided stand in favor of either," but provided for honest labeling that "would permit people to know" what they were buying. Rectified whiskies must indicate on their labels that they were "imitation, compounded, or blended." In the subsequent debate, the House chamber briefly echoed the bitter extremes of controversy that had marked the committee hearing.[14]

A brand new provision, not previously part of food bills, also provoked controversy. Testimony at the hearing caused Mann to add a provision requiring food-package labels to show accurately the contents in terms of weight and measure. Wiley had not previously investigated this problem, but he did so now, providing Mann evidence of shortcomings to exhibit during the House debate. Canners let their opposition be known, and Thomas A. Smith of Maryland spoke against a restraint that had nothing to do with purity.[15]

In no previous congressional debate of a mainline bill had so much

[11] *Ibid.*, 8896–97, 8900. The *Chicago Evening Journal*, June 27, 1906, pictured Mann with his groceries on the top floor of the Capitol. Reprinted in a reelection campaign pamphlet, James Robert Mann Papers, Manuscript Division, Library of Congress.

[12] *Cong. Record*, 59 Cong. 1 ses., 8891.

[13] *Ibid.*, 8891–92.

[14] *Ibid.*, 8891, 8995.

[15] *Ibid.*, 8897–8900, 8903–5, 8983–84; Anderson, *The Health of a Nation*, 193.

attention been given to patent medicines as Mann now devoted to them. The Senate bill put no controls on narcotic nostrums. With the help of Wiley and Samuel Hopkins Adams, Mann had drafted a clause for the House bill as it left the committee requiring medical labeling to report the presence and quantity of alcohol, opium, cocaine, "or other poisonous substances." "The officers of the proprietary association started at once for Washington," Mann later explained. "They insisted that the provision was absolutely new, had been adopted without any hearings, and would be ruinous to their business if enacted into law. Our subcommittee gave them courteous, full and patient hearing. They presented to us an amendment."[16]

The proprietors' proposal would require the listing of any of several drugs on medicine labels if they exceeded a specific maximum amount. This provision, modeled on a Massachusetts law, constituted the largest concession yet made by the Proprietary Association. Wiley considered it no help to the self-dosing public. "The bill might as well not contain anything in regard to patent medicines," he wrote Mann after a conference with fifteen proprietors, "as to allow the quantities mentioned in the proposed amendment to be used without notice. . . . It would simply make the bill a joke." The chief chemist did favor changing the general words "other poisonous substances" to a specific list, believing the word "poisonous" too vague and ill-defined, offering opportunity for endless litigation. Yet Wiley worried that Mann, under pressure, would yield too much. The nostrum makers, Wiley wrote Adams, "I think will get their amendment . . . practically just as they have written it." In conversation and letter Wiley continued to supply Mann with nostrum analyses and clippings. Adams came to Washington to help keep the Illinois congressman staunch for a strongly worded bill.[17]

Mann personally stood firm. He believed, however, that ultimate success demanded duplicity. After castigating the nostrum evil in the House debate, he would seem to retreat by accepting a weakening amendment. Then, knowing that his committee would support more rigorous controls, Mann, at the propitious moment, would reinsert them in the bill. News of Mann's scheme, however, leaked when a reporter overheard the Illinois congressman explaining it to Adams.[18]

This revelation provoked medicine makers to a master plan of coun-

[16] *Cong. Record*, 59 Cong. 1 ses., 8892–93, 9739–40. The amendment was drafted by Congressman William C. Lovering of Massachusetts at the behest of the proprietors: Adams, "Curbing the Great American Fraud," 16–17.

[17] *Cong. Record*, 59 Cong. 1 ses., 8892–93, 8997, 9739–40; Wiley to Mann, March 19, 23, 29, and April 2, 1906; Wiley to Adams, March 26, 1906, Letterbooks, Bureau of Chemistry, General Correspondence, RG 97, National Archives.

[18] *Cong. Record*, 59 Cong. 1 ses., 8892–93, 9739–40.

terduplicity that began to take effect just before the House debate in June. Mann explained the situation to his House colleagues:

> Not daring to fight this bill in the open, not daring to say that they were afraid to state the quantity of narcotics in their drugs, . . . [the proprietors] have falsified in some way about this bill and endeavored to give the country the impression that it was the Senate bill which provided for labeling the narcotics . . . and that it was the House bill that proposed to strike it out, when, as a matter of fact, the Senate bill has nothing upon the subject, and it was the House committee which put it in.[19]

The proprietors' strategy proved remarkably effective, fooling many ardent supporters of stringent controls. Pro-pure-food newspapers, like the *New York Tribune*, pleaded in editorial columns for quashing the House bill and passing the Senate version. Even American Medical Association officials became briefly befuddled.[20]

Mann faced the task, in managing the debate, of exposing the proprietors' ruse without yet acknowledging the ramifications of his own strategy. He attacked narcotic nostrums, especially condemning medicines "advertised in the strongest language . . . for the cure of the opium habit, which . . . themselves contain opium enough to give one the opium habit." In response to a query from Edgar G. Crumpacker of Indiana asking whether labeling opium content would not make it easy for "people with morbid tastes" to satisfy their craving, Mann won applause from the House with his reply: "We can not undertake to prevent the man who is an opium fiend from obtaining opium, but we can undertake to prevent the man who never wishes to take opium from taking it without knowing he is taking it." With information furnished by Wiley, Mann revealed which brand-name remedies contained what dangerous drugs, and cited case histories of addiction and death, particularly the unwitting slaughter of innocent babies by the morphine in soothing syrups.[21]

No champions arose to defend nostrums during the House debate, and many of Mann's colleagues joined him in condemnation. Americans spent $90 million a year, noted Webb of North Carolina, buying some fifty thousand different nostrum brands. "Of all the great civilized nations of the earth," he asserted, "the United States is about the only one that has not a strict law on the subject." For every illness caused by un-

[19] *Ibid.*, 8893.
[20] *Ibid.*; *NY Tribune*, June 21, 1906; Burrow, *AMA*, 81.
[21] *Cong. Record*, 59 Cong. 1 ses., 8905–09, 8982.

clean meat, insisted Slayden of Texas, nostrums caused a hundred cases of poisoning and death, and, whereas "no man who ever ate tainted meat willingly returns to it, . . . many drugs that destroy the moral sense and enslave the bodies and minds of men are eagerly sought for after they have been tried a few times." Slayden chided his fellow congressmen for giving testimonials. "Indeed," he jibed, "Peruna [an alcoholic nostrum] seems to be a favorite congressional drink."[22]

Mann and other members protested the political potency of the Proprietary Association. Slayden termed its influence "a tremendous power which has been able to stay the hands of the reformer time and time again when the people were demanding protection to their health." William H. Ryan of New York cited a letter from a Buffalo proprietor that he regarded as a threat to his reelection. Should the pure-food bill pass, the letter read, Ryan would be "entitle[d] . . . to a holiday." Even as the House debated, new pressures assailed them from proprietors.[23]

The committee amendment on patent medicines came pursuant to Mann's grand strategy, a tougher proposal than he had earlier promised proprietors. Indeed, Mann told the House, the committee had considered, but rejected, an even more stringent proviso: complete formula disclosure on labels. The amendment required a medicine not described in the *United States Pharmacopoeia* or the *National Formulary* and not prescribed by a regularly licensed physician to state on its label the quantity or proportion of any morphine, opium, cocaine, heroin, alpha or beta eucaine, chloroform, cannabis indica, chloral hydrate, or acetanilide it contained, as well as any alcohol in excess of the amount necessary as a solvent or preservative for the active ingredients. Some congressmen, fearing the specified list might not include all poisons that proprietaries might contain, preferred the more general language. Mann explained the litigious potential of the generic term "poison." To strengthen the committee amendment, the exemption of USP and NF articles and physician prescriptions was removed. The prescriptions of regular physicians did not enter the interstate market, and the clause could provide a loophole by letting proprietors hire disreputable physicians to furnish prescriptions wholesale, thus evading the need for labeling dangerous drugs. Thus modified, the amendment was accepted by the House.[24]

Other committee amendments affected the standard-setting provisions of the bill. A recent court decision under the tea act had made

[22] *Ibid.*, 8987, 9070–75.

[23] *Ibid.*, 8,988; Adams, "Curbing the Great American Fraud," 16–17.

[24] *Ibid.*; *Cong. Record*, 59 Cong. 1 ses., 8996–9001.

Wiley and Mann fearful that the House bill placed too much authority in the secretary of agriculture's hands, thus jeopardizing the eventual law's constitutionality. New language, accepted by the House, reduced the secretary's power: he could not "fix" but only "determine and make known" food standards. Nor was he bound to adopt the advice of experts on preservatives, merely to consider their counsel.[25]

Mann's new provision for accurate labeling of weights and measures met strong resistance. "We might as well require the height of a horse to be branded upon him," declared Lemuel P. Padgett of Tennessee, "as to require the weight to be branded on a can of tomatoes." The state of the art, asserted James S. Sherman of New York, himself a canner, would not permit makers of jelly and catsup or canners of corn and peas to meet such a demand. Sherman proposed a substitute, which won House approval, stipulating only that, if a processor labeled the weight or measure of his product on the container, he must do so accurately.[26]

While Sherman succeeded in weakening the committee bill, William Richardson of Alabama sought unsuccessfully to strengthen it. He, like Wiley, deemed coloring and flavoring ingredients in blended whiskey, even though harmless, as adulterants, and he sought to amend the bill to curtail such deception. This prompted one more lively exchange between defenders of the blenders and straight-whiskey stalwarts, highlighted by the rhetoric of Augustus O. Stanley. The Kentucky congressman showed the House a quart of raw alcohol from which the rectifiers devised what they called bourbon, and he defied any member to distinguish "that hellish concoction" from "the genuine article." Counterfeit bourbon, Stanley proclaimed, "will eat the intestines out of a coyote. It will make a whirling dervish out of an anchorite. It will make a rabbit spit in a bulldog's face." Neither Stanley nor Richardson could persuade the House to change the committee's effort to reach a balance between the contesting whiskey factions.[27]

As the final vote approached, several other weakening amendments were rejected, the most important of them seeking to give borax and boracic acid specific authorization as preservatives, if kept at low levels and noted on labels. Adamson's strict states' rights substitute bill also lost by a vote of 44 to 118. Hepburn and Mann's bill then, on June 23, received House approval on a roll-call vote, 241 to 17, with six representatives voting present and 112 not voting. Last-ditch opponents represented the southern strict constructionists.[28]

[25] *Ibid.*, 9001–2.
[26] *Ibid.*, 9052–61.
[27] *Ibid.*, 9062–66.
[28] *Ibid.*, 9068–69, 9075–76.

In contrast with the adamant posture of House members in the conference committee on the meat-inspection amendment, conferees from both House and Senate displayed a willingness to compromise in order to secure a food and drug law. Heyburn, McCumber, and Asbury C. Latimer of South Carolina represented the Senate; Hepburn, Mann, and Ryan of New York negotiated for the House. The Senate bill made more concessions both to commercial interests and to constitutional conservatives than did the House version, and in one major respect this perspective prevailed. The Senate conferees would not accept the House bill provision giving the secretary of agriculture authority to set food standards and to determine the wholesomeness of preservatives. "The Senate has always contended that the power to fix standards should not be given to any man," McCumber explained in presenting the conference report in the upper chamber. Mann told the House that he had once held such a provision "essential" as a method of achieving uniformity and letting producers know what would be required of them. He and his colleagues had been forced to abandon the point because of the Senate's inalterable opposition. The courts would determine food standards, Mann said, as they would have done in any case, and the secretary still had standard-making power under the Agricultural Appropriation Act.[29]

On the whole, Mann thought—and his assessment was correct—the House view had gained in the negotiations. The whiskey provision had been tightened to make it more explicit that rectified liquors must bear the word "compound," "imitation," or "blend." If the Senate definition of "drug," which the conferees accepted, was slightly less rigorous than the House version, the Senate conferees accepted the required labeling of habit-forming drugs. Alcohol was included: the conferees eliminated the exception for alcohol used as a solvent and preservative. Words were also added that seemed to assure that the misbranding provisions covered curative claims. Samuel Hopkins Adams deemed the conferees' patent-medicine provisions "a complete knockout for the Proprietary Association." Moreover, the word "knowingly," a subject of so much previous debate and present in both Senate and House bills, disappeared without comment from the final adjusted version.[30]

The conference report, McCumber told his colleagues, distinctly resembled the bill that had passed the Senate. Senate conferees had accepted parts of the House bill that substantially resembled the Senate

[29] *Ibid.*, 9496, 9738; *Pure Food Bill*, 59 Cong. 1 ses., Senate Doc. 521; Anderson, *The Health of a Nation*, 193–94.

[30] *Cong. Record*, 59 Cong. 1 ses., 9735–40; Adams, "Curbing the Great American Fraud," 16–17.

bill, and House conferees had receded from parts of their bill that differed from the Senate version. "There is nothing," McCumber assured, "making . . . [the conference report] broader or protruding it over State lines in any manner." The conference draft, Mann told his colleagues, although not entirely what the House had wanted, preserved "the vital features." The law would be "a distinct step forward" and would "prove itself to be one of the most valuable and most popular laws ever placed upon the statute books." Wiley thought Mann's efforts in the conference committee had resulted in a law "stronger in its provisions" than either House or Senate bill alone.[31]

With great dispatch, on June 29, both House and Senate accepted the work of their conferees. The next day, the last of the session, in broiling heat, the president came to the Capitol to sign the Food and Drugs Act among nearly a hundred bills that had been hurried through the Congress. After midnight, Roosevelt, donning summer clothes, left by train for Oyster Bay.[32]

"How does a general feel who wins a great battle," Harvey Wiley queried in retrospect, "and brings a final end to hostilities? I presume I felt that way on the last day of June, 1906."[33]

Provisions of the Food and Meat Laws

Signed into law by Roosevelt on the same day, the Food and Drugs Act and the Meat Inspection Amendment embodied in the Agricultural Appropriation Act each printed out to about six pages in the *United States Statutes at Large*. Whereas both laws aimed at safeguarding the nation's food supply, each law did so in a distinctly different way. The contrast resulted from the nature of the problems and the happenstance of historical development.

Hazards undetected by consumers lurked in a steak or a pound of sausage purchased at the butcher shop or a processed ham or a can of roast beef bought at the grocery store. Preventive protection seemed mandatory. Such a system had been in place for fifteen years to protect European customers (and American exporters), but funds had never been sufficient to expand inspection, as the law would have permitted, to give the same assurance of safety to American consumers. Moreover,

---

[31] *Cong. Record*, 59 Cong. 1 ses., 9495–96, 9738–40; Wiley to Mann, July 6, 1906, Letterbooks, Bureau of Chemistry, General Correspondence, RG 97, National Archives.

[32] *Cong. Record*, 59 Cong. 1 ses., 9655, 9740; Genevieve Hoehn Bellis, "Passage of the First Food and Drugs Act," *Food and Drug Rev* 50 (1966), 182–84, 213–15; *Atlanta Constitution*, July 1, 1906. The law appears in chap. 3915, 34 U.S. Stat. 768.

[33] Wiley, *Autobiography*, 231.

the system itself, as Sinclair charged and Neill and Reynolds affirmed, possessed grave flaws.

The new law sought to shore up the old system, expand it, and make it work. Such extended inspection would be expensive. Congress declined to make the packers bear the cost, but "permanently appropriated" from general funds the large sum of $3 million a year to ban from interstate and foreign commerce "meat and meat food products which . . . [were] unsound, unwholesome, or otherwise unfit for human food."

Responsibility remained with the secretary of agriculture, who was to establish rules and regulations to enforce the law, and with his Bureau of Animal Industry. The bureau's corps of inspectors was greatly enlarged to oversee all meat processed for interstate and foreign commerce in all the slaughtering, packing, and canning plants in the land. The law decreed both antemortem and postmortem examination of cattle, sheep, swine, and goats. Carcasses unfit for food purposes must be destroyed in the presence of a government inspector; carcasses and parts thereof suitable for food would be given a stamp or tag stating "Inspected and passed."[34] If a plant manager should refuse to destroy condemned carcasses, the secretary could withdraw inspectors from the plant. Inspectors must have full access to every part of a packing establishment "at all times, by day or night."

Processed products also must be inspected, not only to assure the wholesomeness of the meat, but also to detect dangerous dyes, chemicals, and preservatives. Should these be discovered, destruction must follow. An exception permitted preservatives taboo in the United States to be used in meat products packed for export to countries whose laws accepted such chemicals. Approved meats in cans and pots, and meat wrapped in canvas, must be marked with an "inspected and passed" label. The law forbade selling meat-food products under false and deceptive names; it allowed established trade names that did not distort the truth to continue in use.

Earlier laws had given the secretary of agriculture no control over hygienic conditions in packing plants. The new law did. Aided by "experts in sanitation," he could "prescribe the rules and regulations of sanitation under which such establishments . . . [must] be maintained." Should a plant fail to meet obligatory standards, it lost the right to market its products bearing the government stamp of approval.

[34] Wiley objected to the provision that permitted parts of some sick animals to be used for food. He wrote his sister on June 2, 1906: "I offended The Secretary [Wilson] today by saying I didn't think the flesh of a tuberculous steer was fit to eat. . . . He'll have my scalp next." This letter is in the Wiley Papers.

After October 1, 1906, it became illegal for a person or corporation to offer for shipment or to ship in interstate or foreign commerce any carcasses, parts of carcasses, or meat-food products that had not successfully passed inspection and received the approved government mark. Carriers also violated the law if they accepted for transportation unmarked meat products. Counterfeiting or tampering with the marks, stamps, tags, or labels by which approved meat was identified transgressed the law, as did similar meddling with inspectors' official certificates stating the condition of livestock and processed meat they had examined. Convicted violators might be fined up to $10,000 or be imprisoned for up to two years, or both. Penalties could also result from an attempt to bribe an inspector.

The Biologics Control Act of 1902 had been based on a similar premarketing protective theory. The only serums and antitoxins that could be sold in interstate commerce were those manufactured by firms licensed by the secretary of the treasury. Such firms were subject to periodic random inspection by government scientists from the Marine Hospital Service. No lay consumer and few doctors could examine a vial of vaccine and decide whether it was potent or contaminated. Public protection required premarketing controls.

The Food and Drugs Act, in contrast, rested primarily on different postulates: if the consumer was adequately informed, he could protect himself against deception, even against danger. "When purchasers know *where* a product was made, *when* it was made and *who* made it, and are informed of the *true nature* and *substance* of the article offered for consumption," Robert Allen asserted, "it is almost impossible to impose upon the most ignorant and careless consumers."[35] Some premarketing taboos might be required, aimed at especially hazardous ingredients, but even for narcotic proprietaries that had killed babies and enslaved adults, honest labeling, not the purging of these drugs from formulas, was what the law required. Violations of whatever type would become known only after foods and drugs had reached the marketplace. Then legal remedies came into play. Insanitary premises of manufacture were not per se illegal under the law. "Hereafter," summed up Congressman W. Bourke Cockran of New York, "when you undertake to enter the markets with a package about the contents of which there is any mystery you must do so with its character written plainly over its surface. That is the sum total of this legislation."[36]

The law defined four key words with which it was concerned: the

[35] Robert McD. Allen, "Pure Food Legislation," *Popular Sci M* 34 (July 1906), 53.
[36] *Cong. Record*, 59 Cong. 1 ses., 8993.

types of products—"food" and "drug"—and the kinds of violations—
"adulteration" and "misbranding." "Food" included "all articles used for
food, drink, confectionery, or condiment by man or other animals,
whether simple, mixed, or compound." As to standards of definition for
individual foods, the law remained silent. The House had desired to
give the secretary of agriculture authority to establish such standards to
guide manufacturers and the courts, but the Senate had been dead set
against this power. Indeed, even the year by year authority to set standards that the secretary had been granted in appropriation acts ended in
1906. The House committee had included such authority in its appropriation bill, but on the House floor Charles L. Bartlett of Georgia
made a point of order that succeeded in removing the clause. Wiley and
Secretary Wilson urged the Senate committee to restore this power, but
in vain. Lobbying by the National Food Manufacturers' Association
proved too potent. The Food and Drugs Act limited the secretary's authority to "ascertain[ing] the purity of food products and determin[ing]
what are regarded as adulterations." The baseline definition of purity,
therefore, from which a deviation constituted adulteration, would have
to be established de novo each time a case was taken to court. This task,
as Wiley well knew, would pose massive problems for enforcement officials.[37]

For "drug," part of the law's definition could be precise, because the
statute gave official authority to the standards of "strength, quality, or
purity" of all drugs included in the *United States Pharmacopoeia* and the
National Formulary. If a drug bore a name recognized in these volumes,
it must meet their tests or else be deemed adulterated. However, the law
retreated from this categorical requirement. Its terms permitted USP and
NF drugs to be marketed that varied from official strength, quality, or
purity, provided their labels "plainly stated" their own standard. The
broader definition of "drug" inserted in the Senate bill in 1903, extending coverage to proprietary medicines, made its way into the law. Included was "any substance or mixture of substances intended to be used
for the cure, mitigation, or prevention of disease of either man or other
animals." It was taken for granted that the marketer of each such drug
would set for it a standard of quality and purity. Failure to meet this
professed standard would cause the drug to be adulterated.

"Adulteration" of drugs, therefore, was defined as a deviance from
standards, either those set by the official formularies or those established
by proprietors and made known on labels. Since the law did not provide
a mode for setting food standards, the legislators had to define food

[37] Anderson, *The Health of a Nation*, 197–98; *Cong. Record*, 59 Cong. 2 ses., 1914–15.

"adulteration" in a more elaborate fashion. Food might be adulterated in six major ways. These included the addition of any substance that reduced or injuriously affected a food's quality or strength; the substitution in whole or in part of any "valuable constituent"; and the concealment of damage or inferiority through mixing, coloring, powdering, coating, or staining. Further, in one of its most important and contested provisions, the law declared a food adulterated "if it contain any added poisonous or other added deleterious ingredient which may render such article injurious to health." Here the codfish proviso exempted food protected during shipment by externally applied preservatives that could readily be removed before the foods were consumed. Also defined as adulterated were food substances that consisted "in whole or in part of a filthy, decomposed, or putrid animal or vegetable substance, or any portion of an animal unfit for food, whether manufactured or not, or if it . . . [was] the product of a diseased animal, or one that has died otherwise than by slaughter." Thus, both 1906 food laws combined to safeguard the nation's meat supply.

Confectionery rated a special provision. The presence of specific substances in candy automatically defined it as adulterated: "terra alba, barytes, talc, chrome yellow, or other mineral substance or poisonous color or flavor, or other ingredient deleterious or detrimental to health, or any vinous, malt or spirituous liquor or compound or narcotic drug."

"Misbranding" meant deceptive labeling. A blanket provision banned from the package or label of foods and drugs "any statement, design or device regarding such article, or the ingredients or substances contained therein which shall be false or misleading in any particular." The words of the law went on to single out geographical false branding, labeling inaccurately the place of manufacture. Neither foods nor drugs could parade under false colors, such as an imitation product sold under a genuine article's name, or a product in a package from which the original different contents had been removed. Nor could either food or drug fail to state on its label "the quantity or proportion of any alcohol, morphine, opium, cocaine, heroin, alpha or beta eucaine, chloroform, cannabis indica, chloral hydrate, or acetanilide, or any derivative or preparation of any such substances contained therein." A packaged food, if the label gave the contents in terms of weight or measure, must do so accurately.

Certain concessions regarding adulteration protected prevailing trade practices. Mixtures and compounds bearing their own distinctive names received approval, so long as they did not imitate or appropriate the distinctive name of another article, and did not contain any added poisonous or deleterious ingredients. Articles plainly marked with the word "compound," "imitation," or "blend" also passed muster, and "blend" was defined in the law in a way favoring the whiskey rectifiers, as "a mixture of like substances, not excluding harmless coloring or flavoring ingredients used for the purpose of coloring or flavoring only." The law also specified that manufacturers of proprietary foods that contained "no unwholesome added ingredients" should not be compelled "to disclose their trade formulas, except in so far as" necessary "to secure freedom from adulteration or misbranding."

As a result of the heated arguments over constitutionality, the law was carefully drafted with respect to the limits of interstate commerce. Where Congress controlled internal policy, in the territories and the District of Columbia, the law prohibited the manufacture of adulterated and misbranded foods and drugs. Elsewhere in the nation, Congress forbade any person to introduce such wares into interstate and foreign commerce.[38] It also forbade a resident of a state who had received such an illegal shipment from delivering it, or offering to deliver it, to another person, so long as the product remained in its original unbroken packages. The law defined "person" to include corporation, and violative acts by corporate employees incriminated both the individual and the corporation. Local dealers were protected from unwitting contraventions of the law by a guaranty provision. The wholesaler, jobber, or manufacturer could absolve those in the marketing chain who bought wares from him by signing a guaranty that the products sold were not adulterated or misbranded.

Congress gave the authority to devise rules and regulations for enforcing the Food and Drugs Act to three members of the cabinet, the secretaries of agriculture, the treasury, and commerce and labor. Congress assigned responsibility for policing the food and drug marketplace to Dr. Wiley's Bureau of Chemistry. That bureau should collect and examine specimens. When a sample was discovered to be adulterated or misbranded, the secretary of agriculture should so notify the party from whom the specimen had been obtained, offering him an opportunity to present his case at a hearing. If circumstances then seemed to indicate that the law had been transgressed, the secretary should certify the facts and send the evidence to the United States district attorney responsible for the area in which the violation had occurred. This officer would then be obligated "to cause appropriate proceedings to be commenced and prosecuted in the proper courts."

[38] The food law, like the meat law, contained an exception permitting shipment abroad of goods ordered from a foreign country that conformed to that nation's laws, even though illegal in the United States.

The law authorized two types of legal actions. Violations were defined as misdemeanors for which offending persons could be prosecuted. Conviction for the first offense might bring a fine not to exceed $200. Conviction for each subsequent offense might bring a fine as high as $300, or an imprisonment not exceeding one year, or both penalties together.[39] The meat amendment authorized much higher monetary penalties.

The second enforcement method in the food and drug law provided that adulterated or misbranded goods themselves might be seized by the government, and thus expeditiously removed from channels of trade. This provision, originally part of admiralty law, had been adopted in the Importation of Obscene Literature Act of 1842, and had been part of the mainline food and drug measure since the Paddock bill of 1892.[40] Goods in interstate commerce, or at the end of their journey still in unbroken packages, could be "seized for confiscation by a process of libel for condemnation" secured from a court. If demonstrated to be adulterated or misbranded, the offending food or drug could be destroyed, sold, or returned to the owner to be used in a way not violative of the law. The party responsible for the goods had the right to appear in court and defend their legality, although either intervenor or government could demand a trial by jury over issues of fact. Nothing in the law prohibited both seizure and prosecution actions from being undertaken respecting a single violative product: the first would remove a deceptive and perhaps dangerous food or drug from the marketplace and thus protect the public; the second would punish the offender and perhaps deter him from future crime. So that the public might be kept informed of the results of legal actions taken by the government, the law stipulated that "notice shall be given by publication" after courts had rendered their judgments.

The food and drug law also defined the way in which the secretary of the treasury and the secretary of agriculture should continue to cooperate, as they had been doing under the law of 1902, to keep adulterated and misbranded foods and drugs offered for import from reaching American consumers.

Major changes had occurred in the developing mainline food and drug bill since Congressman Joseph Hawley of Connecticut had, early

[39] For manufacturing violations in a territory or the District of Columbia, the penalty for the first offense could be a fine not to exceed $500 and/or a prison term of up to one year. For subsequent offenses the fine could be doubled; it might be assessed alone, or imprisonment might be decreed without a fine.

[40] Litman and Litman, "Protection of the American Consumer: The Congressional Battle for the Enactment of the First Federal Food and Drug Law in the United States," 316.

in 1881, introduced the National Board of Trade committee's revision of George Wigner's prizewinning draft, itself reflecting the English public analyst's proposed improvements to the British Sale of Food and Drugs Act of 1875. Yet numerous basic elements, especially definitions, from Wigner's draft survived the quarter century of congressional consideration to find their way, in some cases word for word, into the Food and Drugs Act of 1906.[41]

One of the decisions reached by Senate and House conferees dealt with the date on which the law would become effective. The House bill would have put all but one provision of the law into immediate effect upon its enactment. To this the Senate delegates would not agree. The compromise date chosen was January 1, 1907. Nor did Congress, before adjourning, in contrast with the large sum assigned to meat inspection, appropriate a single cent to inaugurate the work of enforcing the Food and Drugs Act.[42] The three cabinet secretaries had six months in which to draft rules and regulations, and Dr. Wiley and his aides six months in which to devise enforcement plans. Before turning to these tasks, however, Wiley joined other participants in and observers of the long struggle in some moments of assessment.

Almost all segments of opinion greeted the Food and Drugs Act with approval. That law, the meat-inspection amendment, and the railroad-rate statute, acclaimed *Collier's*, warranted calling the Fifty-ninth Congress one "that made history." The food bill, contrary to the customary trend, "grew better as it went through the various stages of amendment and conference" and ended up an "excellent measure, . . . an effective safeguard against the interstate traffic in adulterated and misbranded goods." While the food and drug bill did not "appeal to the imagination of the plain people" as did the meat bill, noted *Outlook*, yet "of the two measures" it was "unquestionably the more important." As a result of the act, editorialized the *New York Times*, "the purity and honesty of the food and medicines of the people are guaranteed." "Complaint may be made," suggested the *New York Tribune*, "that the laws passed do not go far enough or are unsatisfactory in this or that detail. But the all important fact is that they do go a long way, and that they blaze a path for future Congresses to follow, if need be."[43]

The patent-medicine provisions particularly were singled out for

[41] Okun, *Fair Play in the Marketplace*, 143–49, 161, 299–302; Stieb, *Drug Adulterations*, 130, 132, 281–83; Litman and Litman, "Protection of the Consumer," 310–29. On Wigner, see chap. 3.

[42] *Cong. Record*, 59 Cong. 1 ses., 9496.

[43] "A Congress That Made History," *Collier's* 37 (July 1, 1906), 9–10; "Against Poison and Fraud," *Outlook* 83 (1906), 496–97; *NY Times*, July 1, 1906; *NY Tribune*, July 1, 1906.

praise. Samuel Hopkins Adams thought them "a complete and over-whelming rout for the Proprietary Association." The new controls, predicted the *Nation*, would deal harmful nostrums a "death-blow." The law was "far better in every respect," asserted the *Journal of the American Medical Association*, than its most ardent supporters could have hoped. "Certainly the powerful Proprietary Association of America has not proved to be so powerful after all."[44] Yet even that trade organization professed satisfaction. Frank J. Cheney, its president, considered it "silly" to require him to relabel Hall's Catarrh Cure just because it contained "a trifling amount of alcohol." But the law's general effect, he said, would be good. "People generally will reason, and reason correctly, that preparations which come up to the requirements of a congressional enactment must be all right, or, certainly, that they are not harmful or dangerous." Even the *National Druggist*, a bitter foe of legislation, termed the final result "not such a terrible thing after all." It gave Wiley "as little power . . . as was possible under any law of the kind that could have been framed." "But let it not be supposed," the editor added, "that the law would have been enacted in its present rather innocuous form but for hard, intelligent and most tactful work on the part of the representatives of the interests it is intended to regulate." Warwick Hough, especially, skillful and persistent champion of the whiskey rectifiers, "fought Dr. Wiley on every occasion, in season and out of season" and "did more than any single individual to clip the wings of this high-flying bird."[45]

Publications representing the interests of pharmacists had paid scant attention to the food and drug bill during its course through the Fifty-ninth Congress. When the bill became law, however, it was welcomed with enthusiasm. The broad definition of drugs, earlier opposed, was now deemed an important advance. The "fakir" will be put out of business, predicted *Drug Topics*, and "the reputable manufacturer" will benefit. *Druggists Circular* deemed the new law a protection to public, small dealer, and manufacturer alike. The statute, asserted Joseph P. Remington, dean of the Philadelphia College of Pharmacy, would work "a peaceful revolution," enhancing drug safety. "The final result," observed the Committee on State and National Legislation of the American Pharmaceutical Association, "seems to be generally accepted as reasonable by all branches of the drug trade."[46]

[44] Adams, "Curbing the Great American Fraud," 16–17; "The Year of Food Laws," 522–23; "The Pure Food Law," *J Amer Med Assoc* 47 (1906), 41–42, 116–17.

[45] *National Druggist* 36 (1906), 210, 372; *National Druggist* cited in *Amer Food J* 1 (July 15, 1906), 9.

[46] *Drug Topics* 21 (1906), 226; *Druggists Circular* 50 (1906), 279, and 51 (1907), 23; *Bulletin*

Spokesmen for other trade groups, which had secured a number of favorable compromises, also greeted the end of the long legislative process with relief, even with favor. The *American Grocer*, long a champion of firm legislation, rejoiced in the changes the new law would bring. Lard would no longer be "cheap and nasty bleached fat." "Currant jelly is going to be pure currant juice and sugar, and not . . . a combination of apple juice, glucose, gelatin, aniline color and with currant flavor." The *American Food Journal*, strong spokesman for a looser law, was "gratified that so many of its ideas were incorporated in the bill as passed, and that it is not nearly as bad as it might have been, considering the lies which have been circulated." Interests represented by this journal anticipated making their own interpretations of the new law prevail when enforcement should begin.[47]

Robert Allen, writing on the eve of victory, rejoiced that the new law would "tend to unify state laws." To gain internal protection to match that henceforth governing interstate commerce, the states would have to maintain equal inspection rigor.[48]

Harvey Wiley, soon to become the central figure in enforcement of the pure-food law, was disappointed in some ways with the measure that had emerged from Congress. Particularly he regretted the absence of standard-setting authority for foods, for which he had lobbied diligently up to the midnight hour. Nonetheless, the chief chemist considered the law more satisfactory than its advocates could have anticipated. "The bill is not as good as we should like it," he wrote one correspondent, "but it is a splendid foundation on which to erect a more perfect structure in the future." To George H. Simmons of the American Medical Association, Wiley elaborated: "When we consider the determined and able efforts which have been continuously made by the opponents of this legislation, . . . we must confess to a feeling of grateful surprise that the measure is as strong as it is." The chief chemist intended to do his best to stamp enforcement policy with his own interpretation of the law he had done so much to bring about.[49]

Wiley had sought to secure from Theodore Roosevelt the pen with which the president had signed the pure-food bill. Senator Heyburn,

of the American Pharmaceutical Association 1 (1906), 301. During the first half of 1906, these journals made very few references to the developing bill.

[47] *American Grocer* 76 (September 26, 1906), 7; *Amer Food J* 1 (July 15, 1906), 16–17.

[48] Allen, "Pure Food Legislation," 55.

[49] Anderson, *The Health of a Nation*, 197–99; Wiley to Porter J. McCumber, June 20, 1906; Wiley to G. A. Ford, June 26, 1906; Wiley to Bernhard C. Hesse, [June 29, 1906]; Wiley to J. W. McCulloch, June 29, 1906; Wiley to Horace Ankeny, June 30, 1906; Wiley to Simmons, July 2, 1906, Bureau of Chemistry, Letterbooks, RG 97, National Archives.

however, had gotten his name in first. This priority was not the one that counted most. In a tribute rare in American annals, this piece of legislation came to bear in popular parlance, not Heyburn's name, nor that of any other member of the Senate or the House. The act became known as the Wiley law. Even before the measure's passage, Heyburn himself had written the chief chemist: "You may rely upon it that for all time your name will be closely associated with . . . any 'Pure food' legislation whatsoever named."[50]

[50] William Loeb, Jr., Roosevelt's secretary, to Thomas R. Shipp, July 12, 1906, Wiley Papers; Heyburn to Wiley, December 30, 1905, Bureau of Chemistry, Incoming Correspondence, RG 97, National Archives.

XII

The Law Interpreted

"Anyone who is fond of sausages and legislation," it has been said, "should not watch either of them being made."
—WILLIAM SCHNEIDER, *Washington Post Book World*[1]

The Historiography of Two Laws

Single laws do not usually loom large in the historiography of a nation. In textbooks by which high school and college students survey American history, the theme of health, let alone laws dealing with public health, has generally received scant attention as compared with politics, diplomacy, and economic development. Yet enactment of the Food and Drugs Act of 1906 and of the simultaneous Meat Inspection Amendment has not gone unnoticed in sweeping accounts of United States history. Indeed, these two laws, or sometimes just one of them, treated as accomplishments of a year or two during the early Progressive era, laws once enacted not then alluded to again, have come to serve as example and symbol of the American nation's concern with the state of its food supply and the condition of its medications. The hero of the episode may be Harvey Wiley, or he may be Upton Sinclair, or both may share the glory. Or Theodore Roosevelt may be accorded major claim to fame, elsewhere, however, appearing as both tardy and reluctant dragon.[2]

In more specialized works dealing with the Progressive period, or with American history in the late nineteenth and early twentieth centuries, authors have been able to devote more space to the food and drug theme. A vast variety of interpretations has been evident. Do authors see roots as deep or shallow? On whom do they bestow principal credit for finally securing the two laws? What elements do they include in the prolaw coalition? Are the food and drug industries stubborn opponents of legislation, major—if clandestine—manipulators seeking to secure

---

[1] Schneider review of David A. Stockman, *The Triumph of Politics*, in *Washington Post Book World*, April 27, 1986, 8.

[2] These generalizations derive from observations of textbooks made over a span of many years.

273

laws, or something of both? Are the two laws best viewed as public-health statutes, consumer-protection measures, or as stratagems by which segments of the food and drug industries sought to get government to solve for them problems that private-sector initiatives had been unable to resolve?

Most of the swirling historiographical currents involving "Progressivism" more broadly have flowed over the subset of events concerned with regulating food and drugs. Special conflicts and controversies have also beset interpretation of the securing of the two 1906 laws. Nor is this small sector of historiography at present calm. The decade of the 1980s has seen a significant amount of scholarship specifically devoted to the enactment of the food and drug act and the meat law, some of it deliberately revisionary—and the judgments often contradictory. A selective survey of the historiography concerning the theme of this book seems an appropriate way to bring it to a conclusion.

In *The Promise of American Life*, published in 1909, Herbert Croly devoted a single sentence to the food and drug law enacted three years earlier. Championing Theodore Roosevelt's intrusion of federal power into private affairs, Croly admitted that such interference always discriminated, aiding some and hurting others, but sometimes must be done. He suggested the pure-food law as an example: it "forbids many practices which have arisen in connection with the manufacture of food products, and discriminates against the perpetrators." The public health, Croly implied, required such legislation.[3]

Walter Lippmann, writing *Drift and Mastery* five years later, assumed the necessity of food and drug laws without mentioning them. Urbanization had made the consumer helpless as an evaluator when buying food, and advertising continually deluded him. Muckraking of foods and patent medicines, although exaggerated, opened the citizen's eyes and turned his stomach. Business must expect, Lippmann asserted, "increasing control in the interests of those who buy."[4]

Benjamin Parke DeWitt, in the first major historical account of *The Progressive Movement*, published in 1915, credited the Progressives with desiring to bring the United States abreast of advanced European nations in social legislation "to strike at poverty, crime, and disease." He cited specific examples, but protection of food and drugs did not make his list.[5]

[3] Herbert Croly, *The Promise of American Life* (Cambridge, MA, 1965; originally published 1909), 191.

[4] Walter Lippmann, *Drift and Mastery: An Attempt to Diagnose the Current Unrest* (Englewood Cliffs, NJ, 1961; originally published 1914), 23–26, 52–56, 91–92.

[5] Benjamin Park DeWitt, *The Progressive Movement: A Non-Partisan Comprehensive Discussion of Current Tendencies in American Politics* (New York, 1915), 24–25, 262, 343, 350–51.

For historians and for the general reading public, the first detailed treatment of the enactment of the two statutes of 1906 came in 1927 with the second volume of Mark Sullivan's *Our Times*. Sullivan had sleuthed and written for Edward Bok in his campaign against patent medicines, and had observed closely and supported "The Crusade for Pure Food" about which he later wrote. His chapter in *Our Times* captures much of the complexity of this crusade. He notes most of the varied participants in the "long agitation": outraged farmers, state and federal food chemists, muckraking journalists, women's club leaders, key members of the Congress. The journalistic attack on nostrums by Bok and Samuel Hopkins Adams receives considerable space, as do repercussions to Sinclair's *The Jungle*. Wiley is recognized as "easily the outstanding figure" in the movement, both as scientist and propagandist. Sullivan does not mention the early efforts in Congress to secure a broad law, plunging into the legislative history with Senators McCumber and Heyburn's bill in 1902, termed the "earliest fruit of the workers for national pure-food legislation." From that point on Sullivan provides a quite detailed narrative, stressing as the reason for postponement of success "furtive obstruction" by food-processing, meat-packing, liquor, and proprietary-medicine interests, bolstered by other sympathetic business groups. Business support for the law receives mention merely in a footnote.[6]

President Roosevelt dominates Sullivan's narrative during the final stages of the campaign for both 1906 laws. "The aggregate of all that worked into the strengthening of Roosevelt's hand," Sullivan summed up, to make it "invincible" by June 1906, included the Neill-Reynolds exposure, indiscreet bragging by whiskey rectifiers, the *Ladies' Home Journal's* and *Collier's'* critiques of patent medicines, and the revelations of food adulteration by Wiley and his state-chemist allies. Sinclair's continuing contact with Roosevelt during the spring of 1906 receives no consideration.

Sullivan's account provided a major source for subsequent scholars, both as to narrative details and interpretation. The laws, their early legislative history neglected, aimed at safeguarding the public health by checking nefarious business practices. The industries to be regulated, with few exceptions, had stubbornly opposed legislation, and had de-

---

[6] Sullivan, *Our Times*, vol. 2, 471–552. See also Sullivan, *The Education of an American*, and Edward L. Weldon, "Mark Sullivan's Progressive Journalism, 1874–1925: An Ironic Persuasion" (Emory University dissertation, 1970). Sullivan had proofs of his chapter on the pure-food campaign checked through several revisions by principal participants, their comments often appearing in footnotes. Before Sullivan wrote *Our Times*, treatises concerning food and drug law prepared to aid lawyers practicing in the field paid some attention to the history of the 1906 act. See, for example, Charles Wesley Dunn, ed., *Dunn's Pure Food and Drug Legal Manual* (New York, 1912–13).

layed it with the aid of shrewd parliamentary maneuvering on the part of friendly congressmen. Finally, opposition was overwhelmed by public opinion, slowly developed by Wiley and his broad coalition, at the climax outraged by muckraking revelations of hazardous patent medicines and unclean meat. President Roosevelt, for Sullivan, is the hero of the drama.[7]

The role of the muckrakers in securing the law became more vigorously asserted, especially in books by C. C. Regier and Louis Filler, although neither downgraded Wiley's pioneer labors. Sinclair's climactic importance in alarming public opinion held firm, indeed became developed in more detail, even as widely varying judgments appeared regarding *The Jungle*'s stature as fiction. Vernon L. Parrington deemed Sinclair's work "art submerged by propaganda," and Ray Ginger termed the novel "a bewildering mass of uninterpreted data" which "fails because it has no integrity." John Chamberlain, on the other hand, thought *The Jungle* a "really respectable novel . . . designed as . . . a call to action," and Filler wrote: "In that generation . . . there was no novel with more lyrical emotion, or a nearer approximation to what was generally thought of as 'genius.' "[8]

Meanwhile, a few historians gave Roosevelt less acclaim than Sullivan had accorded him. Regier cited Wiley's own judgment that the president had received too much credit. Filler argued that the Roosevelt era and the muckraking era coincided, but the latter and not the former was responsible for what was meritorious in food and meat legislation. The president was "involved . . . only incidentally" in the pure-food victory, being mainly the vehicle for weakening compromises. Other historians, like Ginger, accepted Roosevelt's significant responsibility for legislative success, the inadequacy of the laws, however, proving the president's lack of allegiance to real reform.[9]

In 1930 Thomas A. Bailey filled an important hiatus in existing historical accounts by analyzing the pure-food bills introduced into the Con-

---

[7] Harold U. Faulkner, *The Quest for Social Justice, 1898–1914* (New York, 1931), 236–39, and George E. Mowry, *The Era of Theodore Roosevelt, 1900–1912* (New York, 1958), 207–8, provide examples similar to the Sullivan pattern, though briefer.

[8] Regier, *The Era of the Muckrakers*; Filler, *Crusaders for American Liberalism* (New York, 1939), quotation at 163; Vernon L. Parrington, *Main Currents of American Thought: An Interpretation of American Literature from the Beginnings to 1920*, vol. 3, (New York, 1930), 353; Ray Ginger, *Altgeld's America: The Lincoln Ideal Versus Changing Reality* (New York, 1973; originally published 1958), 314–17; John Chamberlain, *Farewell to Reform: The Rise, Life, and Decay of the Progressive Mind in America*, 2nd ed. (New York, 1933), 180, 185.

[9] C. C. Regier, "The Struggle for Federal Food and Drug Regulation," *Law and Contemporary Problems* I (1933), 11–12; Filler, *Crusaders for American Liberalism*, 45, 53–54; Ginger, *Altgeld's America*, 314–17.

gress between 1879 and 1906, suggesting why several single-product statutes had passed and why Congress had delayed so long in enacting a
general law. Bailey did not, however, treat the broader crusade: Wiley's
role, even his name, went unmentioned. Also writing during the same
period, Wiley's former drug deputy, Lyman Kebler, published in pharmacy journals a series of articles on the early proponents of federal food
and drug legislation, articles not so influential as Bailey's among general
historians.[10]

Harvey Wiley, in his *Autobiography*, published in 1930, two years before his death, gave his own account of the pure-food battle. The retired
chief chemist accepted his stature as leader, praised his coalition of allies
including some segments of business converted by his own eloquence,
blasted his enemies, and denied that Roosevelt had "championed the
law in its bitter fight for passage in Congress."[11]

In due course Dr. Wiley himself received some skeptical scrutiny.
T. Swann Harding, in *Two Blades of Grass*, among much laudation included one caveat. The chief chemist's adulteration studies had been
"veritable classics" that became "guidebooks in every laboratory in the
country" engaged in food work. The long effort to secure a law "crys-
tallized under Wiley's skilled touch"; he was "a one-man movement all
by himself, and he carried others with him." Yet Wiley did not possess
the scientific insight to interpret the true results of his own "Poison
Squad" experiments, that preservatives as then used were not harmful.[12]

Hunter Dupree, studying *Science in the Federal Government*, concluded that Wiley's motives in agitating for a law were more complex
than the sheer selfless public interest other authors had taken for
granted. The chief chemist had undertaken the intensive study of adulteration in search of a problem that would save his division from possible extinction in the bureaucratic struggle for survival. In the early years
the Division of Chemistry had done routine research for other sections
of the Department of Agriculture and for other government agencies.
As larger bureaus hired their own chemists, Wiley's domain suffered.
Sugar, the first problem he hoped would provide a substantial mission
for his division, did not work out. Adulteration did, and "gradually en-

[10] Thomas A. Bailey, "Congressional Opposition to Pure Food Legislation, 1879–1906,"
American Journal of Sociology 36 (1930), 52–64. For Kebler's key articles, see above: notes
14 and 36 for chap. 1, note 29 for chap. 2, notes 21 and 34 for chap. 3, and note 6 for chap.
5.

[11] Wiley, *An Autobiography*, quotation at 231. The year before publishing this work, in
The History of a Crime Against the Food Law, Wiley had devoted a long chapter to the
campaign for the law's enactment.

[12] Harding, *Two Blades of Grass*, 45–48, 312–13.

grossed both . . . [Wiley] and his bureau." The chemical revelation of adulterants led to the concept of standards of purity, standards requiring a system of regulation to ensure honestly promoted foods, and thus, not only an investigative, but also an enforcing role for Wiley's bureau. Therefore, power and prestige for its chief accompanied his adoption of the adulteration problem. The new focus of the bureau's energies, Dupree suggested, affected its clients, for it increasingly served consumers more than farmers as producers, the department's traditional responsibility. This shift set up tensions for the future.[13]

The masterful biography of Harvey Wiley by Oscar E. Anderson, Jr., *The Health of a Nation*, appeared in 1958. Based on exhaustive research in primary documents, more detailed than any previous work on the campaign for the pure-food law from the point that Wiley assumed command, taking account of business support for the developing bill to a degree not before achieved in mainline historical scholarship, the book set a new level of thoroughness and balance. While distinctly favorable to Wiley, Anderson did not overlook the chemist's "amazingly few mistakes" or his testiness under criticism, an adjunct of "the eternal problem of the reformer in office." Later scholars were to find some faults with Anderson's account. Otis Graham, for example, held the book flawed by the author's uncritical acceptance of Wiley's own perspective of who was pro and who con on regulation. Yet, despite the later appearance of other works with mildly and even markedly different explanations of the forces achieving the 1906 laws, Anderson's interpretation has stood remarkably well the test of time.[14]

Salvos of revisionary scholarship began in the 1950s to break over the traditional definition of Progressivism. These inevitably altered in contrary directions the ways in which the two 1906 laws came to be viewed.

Richard Hofstadter in *The Age of Reform* (1955) sharply severed the traditional tie between Populism and Progressivism and pointed to a more modern type of agricultural urge underlying the food law: the need for legislation "bearing on the marketing and grading and standardization of agricultural produce." This factor, however, had less influence than another force. By 1906, Hofstadter asserted, echoing a suggestion of Lippmann, "the urban consumer first stepped forward as a serious and self-conscious factor in American social politics." Problems of consumption edged their way into public concern, hitherto dominated by an interest in production. Stirred by muckraking writers, who

[13] Dupree, *Science in the Federal Government*, 176–81.
[14] Anderson, *The Health of a Nation*, quotations at 196 and 255; Otis L. Graham, Jr., *The Great Campaigns: Reform and War in America, 1900–1928* (Englewood Cliffs, NJ, 1971), 177.

were agitating moderate ends with a radical mode of critique, consumers, especially middle-class urbanites, pushed for and secured "something in the form of legislative change and social face-washing." Presumably this somewhat disparaging category included the food and drug laws, although Hofstadter did not discuss this aspect of Progressive legislation in detail. Wiley and Adams go unmentioned, nor is Roosevelt or Sinclair directly linked with the laws of 1906, although Sinclair perhaps receives implied credit.[15]

In *Businessmen and Reform* (1962), Robert H. Wiebe pointed to a major interpretive change that had been evolving with respect to Progressivism and then elaborated his own version of it. For the early historians of the Progressive era, he noted, businessmen had been cast as "villains." The newest trend, however, accorded them the status of prime movers. In this guise Wiebe saw them, businessmen and professionals, members of a new middle class defined in different terms from those employed by Hofstadter. This class, organized in national trade and professional organizations, aspired to a new set of what Wiebe termed "bureaucratic" values. Rather than viewing society in the old way as possessing "predictable motions under natural law," Wiebe's Progressives saw society as characterized by "indeterminate process." The old perspective of government's proper role, as detached from the workaday engines of society's operation, intervening only rarely in times of crisis, could no longer serve. The social order now required a government of "flexible powers and continuous responsibilities."[16]

The pure-food act and the meat law Wiebe included among experiments launched during the Progressive years in "bureaucratic reform." In the "easy years" of Progressivism, up to 1907, the pattern of national legislation was dominated by men who could turn the growing demand for public management to their own ends. Harvey Wiley was just such an "aggrandizing executive," who had clear goals, political savvy, and an alliance of women, doctors, scientists, and even food processors who hoped that moderate regulation would eliminate their marginal competitors. Senator Albert Beveridge was equally ambitious. Both he and Wiley could anticipate that their respective laws would increase their power and enhance their careers. Wiebe did not discuss muckraking in detail, but he attributed to the "exposure" of hazards in the food supply an expansion of business support for regulatory laws. "Businessmen, after all, ate the same pickles and sausages as everyone else." The reve-

[15] Richard Hofstadter, *The Age of Reform: From Bryan to F.D.R.* (New York, 1955), 118, 170–72, 186–89, 193–97.

[16] Wiebe, *Businessmen and Reform*, vii–ix, 19, 42, 48–50, 65–66, 102–3; Wiebe, *The Search for Order, 1877–1920* (New York, 1967), 190–91.

lation of evils needing reform also accelerated a rising power of "the people" within the Republican party, an image and a force, however vague, that President Roosevelt used with masterful effect in countering lobbies opposed to enactment of both 1906 laws, and that members of the Congress also appealed to when voting contrary to business lobby-ists' desires.

Gabriel Kolko, in *The Triumph of Conservatism* (1963), reached down the Progressive lion's throat, grabbed its tail, and pulled the creature inside out. Whereas Wiebe saw business interests supporting national legislation because of a new concept of the advantages to be gained from continuous supervision, Kolko saw a continuation of older patterns, na-ked power plays on the part of the largest elements in industries, includ-ing those packing meat and processing other foods. "It is business con-trol over politics," Kolko wrote, "rather than political regulation of the economy that is the significant phenomenon of the Progressive Era." For him, "progressivism" should more accurately be denominated "po-litical capitalism," an "orderly synthesis of big-business needs and na-tional reform," with "health" and "decency" having nothing to do with the matter. That other than business groups also supported food laws, Kolko considered irrelevant, and he minimized the impact of an aroused public opinion upon the course of events. In his considerable discussion of the long prelude to enactment of the pure-food law, Kolko made Wiley the central figure, but not Wiley as chemical analyst and builder of a broad coalition including consumerist elements. Rather, the chief chemist's conservatism received Kolko's attention. Wiley early had worked at developing glucose adulterants for cane and maple sugar. He insisted that a minor sin, mislabeling, not a major sin, impurity, was what required legislative attention. His closest allies in the fight for the law, especially after the Pure Food and Drug Congress of 1898, were business groups. The law finally passed because the larger and more le-gitimate food processors decided to put their own houses in order and to protect themselves from their less scrupulous competitors. Theodore Roosevelt, always respectful of business, took no leading role in secur-ing this statute. He "merely went along."[17]

The meat-inspection amendment, to which Kolko gave more atten-tion, he interpreted basically in the same way. The packers had taken the initiative in the 1890s by proposing inspection laws when European na-tions placed bans on American pork. The 1906 expansion of inspection

[17] Gabriel Kolko, *The Triumph of Conservatism: A Reinterpretation of American History* (New York, 1977; originally published 1963), 3, 108–10; Kolko, *Main Currents in American History* (New York, 1976), 15–16.

authority represented just another chapter in the same old tale. The major packers wanted a new law even before Upton Sinclair began to write *The Jungle*, a law to reassure Europe once again and also to bring small packers under the same rules that the Chicago oligopolists must follow. When Senator Beveridge introduced his bill, the large packers let it be known they favored it, except for paying and dating, so the ensuing debate related to the terms of the bill, not its enactment per se. Kolko omits mention of packer approaches to one of the president's commissioners and to Roosevelt himself, promising self-reform if given enough time, without the need for new legislation. Kolko acknowledges that "excitement" sparked by *The Jungle* and Neill and Reynolds's report was a factor in getting both laws through Congress, but he underplays public concern, not mentioning the drastic drop in domestic meat consumption. Roosevelt, in Kolko's account, played a more prominent part in getting the meat amendments through Congress than he did with respect to the food and drug bill. Nonetheless, the meat law was assured before the president began to negotiate about terms. Roosevelt, in Kolko's judgment, always held reformers in disdain, "never questioned the ultimate good intentions and social value of the vast majority of businessmen," and never took a stand in behalf of regulation without praising "the basic economic status quo and the integrity of businessmen."[18]

The year after the appearance of Kolko's controversial book, R. James Kane published an article also revisionary with respect to the food and drug law. Kane moved the time of crucial concern backward and the place westward. Ties between Populism and Progressivism became reknit in Kane's argument, for he saw the first significant support for a general food law arising in the Great Plains states during the farmers' revolt. When Wiley's studies of adulteration were "nearly throttled" by his boss, Secretary of Agriculture Wilson, they were kept alive by chemists in the agricultural experiment stations, organized in the Association of Official Agricultural Chemists. And, while the "twelfth-hour impact" of *The Jungle* and Roosevelt's "belated" support helped win the final victory, the indispensable element during the several years preceding the food law's enactment was state chemists and members of the Congress from midwestern states. Neither Populists nor Progressives, Ladd, McCumber, Hansbrough, Heyburn, and Hepburn nonetheless inherited the Populist sense that their section was colonial territory, victim-

---

[18] Kolko, *The Triumph of Conservatism*, 99–108, 111. Ray Ginger calls Kolko's interpretation "often lopsided" but agrees that both 1906 laws were examples of how business sought federal supervision as a barricade against more effective manifestations of public displeasure. From a consumer's standpoint, the meat law was "more ceremonial than efficacious." See *Age of Excess: The United States from 1877 to 1914* (New York, 1965), 351–52.

ized by villainous eastern manufacturers who conspired to dump westward their adulterated wares. The populists had also believed that to
government accrued the responsibility for redressing such grievances.
Holding these views with which their electorates sympathized, coming
from states in which business lobbies had little power, these midwestern
congressmen could safely take the lead in pressing for a broad food and
drug law.[19]

Kane recognized that another major force helped energize the pure-
food campaign, one that was urban, middle-class, and national. Mark
V. Nadel, giving his attention to this component of the crusade, and
developing a theme from Hofstadter, discussed the food laws as an early
victory for the emerging consumer movement. While consumers did
not yet act with a common economic purpose, they had already become
a legitimate political force of considerable weight. Reformers were in
the process of shifting their terminology from "working class" and
"middle class" to "consumer," "common man," and "taxpayer." These
groups, aroused by the muckrakers, "played a great role in the success
of the legislation," a triumph of the people over special interests so that
industry would be regulated for the common good.[20]

As Kane had focused on one segment of the coalition seeking a food
and drug statute, so James G. Burrow concentrated on another, the physicians who composed the American Medical Association. He provided
a detailed account of the AMA's important, if at the eleventh hour inter-
nally conflicting, role in the six years preceding enactment of the law.
Burrow does not insist on the AMA's own evaluation of its primacy, as
"the strongest and most effective" of the forces working for a law, noting that Wiley gave more credit to the women's clubs and the Consumer's League.[21]

A number of other volumes relating to health history appeared in
which, with varying shades of emphasis, the 1906 laws were considered
public-health measures, secured by reformers to control threatening
business practices. Usually Wiley received major credit for leadership,
with the muckrakers of patent medicines and Sinclair's shocking novel
judged responsible for finally arousing the public and the president sufficiently to force Congress into action. Occasionally in these accounts,

---

[19] Kane, "Populism, Progressivism, and Pure Food."

[20] Mark V. Nadel, *The Politics of Consumer Protection* (Indianapolis, 1971), 7–15. Although
more rural than Nadel's population, Wisconsin Progressives as described by David P.
Thelen shared many similar traits. See *The New Citizenship: Origins of Progressivism in Wisconsin* (Columbia, MO, 1972).

[21] Burrow, *AMA*, 67–85.

however, one or another of these principals—even Roosevelt—did not make the cast.[22]

In two health histories, the food and drug law episode becomes evidence serving to support the authors' broader purposes. In *Taking Your Medicine: Drug Regulation in the United States*, published in 1980, Peter Temin interpreted the 1906 act as an outcome of changes in food and drug production and of the shift in distribution from a local community to a national market. The loss of ethical standards that had governed transactions in communities, and the rise of crass commercialism on a nationwide scale, upset many professionals, like Wiley. In their counterattack, these persons directed their aim at the shadiest producers, exaggerating dangers. The examples of food adulteration that Wiley publicized, Temin termed "noteworthy for their triviality." Nor did patent medicines really possess the hazardous character described in muckraking diatribes, even though nostrums were generally no more effective than the drugs physicians prescribed, and even though purchasers lacked knowledge to make reasoned choices. Proprietaries containing opiates, indeed, possessed value by relieving pain suffered during severe illness. What the largely passive new food and drug law sought mainly to achieve was to provide the consumer with more information, so that he could more wisely select among competing products. Reformers had brought government into play to interfere with the free market, but only in a restricted way, insisting on more accurate labeling to ensure fair value for money spent. The law contained loopholes that would benefit large proprietors. Food, not drugs, however, had been the major concern of the long crusade, and the American Medical Association was "largely invisible during these proceedings." If public outrage over meat pushed both bills to passage, Temin held, other forces determined the provisions of the new laws, the desires of the regulated industries and the organizational requirements of Wiley's bureau.[23]

For Temin, his book confined to the history of drug regulation, the Food and Drugs Act of 1906 played a more central role than for Paul Starr, tracing the longer and broader history of American medicine. In *The Transformation of American Medicine* (1982), Starr accepted the thrust of Temin's conclusions that the logic of the 1906 law aimed at improving the functioning of the market by making consumer infor-

[22] Examples are Morton Mintz, *The Therapeutic Nightmare* (Boston, 1965); Dowling, *Medicines for Man*; Milton Silverman and Philip R. Lee, *Pills, Profits, and Politics* (Berkeley, 1979); John Duffy, *The Healers: The Rise of the Medical Establishment* (New York, 1976); and Sonnedecker, *Kremers and Urdang's History of Pharmacy*.

[23] Peter Temin, *Taking Your Medicine: Drug Regulation in the United States* (Cambridge, MA, 1980), 2, 4, 18–37.

mation more accurate, but that the law, in fact, inhibited "only the most arrant fakes." Starr, however, gave the AMA a greater role than did Temin, especially by reprinting and distributing Samuel Hopkins Adams's series on *The Great American Fraud*. Adams's articles, Starr stated, were "to the proprietary drug makers and advertising doctors what the Flexner report five years later would be to the proprietary medical schools: a withering investigation of deceit by commercial interests that contributed to the consolidation of professional authority." The main goal of the AMA's antiquackery campaign, Starr insisted, had been to take credibility away from patent-medicine promoters, who "mimicked, distorted, derided, and undercut the authority of the [medical] profession." Physicians hoped to enhance their own stature, so that patients would buy fewer nostrums and more prescription drugs. The effort was succeeding, and doctors enjoyed an "extraordinary new confidence" during the Progressive years. Starr emphasized the contradiction between the law's intent, to make consumers wiser buyers of proprietaries because of better labeling, and the organized physicians' objective, to get consumers to stop buying such self-dosage wares.[24]

Other historians, not primarily concerned with health, used the food laws of 1906 as evidence to advance the overall arguments of their books. Three such books may be cited as examples: Morton Keller's *Affairs of State* (1977); Irwin and Debi Unger's *The Vulnerable Years* (1978); and Richard L. McCormick's *From Realignment to Reform* (1981).

Keller took a fresh look at "the major theme of American public life during the 1880s and 1890s": "the confrontation with industrialism." He explored the "intense conflict between old values and the pressures generated by massive change." Early governmental intrusions in the economy had been equivocal, based on traditional views of public power but restrained by a residual suspicion of the interfering state. When public health and morals motivated state laws under the police power, in such cases as liquor, oleomargarine, food in general, and drugs, implementation possessed a "special rigor." However, a series of forces thwarted effective regulation on the state level: public indifference, vested interests, divergent state standards, inimical Supreme Court decisions. Early in the new century, that high tribunal looked more favorably upon a broadened federal use of the interstate commerce clause, at a time when large food and meat concerns became especially frustrated with both conflicting state requirements and the competitive practices of their smaller rivals, and when public anxiety peaked about the safety of the

---

[24] Starr, *The Transformation of American Medicine*, 127–34.

food and drug supply. The two federal laws of 1906, in a major new way, made foods and drugs affairs of state.[25]

The Ungers proposed as the emotional essence of Progressivism a feeling of vulnerability. Seeking to contradict Kolko, they praised Progressivism as a genuine effort to offset the abuses of capitalism, a movement that had an "evolving nature" and internal inconsistencies but possessed a distinct core, a popular sense, especially among city dwellers, of jeopardy in confronting "vested interests" that had gained selfish control over the economy and government. The beef trust served as a prime example, but all processed food manufacturers were suspect. Modern chemicals had increased output in agriculture and industry, but had led also to fraud that fabricated artificial butter, doctored spoiled meat, converted raw turnips to canned pears, and vended unlabeled opium as a cure for dread disease. Consumers, alerted by Wiley, then informed more fully by the muckrakers, especially Sinclair, felt increasingly "exposed and unprotected." "Queasy stomachs led to queasy minds," and "the most important stomach of all was T.R.'s." The broad coalition of vulnerable Americans whom the president led in securing the two 1906 laws "cut across class lines and across the ethnic, cultural, and national divisions that had separated the two major parties during the Gilded Age." Formulated by compromise, both laws contained loopholes, but "they were honest attempts to protect the public."[26]

The decline of party influence and the rise of interest group politics, briefly suggested by the Ungers, received elaborate discussion by McCormick. Both in New York state and in the nation, he summed up, the years 1904 to 1909 "unmistakably mark a turning point, when the momentum shifted . . . and the forces of localism and opposition to governmental authority, which had sustained the promotion of commerce and industry but opposed regulation and administration, lost the upper hand to the forces of centralization, bureaucratization, and government action to recognize and adjust group differences." McCormick gave the Progressives a new definition, as reformers who, after having their eyes opened by scandals revealing that business corrupted politics, nonetheless "accepted an industrial society and concentrated their effort on controlling, ordering, and improving it." Without recounting details, McCormick asserted that the first evidence on the national level of the new policy structure, which acknowledged clashing interests and assumed responsibility for adjusting them, came with the 1906 laws to

[25] Morton Keller, *Affairs of State: Public Life in Late Nineteenth Century America* (Cambridge, MA, 1977), viii, 409–20.

[26] Irwin and Debi Unger, *The Vulnerable Years: The United States, 1896–1917* (New York, 1978), 97–141.

regulate railroads, inspect meat for the domestic market, and protect foods and drugs.[27]

A major contribution of the renewed direct attention that has been given during the present decade to the origins of the 1906 laws has been Mitchell Okun's *Fair Play in the Marketplace: The First Battle for Pure Food and Drugs*, published in 1986. The period of Okun's primary concern, 1865 to 1886, has too often been slighted, or omitted altogether. By exploring it in depth, using with insight trade publications and private correspondence, Okun makes abundantly clear the close linkage of some early state laws, especially that of New York, with bills for a national law put before the Congress in Washington. He also establishes the central role of businessmen in this "first battle," and reveals the ethical pressures posed for chemists and other scientists involved in public-health work when regulation came. While there certainly are parallels between these early events and what came after, Okun's judgment, as a reviewer has observed, "borders on the simplistic" in stating that "nothing really changed" from the 1880s to the 1900s "except that the tendencies and technological complexities of modern commerce already present in New York had spread to encompass the rest of the country." This sweeping generalization neglects, among other things, the acceptance of the germ theory, the proliferation of chemical preservatives in commercial food processing, and the broad scope of the coalition created by Harvey Wiley.[28] Moreover, Okun attributed a "final collapse" in the 1880s to the businessmen's movement for a national law, when, in fact, to judge by three articles and a book of the 1980s, business interests had not yet really begun to fight.

Innovative articles by Donna J. Wood and by Ilyse D. Barkan, a book by Wood, and an article by Jack High and Clayton Coppin, stressed the decisive importance of business groups in securing the 1906 laws. None of these authors went so far as Kolko and deemed support for the bills by nonbusiness groups irrelevant. Wood and Barkan concluded that the laws, passed by Congress by overwhelming votes, enjoyed a broad consensus and benefited both manufacturer and consumer.[29]

[27] Richard L. McCormick, *From Realignment to Reform: Political Change in New York State, 1893–1910* (Ithaca, 1981), especially 254–55; McCormick, "The Discovery that Business Corrupts Politics: A Reappraisal of the Origins of Progressivism," *American Historical Review* 86 (1981), 247–74, especially 248, 268.

[28] Okun, *Fair Play in the Marketplace*, 285, 295. Margaret Ripley Wolfe wrote the quoted review, *Amer Hist Rev* 92 (1987), 754–55.

[29] Wood, "The Strategic Uses of Public Policy," and *Strategic Uses of Public Policy*; Barkan, "Industry Invites Regulation"; High and Coppin, "Wiley, Whiskey, and Strategic Behavior."

In 1975 Thomas K. McCraw had argued that neither the "public interest" explanation nor the "capture" by industry thesis, nor, indeed, the
two "in combination" could "adequately characterize the American experience with regulation."[30] Wood sought to place business arguments
in favor of the 1906 food and meat laws within economic theories concerning ways in which government can assist business. Self-interest almost always underlies a given business person's espousal of a proposed
regulatory measure, dictated by the manner in which the bill's provisions might aid in retaining or gaining a competitive advantage. Three
rationales, Wood observed, dominated business presentations favoring
food and drug legislation. According to a general economic interest argument, such laws were needed because expanding production required
enlarging foreign markets, and the shoddy reputation abroad of American processed food thwarted such export efforts. An argument for
shared rules, honesty, and integrity rested on the need to rationalize
contradictory state laws and thus reduce compliance costs, as well as to
protect reputable manufacturers from competitors lowering prices by
using adulterants and deceitful labels. The third argument defended
control over entry to the marketplace and restraint over substitute products by taxation and other means. Established producers favored this
approach to federal protection, hoping to stifle producers of newer,
cheaper goods.[31]

To document these arguments, Wood referred to business testimony
before congressional committees. Especially she cited, to illustrate the
third argument, the trade wars in which makers of butter, cream-of-
tartar baking powder, drugs, and distilled whiskey sought to counter
challenges for market dominance from the makers of oleomargarine,
alum baking powder, proprietary medicines, and rectified whiskey.
While business groups molded the laws' key clauses, Wood concluded,
the interests of business and consumers were "often compatible and occasionally identical." Therefore, the 1906 laws "did seem to have been a
victory for all—except, of course, for adulterators, misbranders, and
those whose newer products threatened the market positions of more
established firms."

The innovative element in Barkan's essay dealt with the need for fu-
sion of two developing, though seemingly contradictory, forces so as to
convert the campaign for a pure-food law, hapless for more than two
decades, into success. One force was rising consumer consciousness, es-

[30] Thomas K. McCraw, "Regulation in America: A Review Article," *Bus Hist Rev* 49
(1975), 159–83, quotation at 179.
[31] Wood, *Strategic Uses of Public Policy*, and "The Strategic Uses of Public Policy," quotation at 432.

pecially in the cities, buyers initially made more literate by the periodical press, finally outraged by muckraking revelations and Wiley's "Poison Squad" reports. Simultaneously, a congeries of managerial, marketing, and political changes—nicely elaborated by Barkan—had brought major business elements to a conviction that a national law was desirable, or at least inevitable. Using their political clout to prevent Congress from acting prematurely, businesses set about preparing for the eventual day. In a scheduled fashion that made Barkan suspicious of deliberate coordination, producers of foods, beverages, and proprietary medicines, between 1902 and 1907, dumped their shoddiest goods on foreign markets. By 1905 and 1906, most producers were ready and "signaled Congress to act." "Political resistance . . . dissolved," and the food and drug law passed a Congress of special interests with only a modicum of opposition.[32]

Barkan took a revisionist position also with respect to the relation between the food law and the meat amendments. It was not the food law that finally swept through Congress on the wave of public alarm about meat. Rather, *The Jungle* upset Americans because its message seemed consistent with what they already had learned about all food. The packers had learned lessons too. When their initial counterattack against *The Jungle*'s charges failed to restore public confidence, they quickly accepted, as in the 1890s, the solution of law. The food and drug movement had taught them that "federal regulation was a strategy of choice," demanded by science and consumer pressure, but also a course of ultimate benefit to themselves.

High and Coppin also broke with traditional explanations while focusing on the role of the divided whiskey industry in the three years preceding passage of the Food and Drugs Act. In traditional accounts, the straight-whiskey distillers had been the public-spirited faction, aiding Wiley in seeking a strong law, one that would put restraints on the adulterating rectifiers who, in turn, sought to block, and did delay, the law's enactment. High and Coppin hold that, as to purity, the blenders could make a better case than could the straight-whiskey producers; that Wiley allied with the latter because they supported his campaign with money and lobbying; and that Wiley shaped the draft bill to please his strong supporters. Wiley's bureaucratic ambitions, therefore, motivated the chief chemist's policies, while both wings of the whiskey industry strove to mold the 1906 law into a weapon in their continuing internecine battle. Thus, High and Coppin concluded, "strategic use of public policy applies not only to firms trying to gain a competitive edge, but

[32] Barkan, "Industry Invites Regulation," quotations at 24 and 25.

also to regulators trying to expand their bureau and further their causes."[33]

During the 1980s other reconsiderations of the Food and Drugs Act reechoed the most prominent earlier interpretation of the law, as a public-health statute secured by a disturbed public to harness hostile industry. This view characterized an article by Richard Curtis Litman and Donald Saunders Litman in the *Food, Drug, Cosmetic Law Journal*. This account is helpful in tracing the evolving bill, indicating in which Congress and under what circumstances provisions appeared that survived into the final version of 1906.[34] A briefer article following the traditional pattern, written by Terra Ziporyn, appeared in the *Journal of the American Medical Association*.[35]

An ingenious new approach to reviving the concept of Progressivism, sometimes declared moribund if not dead, using the two laws of 1906 as a major resuscitating device, came from the pen of Robert M. Crunden in 1982. His book bore the title *Ministers of Reform*.[36] These "ministers" included in their ranks Wiley, Adams, Sinclair, and Beveridge, men reared religiously, most of them in Protestant homes, who chose to make their ethical impact on society from secular professions, "preaching without pulpits." Motivated by "innovative nostalgia," a looking backward for emotional support and secure ideas, the Progressives sought to apply religious canons to economic, social, and political problems, thus oversimplifying solutions during a complex time demanding more instrumental approaches.

The Food and Drugs Act, Crunden believed, "stands out conspicuously as an archetype of how moral indignation could lead to progressive legislation." The convergence of public officials led by Wiley with the muckrakers brought the long crusade for this law to the brink of success. Wiley, an adroit propagandist who possessed political skills, held fast to "a kind of chemical fundamentalism," the ethics of pure food. He underplayed the true dangers of adulteration and held too high hopes for the beneficial results of honest labeling. Adams and other muckrakers, also moved by morality, tended to believe that exposure of evil might lead to repentance. These journalists naively failed to consider adequately what must follow revelation in order to achieve reform. Roosevelt, also a Progressive in Crunden's sense, nonetheless thought the pure-food issue overblown by journalistic exaggeration. This, be-

[33] High and Coppin, "Wiley, Whiskey, and Strategic Behavior."

[34] Litman and Litman, "Protection of the American Consumer."

[35] Terra Ziporyn, "The Food and Drug Administration: How 'Those Regulations' Came to Be," *J Amer Med Assoc* 254 (1985), 2037–39, 2043–44.

[36] Crunden, *Ministers of Reform*, especially 163–99.

sides his suspicion of Wiley's science, might have caused the president to permit the food bill to die. Furor over *The Jungle*, and public identification of meat and food bills as a "single effort," however, led Roosevelt to push hard for them both. The food and drug law as enacted, although an important beginning, revealed the flaws of the Progressive stance. The act "did not require that drugs work, or that food taste good or keep for any specified period of time. It merely required that manufacturers tell the truth on their labels." Honest businessmen, so Progressives anticipated, would obey the law, and decent, informed citizens would buy the accurately promoted foods and drugs. This law resembled other Progressive legislation in its "appearance of radical reform without the substance."

The meat amendment, in Crunden's analysis, shared the food bill's faults, derived from the same moral imperatives. For, despite his surface differences from Beveridge and Roosevelt, Sinclair at heart fit Crunden's Progressive profile. *The Jungle* "remains one of the best examples in the history of literature" of propagandistic art, and the president reacted to it just as did his fellow citizens. To him the meat bill held higher priority than the food bill, because the issue seemed more urgent, and because he felt closer to Beveridge than to Wiley and to the House members who had the bill in charge. Yet, despising the novelist all the while, Roosevelt worked closely with Sinclair, whose novel had precipitated the final crisis, until the modified Beveridge bill became law.

Thus, Crunden's extensive discussion followed the traditional pattern to a considerable degree. The laws resulted, after a long prelude, when finally public indignation reached fever pitch, stimulated by the muckrakers who joined their strident moralistic voices to those in Wiley's coalition. Businessmen, in Crunden's account, are not stark villains. Adulteration was "not a hopeless situation of wicked deception," but a reaction to changing technology, increasing competition, and continuing ignorance about nutrition and food chemistry. Still, businessmen do not appear as proponents of legislation either. The leading actors are Crunden's "Progressives," defined in his imaginative, novel way.

Increasing scholarship in the 1980s has also been devoted specifically to the problem of meat in 1906. Christine Scriabine provided a fresh overview of "Upton Sinclair and the Writing of *The Jungle*." In a probing 1986 dissertation, Suk Bong Suh sought to weigh Sinclair's fiction on the scales of Packingtown's facts. Especially fresh was Suh's comparison of the text of *The Jungle* as it appeared in Socialist periodicals with the text as published by Doubleday, Page.[37] Writing from a journalistic

---

[37] Suh, "Literature, Society, and Culture."

perspective, William Parmenter briefly included the legislative consequences in a survey of *The Jungle*'s impact. Everett B. Miller pointed to
various ways, deriving from advances in veterinary science and education, in which federal meat inspection—despite Sinclair's charges—had
been improving before *The Jungle* came off the press.[38]

Other recent writing has studied the way in which *The Jungle* fit into
the evolving pattern of Packingtown. Robert A. Slayton in *Back of the
Yards* (1986), and James R. Barrett in *Work and Community in the Jungle*
(1987), hold that living conditions of packinghouse workers were worse
than Sinclair described them, but the people more resilient. Hygienic
and laboring conditions in the plants themselves, Barrett concluded,
were even more degrading in fact than in Sinclair's fiction. Louise Carroll Wade followed her book *Chicago's Pride: The Stockyards, Packingtown, and Environs in the Nineteenth Century* (1987), with a paper at an
American Historical Association convention, in which she asserted that
Sinclair overstressed the isolation of the immigrant family and gave an
unduly critical picture of federal meat inspection.[39]

Pure Food: An End and a Beginning

The quarter-century pure-food crusade concluded with the enactment
of two laws during the Progressive period. The securing of that laboriously constructed compromise, the Food and Drugs Act of 1906, has
seemed to require the pluralistic explanation inherent in this book. That
single campaign shared in the complex crosscurrents, institutional and
intellectual, backward-looking and forward-looking, of the broader
Progressive movement.

All major American institutions, forced into change by rapidly developing technology, had shifted from a local to a national orientation:
transportation, manufacturing, management, the sources of news. The
process itself had brought stresses and strains, puzzlement and anxiety,
a perceived dire challenge with a plethora of possible resolutions. A
growing agreement emerged that, since problems had become national,

[38] William Parmenter, "*The Jungle* and Its Effect," *Journalism History* 10 (Spring–Summer 1983), 14–17, 33–34; Miller, "How Important was Upton Sinclair's *The Jungle* to Federal Meat Inspection?"

[39] Robert A. Slayton, *Back of the Yards: The Making of a Local Democracy* (Chicago,
1986); James R. Barrett, *Work and Community in the Jungle: Chicago's Packing House Workers, 1894–1922* (Urbana, IL, 1987); Wade, "Upton Sinclair and Packingtown." Barrett has
recently published a new edition of *The Jungle* with scholarly apparatus (Urbana, IL,
1988), and Gene DeGruson has published *The Lost First Edition of Upton Sinclair's* The
Jungle (Memphis and Atlanta, 1988), the version that appeared in the socialist newspaper
Appeal to Reason.

solutions too must be equally encompassing. Many issues seemed too big and complex for any agency short of the government in Washington to arbitrate and enforce decisions. Matters involving science especially seemed appropriate for such national consideration.[40] The food Americans ate and the drugs they took became—in Morton Keller's phrase— "affairs of state."[41]

Private groups organized nationally and sought to make their weight felt in the process of decision making. Such were the business trade associations that both competed and cooperated in trying to frame a food and drug bill friendly to their concerns, and such were the state chemists, physicians, and women who supported Harvey Wiley's vision of a law. Some segments of society, like the socialists whom Upton Sinclair supported, had more extreme versions of the degree of social and economic change the nation needed. The "new interventionism"[42] of the Progressives who became dominant, however, plotted a more moderate course, striving for piecemeal updating of institutions while trying to retain values long cherished in the American tradition. This required much jousting over particulars, especially in the halls of Congress.

The blueprint by which the federal government should handle food and drug issues revealed just such sharp and continuing debate. Business groups wanted the national government to be a tolerant policeman, enforcing basic ground rules to thwart unscrupulous competitors, ending the chaos of divergent and sometimes ludicrously severe state laws, validating products to reassure consumers both within the nation's borders and overseas. Most of the larger elements of food processing and drug manufacturing viewed the laws as they finally emerged from Congress as generally satisfactory, granted they be reasonably enforced. These industries recognized they had assumed a continuing obligation, a new kind of partnership with government. Constant vigilance would be required to assure that constant surveillance would prove more benefit than burden.

No food and drug law would have passed the Congress in 1906 because of business desire alone. As Oscar Anderson concluded, "support from commercial interests simply was not decisive."[43] The crusade rallying around the "pure food" slogan required, and finally secured, wide popular support. At the end "pure" came to mean an absence from meat of the nauseating ingredients Sinclair had alleged, an absence from pro-

[40] Dupree, *Science in the Federal Government*, 289–93.

[41] Keller, *Affairs of State*.

[42] John Whiteclay Chambers II, *The Tyranny of Change: America in the Progressive Era, 1900–1917* (New York, 1980), vi, 107–8.

[43] Anderson, *The Health of a Nation*, 195.

cessed foods of the poisonous preservatives Wiley had condemned, an absence from patent medicines of the dangerous narcotics Adams had excoriated. Shock and fear about such dangers in the diet and hazards in packaged self-dosage medicines crested in the spring of 1906, adding both urban and rural supporters, the nucleus of a consumer movement, to the allies Wiley already had enlisted. Concern for the nation's health was the salient component in the expanding coalition. Both 1906 laws can properly be considered both consumerist and public-health legislation.

Earlier—and still in 1906—"pure" also had possessed another, an older, a moral, meaning as a synonym for righteous, honest. Prior to his "Poison Squad" experiments, Wiley had almost always interpreted purity in this way. "The evils of fraud," he told a House committee, were "demoralizing." "No man can continually deceive his customer and retain that high moral sense which is the very soul of trade." The chief chemist could even go to the extreme of asserting that purity did not necessarily imply safety: "Pure" meant merely labeled with scrupulous accuracy.[44]

Other campaigners, Alexander Wedderburn and Senator Porter McCumber among them, waved the pure-food banner with a similar flourish. President Roosevelt also made the case in moral terms. The crusade for food and drug control shared with overall Progressivism a deep worry about "purity": business, government at all levels, social conduct, even the bloodlines of the nation's populace seemed threatened with pollution and required cleaning up.[45]

The reassertion of traditional moral values, as Robert Crunden has made abundantly clear, led to an oversimplification of complex issues, blunting instrumental solutions that Progressives hoped for and that the situation demanded.[46] In the pure-food campaign, purity defined as honesty led to unrealistic expectations about the redeeming value of accurate labeling. Also, Wiley, in forecasting that the enactment of a law would so reform the ethics of businessmen that perhaps not a single new inspector would be needed to police the marketplace, displayed a na-

[44] House *Hearings . . . on The Pure Food Bills*, 57 Cong. 1 ses., 257.

[45] Joseph Lincoln Steffens, *The Shame of the Cities* (New York, 1948; originally published 1904); David J. Pivar, *Purity Crusade: Sexual Morality and Social Control, 1868–1900* (Westport, CT, 1973); Mark Thomas Connelly, *The Response to Prostitution in the Progressive Era* (Chapel Hill, NC, 1980); John Higham, *Strangers in the Land: Patterns of American Nativism, 1860–1925* (New Brunswick, NJ, 1955); Robert E. Bouwman, "Race Suicide: Some Aspects of Race Paranoia in the Progressive Era" (Emory University dissertation, 1975).

[46] Crunden, *Ministers of Reform*.

ïveté (or a deceptive stratagem) quickly abandoned when enforcement of the law actually began.[47]

Like other issues arising during the Progressive years, the food and drug campaign came to transcend loyalty to political party. Even back in 1886, when a food issue first engrossed the Congress, some members commented with amazement that the conflict between butter and oleomargarine had caused party allegiances and other political alliances to break apart. In 1906 such fragmentation and realignment seemed to be recurring, producing a sense of surprise similar to that of twenty years before. Henry C. Adams, former food and drug commissioner of Wisconsin, had now come to the House of Representatives, where he was Wiley's fervent ally in supporting the food and drug bill, and soon would accept the president's call to try to work out a compromise on the meat-inspection amendment. Writing Wiley in January 1906 about the pure-food bill's prospects, Adams commented:

> The situation in the House is decidedly interesting. There is marked division in the republican membership and an equally marked division in the democratic membership. There seems to be a constant shifting of lines of division in the political parties not only in the House but all over the country. There are so many Roosevelt democrats and so many Folk republicans scattered around that nobody knows exactly where we are at. The party labels are fast fading in this peculiar period of American political history and they are liable to disappear altogether.[48]

Party labels would in due course receive challenge from Theodore Roosevelt, but parties did not disappear. In the novel atmosphere that Representative Adams described, however, two food bills were enacted into law. The president became involved with both. In the food, drug, and meat historiographical parade, Roosevelt has donned many hats: as heroic cowboy romping on stage for an exciting last-minute rescue; as weasely conniver with Republican businessmen and congressmen to secure laws needed and demanded by business; as responsible public servant working among contentious factions to gain by skillful compromise modest advances in the public interest. A latecomer to the food and drug crusade, the president played a minor but important role in adding to the final momentum toward enactment of the law. His position in framing the compromise for meat inspection was more central.

---

[47] House *Hearings on the Pure-Food Bills*, 59 Cong. 1 ses., 342.
[48] Adams to Wiley, January 15, 1906, Wiley Papers. Adams refers to Joseph W. Folk, crusader against corruption as St. Louis district attorney and then Missouri governor.

A defender of the American business system, Roosevelt recognized that it needed restraining so as better to serve the public interest. He pioneered using the office of president as a significant force in the legislative process, the moderate pure-food bills of 1906 benefiting from this innovative concern.

Harvey Wiley's role has varied less extremely than that of Roosevelt in this special province of historiography, but with a similar rhythm. He too has been interpreted as more closely allied with businessmen than with reformers cherishing an unalloyed devotion to the public health, with a consequent undue flabbiness in his fidelity to adequate legislative goals. Wiley's career ambitions have been given equal weight with, perhaps precedence over, his genuine concern for improving the food and drug supply in the interest of consumers. Still, for most historians, Wiley stood at the center of the entire campaign from his arrival in Washington in 1883.

The chief chemist did indeed emerge a quadruple-threat leader, as scientist, propagandist, organizer, and strategist of the pure-food cause. Self-confident and ambitious, he certainly believed that his bureau was the appropriate base from which the food and drug supply could be properly regulated in the public interest. Pragmatic as to means, Wiley recognized that compromise, even with his most bitter antagonists, was the one sure course toward legislative accomplishment. A moral man molded by the intellectual climate of his upbringing, Wiley trusted too confidently in the ability of the average consumer to buy wisely if adequately informed. Nonetheless, Wiley was a sincere crusader, committed absolutely to securing as strong a law as his unflagging dedication to the cause and the complex political situation would permit.

The end of the protracted legislative process heralded, of course, the beginning of regulation under the law. What the Food and Drugs Act would really mean to the nation, only the manner of its enforcement could reveal. All parties involved in its framing would seek to influence the way in which it would be applied. Two figures stood at the center of the regulatory stage, ready to play their roles. Under the law Wiley was cast as chief regulator, no longer needing—he thought—to compromise. He began to plan his program of stringent enforcement. Roosevelt, long suspicious of the chief chemist down the ladder of government, responsible to many constituencies, not least to business interests concerned with foods and drugs, waited warily in the White House to see how Wiley would manage his mandated duties. The beginning of the regulatory drama promised action as flamboyant as that displayed in the final act of the pure-food legislative drama during the spring and early summer of 1906.

Index

Abbott, Wallace C., 118
Abraham, 87
acacia, 29
Accum, Fredrick, 41–43, 45
acetanilide, 115, 120, 202, 259, 266
aconite, 114
Adams, Henry C.: pilots 1902 oleomarga-
    rine bill through Congress, 162; helps
    negotiate compromise on meat-inspec-
    tion bill, 246–48; dies, 247n; on non-
    party nature of pure-food issue, 294
Adams, Samuel Hopkins: on Roosevelt,
    191; background, 199; *Collier's* series on
    proprietary medicines, 199–204, 293; se-
    ries on fake clinics, 203; confers with
    Wiley, 203, 219–20; praised at House
    hearings, 218–19; influence of, 254; helps
    draft proprietary medicine provision,
    257; evaluates law, 261, 270; in historiog-
    raphy, 275, 279, 284, 289
Adamson, William C., 162–63, 253, 255, 260
Addams, Jane, 186, 202, 233
adulteration of drugs: imported from
    abroad, 6–17; in West and South, 11, 21,
    48; testimony before 1848 House com-
    mittee, 12; threat to medical progress,
    31; Diehl's analysis, 53; National Board
    of Trade assessment, 55; New York and
    Massachusetts analyses, 65, 120; as de-
    fined in 1906 law, 265. *See also* names of
    individual drugs
adulteration of feedstuffs, 103, 122

adulteration of fertilizers, 103, 122–23
adulteration of foods: ancient, 3; Beck's
    analyses, 31–32; milk in New York, 39;
    Accum's analyses, 41–42; Hassall's anal-
    yses, 43–44; Angell's charges, 46–52, 58–
    60, 66, 68; Kedzie's and Smart's anal-
    yses, 53; Wigner's and the National
    Board of Trade's assessments, 55; Wi-
    ley's investigations, 102–6, 126, 128; early
    interest by Department of Agriculture,
    103; investigations funded by Congress,
    103; canned goods, 109–10; study by
    AOAC, 123–24; canned meat, 139; testi-
    mony at Mason hearings, 141–45; testi-
    mony before 57th Congress committees,
    158–59, 163; in 1891 memorial, 184; Mc-
    Cumber mentions, 206; Mann's sum-
    mary in House debate, 256; defined in
    1906 law, 265–67; impact on consumers,
    285. *See also* names of individual foods
Affairs of State, 284–85
Age of Reform, The, 278–79
agricultural depression, 72–73, 79–81
Albany Medical College, 8
alcohol, 7, 30, 116, 218, 220, 259, 266
Aldrich, Nelson W., 160, 172, 194–96, 205–
    6, 209
Allen, Martha M., 186
Allen, Robert McDowell, 209, 220; works
    within National Association of State
    Dairy and Food Departments, 179; leads
    committee to see Roosevelt, 180, 186,

297